The Practice of Multicultural Group Work

Visions and Perspectives from the Field

Janice L. DeLucia-Waack
SUNY Buffalo

Jeremiah Donigian
SUNY Brockport

THOMSON
™
BROOKS/COLE

Australia • Canada • Mexico • Singapore • Spain
United Kingdom • United States

THOMSON
™
BROOKS/COLE

Publisher/Executive Editor: *Lisa Gebo*
Acquisitions Editor: *Marquita Flemming*
Assistant Editor: *Shelley Gesicki*
Editorial Assistant: *Amy Lam*
Marketing Manager: *Caroline Concilla*
Marketing Assistant: *Mary Ho*
Advertising Project Manager: *Tami Strang*
Signing Representative: *Tricia Caruso and Tim Kenney*
Project Manager, Editorial Production:
  Rita Jaramillo
Print/Media Buyer: *Doreen Suruki*

Permissions Editor: *Kiely Sexton*
Production Service: *Sara Dovre Wudali,*
  Buuji, Inc.
Art Editor: *Vernon Boes*
Copy Editor: *Linda Ireland, Buuji, Inc.*
Illustrator: *Eunah Chang, Buuji, Inc.*
Cover Designer: *Andy Norris*
Cover Art: *Judith Harkness*
Compositor: *Buuji, Inc.*
Text and Cover Printer: *Webcom*

Printed in Canada
1 2 3 4 5 6 7 07 06 05 04 03

For more information about our products, contact us at:
Thomson Learning Academic Resource Center
1-800-423-0563

For permission to use material from this text,
contact us by: **Phone:** 1-800-730-2214
Fax: 1-800-730-2215
Web: http://www.thomsonrights.com

Library of Congress Control Number: 2003111363

ISBN 0-534-56038-5

Brooks/Cole—Thomson Learning
10 Davis Drive
Belmont, CA 94002
USA

Asia
Thomson Learning
5 Shenton Way #01-01
UIC Building
Singapore 068808

Australia/New Zealand
Thomson Learning
102 Dodds Street
Southbank, Victoria 3006
Australia

Canada
Nelson
1120 Birchmount Road
Toronto, Ontario M1K 5G4
Canada

Europe/Middle East/Africa
Thomson Learning
High Holborn House
50/51 Bedford Row
London WC1R 4LR
United Kingdom

Latin America
Thomson Learning
Seneca, 53
Colonia Polanco
11560 Mexico D.F.
Mexico

Spain/Portugal
Paraninfo
Calle/Magallanes, 25
28015 Madrid, Spain

This book is dedicated to all those who work toward establishing world peace and human understanding.
—Janice and Jerry

In addition, I would like to acknowledge Muli Sinha and the faculty of Eisenhower College, my alma mater, who believed that World Studies was the core of a liberal arts education.
—Janice

About the Authors

Janice L. DeLucia-Waack (Ph.D.) has been an Associate Professor in the Department of Counseling, School, and Educational Psychology at the University at Buffalo, SUNY, since 1998. She is the program director for the School Counseling master's program, and she teaches two courses, Advanced Group Counseling Theory and Practice, and Group Work in the Schools, related to groups for graduate students. She received a bachelor's degree in Psychology from Eisenhower College, a master's degree in Family Studies from the University of Maryland, and a Ph.D in Counseling Psychology from Pennsylvania State University after completing a predoctoral internship in Psychology at the University of Buffalo, SUNY, Counseling Center. She began her academic career teaching group counseling courses at Purdue University. Her counseling and research interests include: groups, eating disorders and body image, children of divorce, supervision, and multicultural counseling.

Dr. DeLucia-Waack is the author of two books, *Multicultural Counseling Competencies: Implications and Challenges for Practice* and *Using Music in Children of Divorce Groups: A Session-by-Session Manual for Counselors*. She is also the coauthor of two books, *Group Work Experts Share Their Favorite Activities: A Guide to Choosing, Planning, Conducting and Processing* and *Handbook of Group Counseling and Psychotherapy*. She is a former editor of the *Journal for Specialists in Group Work*. In addition, she has authored or coauthored more than 50 journal articles, book chapters, and journal editorials. She was also the recipient of the 2001 Association for Specialists in Group Work President's Award, and was made a Fellow by the same association in 1998. Also in 1998, she received the Distinguished Counselor Educator Award in the state of Indiana and the Association for Specialists in Group Work's Professionals Advancement Award. In 1994, she received the Outstanding Research Article Award in the *Journal for Specialists in Group Work* and the Association for Specialists in Group Work's President's Award.

Jeremiah Donigian (D. Ed.) is past president of the Association for Specialists in Group Work. He is a Fellow in ASGW and has received its Eminent Career Award. He is a member of the American Counseling Association, and a clinical member and approved supervisor of the American Association of Marriage and Family Therapy. Dr. Donigian is Professor Emeritus from the Counseling Education Department at the State University of New York at Brockport. He has coauthored *Critical Incidents in Group Therapy* (2nd edition, 1997), *Systemic Group Therapy: A Triadic Model I* (1999), and *Making Task Groups Work in Your World* (2001). He continues his private practice in marriage, family, and group therapy. He also has served as a consultant to various organizations and systems and has conducted workshops and seminars at the local, state, regional, national, and international levels.

Dr. Donigian shares his life with Anna, to whom he has been married for over 40 years, and his two daughters: Melissa, who is a school counselor, and Rebecca, who is an elementary school teacher.

Contents

CHAPTER 8

Counseling/Therapy Group Vignette #1:
The Assertiveness Group and the Bomb   190

CHAPTER 9

Counseling/Therapy Group Vignette #2:
An Adolescent Boys' Group and the Missing Member   220

CHAPTER 10

Counseling/Therapy Group Vignette #3:
A Gender Orientation Group—Where Do We Fit?   246

CHAPTER 13

Suggestions for Best Practices in Multicultural Group Work 309

"Dad, you think of yourself as a colored man.
I think of myself as a man."
—Sidney Poitier to his father in the movie
Guess Who's Coming to Dinner?

Preface

It is not customary for the Preface to be written by or be about one of the coauthors. Normally it is to be the expression of both. In this instance, however, we felt that Jerry's voice conveyed universal concerns and feelings held by those who struggle with the task of trying to understand and explain the meaning of the term *multicultural.* We also felt his concerns captured the spirit and purpose for which this book was written. Therefore, it is for these reasons that we have chosen to break from the norm. The following text is in Jerry's voice.

When Janice and I agreed to write this book, I had not anticipated what was to befall me as I undertook the task of writing my designated sections. I was struck with my own personal struggle or, if you will, writing block. The experience was very unfamiliar to me. It was not the usual writer's block. It felt more like resistance. Acknowledging it as that, I began a process of introspection. I questioned why I was so resistant to writing after Janice and I had been so excited about the concept of writing a book such as this. After all, was I not as instrumental as she for conceiving it? Clearly, I believed we had established that it was needed. So what was holding it up? The more I pondered this question, the less pleased I was with the recurring answer that I kept facing. It was the lack of consensus and confusion that surrounded the terms *multicultural* and *ethnicity* that was casting a shadow over my ability to begin.

Upon reviewing the literature, I found that the words *ethnicity* and *culture* are sometimes used interchangeably by authors. For example, "Ethnicity refers to a common ancestry through which individuals have evolved shared values and customs. It is deeply tied to the family, through which it is transmitted" (McGoldrick, Giordano, & Pearce, 1996, p. 1). These same authors state, "Every family's background is multicultural. All marriages are, to a degree, cultural intermarriages. The multiple parts of our cultural heritages often do not fit easily into description of any one group" (p. 6).

Bowman (1996) cogently suggested that the reason for confusion rests with the use of terminology. Several others have confirmed her conclusion. Rollock and Terrell (1996) defined the term *ethnicity* as referring "to shared heritage of a societal subgroup and the mutual identification of its members based on a common upbringing, shared activities and experiences and culture" (p. 115). They referred to culture as being "the way of life of a group, providing a meaning system shaped by the group's lived experiences and transmitted across generations to help guide members in interacting with their world" (p. 115). Yinger (1976) offered another view of an ethnic group as being "a segment of a larger society whose members are thought by themselves and/or others to have a common origin and to share important segments of a common culture, and who, in addition, participate in shared activities in which the common origin and culture are significant" (p. 200).

Adding to the confusion is Benge's (2000) argument against using the term *Native American*. He prefers the words *American Indian,* which he believes are more historically accurate. He states, "They acknowledge the singularity and importance of both our tribal and U.S. heritage. . . . [Therefore,] from this point forward I choose to identify myself as a Cherokee-American instead of a Native American. By, in effect, asserting citizenship in both the Cherokee Nation and the United States of America, I integrate and honor both sides of my unique cultural heritage" (p. 6a). Now add to the confusion Pedersen's (1991) view that if either term *ethnic* or *culture* is too broadly or narrowly defined, we run the risk of assuming that all counseling relationships are multicultural.

After reviewing these authors' writings, I began to understand why I was not finding it easy to break through my resistance. At this point, it only seemed to heighten. Janice's earlier words offered some consolation: "There is no consensus to one multicultural theory of counseling, one definition of multiculturalism, or one set of descriptions for race and culture" (DeLucia-Waack, 1996, p. 3) Imber-Black (1997) consoled me further. In addressing the training of multiculturally competent counselors, she stated that it is insufficient to have only content knowledge of diverse cultures. She advocates that to be truly on the path of becoming a multiculturally competent counselor, one not only needs to have researched and read and had a cognitive experience of other cultures, but one needs to have had experiential/affective experiences with them as well. In addition, she holds that counselors would do well to study their own cultural origins.

So there I had it—the Rosetta stone to my resistance. There is strong evidence that *culture* and *ethnicity* are interchangeable terms for some, but not for others. Perhaps the meanings of these terms are best left to individual interpretation. Most important, however, is the need for group leaders to study, research, and experience as many cultural groups as possible, including their own. Further, group leaders need to be aware that each group member they face represents a culture unique to that person. Therefore, group leaders need to approach each group session with what Dyche and Zayas (1995) referred to as cultural naiveté. They advocated that counselors learn from their clients' storytelling about their experiences with acculturation and migration. This approach has a here-and-now appeal and avoids practicing multicultural counseling based on assumptions drawn from previous cognitive experiences.

Finally, I found direction. This book had to state its limitations regarding multicultural group work, and then its intentions. First, it is limited to the reader's own cognitive and affective experiences with persons of different cultures. The intentions of the book are to expose readers to 11 group leaders whose own cultural representations reflect individual and unique families of origin, regions, and migration and acculturation experiences. Thus, by no means will we claim that this book represents the whole of multicultural group work. Instead, it is our intention to present to our readers how persons of various cultural backgrounds may interpret events that occur in multicultural groups when they are members, and then again when they are leaders. It is our desire that readers will be personally affected as a result of being exposed to group leaders who relate how their cultural and ethnic heritage may influence the way they lead multicultural groups. Furthermore, we hope readers will consider bringing their own "cultural naiveté" to each of their group sessions and will view each member's storytelling as being unique to that person's own acculturation experiences.

Additionally, we think it is essential for group leaders to recognize how the purposes of task groups, psychoeducational groups, and counseling and therapy groups may interact with different cultural values and expectations. Group leaders must learn how to effectively utilize the inherent power that rests within the collective diversity of the groups they lead. It follows, therefore, that another of our intentions is to offer an initial step in the direction that helps group leaders learn how to effectively access this dimension of their groups.

The interactions between race, culture, community, family, and individual values are incredibly complex and need to be taken into consideration when conceptualizing multicultural group work. Group stages and group processes are constants that are present regardless of the complexwity of the group's participants (including the leaders). However, cultural diversity increases the complexity and diversity of member, leader, and group-as-a-whole interactions. Therefore, behaviors need to be considered within the context of the members' and leaders' personal worldviews.

We draw from group counseling theory the acknowledgment and utilization of a key ingredient to group process—what Arredondo (1994) refers to as each individual's "multidimensional identities" (p. 310). Yalom (1985) suggested that diversity is an essential element in effective group counseling; in "heterogeneous groups for long-term intensive interactional group therapy . . . the therapist strives for maximum heterogeneity in the patient" (pp. 264–265). This statement can be applied to other areas of group work as well. It can be assumed that the greater the cultural diversity within a group, the greater the heterogeneity—and thus, the group is likely to be more effective. Therefore, the primary purpose of this book is to help those who lead multicultural groups learn how to do so effectively.

We would like to thank the following reviewers for their helpful and constructive comments:

Mary Jo Blazek, University of Maine–Augusta
James Borling, Radford University
Nick Colangelo, University of Iowa
C. Timothy Dickel, Creighton University
Sharon Horne, The University of Memphis
LaVerne Jordan, Oliver Nazarene University
William B. Kline, Idaho State University
Kurt L. Kraus, Shippensburg University of Pennsylvania
Carolyn Magnuson, Lincoln University of Missouri
Daniel Sonkin, Sonoma State University

Introduction

HOW THIS BOOK IS ORGANIZED

The book develops through four parts. Part I, *Introduction to Multicultural Group Work*, is comprised of two chapters. Chapter 1, *Training Multiculturally Sensitive Group Leaders*, discusses the considerations that need to be given in the training of multicultural group leaders, while Chapter 2 addresses *Cultural Values and Their Impact on Group Work*. Part II, *Autobiographies of Respondents*, introduces the reader to each of the contributing experts through autobiographical sketches based on their responses to the following questions. The experts were asked to first answer these questions about themselves, and then provide the readers with a context for their answers:

1. Describe who you are in terms of age, race, any physical disability, sexual orientation, ethnicity and culture, family patterns, gender, socioeconomic status (SES), and intellectual ability (educational background).
2. How do you see yourself as a unique individual based on your ethnic, cultural, and family background?
3. How does your background contribute to your view of how groups work?
4. What strengths do you bring to groups based on your cultural background and beliefs? What limitations do you bring as well?

Part III, *Responses to Multicultural Group Work Vignettes*, has eight chapters that include four group counseling/therapy vignettes, two psycho-educational group vignettes, and two task group vignettes. Each vignette presents a critical incident that occurs in a group, along with experts' responses from two positions: First, as members of the group, and second, as leaders of the group. Three different experts were asked to address two preassigned vignettes (with the exception of Counseling/Therapy Group Vignette #1 and Task Group Vignette #1, which had two experts each). The experts were first aked to read the vignette and imagine what they would think of this group if they were members of it. They responded to the following questions based on being a member of the group:

1. Identify the multicultural issues that need to be taken into consideration for you as a member.
2. Explain how your ethnic and cultural background affected the way you would respond as a member.
3. Explain how your ethnic and cultural background may or may not inhibit the way you respond to the situation as a member.
4. Explain how your ethnic and cultural background may have influenced your choice of the response you made over any other that you may have been considering as a member.
5. As a result of the response you chose, identify the consequences you might anticipate as a member.
6. From your position as a member, explain what the most glaring or outstanding aspect was of the situation which impacted you from your ethnic and cultural orientation.

The experts were then asked to read the vignette again and imagine what they would think of this group if they were the leader. They responded to the following questions based on being a leader of the group:

1. If this type of incident would not occur in your group, explain why it would not.
2. Identify the multicultural issues that need to be taken into consideration for you as a leader.
3. Explain how your ethnic and cultural background affected the way you would respond as a leader.
4. Explain how your ethnic and cultural background may or may not inhibit the way you respond to the situation as a leader.
5. Explain how your ethnic and cultural background may have influenced your choice of the response you made over any other that you may have been considering as a leader.
6. As a result of the response you chose, identify the consequences you might anticipate as a leader.
7. From your position as a leader, explain what the most glaring or outstanding aspect was of the situation which impacted you from your ethnic and cultural orientation.

8. Based on the composition of this group, what multicultural issues (etic and emic) need to be taken into consideration as the incident is addressed in group?

In each vignette chapter, the authors offer a summary and analysis of the experts' responses in their roles as group members and group leaders. The authors present similarities and differences among the experts' responses, and they cite the degree of congruence the experts' responses had with their stated cultural and ethnic backgrounds.

Part IV, *Conclusions*, consists of two chapters: Chapter 12, *What Have We Learned?*, and Chapter 13, *Suggestions for Best Practices in Multicultural Group Work*. In the former chapter, the authors draw upon the ideas presented throughout the first three parts of the book and give a singular voice (and message) based on all that has been said. Included in this chapter is the rationale for how the traditionally Eurocentric concepts of group processes and group factors apply to multicultural group work. In the last chapter, the authors offer guidelines for best practice of multicultural group work.

Introduction to Multicultural Group Work

These introductory chapters are intended to lay a foundation and backdrop for the autobiographies and reactions to group vignettes that follow. The first chapter in this section provides an overview of the training of multiculturally competent group workers and makes specific suggestions for training activities. The second chapter identifies values inherent in traditional methods of group work, and compares and contrasts these values to different cultural beliefs and worldviews.

There is a need . . . "for counselors to transcend their own ethnocentric thinking about the content and process of group counseling as they strive to more respectfully and ethically address the needs and perspectives of persons who come from cultural-racial backgrounds different from their own."
(D'Andrea, 2003, p. 265)

1 CHAPTER | Training Multiculturally Sensitive Group Leaders

Vicki Bowman's (1996) model for multicultural training in general suggested three levels of interpersonal awareness: (a) know yourself; (b) know about others, specifically other cultures, lifestyles, and their values; and (c) know about how one relates to others, emphasizing the cultural differences in interpersonal behavior. Atkinson, Kim, and Caldwell (1998) emphasized the assessment of client values, level of acculturation, locus of problem's etiology, and the group worker's goal of helping as essential to effective multicultural counseling. Our model has incorporated these suggestions as well as extended them to focus specifically on how to incorporate diversity within group work. The suggestions build on each other and are discussed in an ascending order: (a) Examine your own cultural and ethnic values and racial identity to understand who you are as a person; (b) examine your beliefs about group work and the inherent assumptions within the Eurocentric view of group work; (c) learn about other cultures in terms of what they value and how it may affect group work; and (d) develop your personal plan for group work that emphasizes and utilizes cultural diversity. Each suggestion is discussed in terms of specific recommendations for group leaders individually, followed by a discussion of systematic ways to incorporate multicultural awareness into group work curriculum.

EXAMINING YOUR OWN CULTURAL AND ETHNIC VALUES AND RACIAL IDENTITY

Group leaders must first examine how their cultural assumptions affect their work with clients. For example, Greeley et al. (1992) stated:

> Strict adherence to time schedules, reliance on standard English and verbal, behavioral, or emotional expressiveness are not uniformly valued across class or cultures. Misunderstandings that arise from variations in communication or from assumptions of the uniformity or homogeneity of cultures may lead to alienation within the group and an inability to develop a supportive counseling relationship with members. (p. 203)

Group leaders must learn to recognize and separate their own cultural assumptions from the assumptions of their chosen theoretical orientation and those basic to group dynamics. Once the influence of culture and theoretical beliefs on their approach to group counseling is recognized, group leaders are more aware and communicate more directly that how they approach counseling, and specifically group counseling, is from their own, rather than a universal, perspective—and thus, such leaders are more sensitive to differing perspectives.

Exploration of Cultural Heritage and Background

Each person has her own worldview. It is influenced by a myriad of factors and groups of people: who she is as a person, the values of her family as she grew up, the community she identified with as a young person, the community she now identifies with, religious or spiritual values, the values of the cultural group she identifies with, and the values of the racial group she identifies with. In addition, unique individual factors such as sexual orientation, education, geographic location, and the influence of a physical or emotional or learning disability all combine to make each person unique.

Exploration of Worldview and Background

It is essential for group leaders to understand where their values come from and the impact of their values on life choices, and to be able to separate their personal values from those they have about the counseling and group process (or at least acknowledge how their personal values may affect the values they hold about counseling).

There are a number of things you can do to increase self-awareness. Group leaders must understand the impact of potential biases on the kinds of issues they attend to, the potential interventions they may select, and how they respond to individual group members. In order to maintain objectivity and use yourself more effectively in counseling relationships and group work, explore the following questions, which will help you sort out your values and determine how they are similar or dissimilar to those of people around you. First, start by listing your values. What is important to you? What do you value? How should people interact with each other respectfully? How should people communicate with each other with dignity and effectively? What makes a person successful? How do people learn and change and grow? Clearly identify which values are your personal values, which things you value because of your theoretical approach to counseling and group work, and which values come from both. Next, list the values of the various groups that you have been or are currently affiliated with. Use a separate column for each group. Start with your immediate family, and then list the values of your extended family, the community you grew up in, your peers as your grew up, the community you live in now, your peers now, your religious community, your cultural group, and your racial group. Then, think about how the following areas of multiculturalism and diversity (Council for Accreditation of Counseling and Related Educational Programs [CACREP], 2001) may influence your values: age, physical disability, sexual orientation, family patterns, gender, socioeconomic status, and intellectual ability (educational level and background). Note where the majority of your current values come from. Also note any conflicts between different sets of values, how you perceive these conflicts, how you resolve such conflicts, and potential problems these conflicts may present.

Imber-Black (1997) suggested cultural genograms as a useful tool in the training of multiculturally competent counselors. Hardy and Laszloffy (1995) presented a model of a cultural genogram with the primary goal of promoting cultural awareness and sensitivity by helping trainees to understand their cultural identity. They suggested two major steps in preparing a cultural genogram: (a) getting organized, and (b) putting it together. The getting-organized step includes defining one's culture of origin, organizing principles and pride/same issues, creating symbols to denote all pride/shame issues, selecting colors to represent each group that comprises a person's culture of origin, and identifying intercultural marriages. The putting-it-together step consists of establishing cultural framework charts; constructing a genogram of at least three generations that identifies intercultural marriages, the composition of each person's cultural identity, and the symbols denoting pride/shame issues; and considering questions to identify the various sociological factors that contribute to cultural identity. McGoldrick and Gerson (1985), in their book entitled *Genograms in Family Assessment*, provided specific directions for creating and interpreting genograms as a way of identifying the influence of family on one's worldview.

Falicov (1995) designed an intervention similar to the cultural genogram with a focus on four key comparative parameters: ecological context, migration and acculturation, family organization, and family life cycle. She suggested that "the integration of these two steps—the cross-cultural comparisons in the four key parameters, and the exploratory, self-reflexive attitudes of the therapist along the same parameters—organizes the comparative framework.

The parameters become road maps to facilitate travel in the client cultural pattern interactions" (p. 378). The ecological context focuses on the inter-actions between the family and the communities to which the family belongs (racial, ethnic, religious, rural-urban); between the families' living and work conditions; and between the family and institutions such as schools and social agencies. Migration and acculturation focuses on migration experiences and destruction in family lives as well as families' education to a new culture. Family organization assesses the ways that family groups are organized, such as primary central relationships, boundaries, roles, and communication styles. Family life cycle emphasizes transitions, crisis points, and the renegotiation of roles precipitated by additions, losses, and changes of status among family members. Integral to Falicov's intervention is the emphasis on the counselor's parallel assessment, the therapist map as she calls it, and the continual com-parison of the therapist map to the map of the family the therapist is working with. Continual assessment and monitoring of potential cultural biases that the counselor may be bringing to counseling is critical.

Bowman (1996) suggested a series of activities that can be done individu-ally or as part of a class to help group leaders explore their heritage: *Roots* papers, which outline family history, values, and experiences; *Draw Your Culture*, which involves the drawing of symbols, designs, or events that have influenced one in one's culture, and the *Cultural Coat of Arms*, which identifies a symbol for one's culture, a favorite cultural food, the number of generations the family has been in the United States, an artifact of culture that is in one's home, and a common stereotype of this cultural group. In addition, examples of several activities that may be used to help group leaders and group members explore their cultural backgrounds have been outlined in a publication by the Association for Specialists in Group Work (ASGW) entitled: *Group Work Expert Share Their Favorite Activities: A Guide to Choosing, Planning, Conducting, and Processing* (DeLucia-Waack, Bridbord, & Kleiner, 2002).

Asner-Self (2002) described an activity entitled *Country-of-Origin Fairy Tales*. This activity utilizes the fairy tale Hansel and Gretel as a starting point to illuminate the cultural assumptions and values that are embedded in our fairy tales. A second part of the activity asks group members to recall fairy tales from their cultural background and to then identify the cultural assump-tions and values embedded within them. Lastly, group members are asked to compare and contrast these assumptions and values and to ponder how they influence group members' worldviews and relational patterns.

Hulse-Killacky (2002) described a brief activity to prompt discussion of cultural differences and family backgrounds in the beginning part of group work. She simply asks members to state their names, how they got their names, whether they like their names, and what names they would choose if they don't like their names. Hulse-Killacky noted that one comment often made during the processing of this activity is "I have learned some added information about each person's culture and family."

Hulse-Killacky, Killacky, and Donigian (2001) often use an activity that promotes community building in group work. They ask the group to discuss three important questions that emphasize the influence of both the individual and the group as a whole: Who am I? Who am I with you? Who are we together? Although these three questions were not designed specifically for multicultural group work, they are useful in asking group members in any kind of group to examine how they see themselves as individuals, in relationship to others, and as part of the bigger group. Group members' answers may differ based on their views of individualism, collectivism, connection, and responsibility as part of the group.

Group leaders must discuss their heritage and values, and discover the similarities and differences between those of various backgrounds. Also, activities focused on knowing oneself must be designed to respect individuals' rights to inquiry, encourage honest dialogue, and avoid judgment in order to heighten feelings of self-worth and empowerment (Bowman, 1996). Verbalizing similar and different values, along with discussing how to respect differences and utilize them to increase group problem-solving, is essential to effective group work.

Confronting Racism and Prejudice

Chung (2003) extended the idea of group leaders understanding their own values and the similarities and differences between their values and other people's values even a step further. She stated:

> [G]roup leaders must undergo an in-depth examination of their own racial/ethnic identity, honestly examining personal prejudices, stereotypes, and biases. This calls for assessment of their own socialization and conditioning with regards to other racial or ethnic groups, the prejudice and bias towards that group, as well as, the stereotypes they hold of that group. They must be aware, understand, acknowledge and accept issues of racism, discrimination, and oppression, as well the concept of White privilege. This requires that group leaders be able to identify and be aware of countertransference issues. (p.10)

For example, female group leaders may face problems with Asian men who come from a male-dominated culture, requiring the female leaders to deal with their own feelings about men. In turn, Asian men may be conflicted about having a woman in a leadership position. If these issues are not understood and addressed, group interaction may be inhibited.

D'Andrea (2003) made several important points related to racism and prejudice that white group leaders in an increasingly multicultural society must be aware of. In a chapter on the impact of racial identity development of group leaders and members on group effectiveness, he noted that nonmajority racial-cultural identity models of development all emphasize the following points:

1. Members of the dominant racial-cultural group in the United States (white, English-speaking persons of Western European descent) continue to disproportionately benefit from a host of social, educational, economic, and personal privileges and advantages that individuals from racially dis-

empowered minority groups do not (Cross, 1995; D'Andrea & Daniels, in press; Helms, 1995; Scheurich, 1993; Scheurich & Young, 1997.)

2. A number of sociopolitical factors have been identified as playing key roles in maintaining the social inequities that continue to exist in the United States. These include the way various forms of racism, racial stereotyping, discrimination, and cultural oppression continue to be played out in our contemporary society.

3. Not only do the complex problems of racism, racial stereotyping, discrimination, and cultural oppression help to sustain an unfair and racially stratified structural arrangement in our nation, but these sociopolitical factors also have an impact on the psychological development of white and non-white persons in our nation.

4. According to most racial-cultural identity development theorists, persons who are victimized by various forms of racism and cultural oppression commonly rely on other persons within their own racial-cultural group for psychological support and assistance as they strive to cope with the stressors of life and make sense of who they are. This results in the development of a *group referenced identity*: a unique identity that often provides persons of color with a heightened sense of personal power and support that is linked to the collective survival and progress of their group and fosters the development of healthy individual racial-cultural identities.

5. Differences in racial-cultural identity development reflect some of the within-group differences that are exhibited by persons who come from similar racial-cultural groups and backgrounds. These differences have many important implications for multicultural counseling in general and the challenges practitioners face when they find themselves working in racially heterogeneous group counseling settings in particular (Merta, 1995.)

6. To run racially heterogeneous groups in an effective, respectful, and ethical manner, counselors need to be able to accurately assess how their clients' and their own level of racial identity development affects the counseling process. (D'Andrea, 2003, p. 267)

What is most striking in D'Andrea's statements is the impact of racism and prejudice. How often do group leaders who are of the dominant racial-cultural group give lip service to such concepts without truly understanding or comprehending the impact of racism and oppression on the daily existence of others? D'Andrea (2003) eloquently summed up our thoughts on this question: "Members of the dominant racial-cultural group in the United States (White, English-speaking persons from western European descent) continue to disproportionately benefit from a host of social, educational, economic, and personal privileges and advantages that individuals from racially-disempowered minority groups do not" (p. 267).

In discussing a related concept, Friere (1983) described three effects of oppression: (a) existential duality, (b) self-deprecation, and (c) fatalism. He postulated that the oppressed are, at the same time, both themselves and the oppressor whose image they have internalized. Friere stated:

This internalization of the oppressor's views fuels self-deprecation, as the oppressed realize that many of their efforts to progress are fruitless. Finally, a sense of fatalism results from the historical and sociological powerlessness they have experienced. Such concepts must be taken into consideration when working with clients of different races as the manifestations of oppression resemble mental illness and personality disorders if not interpreted within the context of their lives. (p.72)

As a next step in the self-awareness process, Bowman (1996) suggested a series of activities to explore personal beliefs and attitudes about racism, power, and privilege. In *Circle Break-in* (Katz, 1978), participants "get in touch with the power they have in this country as Whites to exclude non-Whites from the privileges of the majority race" (Bowman, 1996, p. 19) by creating a circle and not allowing certain participants to join in. In *Create Your Prejudice Hierarchy* (Katz, 1978), participants create a hierarchy of their prejudices in an effort to identify and discuss their biases and what they can do about them. "Guilt and defensiveness require time and a safe environment. Students need the opportunity to come to terms with concepts and experiences of prejudice, racism, and oppression. Many trainees have never heard of White privilege let alone considered its implications (Bowman, 1996, p. 19).

Beck (2002) described an activity in which people are asked to examine potential biases and prejudices they may hold about persons of different cultural, ethnic, racial, and lifestyle groups by placing labels on each person's back and then asking the others to interact with them without revealing the labels, but based on traditional perceptions, stereotypes, and biases that people may hold about the label. Processing questions highlight such issues as: what it felt like to be treated differently based on a label or stereotype, what it was like to watch others being discriminated against, and changes in behavior as a result of this activity.

Exploration of Racial Identity Development

Everyone has a racial and cultural identity, and it is important to begin by emphasizing how this identity shapes a person's unique identity and how it influences the way in which a person interacts with others. Most importantly for group leaders, this identity shapes their views of counseling and clients, specifically and in general. In a chapter on generalizing racial identity interaction theory to groups, Helms (1984) emphasized the importance of the relationship between groups and racial identity for two different reasons. First, individuals do not develop their sense of racial identity development in a vacuum. In fact, she stated: "individuals do not develop a sense of racial identity independently of group interactions, but rather it evolves in response to various group-level socialization experiences from which the person makes inferences about herself or himself" (p. 187). Secondly, Helms discussed the impact of the racial identity of specific group members on group functioning. She noted: "racial identity issues may be undercurrents . . . which, if left untreated, can contribute to the group's demise of this functionality" (p. 189). Helms noted that while racially homogenous groups may have an easier time of managing racial identity issues than racially mixed groups, group differences in racial identity still have an impact on specific group members, even if they are of the same race. For racially mixed groups, Helms suggested that race proportion is an issue. For racially homogenous groups, she suggested that the number of individuals within each stage of racial identity may determine the direction of group.

Racial identity development significantly affects group members' behavior and perceptions of others, as well as group process and dynamics. If racial identity development is based on an individual's perceptions of himself as a member of a cultural group and an individual's perceptions of other cultural groups, then it makes sense that racial identity development of group members will significantly affect what happens in groups (D'Andrea, 2003). Depending on their stage of racial identity development, members may have strong preferences regarding the race and ethnicity of the group leader, and the composition of group members. Their racial identity development may also influence what they are willing to disclose in group, their perceptions of problems, and their selection of solutions.

Several models have been suggested for racial identity development that are applicable to both group members and leaders. Most are specific to a cultural group or race, recognizing that while there are some similarities in the stages, there are unique differences for each cultural group. Differences may reflect relationships with the dominant culture, oppression, racism, and prejudice. We will briefly review several different models of racial identity development and the assessment measures that are used with these models.

Sue and Sue (1999) developed a generic theoretical framework called the racial-cultural identity development model based on the similarities they noted in culture-specific racial identity development models. They noted that "at each level or stage of racial-cultural identity development, individuals typically exhibit corresponding attitudes and beliefs about (a) the self, (b) other members of the same minority group, (c) persons from other minority groups, and (d) individuals in the dominant racial-cultural group in the United States" (p. 128). Five stages were identified: conformist, dissonance, resistance and immersion, introspection, and integrative awareness. In the *conformist* stage, due to the pressures and stress of being racially and culturally different, individuals typically internalize negative attitudes and beliefs about their own cultural group and idealize all aspects of the dominant cultural-racial group. The *dissonance* stage is characterized by a sense of confusion about one's racial-cultural identity. There is growing awareness of racism and oppression and appreciation for some of the positive aspects of one's cultural background. The *resistance and immersion* stage is marked by an idealization of the group of color and the denigration of whites. Self-discovery occurs as people in this stage immerse themselves in learning as much as they can about their racial-cultural values, beliefs, history, and heritage. Individuals enter the *introspection* stage motivated to explore issues related to their own sense of personal independence and economy as well as to rethink the way they relate to other persons and their racial-cultural group. There is a shift away from the unequivocal acceptance of one's own racial-cultural group and some reaching out to members of other minority groups and the dominant group. The *integrative awareness* stage is characterized as a more complex integrative racial identity with a new worldview and revitalized personality (D'Andrea, 2003).

Models of Asian Racial Identity Development   Kim's model (1981), based on narratives from third-generation Japanese-American women, incorporates the influence of acculturation, exposure to cultural differences, and environmental negativism to racial differences, personal methods of handling race-related conflicts, and the effects of groups or social movements on the Asian-American individual. The *awareness* stage begins around the age of 3 with the child's family members serving as her significant ethnic group model. The *white identification* stage begins upon entering school. The realization of differences may lead the child to self-blame and a desire to escape from her own racial heritage by identifying with white society. The *awakening to social political consciousness* stage means the adoption of a new perspective, with the primary results being the abandonment of identification with white society and a consequent understanding of oppression and oppressed groups. The *redirection* stage consists of a renewed connection with one's Asian-American heritage and culture. Anger against white racism may become a defining theme, with concommitment increases of Asian-American pride. The *incorporation* stage represents the highest form of identity evolution with the development of a positive and comfortable identity as an Asian American and respect for other racial and cultural heritages.

Chinese Model of Racial Identity Development   Sue and Sue (1971) proposed four different Chinese-American personality types based on level of acculturation: (a) *traditionalist*: a person, typically foreign-born, who internalizes traditional Chinese customs and values, resists acculturation forces, and believes in the "old ways"; (b) *assimilationist*: a person who rejects Asian values, adopts American culture, and tends to identify herself as an American; (c) *marginal person*: an individual who rejects both American and Asian cultures and feels alienated from both cultures; and (d) *bicultural Asian American*: a person who is in the process of forming a positive identity and who is ethnically and politically aware.

Japanese Model of Racial Identity Development   Kitano (1982) proposed a model of Japanese-American role behaviors. Four types were formulated: (a) *positive-positive*, in which the person identifies with both Japanese and white cultures without role conflict; (b) *negative-positive*, in which there is a rejection of white culture and acceptance of Japanese-American culture with accompanying role conflict; (c) *positive-negative*, in which the person accepts white culture and rejects Japanese culture with accompanying role conflict; and (d) *negative-negative*, in which the individual rejects both cultures.

Models of Latino Racial Identity Development　Ruiz's model (1990), based on case studies of Chicanos/Latinos, proposes a five-stage model of Latino identity development. During the *causal* period, Latinos experience messages from the environment and significant others that negate their ethnic heritage, and thus there is a failure to identify with Latino culture. During the *cognitive* period, as a result of the negative and distorted messages, three erroneous belief systems of Latino heritage become incorporated into mental sets: (a) there is an association of ethnic group membership with poverty and prejudice, (b) assimilation to white society is seen as the only means of escape, and (c) assimilation is seen as the only possible road to success. During the *consequence* period, fragmentation of ethnic identity becomes very noticeable. The person feels embarrassed by ethnic markers, which leads to an estrangement from and rejection of Latino heritage. During the *working through* stage, the person is unable to cope with the psychological distress of ethnic identity conflict. He is no longer able to pretend to identify with an alien ethnic identity and is propelled to reclaim and reintegrate his ethnic identity fragments. During *successful resolution*, there is greater acceptance of the individual's culture and ethnicity, resulting in improvement of self-esteem and a sense of ethnic identity representing positive and success-promoting resources.

A Model of African-American Racial Identity Development　Helms (1984) suggested a four-stage model. In the *preencounter* stage, there is a denial of the importance of race and an idealization of Euro-American values. In the next stage, *encounter*, there is confusion of black identity in the previous idealization of whites. In the *immersion-emersion* stage, the attitude is primarily a pro-black/anti-white one, with a denial of whites and an idealization of blacks. In the final stage, *internalization*, there is primarily an identification with blackness but also a tolerance and acknowledgement of whites.

Models of White Racial Identity Development　Several authors (Helms, 1984; Ponterotto, 1988; Sabnani, Ponterotto, & Borodovsky, 1991) have suggested a racial identity development model for Anglo Americans. The first stage is called *preexposure/precontact* and occurs when there is an absence of self-awareness as a racial being. People in this stage typically accept group stereotypes and have no awareness of multicultural issues or of living in an oppressive society. They do not question the Euro-centered worldview. The second stage is called *conflict*. The conflict is between cultural norms and humanitarian values. People in this stage have an increasing awareness of racism and begin the process of self-examination of the assumptions of their culture often resulting in guilt, anger, and depression. The third stage is called *prominary/antiracism* and is typified by an overidentification and paternalism toward multicultural persons. The fourth stage consists of a *retreat* into the white culture as a result of the feelings of rejection, defensiveness, and fear. At this point, the person needs to work through his own feelings. The final stage is called *redefinition and integration*. Individuals at this stage internalize their white identity with ownership and pride. At the same time, they value cultural differences and promote a culturally transcendent worldview.

Helms (1995) presented an updated model of white racial identity development called "white racial identity ego statuses." The *contact* status occurs when whites exhibit satisfaction with a racial status quo and are oblivious to racism. If racial factors influence decisions, they do so in a simplistic manner. The *disintegration* status occurs when white persons experience a sense of disorientation and anxiety as a result of facing unresolvable racial moral dilemmas that force the person to choose between own-group loyalty and humanism. The *reintegration* status is characterized by the idealization of one socioracial group and intolerance for other groups. This *pseudoindependence* status typically consists of intellectual commitment to one's own socioracial group with a tolerance of the other groups. The *immersion/emersion* status consists of a search for the personal meaning of racism and cultural oppression as well as the ways in which one benefits from being a part of the dominant racial group.

Related Concepts: Ethnic Identity, Acculturation, and Biculturalism

The constructs of ethnic identity, acculturation, and biculturalism are relevant to the discussion of racial identity development and group work. We will briefly define them, suggest measures of assessment, and comment on their potential impact on group work. *Acculturation* refers to the processes within which ethnic groups adapt to mainstream culture with varying degrees across the different social-cultural contexts (Epsin, 1987). Language proficiency is viewed as a key component of acculturation. Furthermore, Berry (1995) defined psychological acculturation as "the process by which individuals change, both being influenced by contact with another culture and by being participants in the general acculturative changes under way in their own culture" (p. 460).

The term *biculturalism* represents a revision of the construct of acculturation. Specifically, biculturalism can be characterized as a bidimensional model of acculturation (Szapocznik et al., 1984). LaFromboise, Coleman, and Gerton (1995) viewed bicultural individuals as acquiring the second culture through an alternation method: "The alternation method of second-culture acquisition assumes that it is possible for an individual to know and understand two different cultures. It also presupposes that an individual can alter his or her behavior to fit a particular social context" (p. 382). So instead of an "either-or" process in which moving toward the mainstream culture necessarily presupposes the loss of values, beliefs, and behaviors of the home culture, biculturalism assumes proficiency in both cultures.

Another related and correlated concept is that of *ethnic identity*. Nesdale, Rooney, and Smith (1997) defined ethnic identity as the magnitude to which an individual appreciates and actively engages in her own cultural values, traditions, beliefs, and behaviors. Phinney (1995) described ethnic identity as being "that part of an individual's self-concept which derives from the knowledge of membership in a social group, together with the value and emotional significance related to the membership" (p. 58). During the establishment of one's identity, ethnic heritage is a strong influence:

> In a pluralistic society (e.g., the United States) in which multiple ethnic groups with different minority statuses exist, the process of ethnic identity development involves a minority person's attempt to simultaneously locate himself or herself psychologically and socially to one's ethnic group and the majority group. Thus, ethnic identity represents a social-psychological outcome that is based on an assessment of the "fit" between a minority person's ethnic self and other ethnic social systems in the environment." (Kwan, 2000, pp. 142–143)

Biculturalism, acculturation, and ethnic identity may all affect a group member's self-esteem, interpersonal behavior, and thus her participation in psychoeducational, counseling, and therapy groups. Phinney, Cantu, and Kurtz (1997) reported that ethnic identity was a significant predictor of self-esteem for African-American, Latino, and white adolescents. Cavazos and DeLucia-Waack (2003), in a study of self-esteem and ethnic identity of Latino adolescents enrolled in bilingual and regular education programs, found that those students enrolled in a bilingual education program were (as hypothesized) more acculturated to their Latino ethnic group, as indicated by significantly higher levels of the use of the Spanish language within and outside the family context. They also reported significant differences between predictors of self-esteem based on whether students attended a bilingual education program or a regular education program. For the students enrolled in a bilingual education program, grade point average (GPA), total number of years of living in the United States, and affirmation, belonging, and commitment of the multigroup Ethnic Identity Measure together significantly predicted self-esteem. For Latino students enrolled in a regular education program, none of the variables (GPA, total number of years living in the United States, or acculturation and ethnic identity) proved to significantly predict self-esteem. Thus, it seems essential to assess acculturation, bilingualism, and ethnic identity, as these may impact racial identity development and, thus, perceptions of other group members and subsequent participation in group work.

The Impact of Racial Identity Development on Group Process   To further support the importance of understanding group leaders' and group members' racial identity development, Helms (1990) adopted her model of relationship types for individual counseling to the relationship between group members and group leaders and suggested the potential impact of these relationships on group interaction, dynamics, and effectiveness. Helms suggested that it is useful to assess the racial identity development of both the group leader and specific group members as well. She describes four types of leader-member relationships. *Parallel relationships* are those in which the group leader and a coalition of the group share the same or analogous stages of racial identity. For example, in all-white groups, parallel relationships between leaders and a coalition of the group occur when both are in the contact or disintegration stage. For an all-black group, parallel relationships occur when leaders and a coalition share the same stage of black identity. And for groups that are racially heterogeneous, parallel relationships would include the *preen-counter/reintegration, internalization/autonomy,* and perhaps the *encounter/disintegration* status. The common theme in parallel relationships is inertia, because the majority of the participants in the group, including the group leader, are all at the same stage, and thus, share similar worldviews, which makes it difficult for them to challenge one another to move beyond their common world. It makes sense that some heterogeneity in racial identity development is useful to group productiveness.

Regressive relationships are characterized by a coalition of members whose stage of racial identity development is more advanced than that of their leader; thus, the major theme of this type of relationship is regression (Helms, 1990). Group leaders' attempts to influence coalitions in their view of racial issues are no longer functional because they are not at the level that is needed.

Crossed relationships occur when the group leaders' stage of identity development is conceptually opposite from that of a coalition of members; thus, relationships tend to be combative. Helms (1990) gave the example of a group leader who is in the role of authority while the coalition is in the role of partner or follower.

Progressive relationships, as described by Helms (1990), appear to be the most useful and desirable ones in group work. In this type of relationship, the group leader is at a stage of racial identity that is more developed than those of the coalition of group members. The general theme in progressive relationships is movement and energy, with the leader encouraging the coalition to move beyond its present level of development.

Summary   It is essential that group leaders establish what their values are and how these values affect their theoretical orientation and their work with clients. Earlier we explained the importance of group leaders understanding themselves as cultural beings and how such understanding promotes effective group work by decreasing the amount of bias toward issues, interventions, and individual members. Consistent with this position regarding group leaders and their values, we asked 11 experts in the fields of multicultural counseling and group work a series of questions that were intended to help them identify their value orientations and the influence of their cultural heritages. We then asked them to identify how these values influence their views of counseling and group work. (See the list of questions in the Introduction.) Their descriptions of themselves as multicultural people and group leaders can be found in Parts II and III of this book. It is essential to understand the respondents' cultural heritage in order to have a framework within which to understand their comments, theoretical approaches, and suggested interventions.

When you read the autobiographies of the 11 multicultural experts in group work and their responses to the different group vignettes, you will probably be struck by the respondents' descriptions of themselves. For some, gender and age play a significant role in how they view themselves and in their worldviews. For others, the influences of extended family, community, and ethnic groups are great. Sexual orientation (and the decision about whether or not to disclose it) is a key factor in several reactions to the vignettes. You will also notice that sometimes it is relatively easy for our respondents to identify whether their beliefs and values come from an identification with a specific cultural or ethnic group, a geographic region, or religious beliefs, while at other times it is not clear to the reader (or even to the respondent) exactly how they developed particular beliefs or values.

Kalodner (2002), as part of the panel discussion at the ASGW national conference on multicultural group work, noted that it was easy for her to identify who she was as a result of her background. The difficulty for her was in sorting out how being a woman, being Jewish, being married to a Hispanic man, and being educated influenced her uniquely as a person. She added that in some ways, it was easier for close friends and people who knew her well to point out aspects of herself that seemed to result from her different influences.

It seems that the process of self-examination is more important than the end result. Group leaders continually need to ask themselves: What are my values? Where did they come from? How do they influence my behavior in group? How do they influence my behavior toward members of different cultural groups? Am I in some way trying to impose my values upon others?

EXAMINING YOUR BELIEFS AND INHERENT ASSUMPTIONS

The next step is to examine your theoretical approach toward group work within the context of your worldview and personal values. How does what you believe about people and about how they learn, change, and grow influence your style of group work? And specifically, how do groups work, and what makes them effective?

Most traditional counseling theories are based upon Eurocentric assumptions about relationships. "When many of the traditional theoretical orientations were originally formulated, individual differences due to culture, gender, class, or other variables were not taken into account. . . . These theories, and techniques, therefore, may not be applicable to all cultural and ethnic groups as most are more value-laden than value-free" (Kincade & Evans, 1996, p. 93). In their chapter entitled "Counseling Theories, Process, and Interventions in a Multicultural Context," Kincade and Evans identified the implicit Eurocentric assumptions of several theoretical approaches to counseling and potential conflicts with other cultural values. The two areas they focused on were: how change occurs, and the role of the group worker and counseling techniques. For instance, they suggested that the person-centered approach may be problematic to cultures, such as an Asian culture, that stress seeking help from an older and wiser person, since the group worker may tend to reflect more than give direction. For the cognitive-behavioral approach, Kincade and Evans noted that some cultures may value the problem focus and the concentration on thoughts, rather than feelings. These authors also reviewed several other approaches (Gestalt, psychodynamic) in terms of their applicability to multicultural populations and suggested that many counseling theories include specific embedded assumptions about how individuals, families, and communities function, change, and interact.

DeLucia-Waack (1996) also discussed the implicit assumptions in traditional approaches to group work. She suggested that there are several Eurocentric assumptions of group counseling that must be taken into account when working with multicultural groups. The first is the individual as a focus of treatment. Independence and self-sufficiency is valued in Anglo culture, but other cultures emphasize family, cooperation, and group loyalty. The second implicit Eurocentric assumption is the importance of verbalization. "Several of Yalom's (1985) therapeutic factors of group counseling are based on the Eurocentric assumption that people need to self-disclose. . . . Talking is essential to these therapeutic factors, with the implicit expectation that members speak English within the group. This is one perspective; others emphasize silence" (DeLucia-Waack, p. 164).

A third assumption discussed by DeLucia-Waack (1996) is the importance of unstructured interaction between group members. The idea behind this is that as group members interact without structure, they will display typical relationship patterns and problems, and thus be able to work on changing and improving their relationships. However, some cultures view group workers as experts or elders; members from these cultures may not interact without being asked to, or may act within prescribed relationship patterns dictated by gender, class, or other social standards. Also related are the implicit assumptions about the role of the group leader. Group leaders may take the stance of not sharing much personal information about themselves or making direct suggestions about members' problems. Some cultural norms limit member interaction because the members do not have a personal relationship with the leader and do not know much about her. In addition, members of some cultural groups may desire direct suggestions and interventions, and may be disappointed and/or leave the group if they receive none.

The last implicit assumption of traditional group counseling that DeLucia-Waack (1996) discussed is the importance of taking risks and trying out new behaviors. Group leaders often emphasize the use of role-play and other activities to practice new behaviors. "It is difficult for some individuals to not be perfect in group and to attempt new behaviors with others watching. Cultural norms may suggest that individuals lose face if they do not succeed with others watching or that they have shamed a family member or friend by involving them in a role-play situation" (DeLucia-Waack, p. 166). The next chapter will discuss in more detail the assumptions inherent in traditional models of group work and how these may be similar or dissimilar to the values of other cultures and of persons from diverse backgrounds.

The next step in the assessment process is an examination of how your values impact your view of group work. As a group worker, it would be helpful to start by asking yourself: What is my theoretical orientation toward group work? What does it suggest about how change occurs? What does it suggest about the relationship between the group worker and the group member? How does this fit or not fit with my personal beliefs? If there is a conflict, how will I reconcile it? How are the assumptions of my counseling approach toward group work similar or dissimilar to other cultures' beliefs about change, seeking help, and relationships in general?

Table 1.1 lists issues related to diversity that cultures differ on in terms of their perspective, such as time, relationship structure, worldviews, and communication patterns that affect group process and dynamics. Pack-Brown and Fleming (2003) suggested a series of questions that group counselors might use to compare and contrast their worldviews with those of potential group members:

- What are the racial, ethnic, and cultural situations of each group member?
- What goals for the group does each member have?
- What are possible cross-cultural issues that may be evidenced in group?
- What possible thematic cultural value and beliefs system differences and similarities might be evidenced in group?
- What is my personal level of racial identity development?
- How will I assess each group member's racial identity development?
- What is my personal theory of effective group work with diverse and multicultural populations? (p. 190)

Pack-Brown and Fleming (2003) also suggested several African-centered values that are applicable to different cultures' worldviews and group assumptions. They include interconnectedness, group emphasis, collectivism, communication, time, history, power, and respect. Bolyard and Jensen-Scott (1996) presented a table describing a multicultural approach to crisis intervention that suggests several major themes related to value orientations: the nature of humankind, people/nature, time, activity, and relational (pp. 223–224). Torres Rivera, Wilbur, Roberts-Wilbur, and Phan (1999) also suggested, specifically for Latino clients, a series of topics and issues that are important to assess: time, money, relationships, friendship, intimacy, love, sexuality, parenting, commitment and responsibility, center of focus, communication and negotiation, thought, logic, decision making, power, rules, projects and process, and morality. Foeman (1991) suggested five goals for race-relations training that are relevant to training multicultural group leaders. They are: (a) discussion of race-related issues (demystification), (b) articulation of other groups' perspectives, (c) examination of other groups' perspectives, (d) finding validity in other groups' perspectives, and (e) utilizing others' perspectives in order to work together toward common goals more effectively.

As an integration of several of these themes, Table 1.1 can be used as a guide to assess your values for issues that are potentially relevant to diversity.

Table 1.1 | Issues Related to Diversity
and Differences in Perspectives Issue

Issue	Possible Perspectives
Relationship structure	Formal . . . informal
	Collateral . . . hierarchial
	Same-sex . . . opposite-sex interactions
	Male . . . female roles
Focus of treatment	Family . . . group . . . individual
Perception of authority figures	Respect . . . mistrust
	Inherited . . . achievement
	Within family . . . from outside
Time orientation	Clock . . . quorum time
Temporal focus	Past . . . present . . . future
Intrapersonal focus	Thoughts . . . feelings
Silence	Respectful . . . resistant
Talking	Attention-seeking . . . establishing relationship
Locus of control	Internal . . . external
	Individual . . . family . . . community
Nature of humankind	Good . . . evil
Relationship between people and nature	Mastery . . . harmony . . . subjugation
Expressiveness	Behavioral . . . emotional . . . verbal
Activity	Being . . . being-in-becoming . . . doing
Relational aspects	Lineality . . . collaterality . . . individualism
Worldview	Formism . . . contextualism . . . mechanism . . . organism
Communication patterns	Verbal . . . nonverbal
	Direct . . . indirect
	I . . . you statements
Physical contact	Between family . . . friends . . . strangers
Self-esteem	Achievement . . . relationships

Possible perspectives are listed in the righthand column to suggest some potential differences in worldviews. As you choose your perspective on these critical issues, think specifically about how the group process works and what makes groups effective.

LEARNING ABOUT OTHER CULTURES

Another step in the self-assessment process for group leaders is studying and understanding different cultures in terms of how cultural norms and values influence interactional styles, perceptions of problems, and perceptions of interventions and change relevant to group counseling. Group leaders must find guidelines and frameworks that organize cultural information but still remain flexible enough to recognize when a client's behavior and/or attitudes differ from cultural norms. "Perhaps we should think of the emic approach not so much as a 'multicultural cookbook' than as a cultural thesaurus" (Cheatham, 1994, p. 295). Thus, it is important to utilize information about cultures in general as a background upon which to collect data and to generate hypotheses both as a group counselor and as a person living in a multicultural world. As a group counselor, it is important to collect data about different cultures' values related to group counseling on topics such as authority figures, self-disclosure, relationship styles, interactional patterns, and perceptions of mental health and change. The distinction between emic and etic is important as one learns about similiarities and differences between cultures. Draguns (1976) distinguished between emic and etic as follows: *Emic* refers to the viewing of data in terms of being indigenous or unique to the culture in question, and *etic*, to the viewing of data in light of categories and concepts external to the culture but universal in their applicability (p. 2).

While it is not possible to be an expert on all cultures, group leaders must learn about and experience different cultural perspectives. It is not enough to read about cultures; some element of experience must be included as well. The goal of learning about other cultures is not to memorize their values and beliefs but to come to an understanding of how cultures differ and to develop an appreciation of these differences. Many multicultural counseling experts (D'Andrea, 2003; Hardy & Laszloffy, 1995; Torres Rivera, 2003) emphasize the importance of not just reading about other cultures, but living them as well. Personal interactions are necessary to understand and integrate different cultural perspectives and relationship dynamics.

Much has been written in the fields of counseling and psychology about different cultures, cultural values, and their impact on counseling. A reference list is provided at the end of this chapter that includes professional literature and videos about different cultures and multicultural issues.

Popular literature and movies also provide some good examples of lifestyles and values of other cultures. The most well-known examples of literature include: *The Joy Luck Club* (Tan, 1989), *I Know Why the Caged Bird Sings* (Angelou, 1970), *The Color Purple* (Walker, 1983), and *Bury My Heart at Wounded Knee* (Brown, 1970). Popular movies include: *Dances with Wolves, Come See the Paradise, Boyz'n the Hood*, and *American Me*. The list of suggested resources at the end of this chapter includes popular literature and movies that provide the reader with an in-depth look at other cultures.

Finally, it is not enough to simply read about other cultures; one needs to experience them as well. Many cultural activities and experiences are available in most communities; one simply needs to seek them out. Most universities offer coursework about other cultures and different groups of people. For example, popular courses include Psychology of Women, Counseling People with Disabilities, Psychology of African Americans, Latino Literature, and Study of Non-Western Religions, to name just a few. Cultural immersion experiences and language training are other ways to begin to understand other cultures.

In addition to these activities, Johnson et al. (1995) suggested consultation or coleadership of minority group work and/or actively taking inventory of the needs of minority groups in the community. In addition, volunteering in an urban or multiracial school would provide another chance to interact with and learn about people from other cultures. Phan and Torres (2003) made several suggestions for group leaders who work with linguistically different clients that are also applicable for anyone learning about different cultures. Their suggestions include: learn or become familiar with a language other than English; be aware of one's own linguistic biases and understand where these biases come from; view movies and read ESL (English as a Second Language) textbooks to understand the thinking process of linguistically different people; gain familiarity with ethnic neighborhoods to understand how people communicate in their own language; learn and know important phrases in clients' languages in order to establish credibility and respect with linguistically different clients; and be flexible and comfortable with ambiguity in order to allow clients to create their own structure in groups.

Pedersen (2002) suggested a group activity in which someone from another culture is interviewed and group members then assess the level of emotion exhibited by the person who was interviewed. Processing questions for this activity focus on how the attributions about emotions were made by individual group members, similarities and differences between perceptions and what the person interviewed reported in terms of emotion, and how often misperceptions may occur between individuals and potential reasons for misperceptions.

Another activity that has been suggested by Pack-Brown (2002) is called *Drumming*. Drumming is an Afrocentric approach to group work. It is a diversity-competent exercise espousing a collectivistic view of groups built around the African values of Umoja (oo-MOH-jah), which means unity, and Ujima (oo-JEE-mah), which means collective responsibility. The foundation upon which this group activity is constructed is the reality of "I am because we are." Group leaders continuously build on the African value of Kujichagulia (koo-ji-chah-goo-LEE-ah), which means self-empowerment, to promote "self-in-relation" among and between group members. Group members are taught to perceive "self" as a member of the community (the group) and to assume responsibility for promoting both individual and collective self-esteem and empowerment within group process and dynamics. This activity not only provides information about the African-American culture but also emphasizes group community building and the balance between I and we.

Garrett (2002) outlined an activity called *The Four Directions*. It informs members about a traditional Native American symbol, the Medicine Wheel, which emphasizes the cyclical nature of the world and the self. Both the world and the self are composed of four basic dimensions represented by the Four Directions—East, South, West, and North. This activity asks members to explore their spirituality based on the characteristics of these four dimensions. Along the same theme, John Lawrey (2002) suggested a college classroom ice-breaker exercise that utilizes a Native American council format. He utilizes the Native American Talking Stick and Council process to help members share objects of value with classmates and to promote self-disclosure and discussion of what they value, and why.

Several training techniques have been utilized to teach multicultural counseling skills. The Critical Incidents Method (Sue, 1981) involves a delineation of barriers to counseling and a generation of counseling methods appropriate to persons (described in vignettes) of varying cultural backgrounds. The Facilitating Interracial Groups (FIG) and the Counseling Ethnic Minorities techniques (McDavis & Parker, 1977; Weeks, Pedersen, & Brislin, 1977) are other methods that help to integrate knowledge about various cultures with the planning of culturally sensitive interventions. The FIG exercise, for example, teaches students how to organize and facilitate multicultural group experiences by discussing the literature on cross-cultural group facilitation, having students watch videotapes of models conducting an interracial group and critique the sessions, and having each student role-play the facilitator's role. Pedersen's (1983, 1988) Triad Model of Cross-Cultural Counseling Training also focuses on the application of counseling skills to multicultural counseling.

Much of what has been suggested in the professional literature and what is considered standard in terms of readings, videos, and activities in multicultural training does not focus specifically on multicultural group work. It is important to first acquire and integrate knowledge of cultural values, and then to begin examining the impact of different values and relationship patterns on group stages, dynamics, and member behavior. Conyne (1998) adapted Hansen's (1972) *What to Look for in Groups* "to include and be responsive to multicultural dimensions that are important in group life, and to provide a set of guidelines for using this approach" (Conyne, p. 23). Group leaders can use group simulations, group videos, or actual groups (with permission, of course) as a stimulus for this activity. They observe the group interactions and then answer a series of questions focused on the following areas: participation, influence, decision-making procedures, task functions, maintenance functions, group atmosphere, membership, feelings, and norms. Questions include: How might silence be related to cultural differences? In general, what cultural similarities and differences might be influencing a member's involvement, and how are they affecting the group? Are some members resentful that they have to make a special attempt to understand another member's culture? Do members of different cultural backgrounds overtly disagree or agree with each other? Answering these questions is a beginning in examining the impact of cultural values on group interaction.

As you read, watch, and have experience as a group worker, you need to begin to process and integrate the information you gain from these sources to determine what it says about future group work interactions. Such information can help you answer the following questions: What cultural values may help members to seek group work, and what values might inhibit them from seeking group work or from participating in group sessions? What cultural values may help group members to connect with the group leader or other group members, and what cultural values might inhibit their connection with the group leader or other members? What cultural values support the traditional concept of group work, and what cultural values are in conflict with it? How do these values vary within a culture? How does acculturation affect these values? Refer back to the perspectives you identified in Table 1.1 and compare them with the cultural values that you learn about and experience. We encourage you to begin thinking about what these cultural values mean in terms of how potential group members might behave in the group and the impact their behavior may have on the group process.

Although we have been stressing the importance of learning about values, beliefs, and worldviews within a culture, one cannot make blanket assumptions about persons based on their cultural affiliation. Chung (2003), in discussing Asian Americans, points out some issues that are important to consider for all cultures. The first issue is the importance of intergroup differences. Chung noted that there are potentially 40 groups of persons who are considered Asian American. She stressed, "each group has its own distinct historical and social-political backgrounds, languages, identity issues, cultures and challenges encountered in mainstream society" (p. 200–201). As an example, Japanese Americans present very different issues and dynamics in a group than Chinese Americans whose ancestors migrated to the United States to become laborers and never faced internment.

The second issue of importance is intergroup conflict. Chung (2003) presents the example of a teacher who, thinking she was displaying cultural sensitivity, placed Chinese and Japanese students together to work on a class project. The teacher was confused when the students refused to work together. Chung noted, "given the sociopolitical and historical background between China and Japan, this was not surprising. The Japanese attacks in China during World War II have intergenerational impacts and may result in tension between Chinese and Japanese students" (p. 201).

The third issue is intragroup differences. Chung (2003) emphasized the importance of understanding intragroup differences as well as differences between cultural groups. She suggested that premigration and postmigration experiences significantly influence worldview, adjustment problems, and acculturation; for example, the first wave of Southeast Asian refugees experienced fewer adjustment problems in the United States than subsequent waves of refugees due to differences in education, English proficiency, and premigration trauma experiences (Chung & Okazaki, 1991).

D'Andrea (2003) discussed 31 competencies developed by the Association for Multicultural Counseling and Development, several of which emphasize the importance of being able to accurately identify and respectfully address the unique cultural-racial differences that persons from diverse client populations exhibit in individual and group counseling. These competencies emphasize that not only must counselors be knowledgeable of the between-group differences that commonly mark the psychological development of persons from diverse cultural-racial groups, but they also must understand the numerous within-group differences that are routinely manifested among individuals from the same cultural-racial background (D'Andrea & Daniels, in press).

Yau (2003), in his article on guidelines for group work with international students, noted the complexity in working with international students. Issues of biculturalism and acculturation are different for international students because most of them return to their country of origin. Yau stated, "a host of problems encompass culture shock and these include economic adjustments, psychological distress, and personal problems"(p. 254). Thus, the need for counseling services for international students is great. More specifically, two very different but related areas of services are needed for international students: helping them adjust to American culture, and later helping them make the adjustment back to their native countries.

DEVELOPING YOUR PERSONAL PLAN FOR GROUP WORK

Throughout this chapter, we have suggested ways for group leaders to understand themselves and others as a beginning point in working toward developing and implementing effective multicultural group work interventions. This series of steps for group leaders in their development as multiculturally sensitive group leaders can be summarized as follows.

1. **Clarify your personal values.** Know what is important to yourself as an individual and as a member of your cultural groups. Identify what you considered to be important values and beliefs, and how you perceive people as interacting in a productive and helpful way.

2. **Clarify the values inherent in your theoretical approach to group work.** What thoughts, feelings, and behaviors are viewed as healthy and productive? Conversely, what thoughts, feelings, and behaviors are viewed as unhealthy and unproductive? What behaviors do you expect of clients and group members as they come to counseling and group work? Table 1.1 provides the frame of reference for this examination.

3. **Identify particular situations where your personal and/or theoretical values, beliefs, and assumptions may conflict with the values of a person from another culture diverse background.** Identify how you will avoid imposing your values on that person. Think specifically about your values regarding what constitutes a family, how people show respect toward each other, and how people should solve problems and conflicts. Table 1.1 can be useful in this exploration.

4. Identify particular situations where values inherent in your approach to group work may conflict with the values of a person from another culture or diverse background. Identify how you will avoid imposing your values on the other person, how you will discuss these potential differences with the person, and possible options for resolving any conflicts so you can still work effectively with the person. Think about these options specifically in terms of what you think are appropriate goals for counseling and group work, including the types of interventions you could make in and outside of group. Consider what you believe to be appropriate and best for group members who might be different from others based on their cultural beliefs and worldviews.

5. Identify particular situations, presenting problems, and specific group members that might lead you, because of conflicts with your personal values and beliefs, to refer a member to another group or counseling professional. Most people have some types of problems or certain issues that they acknowledge they may have difficulty working with. It is usually easiest for people to identify clients with behavioral problems that they cannot work with: men who batter, or women who are contemplating abortion. It is more difficult for counselors to acknowledge that, because of personal beliefs, they may be uncomfortable working with someone from a different culture. It is important to identify your own personal biases so that they can be addressed in supervision or consultation, or so clients can be referred to counselors who may be more effective with them.

6. Identify potential situations in group where values of group members may be in conflict. Identify how you will help members avoid imposing their values on another person, how you will discuss these potential differences between group members so that members will learn about and from each other, and possible options for resolving conflicts and having diverse group members work effectively together. Differences in cultural background, religion, racial identity development, gender, age, SES, lifestyle, and disabilities affect individuals' worldviews, goals for group work, and interactional styles. Think about what you know about making groups safe and productive based on your personal beliefs and theoretical approach to group work. Then contrast that with the approaches of other cultures to group work, healing, and styles of interaction.

7. Identify situations when you will need supervision or to consult with other group leaders to discuss biases in group work. There is an old adage in psychotherapy training that the more we talk about countertransference, the less likely we are to act it out with a client. It makes sense to be aware of our own potential for countertransference, especially with regard to our prejudices and biases toward certain groups or types of people. We must make every effort to connect with our group members and to provide them with the best treatment possible.

8. Identify a list of sources to which you can refer for information about different cultures, acculturation, and potential conflicts and issues related to group work. The list at the end of this chapter provides some of this material; however, such a collection needs to be constantly updated.

CONCLUSIONS

We have recommended a series of steps for group leaders to take as they work toward achieving multicultural group work competency. These steps include: (a) examining your own cultural and ethnic values and racial identity to understand who you are as a person, (b) examining your beliefs about counseling and group work and the inherent assumptions within the Eurocentric view of group work, (c) learning about other cultures in terms of what they value and how this may affect their relationships in group work, and (d) developing a personal plan for group work that emphasizes and utilizes cultural diversity. In some ways, multicultural understanding is a never-ending process. New information is always being developed about different cultures, and new clients who are potential group members will always be walking through our doors. Thus, you need to constantly think about how your knowledge of cultures and cultural values affects how you lead groups, and about how the cultural orientation of group members affects the way they participate in groups.

RESOURCES ON CULTURE AND MULTICULTURAL ISSUES

Professional Resources

Journals Relevant to Culture

American Psychological Association Multicultural Journal (www.apa.org)

Journal of Counseling and Development (www.counseling.org/resources/journals.htm)

Journal of Multicultural Counseling and Development (www.counseling.org/resources/journals.htm)

Multicultural Review (www.mcreview.com)

Books and Chapters Related to Multicultural Group Work

General

Brinson, J. A., & Lee, C. C. (1997). Culturally-responsive group leadership: An integrative model for experienced practitioners. In H. Forester-Miller & J. A. Kottler (Eds.), *Issues and challenges for group practitioners* (pp. 43–56). Denver, CO: Love.

Cartledge, G. (1996). *Cultural diversity and social skills instruction: Understanding ethnic and gender differences*. Champaign, IL: Research Press.

D'Andrea, M. (2003). Considerations related to racial identity development for group leaders and members. In J. DeLucia-Waack, D. Gerrity, C. Kalodner, & M. Riva (Eds.), *Handbook of group counseling and psychotherapy* (pp. 265–282). Thousand Oaks, CA: Sage.

DeLucia-Waack, J. L. (1996). Multicultural group counseling: Addressing diversity to facilitate universality and self-understanding. In J. L. DeLucia-Waack (Ed.), *Multicultural counseling competencies: Implications for training and practice* (pp. 157–195). Alexandria, VA: American Counseling Association.

Lotan, R. A., Shulman, J. H, & Whitecomb, J. A. (1998). *Groupwork in diverse classrooms: A casebook for educators*. New York: Teachers College Press.

Merta, R. J. (1995). Group work: Multicultural perspectives. In J. G. Ponterotto, J. M. Casas, L. A. Suzuki, & C. M. Alexander (Eds.), *Handbook of multicultural counseling* (pp. 567–585). Thousand Oaks, CA: Sage.

Phan, L. T., & Torres Rivera, E. (2003). Language as it impacts group dynamics in counseling and psychotherapy groups. In J. DeLucia-Waack, D. Gerrity, C. Kalodner, & M. Riva (Eds.), *Handbook of group counseling and psychotherapy* (pp. 283–294). Thousand Oaks, CA: Sage.

Torres Rivera, E., Garrett, M. T., & Crutchfield, L. B. (2003). Multicultural interventions in groups: The use of indigenous methods. In J. DeLucia-Waack, D. Gerrity, C. Kalodner, & M. Riva (Eds.), *Handbook of group counseling and psychotherapy* (pp. 295–306). Thousand Oaks, CA: Sage.

African Americans

Jordan, J. M. (1991). Counseling African American women: Sister-friends. In C. Lee & B. Richardson (Eds.), *Multicultural issues in counseling: New approaches to diversity* (pp. 49–63). Alexandria, VA: American Association for Counseling and Development.

Pack-Brown, S. P., & Fleming, A. (2003). An Afrocentric approach to counseling groups with African-Americans. In J. L. DeLucia-Waack, D. Gerrity, C. R. Kalodner & M. T. Riva (Eds.), *Handbook of group counseling and psychotherapy* (pp. 183–199). Thousand Oaks, CA: Sage.

Pack-Brown, S. P., & Whittington-Clark, L. E. (2001). *"I am because we are!" Afrocentric approaches to group (A diversity competent model)*. Farmingham, MA: Microtraining.

Pack-Brown, S. P., Whittington-Clark, L. E., & Parker, W. M. (1998). *Images of me: A guide to group work with African-American women*. Needham, MA: Allyn & Bacon.

Asians

Chung, R. Y. (2003). *Group counseling with Asians*. In J. L. DeLucia-Waack, D. Gerrity, C. R. Kalodner, & M. T. Riva (Eds.), *Handbook of group counseling and psychotherapy* (pp. 200–212). Thousand Oaks, CA: Sage.

Individuals with Disabilities

Seligman, M. & Marshak, L., (2003). Group approaches for persons with disabilities. In J. L. DeLucia-Waack, D. Gerrity, C. R. Kalodner, & M. T. Riva (Eds.), *Handbook of group counseling and psychotherapy* (pp. 239–252). Thousand Oaks, CA: Sage.

Gay, Lesbian, Bisexual, and Transgendered Individuals

Horne, S., & Levitt, H. (2003). Counseling groups with gay, lesbian, bisexual, and transgendered clients. In J. L. DeLucia-Waack, D.Gerrity, C. R. Kalodner & M. T. Riva (Eds.), *Handbook of group counseling and psychotherapy* (pp. 224–238). Thousand Oaks, CA: Sage.

Latinos

Torres Rivera, E. (2003). Psychoeducational and counseling groups with Latinos. In J. L. DeLucia-Waack, D. Gerrity, C. R. Kalodner & M. T. Riva (Eds.), *Handbook of group counseling and psychotherapy* (pp. 213–223). Thousand Oaks, CA: Sage.

Native Americans

Garrett, M. T. (2003). Sound of the drum: Group counseling with Native Americans. In J. L. DeLucia-Waack, D. Gerrity, C. R. Kalodner, & M. T. Riva (Eds.), *Handbook of group counseling and psychotherapy* (pp. 169–182). Thousand Oaks, CA: Sage.

International

Yau, T. Y. (2003). Guidelines for facilitating groups with international college students. In J. L. DeLucia-Waack, D. Gerrity, C. R. Kalodner & M. T. Riva (Eds.), *Handbook of group counseling and psychotherapy* (pp. 253–264). Thousand Oaks, CA: Sage.

Journal Articles Related to Multicultural Group Work

General

Association for Specialists in Group Work (ASGW) (1999). Association for Specialists in Group Work principles for diversity-competent group workers. *Journal for Specialists in Group Work, 24,* 7–14.

Conyne, R. K. (1998). What to look for in groups: Helping trainees become more sensitive to multicultural issues. *Journal for Specialists in Group Work, 23,* 22–32.

DeLucia, J. L., Coleman, V. D., & Jensen-Scott, R. L. (1992). Cultural diversity in group counseling. *Journal for Specialists in Group Work, 17,* 194–195.

DeLucia-Waack, J. L. (1996). Multiculturalism is inherent in all group work. *Journal for Specialists in Group Work, 21,* 218–223.

DeLucia-Waack, J. L. (1999). Exploring multicultural group work from a variety of perspectives. *Journal for Specialists in Group Work, 24,* 339–341.

Greeley, A. T., Garcia, V. L., Kessler, B. L. & Gilchrest, G. (1992). Training effective multicultural group counselors: Issues for a group training course. *Journal for Specialists in Group Work, 17,* 196–209.

Haley-Banez, L., & Walden, S. L. (1999). Diversity in group work: Using optimal theory to understand group process and dynamics. *Journal for Specialists in Group Work, 24,* 404–422.

McRae, M. B. (1994). Interracial group dynamics: A new perspective. *Journal for Specialists in Group Work, 19,* 168–174.

African Americans

Franklin, R. E., & Pack-Brown, S. P. (2001). Team brothers: An Africentric approach to group work with African-American male adolescents. *Journal for Specialists in Group Work, 26(30),* 237–245.

Gainor, K. A. (1992). Internalized oppression as a barrier to effective group work with Black women. *Journal for Specialists in Group Work, 17,* 235–242.

Portman, T. A. A., & Portman, G. (2002). Empowering students for social justice (ES2J): A structured group approach. *Journal for Specialists in Group Work, 27,* 16–31.

Rollock, D., Westman, J., & Johnson, C. (1992). A Black student support group on a predominantly White university campus: Issues for counselors and therapists. *Journal for Specialists in Group Work, 17,* 243–252.

Williams, C. B., Frame, M. W., & Green, E. (1999). Counseling groups for African-American women: A focus on spirituality. *Journal for Specialists in Group Work, 24,* 260–273.

Asians

Chen, M., & Han, Y. S. (2001). Cross-cultural group counseling with Asians: A stage-specific interactive approach. *Journal for Specialists in Group Work, 26,* 111–128.

Fukuyama, M.. A., & Coleman, N. C. (1992). A model for bicultural assertion training with Asian-Pacific American college students: A pilot study. *Journal for Specialists in Group Work, 17,* 210–217.

Leong, F. T. (1992). Guidelines for minimizing premature termination among Asian American clients in group counseling. *Journal for Specialists in Group Work, 17,* 218–228.

Individuals with Disabilities

Corrigan, M. J., Jones, C. A., & McWhirter, J. J. (2001). College students with disabilities: An access employment group. *Journal for Specialists in Group Work, 26,* 319–338.

Gordon, P. A., Winter, R., Feldman, D., & Dimick, D. (1996). Group work for persons with multliple sclerosis. *Journal for Specialists in Group Work, 21,* 243–251.

Rose, S. R. (2001). Group work to promote the occupational functioning of Ethiopian minority men with disabilities who have immigrated to Israel. *Journal for Specialists in Group Work, 26,* 144–155.

Gay, Lesbian, Bisexual, and Transgendered Individuals

Firestein, B. A. (1999). New perspectives on group treatment with women of diverse sexual identities. *Journal for Specialists in Group Work, 24,* 306–315.

Latinos

Gloria, A. M. (1999). Apoyando estudiantes Chicanas: Therapeutic factors in Chicana college student support groups. *Journal for Specialists in Group Work, 24,* 246–259.

Torres Rivera, E., Wilbur, M. P., Roberts-Wilbur, J., & Phan, L. (1999). Group work with Latino clients: A psychoeducational model. *Journal for Specialists in Group Work, 24,* 383–404.

Native Americans

Appleton, V. E., & Dykeman, C. (1996). Using art in group counseling with Native American youth. *Journal for Specialists in Group Work, 21,* 224–231.

Colmant, S. A., & Merta, R. J. (1999). Using sweat lodge ceremony as group therapy for Navajo youth. *Journal for Specialists in Group Work, 24,* 55–73.

Dufrene, P. M., & Coleman, V. (1992). Counseling Native Americans: Guidelines for group process. *Journal for Specialists in Group Work, 17,* 229–234.

Garrett, M. T., & Crutchfield, L. B. (1997). Moving full circle: A unity model of group work with children. *Journal for Specialists in Group Work, 22,* 175–188.

Garrett, M. T., Garrett, J. T., & Brotherton, D. (2001). Inner Circle/Outer Circle: A group technique based on Native American healing circles. *Journal for Specialists in Group Work, 26,* 17–30.

Garrett, M.T., & Osborne, W.L. (1995). The Native American sweat lodge as a metaphor for group work. *Journal for Specialists in Group Work, 20,* 33–39.

Kim, B. S., Omizo, M. M. & D'Andrea, M. J. (1998). The effects of culturally consonant group counseling on the self-esteem and internal locus of control orientation among Native American adolescents. *Journal for Specialists in Group Work, 23,* 145–163.

Roberts-Wilbur, J., Wilbur, M., Garrett, M. T., & Yuhas, M. (2001). Talking circles: Listen, or your tongue will make you deaf. *Journal for Specialists in Group Work, 26,* 268–284.

International

Conyne, R. K., Wilson, F. R., & Tang, M. (2000). Evolving lessons from group work involvement in China. *Journal for Specialists in Group Work, 25,* 252–268.

DeLucia-Waack, J. L. (2000). International group work. *Journal for Specialists in Group Work, 25,* 227–228.

Lev-Wiesel, R. (2002). A model for promoting community cohesion in response to conflict. *Journal for Specialists in Group Work, 27,* 32–42.

Pan, P. J. D. (2000). The effectiveness of structured and semistructured Satir model groups on family relationships with college students in Taiwan. *Journal for Specialists in Group Work, 25,* 305–318.

Queener, J. E., & Kenyon, C. B. (2001). Providing mental health services to Southeast Asian adolescent girls: Integration of a primary prevention paradigm and group counseling. *Journal for Specialists in Group Work, 26,* 350–367.

Rose, S. R. (2001). Group work to promote the occupational functioning of Ethiopian minority men with disabilities who have immigrated to Israel. *Journal for Specialists in Group Work, 26,* 144–155.

Shakoor, M., & Fister, D. L. (2000). Finding hope in Bosnia: Fostering resilience through group process intervention. *Journal for Specialists in Group Work, 25,* 269–287.

Shechtman, Z., & Perl-Dekel, O. (2000). A comparison of therapeutic factors in two group treatment modalities: Verbal and art therapy. *Journal for Specialists in Group Work, 25,* 288–304.

Videos Relevant to Multicultural Counseling

General

Carlson, J., & Arnold, M. (1998). *Culture-sensitive therapy.* [Motion Picture]. (Available from Insight Media at www.insightmedia.com).

Comas-Diaz, L. *Ethnocultural psychotherapy.* [Motion Picture]. (Available at www.apa.org/videos/4310240.html).

Cross, W., & Jackson, B. (1994). *Cultural identity theory: Origins, present, and future status.* [Motion Picture]. (Available from Insight Media at www.insightmedia.com).

Davis, D. P., Prieto, L., Reynold, A. L., & Vazquez, L. A. *Multicultural counseling: Issues of diversity (Internal self-talk).* [Motion Picture]. (Available at www.emircotraining.com).

Davis, D. P., Stone, G., Sue, D. W., & Vazquez, L. A. *Multiculturalism: Issues in counseling and education.* [Motion Picture]. (Available at www.emircotraining.com).

Giordano, J. *Ethnic sharing.* [Motion Picture]. (Available at www.emircotraining.com).

Ivey, A., & Pier, P. T. (1996). *Family and community genograms in multicultural counseling: Psychotherapy as liberation.* [Motion Picture]. (Available from Insight Media at www.insightmedia.com).

Sue, D. W. (1989). *Barriers to cross-cultural counseling.* [Motion Picture]. (Available from Insight Media at www.insightmedia.com).

Sue, D. W. (1989). *Cultural identity development.* [Motion Picture]. (Available from Insight Media at www.insightmedia.com).

Sue, D. W. (1990). *Culture-specific strategies in counseling.* [Motion Picture]. Sue, S. *Science, ethnicity, and bias: Where have we gone wrong?* [Motion Picture]. (Available at www.emicrotraining.com).

Unknown. (1983). *Constructing the multigenerational family genogram: Exploring a problem in context.* [Motion Picture]. (Available from Insight Media at www.insightmedia.com).

Unknown. (1992). *Multicultural counseling: Ethnic issues* (Vol. 1). [Motion Picture]. (Available from Insight Media at www.insightmedia.com).

Unknown. (1992). *Multicultural counseling: Diversity issues.* (Vol. 2). [Motion Picture]. (Available from Insight Media at www.insightmedia.com).

Unknown. (1999). *Cultural diversity in mental health counseling.* [Motion Picture]. (Available from Insight Media at www.insightmedia.com).

Asian Cultures

Leong, F., Iwamasa, G., & Sue, D. W. (1998). *Innovative approaches to counseling Asian-American people.* [Motion Picture]. (Available from Insight Media at www.insightmedia.com).

Sue, D. W. *Guidelines for counseling Asian-American clients.* [Motion Picture]. (Available at www.emicrotraining.com).

Unknown. (1990). *Ethnicity and counseling: Vietnamese clients.* [Motion Picture]. (Available from Insight Media at www.insightmedia.com).

Native American Cultures

LaFromboise, T. (1994). *Counseling and therapy with Native-American Indians.* [Motion Picture]. (Available from Insight Media at www.insightmedia.com).

Martinez, A., & Martinez, N. (1999). *Innovative approaches to counseling Native-American Indian people.* [Motion Picture]. (Available from Insight Media at www.insightmedia.com).

Ryan, R. *The healing road: The Native American tradition.* [Motion Picture]. (Available at www.emicrotraining.com).

Unknown. (1990). *Ethnicity and counseling: Native-American clients.* [Motion Picture]. (Available from Insight Media at www.insightmedia.com).

Gay, Lesbian, Bisexual, and Transgendered Lifestyles

Banez, L., & Chen-Hayes, S. (2001). *Lesbian, bisexual, gay and transgendered counseling: LBGT counseling: Awareness and knowledge.* (Tape 1). [Motion Picture]. (Available at www.emicrotraining.com).

Banez, L., & Chen-Hayes, S. (2001). *Lesbian, bisexual, gay and transgendered counseling: LBGT counseling: Skill-building vignettes.* (Tape 2). [Motion Picture]. (Available at www.emicrotraining.com).

Garnets, L. *Sexual orientation in perspective.* [Motion Picture]. (Available at www.emicrotraining.com).

Hayes, S. C., & Haley-Banez, L. (2000). *Lesbian, bisexual, gay, and transgendered youth: Affirmative practice in school and families.* [Motion Picture]. (Available from Insight Media at www.insightmedia.com).

Unknown. *The gay gene.* [Motion Picture]. (Available from Films for Humanities and Sciences at www.films.com).

Latino Cultures

Aponte, H. (1990). *Ethnicity in family therapy: Structural therapy with a Hispanic family.* (Vol. 2). [Motion Picture]. (Available from Insight Media at www.insightmedia.com).

Arredondo, P. (1994). *Latina/Latino counseling and psychotherapy.* [Motion Picture]. (Available from Insight Media at www.insightmedia.com).

Unknown. (1990). *Ethnicity and counseling: Mexican clients.* [Motion Picture]. (Available from Insight Media at www.insightmedia.com).

Unknown. *Hispanic education at the crossroads.* [Motion Picture]. (Available from Films for Humanities and Sciences at www.films.com).

Vasquez, L., Santiago-Rivera, A., & Orjuels, E. (1998). *Innovative approaches to counseling Latino/Latina people.* [Motion Picture]. (Available from Insight Media at www.insightmedia.com).

African-American Culture

Aponte, H. (1990). *Ethnicity in family therapy: Structural therapy with a Black family.* (Vol. 1). [Motion Picture]. (Available from Insight Media at www.insightmedia.com).

Courtland, L. (1998). *Counseling African Americans—Part I: Counseling African American men.* (Vol. 4). [Motion Picture]. (Available at www.counseling/org/enews/volume_1/0104a.htm).

Cross, W. E. *Shades of Black: Diversity in African American identity.* [Motion Picture]. (Available at www.emicrotraining.com).

Hardy, K. V. (1995). *The psychological residuals of slavery.* [Motion Picture]. (Available from Insight Media at www.insightmedia.com).

Jordan, J. (1998). *Counseling African Americans—Part II: Counseling African American women from a culturally sensitivity perspective.* [Motion Picture]. (Available at www.counseling/org/enews/volume_1/0105a.htm).

Parham, T. A. *African-American counseling and psychotherapy.* [Motion Picture]. (Available at www.emicrotraining.com).

Parham, T. A. & Ajamu, A. (1999). *Innovative approaches to counseling African descent people.* [Motion Picture]. (Available from Insight Media at www.insightmedia.com).

Unknown. *Black America and the education crisis*. [Motion Picture]. (Available from Films for Humanities and Sciences at www.films.com).

Unknown. (1990). *Ethnicity and counseling: African-American clients*. [Motion Picture]. (Available from Insight Media at www.insightmedia.com).

Prejudice

Unknown. *Color-blind: Fighting racism in school*. [Motion Picture]. (Available from Films for Humanities and Sciences at www.films.com).

Unknown. *Cultural bias in education*. [Motion Picture]. (Available from Films for Humanities and Sciences at www.films.com).

Unknown. *Throwaway teens*. [Motion Picture]. (Available from Films for Humanities and Sciences at www.films.com).

Unknown. *Unequal education*. [Motion Picture]. (Available from Films for Humanities and Sciences at www.films.com).

POPULAR RESOURCES

Movies

African American Culture

Avildsen, J. G. (Director). (1989). *Lean on me*. [Motion Picture]. United States: Twentieth Century Fox.

Campus, M. (Director). (1973). *The mack*. [Motion Picture]. United States: Charter Entertainment.

Dickerson, E. R. (Director). (1992). *Juice*. [Motion Picture]. United States: Paramount Pictures.

Freedman, J. (Director). (1987). *Native son*. [Motion Picture]. United States: Monterey Home Video.

Hughes, A. & Hughes, A. (Directors). (1993). *Menace II society*. [Motion Picture]. United States: New Line Studios.

Jewison, N. (Director). (2000). *The hurricane*. [Motion Picture]. United States: Universal.

Lee, S. (Director). (1992). *Malcolm X*. [Motion Picture]. United States: Schlessinger Media.

Lee, S. (Director). (1996). *Get on the bus*. [Motion Picture]. United States: Columbia/Tristar.

Lee, S. (Director). (2000). *Bamboozled*. [Motion Picture]. United States: New Line Studios.

Littman, L. (Director). (1999). *Having our say: The Delany sisters' first 100 years*. [Motion Picture]. United States: Columbia/Tristar.

Markowitz, R. (Director). (1996). *The Tuskegee airmen*. [Motion Picture]. United States: HBO Home Video.

Nair, M. (Director). (1992). *Mississippi masala*. [Motion Picture]. United States: Columbia/Tristar.

Parker, A. (Director). (1988). *Mississippi burning*. [Motion Picture]. United States: Metro Goldwyn Mayer.

Petrie, D. (Director). (1961). *A raisin in the sun*. [Motion Picture]. United States: Columbia/Tristar.

Price-Bythewood, G. (Director). (2000). *Disappearing acts*. [Motion Picture]. United States: HBO Studios.

Reid, T. (Director). (1996). *Once upon a time . . . When we were colored*. [Motion Picture]. United States: Republic Studios.

Reynolds, R. (Director). (1997). *187*. [Motion Picture]. United States: Warner Studios.

Robinson, P. A. (Director). (2000). *Freedom song.* [Motion Picture]. United States: Turner Home Video.

Sargent, J. (Director). (1997). *Miss Evers' boys.* [Motion Picture]. United States: HBO Studios.

Sayles, J. (Director). (1996). *Lone star.* [Motion Picture]. United States: Twentieth Century Fox.

Singleton, J. (Director). *Rosewood.* [Motion Picture]. United States: Warner Studios.

Singleton, J. (Director). (2000). *Shaft.* [Motion Picture]. United States: MGM Studios.

Speilberg, S. (Director). (1997). *Amistad.* [Motion Picture]. United States: Universal Studios.

Tillman, G. (Director). (1997). *Soul food.* [Motion Picture]. United States: Twentieth Century Fox.

Yakin, B. (Director). (2000). *Remember the titans.* [Motion Picture]. United States: Disney.

Zwich E. (Director). (1989). *Glory.* [Motion Picture]. United States: Columbia/Tristar.

Native American Cultures

Apted, M. (Director). (1992). *Thunderheart.* [Motion Picture]. United States: Columbia/ Tristar.

Costner, K. (Director). (1990). *Dances with wolves.* [Motion Picture]. United States: MGM.

Everett, D. S. (Director). (1993). *Running brave.* [Motion Picture]. United States: Tapeworm.

Eyre, C. (Director). (1998). *Smoke signals.* [Motion Picture]. United States: Miramax Home Entertainment.

Mann, M. (Director). (1992). *The last of the Mohicans.* [Motion Picture]. United States: Fox Home Entertainment.

Margolin, S. (Director). (1997). *Medicine River.* [Motion Picture]. United States: United American Video.

McDonald, B. (Director). (1995). *Dance me outside.* [Motion Picture]. United States: Unapix Studios.

Sackheim, D. (Director). (1996). *Grand Avenue.* [Motion Picture]. United States: HBO Studios.

Strand, P. (Director). (1942). *Native land: Nomads of the dawn.* [Motion Picture]. United States: Wellspring Media.

Wacks, J. (Director). (1988). *Powwow highway.* [Motion Picture]. United States: Anchor Bay Entertainment.

Asian American Cultures

Attenborough, R. (Director (1982). *Gandhi.* [Motion Picture]. United States: Columbia/Tristar.

Bui, T. (Director). (1999). *Three seasons.* [Motion Picture]. United States: USA Films.

Cohen, R. (Director). (1993). *Dragon: The Bruce Lee story.* [Motion Picture]. United States: Universal Studios.

Franklin, S. (Director). (1937). *The good earth.* [Motion Picture]. United States: Warner Studios.

Hicks, S. (Director). (2000). *Snow falling on cedars.* [Motion Picture]. United States: Universal Studios.

Kelly, N. (Director). (1991). *Thousand pieces of gold.* [Motion Picture]. United States: Hemdale Home Video I.

Lee, A. (Director). (1993). *The wedding banquet.* [Motion Picture]. United States: Twentieth Century Fox.

Lee, A. (2000). *Crouching tiger, hidden dragon.* [Motion Picture]. United States: Sony Pictures Classics.

Lo, C. M. (Director). (2002). *Catfish in Black bean sauce.* [Motion Picture]. United States: First Look Pictures.

Nair, M. (Director). (1997). *Kama sutra: A tale of love.* [Motion Picture]. Unites States: Vidmark/Trimark.

Nair, M. (Director). (2001). *Monsoon wedding*. [Motion Picture]. United States: IFC Productions.

Parker, A. (Director). (1990). *Come see the paradise*. [Motion Picture]. United States: Twentieth Century Fox.

Scorsese, M. (Director). (1997). *Kundun*. [Motion Picture]. United States: Touchstone Video.

Stone, O. (Director). (1993). *Heaven and earth*. [Motion Picture]. United States: Warner Studios.

Tianming, W. (Director). Minglun, W. (Screenwriter). (1999). *King of masks*. [Motion Picture]. United States: Columbia/Tristar.

Wang, W. (Director). (1989). *Eat a bowl of tea*. [Motion Picture]. United States: Columbia/Tristar.

Wang, W. (Director). (1993). *The joy luck club*. [Motion Picture]. United States: Hollywood Pictures.

Latino Cultures

Arau, A. (Director). (1993). *Like water for chocolate*. [Motion Picture]. United States: Miramax.

Availes, A. (1994). *Mi vida loca*. [Motion Picture]. United States: HBO Studios.

Avila, C. (Director). (2000). *Price of glory*. [Motion Picture]. United States: New Line Studios.

Escobedo, M. (Director). (2001). *Rum and coke*. [Motion Picture]. United States: Delta Studios.

Loach, K. (Director). (2000). *Bread and roses*. [Motion Picture]. United States. Studio Home Entertainment.

Marin, C. (Director). (1987). *Born in east L.A*. [Motion Picture]. United States: Goodtimes Home Video.

Menendez, R. (Director). (1988). *Stand and deliver*. [Motion Picture]. United States: Warner Studios.

Nava, G. (Director). (1984). *El super*. [Motion Picture]. United States: New Yorker Films.

Nava, G. (Director). (1995). *Mi familia*. [Motion Picture]. United States: American Playhouse.

Nava, G. (Director). (1997). *Selena*. [Motion Picture]. United States: Warner Studios.

Redford, R. (Director). (1988). *The milagro beanfield war*. [Motion Picture]. United States: Universal Studios.

Sargent, J. (Director). (2000). *For love or country*. [Motion Picture]. United States: HBO Studios.

Valdez, L. (Director). (1987). *La bamba*. [Motion Picture]. United States: Columbia/Tristar.

Wise, R. (Director). (1961). *West side story*. [Motion Picture]. United States: MGM Studios.

Lesbian, Gay, Bisexual, and Transgendered Lifestyles

Demme. J. (Director). (1993). *Philadelphia*. [Motion Picture]. United States: Columbia/Tristar.

Epstein, R., & Friedman, J. (Director). (1996). *Celluloid closet*. [Motion Picture]. United States: Columbia/Tristar.

Nichols, M. (Director). (1996). *The birdcage*. [Motion Picture]. United States: HBO Studios.

Sagliotti, J. (Director). (1984). *Before stonewall*. [Motion Picture]. United States: First Run Features.

Sagliotti, J. (Director). (1999). *After stonewall*. [Motion Picture]. United States: First Run Features.

Spottiswoode, R. (Director). (1993), *And the band played on*. [Motion Picture]. United States: HBO Studios.

Inner-City Culture

Deniro, R. (Director). (1993). *A Bronx tale*. [Motion Picture]. United States: HBO Studios.

Kaye, T. (Director). (1998). *American history X*. [Motion Picture]. United States: New Line Studios.

Kouf, J. (Director). (1997). *Gang related*. [Motion Picture]. United States: Orion Home Video.

Olmos, E. J. (Director). (1992). *American me*. [Motion Picture]. United States: MGM Studios.

Singleton, J. (Director). (1991). *Boyz 'n the hood*. [Motion Picture]. United States: Columbia/Tristar.

Books

African American Culture

Angelou, M. (1970). *I know why the caged bird sings*. New York: Random House.

Cary, L. (1991). *Black ice*. New York: Knopf.

Ellison, R. (1990). *Invisible man*. New York: Random House.

Giddling, P. (1984). *When and where I enter: The impact of Black women on race and sex in America*. New York: W. Morrow.

Haley, A. (1966). *The autobiography of Malcom X*. New York: Grove Press.

Hansbery, L. (1959). *A raisin in the sun*. New York: Vintage Books.

Hooks, B. (1995). *Killing rage: Ending racism*. New York: Holt, Rinehart & Winston.

Hoyt-Goldsmith, D. (1993). *Celebrating Kwanza*. New York: Holiday House.

Hurston, Z. N. (1990). *Their eyes were watching god*. New York: Harper & Row.

Lee, H. (1961). *To kill a mocking bird*. Toronto: McCelland & Stewart.

McCall, N. (1994). *Makes me wanna holler: A young Black man in America*. New York: Random Books.

Morrison, T. (1970). *The bluest eye*. New York: Holt, Rinehart & Winston.

Morrison, T. (1987). *Beloved*. New York: Alfred A. Knopf.

Mosley, W. (1995). *RL's dream*. New York: W.W. Norton.

Nayor, G. (1986). *The women of Brewster Place*. New York: Penguin Books.

Schuyler, G. (1969). *Black no more*. College Park, MD: McGrath.

Walker, A. (1983). *The color purple*. New York: Pocket Books.

Wright, R. (1940). *Native son*. New York: Harper & Row.

Inner-City Culture and Racism

Anyon, J. (1997). *Ghetto schooling*. New York: Teachers College Press.

Kozol, J. (1992). *Savage inequalities: Children in American schools*. New York: Perennial Press.

Rose, J, (1990). *Lives on the boundarties: A moving account of the struggles and achievements of the America's unprepared*. New York: Penguin.

Biracial Cultures

Moraga, C., & Anzaldua, G. (1981). *This bridge called my back: Writings by racial women of color*. Watertown, MA: Persephone Press.

Native American Cultures

Brown, D.A. (1970). *Bury my heart at wounded knee: An Indian history of the American west*. New York: H. Holt.

Dorris, M. (1987). *Yellow raft blue water*. New York: Henry Holt.

Edrich, L. (1989). *Tracks*. New York: Harper Perennial.

Hogan, L. (1992). *Mean spirit*. New York: Ivy Books.

Silko, L.M. (1999). *Gardens in dunes*. New York: Simon & Schuster.

Asian Cultures

Buck, P. S. (1932). *The good earth.* New York: Washington Square Press.

Chao, P. (1997). *Monkey king.* New York: HarperCollins.

Fadiman, A. (1998). *The spirit catches you and you fall down: A Hmong child, her American doctors, and the collision of two cultures.* New York: Farrar, Straus & Giroux.

Houston, J., & J. Houston (1974). *Farewell to Manzanar.* New York: Bantam Books.

Kingston, M. (1980). *China men.* New York: Knopf.

McCunn, R. (1988). *Thousand pieces of gold.* Boston: Beacon Press.

Sone, M. (1953). *Nisei daughter.* Boston: Little Brown.

Tan, A. (1989). *The joy luck club.* New York: Putnam.

Tan, A. (1991). *The kitchen god's wife.* New York: Putnam.

Tan, A. (2002). *Bonesetter's daughter.* New York: Ballantine Books.

Yeh Mah, A. (1999). *Falling leaves : The true story of an unwanted Chinese daughter.* New York: Broadway Books.

Latino Cultures

Allende, I. (1985). *The house of the spirits.* New York: A.A. Knopf.

Allende, I. (1993). *The infinite plan.* New York: HarperCollins.

Bourgeois, P. (1996). *Search of respect: Selling crack in El barrio.* Boston: Cambridge University Press.

Cisneros, S. (1983). *The house on Mango Street.* New York: Vintage Books.

Cisneros, S. (1992). *Women hollering creek.* New York: Vintage Books.

Esquivel, L. (1992). *Like water for chocolate.* New York: Doubleday.

Hijuelis, O. (1989). *The mambo kings play songs of love.* New York: Farrar, Straus & Giroux.

Mirande, A. (1997). *Hombres y machos: Masculinity and Latino culture.* Boulder, CO: Westview Press.

Ramirez, R. (1999). *What it means to be a man: Reflections on Puerto Rican masculinity.* Piscataway, NJ: Rutgers University Press.

Rodriguez, R. (1983). *Hunger of memory: The education of Richard Rodriguez.* New York: Bantam Books.

Rouse. I. (1993). *The Tainos: Rise and decline of the people who greeted Columbus.* New Haven, CT: Yale University Press.

Wells, R. (1996). *The divine secrets of the Ya-Ya sisterhood.* New York: Penguin.

Lesbian, Gay, Bisexual, and Transgendered Lifestyles

Brown, R. (1977). *Rubyfruit jungle.* New York: Bantam Books.

Hardy, J.E. (1994). *B-Boy blues.* New York: Alyson.

Jennings, K. (1994). *Becoming visible: A reader in gay and lesbian history for high school and college students.* Los Angeles: Alyson.

Marcus, E. (1993). *Is it a choice?: Answers to 300 of the most frequently asked questions about gays and lesbians.* New York: HarperCollins.

Reid, J. (1977). *The best little boy in the world.* New York: Ballantine.

Shyer, C., & Shyer M. F. (1996) *Not like other boys—Growing up gay: A mother and son look back.* New York: Houghton Mifflin.

Singer, B. L. (1994) *Growing up gay/Growing up lesbian: A literary anthology.* New York: The New Press, City University of New York. (Originally published as *Growing Up Gay.* 1993.)

Warren, P. (1988). *The front runner.* New York: New American Library.

Woog, D. (1995). *School's out: The impact of gay and lesbian issues on American schools*. Boston: Alyson.

Jewish Culture

Potok, C. (1967). *The chosen*. New York: Simon & Schuster.

Individuals with Disabilities

Kisor, H. (1990). *What's the pig outdoors?*. New York: Hill Wang.

Neugeboren, J. (1997). *Imagining Robert*. New York: William Morrow.

Nolan, C. (1988). *Under the eye of the clock*. New York: St. Martin's Press.

*Ethnocentrism is the phenomenon underlying much
of the insensitivity to culturally different clients. It
is based on a hierarchial view of values and assumes
that one's value system is best or better than others.
For example, many group counselors believe that
emotional openness is better than inhibition.*
(Leong, 1992, p. 220)

Cultural Values and Group Work

CHAPTER | **2**

The goal of this chapter is to summarize and make you aware of different worldviews and how they may accentuate or impede individuals' initial willingness to participate in a group and their interactional patterns during group sessions. We want to make you aware of some of the key Eurocentric assumptions that you may possess as a result of your theoretical approach to group work. The idea is that if you are aware that the beliefs you hold are based on your own view of the world and recognize that these beliefs may not be held by members of your group, then you are freer to discuss differences in values and beliefs than if you assume that everyone holds these beliefs and, possibly, put off group members in the process. Leong (1992) framed it nicely when he said, "The tendency to use one's framework as if it were universal is not unique to Western groups, but it behooves us to become aware of that tendency" (p. 228).

Following is a discussion of some of the Eurocentric assumptions of counseling that often affect how group work is conceptualized and enacted. Potential value conflicts with other cultures will be highlighted to provide a context within which to view obstacles to traditional group work and areas of needed growth and change for future group work. Remember that we are discussing cultural values in terms of generalities here. As we stressed in Chapter 1, in discussing racial identity development, assimilation, acculturation, and ethnic identity all significantly affect an individual's adaptation of cultural values.

INDIVIDUAL AS FOCUS OF TREATMENT: INDIVIDUALISM VERSUS COLLECTIVISM

Probably the most obvious bias in the Eurocentric approach to group counseling is the focus on the individual as the recipient of treatment. Even in group work, people typically participate in a group as individuals, not knowing other members and certainly not coming as part of an already established group of family or friends. Bringing together individuals in a group setting implies that working with *one* individual can change this person's life, behavior, and relationship patterns, which directly contradicts many cultures' beliefs related to interdependence, community, and selflessness. Leong (1992) suggested that this belief implies that "independence and self-sufficiency are signs of maturity, whereas interdependence and group loyalty are characteristics of individuals who are not self-actualized" (p. 220).

In contrast to the theme of individualism, Chen (1995) listed several general characteristics of Chinese clients that represent the importance of family over the individual: a strong sense of parental authority and dignity, significance of maintaining the integrity and reputation of one's family, emphasis on collective/societal needs, and great respect for the elderly. Paniagua (1998) noted that for Asian persons, family comes first, and extended family is included as well. Chung (2003) sums it up nicely:

> [I]n general, the Asian populations, come from the collectivist cultures that emphasize family community and value strong interdependent relationships where priority is given to the collective goals over personal goals to avoid confrontation so as to maintain harmony with their in-groups and extended family and community. This results in defining oneself in terms of their in-group relationship. In contrast, individualistic cultures, such as the United States and other Western cultures, focus on individualism, independence, competitiveness, personal goals over group goals, feelings of distinction from their social networks, the acceptance of confrontation within in-groups, and defining oneself independently from the in-group to which they belong. (p. 202)

Positively, Chung goes on to emphasize that the collective nature of the Asian culture is consistent with group work as an effective and appropriate intervention.

Personalismo is a communication style that emphasizes personal interactions and is often manifested as interdependence and cooperation. As interpersonal behaviors are perceived as more important than task accomplishments, external characteristics (e.g., money and possessions) are of secondary value. For example, Latinos and Latinas who emotionally and personally support their families are more highly valued by family members than those who esteem prestige and status (Gloria, 1999, p. 249).

To illustrate the extreme of collectivism, Silverstein (1995) suggested that the identity of the Chassidic ultra-orthodox Jewish woman is incomplete without its association to family and children. Thus, focusing on her as an individual may not make sense to her, or may alienate her and cause her to leave group counseling prematurely. The focus on individuals and the value of self may be important in some cultures, but in others, the value of the family, cooperation, and group loyalty is emphasized.

In the Maori tribe in New Zealand, the tribe or family name is more important than the individual name, which illustrates the tribe's collectivist culture (Chung, 2000). Chung noted, as a symbol of how "We-ness" is more important than "I-ness," that when Chinese people ask for your name, they are asking for your family name, not your first name. Courtland Lee (1997) illustrated this concept further in his description of the Hongi welcome ceremony of the Maori people. They introduce themselves by completing the following sentences: *My mountain(s) is/are . . ., My river(s) is/are . . ., My tribe is . . .,* and *I am . . . .*

Chung (2000) noted that Brazilian culture is group-oriented, and thus the focus is on social relationships, and not on "me." For Latinos, Paniagua (1998) emphasized the concept of *familismo,* the importance of the family before the individual; thus, the family must be included in counseling in order to effect change.

Furthermore, although group counseling literature recognizes marital group counseling as a viable form of treatment and occasionally prescribes group counseling for families, traditionally groups are composed of individuals who do not know each other. The assumption is that individuals who know and interact with each other outside of group will form coalitions and alliances in group based on preestablished roles and patterns of interaction that may negatively affect group cohesiveness. This again contradicts the collective nature of many cultures and the emphasis on seeking helping first from family and community.

VALUE OF THOUGHTS AND THINKING

In another direction, the traditional Eurocentric focus has been on the individual's thoughts, feelings, and behaviors in a group setting. Other cultures, particularly Eastern cultures, emphasize the interconnectedness of the mind and body (Ying, Lee, Tsai, Yeh, & Huang, 2000). Garrett and Garrett (1994) suggested that spirituality is essential for Native Americans; harmony comes from a person's connection with all parts of the universe, with everything and everyone having a purpose and value.

GROUP AS A TREATMENT MODALITY

All societies have rituals that take place in a group setting, with various functions: festivities, prayer, and/or healing. Not all cultures, however, perform healing rituals within a group setting. Yet the Eurocentric assumption of traditional group work is that working as a member of a group is more powerful than working in individual therapy, and thus, the Western view stresses the importance of group work. Many other cultures also value the healing powers of a group and may encourage members of these cultural groups to accept and participate in counseling groups. Banawi and Stockton (1993) suggested that Muslims celebrate several religious feasts in a group setting as well as daily prayer. Thus, for Muslims, "group therapy can be seen as an optimal setting and a way for Muslims to experience personal growth. The individual in Islam is an independent member of the group who makes decisions to satisfy his needs and interests without hurting the group" (p. 154).

Similarly, Native American values have traditionally emphasized group work, sharing, and cooperation (Garrett & Garrett, 1994). Native American group techniques include the Sweat Lodge and the Inner/Outer Circle. The Sweat Lodge (Colmant & Merta, 1999; Garrett & Osborne, 1995) emphasizes honesty, endurance, and community. The Inner/Outer Circle (Garrett, Garrett, & Brotherton, 2001) is based on the principles of community contribution, sharing, acceptance, cooperation, and awareness of relationship.

The Japanese culture holds the group in high regard; in essence, most Japanese people belong to multiple groups. Takahashi (1991) goes so far as to say that Japanese work groups function better than American work groups because of two psychological elements: *amae*, the presumption upon others' benevolence, and *gaman*, the curtailment of egoism for the sake of others. The Maori tribe in New Zealand also values the group; it utilizes a group of elders to decide family, community, and governmental issues (Chung, 2000).

IMPORTANCE OF VERBALIZATION AND SELF-DISCLOSURE

Although many cultures function in groups and value collective participation, what occurs in some cultural groups is very different from the expected behavior, norms, and interactional styles in traditional counseling and therapy groups. Several of Yalom's (1985) therapeutic factors of group counseling are based on the Eurocentric assumption that people need to self-disclose. Corrective recapitulation of the primary family group emphasizes the reliving of early familial conflicts in order to resolve them, whereas interpersonal learning focuses on gaining insight into past and present relationships and then making changes based on this insight. Imparting of information also utilizes group discussion to share instructions about mental health and how to deal with life's problems. Yet many cultures may hold values that prohibit the sharing of personal information, especially problems, as that may bring shame not only on the individual group member, but on the family as well.

Talking is essential to these Eurocentric therapeutic factors, with verbal disclosure being seen as a sign of group participation, trust, and cohesiveness. This position espouses that (a) a responsible person talks so that something can be accomplished; (b) silence does not accomplish anything; and (c) a person who is quiet is either not very bright or does not have any ideas. For example, African Americans may engage in emotional verbal dialogue and tend to distrust members who do not verbalize their thoughts (Greeley et al., 1992). Other cultures, however, emphasize the value of silence and listening to gain wisdom. The Asian position, for example, states that (a) it is better to be silent than to ramble on and say nothing or to say something that is not well thought out; (b) a talkative person does not think very much because he is too busy talking; and (c) a talkative person is essentially an attention-seeker or show-off. Lack of understanding of Asian members' silence may lead counselors to erroneously interpret their behavior as resistance or apathy (Greeley et al., 1992, pp. 203–204). Rose (2001) quoted an old Ethiopian proverb suggesting the wisdom of listening: "If one person talks, everyone can hear; if everyone talks, no one can hear."

Cultural differences are evident in the content as well as the amount of verbalization. Group counseling theory assumes that individuals will disclose to other members (initially strangers) significant life events, relationships with significant others (including family members), and personal thoughts and feelings. Catharsis as a therapeutic factor (Yalom, 1985) also emphasizes experiencing and expressing feelings. Cultures, however, may view self-disclosure differently. In some cultures, it is appropriate only within the family, within same-sex groups, or to authority figures but not to peers; in others, self-disclosure is inappropriate under any circumstances. Chen (1995) suggested that, in general, Chinese culture values thinking and doing more than feeling, which may interfere with the open expression of emotions. More importantly, Chen noted that Chinese children are taught to present their emotions in an implicit manner through mutually recognized nonverbal exchanges rather than through verbalizations or physical acts. Chung (2003) noted that many Asians are uncomfortable with direct communication, and so the goal of group counseling that emphasizes direct and honest feedback may conflict with their beliefs about not openly expressing feelings and not drawing attention to oneself.

The altruistic role of the group member also focuses on verbalization to other members. In the role of helper, members are expected and encouraged to express support, give suggestions and advice, and share common experiences as a way of connecting (the therapeutic factor of universality). Members' willingness to share feelings and reactions with each other is essential to each person learning how they are perceived and the impact of their behaviors on others. Challenge and confrontation are important in helping members learn about themselves. The Asian tradition, however, values a nonconfrontive stance; it is impolite to put someone on the spot and to interrupt others (Greeley et al., 1992; Leong, Wagner, & Kim, 1995). For Native Americans, direct confrontation must be avoided because it disrupts the harmony and balance that are essential to being (Garrett & Garrett, 1994). In contrast, Islamic values parallel some of the traditional values of group counseling, emphasizing that group members are expected to express their personal views and feelings and to extend help and exchange feedback among themselves (Banawi & Stockton, 1993).

Support and empathy can be shown nonverbally as well as verbally, but the Eurocentric view emphasizes giving suggestions, sharing common experiences, and challenging, all of which tend to be done verbally. Consequently, the Eurocentric emphasis in traditional group counseling has been on verbalization of feelings, thoughts, experiences, and reactions. With the expectation of verbalization in traditional group work comes the American definition of assertiveness: Speak clearly, speak directly to the person, use "I" statements, and maintain eye contact. Some cultures, such as Latino and Israeli, endorse similar beliefs, while others are in direct conflict with this stance.

Eye contact itself is an important issue. We often tell group members, "Look directly at and speak directly to the person you want to communicate with." Yet, in some cultures, this violates a very important norm. Garrett and Garrett (1994) suggested that the Native American communication style emphasizes nonverbal communication, with moderation in speech and avoidance of direct eye contact as communicating respect, especially for elders or authority figures.

A similar dilemma may arise for Native Americans who take their cues for behavior based on the structure of the situation. For example, Garrett (2003) noted that while Native Americans generally take a nonaggressive and noncompetitive approach to life, competition and aggression are considered acceptable as part of sports competitions. However, if a counseling or therapy group does not provide structure or suggestions in terms of desired behavior, Native American group members may not actively participate or ask for feedback.

IMPORTANCE OF UNSTRUCTURED INTERACTION BETWEEN MEMBERS

As counseling groups become established, members interact with each other as they do in important relationships outside of group. Thus, patterns in relationships and areas of difficulty for individual members are displayed in group sessions. Members' interactions with other members parallel their interactions with peers, while their reactions to counselors correspond to their reactions to other authority figures. Differences in relationship style based on gender and age will appear (e.g., a woman may be able to be appropriately assertive with a same-age woman, her age and gender peer, but not with an older woman, an authority figure in terms of age, or a same-age man, a peer but a different gender). If individuals talk and behave spontaneously and without structure, then these relationship patterns will be acted out. It is assumed that when individuals have a reaction or contribution to make, they will do so. Members do not usually raise their hand and wait to be called on. Yet, in some cultures, something on that order may be the norm when authority figures are present. For example, individuals from Asian cultures who highly regard persons of authority may not speak unless specifically addressed by the leader (Greeley et al., 1992).

Consequently, cultural norms that prescribe an order or structure of participation mediate, but do not destroy, group process. Such cultural norms must be identified and discussed in order to facilitate accurate perceptions of an individual's behavior in group. For instance, in the Chassidic ultra-orthodox Jewish culture, all social interactions are clearly prescribed. Interactions between the sexes are minimal, and subjects of conversation are determined by the relationship between the persons (Silverstein, 1995). Muslim beliefs also guide interactions between genders, so it may be useful to have coleaders of both genders (Banawi & Stockton, 1993). Such restrictions make participation in group counseling particularly difficult, if not impossible, for some persons. As the United States in general and group work specifically become more multicultural in focus, counselors and clients must "improve the accuracy of their own and members' interpretations of others' behaviors, particularly if such behaviors are culturally bound" (Greeley et al., 1992, p. 205).

The one instance where groups tend to be structured is in starting and ending at a prescribed time to create safety and trust for the group. Other cultures, however, particularly Latino and Native American, view time very differently. People from such cultures may push boundaries by arriving late or being willing to stay beyond the prescribed time. In these cultures, functions begin when everyone arrives and end when everyone leaves or the tasks are done. The concept of time is very different between cultures, and this difference must be taken into consideration.

IMPORTANCE OF TAKING RISKS AND TRYING OUT NEW BEHAVIORS

Yalom's (1985) therapeutic factors of development of socializing techniques, imitative behavior, interpersonal learning, and corrective recapitulation of the primary family group occur as a result of experimenting with new behaviors and relationship skills within the group. Members take risks and try out new behaviors such as expressing feelings, being assertive, and asking for help. They may also practice behaviors they want to use outside of group with significant others in their lives through the technique of role-playing. Role-playing involves practicing new behaviors, making mistakes, and receiving feedback about the impact of behaviors on others, and possibly on how to change and/or improve behaviors.

It is difficult for some individuals to "not be perfect" in group and to attempt new behaviors with others watching. Cultural norms may suggest that individuals will lose face if they do not succeed with others watching or that they will shame a family member or friend by involving them in a role-play situation. Leong et al. (1995) suggested that "the concept of openly expressing feelings and possibly drawing attention to oneself might be culturally inconsistent and extremely confusing" (p. 220). Thus, for members of some cultural groups, taking a risk in public may not only be a new behavior, but may also violate a norm. Other cultures, such as Islam, emphasize the usefulness of groups in providing support, feedback, and advice to each other, similar to what is traditionally expected in psychoeducational and counseling groups (Banawi & Stockton, 1993). Garrett and Garrett (1994) suggest that the Native American perspective may fall somewhere in between: learning through practice and observation, but speaking softly and having ample time to reflect before responding.

For the Chicano culture, *simpatia* is a cultural pattern of social interaction that emphasizes the promotion and maintenance of harmonious or smooth social and interpersonal relationships. Gloria (1999) commented, "By maintaining harmony, dignity and respect, positive behaviors are emphasized and negative are deemphasized to avoid interpersonal conflict. Latinos/as and non-Latinos/as who deviate from the cultural script of simpatia are often perceived as critical or competitive and are likely to be rejected by those who would adhere to simpatia" (p. 250).

Oftentimes, group leaders try to include silent members, get members involved, and ask members where they were if they missed a group session. Garrett (2003) emphasized the concept of noninterference for Native Americans, which may conflict in some ways with typical group leader behavior. He noted that the belief in immanent justice may, in some instances, prevent Native American group members from providing honest but critical feedback. Garrett quotes an old Indian saying: "One should never speak ill against another, for the wind will carry it to that person, and, eventually, the ill will return on the wind, seven times stronger" (p. 171). He also states:

> [A]bove all, respect for others through patience, openness, and flexibility, ultimately shows respect for oneself and one's community. It is not uncommon in the traditional way for the group to allow or accept a person's withdrawal without question or expectation. In addition, that person is to be welcomed back into the group without a required explanation for his and her absence. There is no need to interfere by asking what is wrong, or offering solutions. Respect for another dictates that when a person is ready to share information, he or she will do so. Likewise, if a person is in need of assistance or help, he or she will ask. (p. 172)

ROLE OF THE GROUP LEADER

Gladding (1991) suggested that the role of the group counselor is to influence and motivate others toward group and individual goals without controlling the session and member behavior. Thus, counselors create a safe environment for individuals to examine and explore their personal relationships and problems. Yalom (1985) suggested two roles for the group leader: the technical expert, and a model-setting participant. The technical expert shares her knowledge of group process and group interventions, whereas the model-setting participant actively models behaviors for members to imitate. Yalom's (1995) research also identified four types of leader behavior: executive functions (focusing on procedural norms such as starting and stopping on time, one person speaking at a time), meaning attribution (interpreting what members are doing and learning in the group), emotional stimulation (helping members integrate affect, thinking, and behavior), and caring and empathy. While the counselor may initially perform most of these functions, Yalom (1995) postulated that during the working stage of a group, members share these four types of behavior with the leader. Consequently, although group counseling theory and research ascribes certain behaviors primarily to group leaders, it also assumes that all persons, members and leaders, will work together in a cooperative and collaborative manner.

Cultural norms may conceptualize the relationship between group leader and member differently. For example, "in most Asian cultures, interpersonal relations tend to be hierarchical with a strong respect and loyalty to authority. Hence, Asian American clients in groups will tend to view the counselor as the authority and expect him or her to have special expertise and power and to direct the group process" (Leong, 1992, p. 223). Chung (2003) noted that the group leader is seen as the expert with credibility, and thus is considered an authority figure and viewed with respect and paternalism.

Native Americans and Hispanics also may bestow reverence and attribute knowledge and wisdom to persons in authority positions (Greeley et al., 1992). Latino clients "may be experienced by therapists as generally more polite, formal, less overtly angry and argumentative. . . Yet care must be taken to recognize that the seemingly 'nicer' personality styles of Latinos can be as interpersonally problematic as the more disruptive styles of non-Latino patients" (Organista et al., 1993, p. 230).

Some cultures regard authority figures as experts on all areas of life and expect the counselor to direct not only the process but also the content of group sessions, and to make specific suggestions about what members should do. Organista et al. (1993) recommended cognitive behavior therapy with Latino clients because they often expect immediate symptom relief, guidance and advice, and a problem-centered perspective. Paniagua (1998) suggested that structured behavioral approaches and family therapy may work well with Native-American and Asian clients due to their desire for a more directive active approach on the part of the group counselor.

Individuals of some cultures may view suggestions from a counselor as directives that must be followed because the counselor is an authority figure. Such clients may expect to play a more passive role in counseling and may assume that the group leader will be directive but nurturing (Baloglu, 2000). Individuals of other cultures might view the same suggestions as intrusive because they are made by someone outside the family. Such cultures may view authority figures with suspiciousness and lack of trust (Greeley et al., 1992). Fukuyama and Coleman (1992) emphasized that expectations of group leader behavior are influenced not only by cultural values but also very strongly by level of acculturation.

The attributes of a leader also may vary by culture. For example, Japanese culture values leadership, but group members from a traditional Japanese culture may not choose a leader because of her power or strong opinions, but rather because of her ability to help the group form consensus and realize the group's collective wishes. "In Japanese culture, the leader belongs to the group and not the group to the leader" (Takahashi, 1991).

Group counseling theory suggests that leaders should self-disclose, but only with regard to here-and-now events (e.g., I feel very sad when you say this), as opposed to personal experiences and events (e.g., I lost my grandfather, too, about five years ago to cancer). For members from some cultures, this lack of personal information may contribute to the perceived power of the counselor, whereas members of other cultures may desire more personal knowledge from the counselor in order to feel connected. For instance, Organista et al. (1993) advocated that group counselors engage in small talk and self-disclosure (*platica*) with Latino clients in order to be perceived as having social and interpersonal grace and etiquette. Paniagua (1998) emphasized the importance of group counselor self-disclosure and stated that it may be rewarded with gifts from the client. As in other areas, Banawi and Stockton (1993) suggest a little different leadership perspective for Islamic clients: The group leader is to be respected, but members should also express their personal views. Consequently, the Eurocentric emphasis in group counseling theory must be taken into consideration in preparation for assuming a multicultural approach to group counseling.

CONCLUSION

This chapter has provided you with basic assumptions about group work that are inherent in the traditional Eurocentric model of group counseling and theory, and compared and contrasted these assumptions with the worldviews of other cultures. Most cultures have some values that support the concept of groups as a healing mechanism and that encourage growth and change. At the same time, most cultures also have values that conflict with traditional group work assumptions. Therefore, you must be aware of potential biases and conflicts between cultures as you begin thinking about how to lead a multiculturally sensitive group.

Autobiographies
of Respondents

You are about to be introduced to eleven persons who are of diverse cultural and ethnic backgrounds. As you read their stories of acculturation and migration, you will be given a context from which to understand how their backgrounds influenced the way they responded as members and leaders to the group situations presented in Part III. We asked each respondent to answer the following questions about themselves as part of their cultural and social autobiographies:

1. Describe who you are in terms of age, race, any physical disability, sexual orientation, ethnicity and culture, family patterns, gender, socioeconomic status (SES), and intellectual ability (educational background).
2. How do you see yourself as a unique individual based on your ethnic, cultural, and family background?
3. How does your background contribute to your view of how groups work?
4. What strengths do you bring to groups based on your cultural background and beliefs? What limitations do you bring as well?

3 CHAPTER | Cultural, Social, and Family Autobiographies

BEVERLY BROWN

While hard for me to believe, I am nearly 58 years old and thinking about retirement. Not long ago I was reflecting on my career in a manner common for someone in the middle of her career. Was I still experiencing my life as satisfying, or would I prefer to explore differ- ent challenges? I soon real- ized major changes were not needed. I am fortunate

to be in a dynamic profession with challenges and satisfaction from serving others. As a white woman of my generation, I am also fortunate to have two grown children as well as profes- sional opportunities.

Let me tell you about some of the influences on who I am today. My heritage can best be described by my British Isles lineage back to a time soon after the *Mayflower* landed. Puritan protestant values were an important part of the reason why my paternal family came to America from England. Men of the family often worked as ministers, teachers, and lawyers. The thread of Puritan Protestant values carried forward across generations into my childhood experience. My maternal heritage is Welsh, Irish, and English, bringing a lively spirit to our family. Family values, hard work, and strictly living by one's beliefs have remained as family characteristics. As a child, my life seemed idyllic, with little exposure to conflict—a communication skill I did not learn until graduate school. As a young girl, I was highly sensitive and upset when harm came to other people or animals. Later this sensitivity turned into concern for the professional care of others.

My grandparents did not attend college, but my paternal grandfather supported his brother through seminary. My parents also did not attend college but highly valued education and encouraged my two brothers and me to graduate from college. One brother received his bachelor's degree and was successful in business and volunteer work with Boy Scouts. My other brother has been a practicing oncologist for many years. I received three degrees from a midwestern university (B.S., M.S., & Ph.D). My father was successful in business, and we had an upper-middle-class lifestyle. My mother focused on raising children and was highly skilled at keeping peace within the family.

Patterns established in my childhood gave support to family values and service to others. We attended church regularly and often had a family dinner following the service. The extended family also gathered for every holiday and birthday. I particularly remember the many years my father worked with United Cerebral Palsy, later becoming president of the organization. He would show me pictures of children with cerebral palsy and talk to me about attitudes toward people with disabilities. I heard about parental fears that their grown children with cerebral palsy would be institutionalized and receive poor care when they were no longer able to care for them. He would tell me of new legislation on education for children with disabilities and the funds his association was providing for research to cure cerebral palsy. These experiences helped me understand people different from myself and the importance of service to others.

As the years passed, I discovered that both of my own children have disabilities. One has a learning disability and the other a severe hearing loss. I also discovered the cruelty and discrimination experienced by my children because of their disabilities. People would routinely ignore my son because they were afraid of his hearing aid and unsure of his ability to communicate. My daughter would work twice as hard on her academics as most other children and still be criticized by teachers for lack of effort. I wondered how some professionals could be so unaware of their hurtful impact on our trusting, young children. My children have both graduated from college, but I often wonder how many children with disabilities are unable to maintain the confidence they need to continue their education beyond high school.

My early exposure to children with disabilities and my later experiences with my own children have had a profound impact on me—much more than my personal experience of discrimination as a woman. However, my awareness of systemic discrimination against women has helped me understand discrimination against people in other groups. Values from my family and cultural background have brought a passion and determination to stand by beliefs I hold dearly, especially the value and care of all people. These same values have influenced my tendency to be persistent and personally satisfied with my work only when I know I have given my best effort.

Group work has been a means to express my belief in people regardless of differences. The natural process of group development can foster understanding of differences and working together in a democratic manner. I've grown to believe that the success of group work rests heavily on the manner in which members learn to resolve conflict and value one another's differences. For this reason, I work with groups to establish norms for communication about differences. I also work with goals in the group that can unify and bring value to members' diverse experiences.

Strengths I bring to group work might be best described as those related to conflict and working with differences. As a normal and healthy part of relationships and group development, conflict can serve as a powerful energizer to foster open communication. My belief in people and their ability to understand and care for those different from themselves brings a positive edge to the climate of a group, and my understanding of accommodation alternatives for including people with disabilities in group work helps to minimize avoidable difficulties. Although I have worked for many years to become comfortable with conflict, my limitations also rest in this area. I'm still not completely comfortable with conflict. How easy it would be to smooth over conflict rather than work it through. How easy it would be to collude with group members and pretend a conflict does not exist. I am aware of how important it is for me to monitor my first response to conflict and choose to work with the group in a productive manner. Another strength as well as weakness is related to discrimination. While I am highly sensitive to bias and discrimination in group work, I must be aware of my own potential for being intolerant of members who themselves are intolerant of others.

RITA CHI-YING CHUNG

I am a Chinese woman who was born in New Zealand and has lived in New Zealand, Hong Kong, the Philippines, Great Britain, Brazil, and now in the United States. My parents migrated to New Zealand as a result of World War II. As children of immigrant parents, my brothers, sisters, and I spent our childhood and adolescent years working in family businesses that included, at various times, a grocery store and restaurants. My family spoke Cantonese at home, which caused difficulties for me in school because of my poor English-language skills. Because of this, I entered university at a later age under the "mature" student category.

My upbringing causes me to perceive myself as part of a family system and cultural community rather than as an individual. Since most, if not all, of the Chinese people who migrated to New Zealand during World War II were from the Canton region of China, there were already established social networks. The Chinese community encountered racism in New Zealand, making it a natural step to establish a tight enclave community in which language, culture, food, and so on would be appreciated and respected. Within this close-knit community, individuals were seen as part of their family systems as well as their cultural community, both of which were free from prejudice and discrimination. Hence, the community was aware of individual members' behaviors, which allowed for effective provision of social support to its members, but which also, just as critically, provided a method of maintaining the Chinese culture through monitoring and surveillance of its members' behavior. Being part of a family and cultural community appeared natural to me, so it was not until I came to the United States (11 years ago) that I realized how different my perspective was compared to mainstream values in the United States. Having read a large amount of literature on Asian Americans, psychosocial adjustment issues of immigrants, and general cross-cultural and multicultural psychology and counseling, I was fortunate to obtain funding to undertake postdoctoral studies with Dr. Stanley Sue, who had just received a grant from the National Institute of Mental Health (NIMH) to establish a National Center for Asian American Mental Health at the University of California in Los Angeles (UCLA). I arrived in the United States alone and not knowing anyone. Soon after arriving at UCLA, Stan and I were discussing the cultural differences of the people at the Center. The Center was comprised of faculty and students who were Asians or Asian Americans. The postdoctoral fellows came from Pan Asian countries. Although most people at the Center were Asian, it was diverse in terms of the different Asian groups (e.g., Chinese,

Japanese, Filipino, etc.), and there were differences within and between groups (e.g., foreign-born versus U.S.-born). Therefore, it was interesting to observe the interactions of people at the Center in terms of the level of acculturation. One day Stan commented to me that I was "truly bicultural," which surprised me. Not being familiar with the American culture except through my readings, I had assumed that all Asian Americans and people of color in the United States were bicultural. Stan's comment made me realize that not every person of color views the world through a bicultural or multicultural lens. This initiated a personal and professional exploration of how one becomes bicultural. It had been so ingrained in me that I did not realize it was a unique characteristic until Stan pointed that out.

As I reflected on who I was and how I had become this person, I kept coming back to my family. My parents, grandmother, aunties, uncles, siblings, cousins, and the general Chinese community were all part of my makeup and personality. My family and community taught its members to be proud of being Chinese by educating us on the historical, political, sociocultural, psychosocial, and spiritual perspectives of our culture and, most importantly, on the family lineage that goes back several dynasties. We were taught to stand proud and not fight back when the Europeans (the name for white New Zealanders) laughed or ridiculed us. My family taught its members racial socialization, how to deal and cope with racism and discrimination in a positive manner. We were taught how to access resources in the wider society but at the same time maintain our cultural self and integrity. For example, my siblings and I came home from school crying one day after being mocked about our Chinese names. We begged our parents to give us English names, which they did, acknowledging that it was a necessary first step for their children to gain acceptance and access into mainstream culture. However, we were and still are called by our Chinese names by family and community as a symbol of our own cultural identity that helps to maintain our cultural heritage. Through such teachings, we became bicultural, with an ability to access, navigate, and succeed in both cultures in a positive, affirming manner.

The foundation of my world was community and family. Coming from a collectivistic culture, my world consisted of smaller communities within a large community. My family and everyone I knew were individuals whose identities were based on their membership in one or more groups. This was essential for all of us to coexist harmoniously. The foundation for this was interdependence that aimed at peaceful coexistence and sacrificed independence. Social groups that made up the community maintained societal values and beliefs that were the foundation for our world, teaching us about the responsibility of caring for others, respect, and harmony. The emphasis was on others and the world around us, rather than on self. This interdependence facilitates a relationship with the world that is based on coexistence. The importance of others' needs over one's own, however, doesn't inhibit personal growth and development. Rather, this orientation has contributed to my becoming a more holistic person who has the ability to give, think, and feel unconditionally, and still develop a more integrated spiritual self.

The collectivistic viewpoint that places family and community before self provides group members with sensitivity, appreciation, acceptance, understanding, and awareness of other group members' needs; the ability to place the group's needs before individual needs; and an understanding and awareness of the essential elements for the group to function in a productive manner so that each member will benefit. Furthermore, through the experiences of racism and discrimination, my culture has taught me to fight back in a more productive manner, for example, teaching and researching on issues such as social justice, human rights, advocacy and leadership, along with multiculturalism and globalization. These six prominent issues have now become a core of my cultural essence, both personally and professionally, and take into account the specific cultural issues relevant to Asian groups. One of the limitations of this viewpoint is that people do not think in an individualistic manner, which is contrary to the cultural foundation of Western societies. Therefore, the collectivistic viewpoint may hinder the full appreciation, understanding, and acceptance of personal needs and create confusion about how one's self relates to family and community.

BETH A. FIRESTEIN

My name is Beth Firestein, and I work as a Ph.D-level counseling psychologist in private practice in a town of approximately 50,000 people in northern Colorado. I have been in full-time private practice for the past five years. Prior to this, I worked for 10 years at a university counseling center, where I served as the staff psychologist and the administrative director of the Office of Women's Services for Southern Illinois University at Carbondale. I led a variety of theme and process-oriented therapy groups at that counseling center, and I continue to run process-oriented women's therapy groups and a monthly support group for cross-dressers, transgendered, and transsexual individuals as a part of Inner Source Psychotherapy and Consultation Services. I love facilitating therapy groups and am pleased that I have been able to continue developing and expanding this interest.

My personal identity consists of an ethnic, family, and cultural background that is both extremely typical of 21st-century American culture and rather unique. Ethnically, I am the product of my father's Russian-Jewish heritage and my mother's German-Jewish heritage. My father was a first-generation Orthodox Jew from Russia whose parents emigrated from an area of the Ukraine not far from modern-day Kiev in the early 1900s. My father's family settled in Philadelphia, Pennsylvania, where he grew up. My father later converted to Reform Judaism and became a rabbi. My mother's family worked as flour millers from the southern part of modern-day Germany. The majority of her family immigrated to the United States in the early and mid-1800s, where they became business owners and members of the organized Reform Jewish community of Houston, Texas.

My parents met and married in Houston, Texas, and I am the first of four children (three girls and one boy) born into their marriage. I grew up in Houston and then in Austin, Texas. My father led a modest-sized Reform Jewish congregation consisting of a few hundred families deep in the Bible belt of Texas. Our status as outsiders and religious minority members of our community was clearly confirmed in a variety of subtle and not-so-subtle ways. In marked contrast to our family's minority status as Jews in a heavily Christian community, my upbringing was rather typically middle-class, suburban, and "American." Our family was highly acculturated in most respects, and other "differences" we may had as a family were not obvious. Growing up in a Jewish-American family, education was highly prized, and all four children attained a college education. Three of us obtained master's degrees, though I am the only one who has earned a doctorate.

I discovered my bisexual orientation during my teenage and early college years, and this presented some adjustment challenges for my family that continue to this day. Although I was barely aware of the profound implications of my bisexual identity during my teens and early twenties, I am certain that my sexual orientation also contributed to my sense of being "different" and having an "outsider" status in the culture I grew up in. I have enjoyed long-term significant love relationships with both men and women, but have never legally married nor had children. I live now as a 43-year-old, single, professional woman with a lover, a housemate, a cat, and a horse.

My ethnic and cultural background as a Jew in a Christian culture prepared me well for some of the struggles I encountered in coming out as bisexual in a culture that perceives sexual orientation in a strongly dichotomous way. My bisexual identity, in combination with my professional study of sexual orientation issues, has also provided me with an experiential basis for the deep empathy I have been able to extend to my transgendered and transsexual clients. I am comfortable working with a variety of other "outsiders," both individually and in a group context.

The primary impact of my background on my view of how groups work has been to give me a balanced appreciation for both the constructive and destructive potentials of groups. The white, male, Christian, heteronormativity that pervades our culture creates a context of fear, pain, and alienation that affects both those who are "different" and those who are supposed to feel that they belong. Therapy groups often function as microcosms of cultural groups and peer groups, mirroring the complex gender, racial, ethnic, and sexuality-based power relations that are woven throughout the dominant, overlapping cultures. I think that my background contributes strongly to my appreciation of these complexities and my ability to help others understand and navigate these complexities.

My cultural background, beliefs, and current social status also hinder me in some aspects of group work. I am clearly positioned as a card-carrying member of the dominant culture, with significant social, cultural, and economic advantages that are virtually assured to bias me toward some educational and mental health perspectives characteristic of that culture. Yet this apparent identification with elements of the mainstream culture masks ongoing struggles to honor and express my individual differences and my deep alliance with a number of stigmatized subcultures. At times, this may lead me to alternate between powerful identification with emic and etic perspectives in my group work, and transference and countertransference issues can arise in connection with my work with members of particular groups. I may deeply empathize, even overidentify, with individuals whose group membership leads them to struggle with issues of recognition and inclusion, yet fail to recognize and honor the validity of other subcultural mores when an individual's cultural values threaten mainstream or subcultural perspectives that are close to my heart. On balance, I see the mix of dominant and minority perspectives present in my personal biography and individual history to be quite beneficial to the clients I serve in my group work.

MICHAEL TLANUSTA GARRETT

Siyo osda nuwati yoldasu (Hello, things are as they should be, I hope you are well). My name is Michael Tlanusta Garrett. Professionally, I am an assistant professor of counseling in the Department of Human Services at Western Carolina University. I received my Ph.D in counselor education and M.Ed. in counseling and development from the University of North Carolina at Greensboro, and my B.A. in psychology from North Carolina State University. In addition to being the author of numerous articles and chapters dealing with counseling issues surrounding wellness, spirituality, and working with Native people, I have also authored the book *Walking on the Wind: Cherokee Teachings for Healing through Harmony and Balance* (1998), and coauthored the book *Medicine of the Cherokee: The Way of Right Relationship* (1996).

My experience with Native people, both professionally and personally, lends a unique perspective and expertise with Native-American issues and concerns. I have worked as a school counselor with children and adolescents in the schools, with Native-American and other minority students in the university setting, with both perpetrators and survivors of domestic violence and sexual assault in a community agency setting, and with Native people in an urban Indian center serving the local Indian community. My experience in group counseling includes leading and coleading groups with children of domestic violence, women of domestic violence and sexual assault, and court-ordered male batterers, as well as psychoeducational and therapeutic groups with youth in the schools. My specialized focus has been in applying traditional Native-American group concepts and techniques to contemporary group counseling as a way of bridging the cultural gap.

I am a member of the Eastern Band of Cherokee (Kituwah), from the Ani-Gilohi (Long Hair Clan). I am a 31-year-old, married, heterosexual male. Though I am middle-class now, I grew up in a family that was lower-class, with both nuclear family intact and a strong, consistent presence of extended family. Though I have resided in a number of places, both urban and rural, I grew up on the Cherokee Indian reservation in the Smoky Mountains of western North Carolina, where I still reside today. I consider myself biracial, bicultural, multiethnic, and somewhat multilingual. I do not look upon myself so much as a "unique individual" but rather as a member of multiple dynamic circles, including those of family, clan, tribal nation, and community, as well as environmental and universal circles.

Twice in my youth, once in high school and once in college, I was resigned to dropping out of school. When one of my elders questioned my decision, I proclaimed that "school won't help me stand on the street corner any better" and "besides, I don't really belong there." My decision to stay in school at both points is reflective of my current identity and the convergence of many experiences and choices. When I was younger, part of it was that I had nowhere else to go, but part of my decision was based on my belief in the intrinsic value of learning about life—a passion that has followed me to this day.

The influence of my Native upbringing instilled in me the significance of groups as a daily part of life, both in ordinary interaction and in ceremonial participation. I learned the importance of respect, humility, generosity, connection, compassion, listening to the heart and with the heart, and being right here right now. I also learned noninterference as a way of both understanding and respecting the experiences of another person, no matter how painful. As a result, probably one of the biggest lessons I learned from my cultural upbringing was the importance of choice. These are among my greatest strengths as a group counselor, and also my greatest limitations at times.

As a bicultural person, I pride myself on what were once probably survival skills more than anything else, but are now hopefully a gift of multiple perspectives (a continual work-in-progress) to help guide me in both my personal and professional endeavors. I try to be wise enough to know when and how to intervene, and when and how to let it be. If life doesn't show me the difference, I just ask . . . in my own way. As I seek my own harmony and balance, I also seek to honor the greater harmony and balance of all that is. As one elder taught me, "adanvdo aquenvsvi" (home is where the heart is). In other words, from a Native perspective, "sometimes you find something, sometimes, something finds you." The question is: Do you have the courage to keep yourself open to a way of seeing more clearly what was, and what will be? That is both the challenge and beauty of the circle.

THOMAS J. HERNÁNDEZ

Understanding groups is about understanding people and the complex relationships that develop between them. In the 36 years that I have been on this planet, I have discovered that the lens through which I view the world has a profound impact not only on what I see in others, but also on how I see the world. My age, my status as a middle-class citizen, my occupational identity as a counselor and counselor educator, my heterosexuality, and, most importantly in my life, my multiculturality have a strong effect on the way the world looks to me, the way group interactions look to me, and the way I interact in groups.

I grew up as the eldest of three boys in an intact Peruvian-American family. My father took on the traditional role of breadwinner, and my mother the traditional role of caretaker of the family. Contrary to the stereotypical image that many people have about Latino families, it is not only the father, the patriarchal figure, who wields power. The mother also, while carrying a considerable burden in maintaining the household, has a significant amount of power. She determines how to nurture and care for her children, how needs are met and when they are met, and how discipline is carried out. You see, while it was my father who was the disciplinarian, my mother served as the reporter of "behavioral transgressions."

As a Latino, the importance of family and cultural identity is never far from my experience. I value collaborative work and the collective wisdom of the community. I understand that everything and everyone has a "place," a role in the social hierarchy.

The culture I was raised in and my personal set of experiences equally affect the work that I do—that has never been clearer. I see myself as both creating and being created by my world. I was raised with a certain set of cultural norms and values within a society that expects a completely different set of behaviors and values, making my context quite complex. Writing these words reminds me of the struggle Agar (1996) referred to in his discussion of the etic and emic perspectives in ethnographic research and participant observation. Agar talked about the distinction between ourselves and the "other." He argued that where the etic ends and the emic begins is often quite unclear. While we search for ourselves in society, we often try to differentiate from the "other." Agar argued that "we have found the other, and they are us" (p. 20). This is not unlike the struggle to understand one's self in society.

My worldview is such that I see all members of our society as unique. Individuals not only contribute their ethnic, cultural, and family backgrounds to a group, but they also contribute their interpretations of their experiences, teaching us not only what they have experienced but also how they have experienced it. In many ways, I see myself as providing the same uniquenesses because of my experiences. To overgeneralize my experiences based on who I am, however, oversimplifies who I am, who others are, and who the group is. That is, the group will experience me in a multitude of ways. Because of this, what I say about group process must in turn be processed and made uniquely "yours" as you read the reactions to each of the case vignettes.

Perhaps the greatest strength I bring to the group process—either as a group member or as a group leader—is my willingness to accept each member of the group as unique and to learn: (1) what this tells me about the person and/or group I am interacting with, and (2) about myself as I interact in the complex system that is the group. These are also the greatest limitations I bring, in that they require me to listen to both the group members and myself, as an individual and a part of a greater system. I must begin to understand myself and the relationships I have in my context: I must understand who I am culturally and socially if I am to truly participate with others who are working through the same process. This brings me full circle: Understanding difference is not only about knowing typical values, beliefs, norms, and patterns of behavior of another person, but also about knowing the other person and appreciating his uniqueness and what he contributes to the world. This includes the "what" of what makes people different, and the "why" and "how" of their views of the world and of their place within it.

MICHAEL HUTCHINS

I was born in Clinton, Massachusetts, a blue-collar factory town, in October 1943. Both of my parents grew up during the Great Depression in large single-parent, religious Irish-American families. My mother's parents migrated from Ireland in the late 19th century, while my father's family arrived in Maine in the 17th century. My father's father became disconnected from his family when he married an Irish-Catholic immigrant from Boston in the late 19th century. My father's mother died when my father was 10; my mother was 6 when her father died. My father left school in the 8th grade to work; my mother, the youngest in her family, graduated from high school.

Education was very important to my parents, as they did not want their children to experience the insecurity that plagued their early lives. As a result, they sacrificed to ensure that their two children would have educational opportunities. I went through 17 years of Catholic education, attending schools that were well beyond what the family could afford. The local parish assisted me socially, spiritually, and financially. As a result, I was able to attend a Xavierian Brothers prep school and a Jesuit college. In those schools, most of my classmates were of a socioeconomic class well above my own.

From my parents I learned the importance of the extended family, the role of religion as a centerpiece in life, the value of education and hard work, and the importance of active involvement in the community in which I live. My father was committed to avoiding conflict at all cost. My mother believed in talking through dissonance. At times, discussion was lively; at other times, nonexistent. Under no circumstances were we to discuss sexuality. As a result, I learned that I could not discuss my attraction to men. These rules for being in the world seemed consistent with the rules learned by my Irish-Catholic working-class peers.

After college, I volunteered with the Jesuit Lay Volunteer Corps and taught in a secondary school in Baghdad, Iraq. For the first time, I lived in a culture that was very different from the one in which I was raised. I learned about different forms of Christianity and Islam, and I learned that the world is not as homogeneous as I had been led to believe. However, it was still not a safe place to explore sexuality and my attraction to men.

It was in Baghdad that I first began to question social rules. I had not acknowledged my sexual attraction to men and had learned to read my environment carefully, lest anyone suspect that I might be homosexual. (My mother would later use the word *queer* in attempting to understand.) I had observed other men throughout my life and had some understanding of how men were "supposed" to behave. I also knew that my experience of the world was different . . . and often lonely. In Iraq, I learned that there are many different ways of being-in-the-world. I had read about differences as a college student. Now, I was beginning to experience differences. I did not yet know what it was like to live differently.

Upon my return to the United States, I got my master's degree in counseling and became a school counselor in Baltimore, Maryland. During this time, I engaged in secretive sexual connections with other men, none of us acknowledging that we were gay men. I was married two weeks before the Stonewall riots in 1969. During the Vietnam War, I worked in opposition to the war. I also had a son. In 1971, I moved to Moscow, Idaho, to begin a doctoral program. As I packed up the family, I didn't even know where Idaho was.

Over the next three years, I again learned about diversity. I lived in rural America and worked with folks who had grown up in the Mormon church. Again I encountered new structures and different worldviews. I also learned about group work as a doctoral student. One of my mentors introduced me to groups and to collaborative decision making. These were new concepts for me. They challenged my belief in individual decision making and introduced me to new paradigms for working together. I was intrigued. Upon graduation from the University of Idaho, I took a teaching position at Oakland University in Rochester, Michigan. My primary reason for taking this position was to learn more about group work.

Throughout these years, I kept my attraction to men quietly within myself. I had been having sexual experiences with males from early adolescence on, but I believed that when I was married my attraction to men would cease. This was not the case. In Michigan, I began to face this attraction directly. I met a man who was to become my lover. As a result of this relationship, I learned that my attraction to men was significant. I then moved west to take a different teaching position, and my daughter was born. My lover moved west a year after I did. Over the next several years, I would leave my marriage, move back to Detroit to be with him, leave that relationship and return to the west, and eventually settle in Tucson.

These were years of turmoil. I left academia and the counseling profession. Later, I learned that this experience of life change is common for many middle-class, white gay men of my generation. As I was going through these changes, I had no information about sexual identity development. Primarily, I knew that my world seemed very different from that of most of my colleagues.

Once I became willing to integrate my sexual orientation into my greater sense of self, I was prepared to return to the world of counseling. I had worked in juvenile corrections and had seen young men of different cultures struggling to make their way in the world of the white majority. I had learned that oppression was a part of the world in which I lived. I believed that I could make a difference in confronting oppression and that I had a unique perspective that I needed to share. By this time, I also had learned that group work was a powerful tool for addressing social issues. It was now time to put my learning into practice.

Throughout the years, I have worked in a variety of settings and with people from a wide range of cultures and ethnic groups. I have had my worldview challenged regularly and have, I hope, become more tolerant, accepting, and celebratory of different ways of being-in-the-world. In addtion, the perceived need to hide who I was, and the attendant pain and loneliness of such secretiveness, helped me to develop compassion, understanding, and tolerance. Such experiences also have helped me to recognize that I continue to carry, within myself, prejudices that get in my way as I move through life.

As a result of my life experience, I have learned the power of group work. Through the group process, we break through the differences and come to know each other. I also have learned that it is not always through verbal, insight-oriented group work that the most significant changes occur.

In working with folks from different cultural groups and of different ages, I have discovered that experiential group work is sometimes the most effective tool for learning. As a school counselor and secondary school teacher, I tried to create an environment where each student felt valued. Through these experience, I discovered that not all members of society learn intellectually. For example, many of my students were more effective when they were invited to experience the world. During my early years as a teacher and counselor, I became committed to experiential learning, and I continue with that commitment. In many groups, the collaboration on multidimensional tasks brings people to a much clearer understanding of who they are, who they are with each other, and who the group or community-as-a-whole is. It is also important to look at the group from the position of those who are excluded.

I believe that my experiences in different cultures have given me a broad perspective. My education in Catholic schools taught me observation and thinking skills. My development as a gay man has helped me to see the world from the perspective of an outsider. My commitment to justice and equality helps me to be compassionate and willing to work diligently for inclusion.

My experiences as a "hidden" person taught me to read the environment carefully. Often the world in which I lived was not safe. I became familiar with feeling like I was on the outside of most groups, and I learned about the loneliness of being different. When I began to learn counseling skills, and later group work skills, I was determined to do whatever I could to make the community a little safer for those who are different. In Iraq, I listened to young men who were not often heard or included, and as a school counselor, I attended to those students who had many ideas yet did not feel safe in large groups. I knew those experiences well.

My life experiences have led me to read feminist resources, gay literature, and chaos theory. Additionally, I have been involved in a variety of groups, both as a participant and as a leader. I believe that each of us makes a difference in the world and our task is to determine what kind of difference we wish to make. As a result, I like to believe I am the type of group leader who shares the leadership role with all group members. I believe that the power in the group comes from the energy of people working together, so I encourage to participate all members. Often, this participation takes the form of some experiential exercise, which then gets "processed" by the group. I invite group members to see their experiences in the group as metaphors for who they are and how they live their lives.

One of my favorite ways to work with people in a group is to collaborate to create an experience and then invite members to explore "what" was done, "how" it was done, and with what "effect." We explore what we learn about ourselves as a result of the experience, what we have learned about our relationships with others in the group, and what we have learned about the group-as-community. Exploring these areas is a result of the lessons I learned as a developing gay man, as a graduate of Roman Catholicism, and as a counseling practitioner. At times, I celebrate my heritage. At other times, I work diligently to transcend it. Sometimes, my assumption of privilege has made it difficult to recognize limitations. I may not always see my prejudices, nor recognize that I am contributing to oppression. I continue to explore.

CYNTHIA KALODNER

When asked to describe myself when I meet someone new, I typically respond, depending on whom I am meeting and under what circumstances, that I am Elena and Noah's mom, Roberto's wife, or a professor of counseling psychology. These mini-descriptions highlight the relevance of my most important self-defining roles. However, to define myself in terms of age, race, physical disabilities, sexual orientation, ethnicity and culture, family patterns, socioeconomic status (SES), and intellectual ability (or educational background), as I am asked to do here, goes far beyond my normal introduction. So, I am a white, nondisabled, straight woman of Jewish background who is approaching 40 years of age. I come from a two-parent, dual-career family with one brother and a middle-class background. I went to public schools in Philadelphia and to state universities in New Jersey and Pennsylvania for my undergraduate and graduate education.

As I grew up, both of my parents were involved in my life. We had family dinners almost nightly; my mom cooked, and my dad cleaned up. I remember celebrating all the Jewish holidays with my aunts, uncles, and cousins. My parents recently celebrated 45 years of marriage. Both of my parents are well educated and spent their careers as teachers in public schools. My younger brother, who is now a financial planner, lives in New Jersey; he is married and has three children close in age to my own two children. I view my "family" as including the nuclear one (those who live with me), along with my mom, dad, brother, his wife and children, aunts, uncles, cousins, and my husband's family of origin.

The characteristic that has the most relevance for my responses to the critical incidents in the case vignettes may be my cultural background as a Jewish female. I am sure that being white, straight, and nondisabled also have influenced me, but the affects are less clear, since they keep me in the majority, while being Jewish makes me a member of a minority group. In some places, being female also has resulted in my being in the minority.

My parents raised me in a family surrounded by Jewish people, education, ceremonies, foods, holidays, and expressions. Judaism has three major distinct sects—Orthodox, Conservative, and Reform. My background is in the Conservative movement (not to be confused with the political term *conservative*, which does not define me at all!), which tends to be more religious and traditional than the Reform movement, but less so than the Orthodox. My Conservative Judaism background has been profoundly influential in my life. I notice the importance of my Jewish culture, especially in places where there are fewer Jewish people, and especially as my children get older and interact in a non-Jewish world. When one of my Jewish colleagues used a Yiddish expression, I was really pleased to hear words that reminded me of my parents. I use these kinds of expressions in my teaching, though I have to stop and explain what I mean by a *mensch* or a *nebbish*.

Despite the importance of my Jewish culture to me, I married a non-Jewish man of Latin-American background. To my Jewish cultural world, I have added Spanish language, Latin-American foods, and a sense of what it is like to live in other countries. This intermarriage, along with the circumstances that surround it, has influenced me and my values.

Being female also has been influential. Sometimes I have been the only female professional in a room full of more senior male colleagues. This interesting dynamic has not been a problem for me, but has provided me with some entertaining stories to tell. Being female is meaningful in that it comes with certain roles and responsibilities. Some of these are a function of being a woman (childbearing, breast-feeding), but others are more societal. For me, these issues relate to the balance of family and career.

Having children is another part of my world that has a profound effect on what is important to me. Although I am not sure if this is cultural, I understand now, better than I ever could before having children, the nature of love and dependence, interdependence and independence. My children's smiles and laughter are much more important to me than anything I do in the office. This may be a reflection of my Jewish background, since children are viewed as central to the life of the Jewish family, especially the Jewish mother.

I tend to rely on my theoretical views and training in group work to explain how groups work, though I am sure that being who I am in a cultural context does influence my choices related to group work. My cognitive-behavioral theoretical framework and my group training in Yalom-style process groups combine to form my leadership style. One might wonder if there is a relationship between my cultural background and the choice of cognitive-behavioral theory and Yalom-style groups. I am not sure. Maybe my cultural world has influenced my enthusiasm for groups as a therapeutic intervention. Since the Jewish culture values interdependency and a sense of community, group modalities make sense to me.

I can imagine that my background might influence the kinds of groups I prefer to lead, the people I choose as coleaders, and the kinds of interventions that I make in a group setting. I have led many different types of groups. The most structured ones have been psychoeducational groups on themes such as stress and time management or study skills. I have also led several structured behaviorally oriented weight loss groups. The majority of my group experience has pertained to eating disturbances and disorders. Those groups, led as counseling or psychotherapy groups, typically followed a semistructured format, in which I sometimes brought in a theme for discussion. The empirically supported treatment for bulimia nervosa is what I like to start with for this type of group. Finally, I have been the leader in general therapy groups, with very little structure. Overall, at this point in my career, I am comfortable with some degree of structure in my counseling and psychotherapy group work, although I have worked with some coleaders who preferred less leader direction. Psychoeducational groups are necessarily structured, including a didactic component.

One important strength I bring as a group leader is a sincere commitment to the use of groups as a modality for working with clients. I think this commitment to group work is a major asset, since my belief in the power of the modality is likely to influence the development of the group. I am a leader who carefully plans groups, including the selection and screening of members and session-by-session considerations. It is a strength that I prepare prospective members for their experience in group work. Additionally, I am knowledgeable about the theory and practice of group work, and draw on this knowledge in my work in groups. I refer to the literature on groups when forming a new kind of group, and I collect data to study the effectiveness of group interventions.

Depending upon one's idea of what is "right" for groups, I may be seen as being too directive or active as a group leader. I have a bias toward empirically supported treatments when they are available. Although my belief in the power of groups is a strength, it may also keep me from seeing when a group may not be the most effective intervention for a client.

BOGUSIA MOLINA

I am a great-granddaughter of the people of the land—*Polanie* in Polish. I come from a rich Polish, Hungarian, Austrian, and German background. My maternal grandmother, who was one of my best teachers, used to say, "I never had to leave my town, yet I got to live in three different countries." My ancestors lived in the same geographic location, Southern Poland. Like any place on our mother Earth, it is a very beautiful one. The location had many creeks and valleys—mountains where sheep would wander about, where the winds would dance through the fields littered with hay stacks, where children danced in circles and sang and enjoyed nature's gifts of apple trees, raspberry bushes, plum trees, and hazelnuts, where the paths were filled with lilies of the valley, peonies, tulips, roses, and many other flowers.

In that location, children and families were part of a community. There were always people on the street, and anyone might stop a child and say, "School ended two hours ago. What are you doing in the mountains all by yourself?" We had no telephones until I was about 12, but everyone seemed to have a "spirit telephone." My parents and grandparents knew what I did and did not do at school long before I put my feet through the door and had a chance to explain my version of the story. And people helped one another. When our elderly neighbor was too tired, my dad and uncles all got together and helped to kill his pig, with a special ritual of prayers and songs, so that his family would have plenty of meat to last through the upcoming winter.

Although people tended to be punctual and aware of time when they went to work and school, time had a different meaning when family gatherings took place. Gatherings would start at an official time, but people came and left whenever the time felt right. Nature had a way, however, of teaching us the importance of time. There was time to get up, when the sun was up, so that we could help with chores before going to school or work. Watering plants, getting milk from a neighbor who had a cow, and feeding rabbits were my favorite tasks. There was time to get the potatoes picked and hazelnuts gathered and cabbage processed into kraut as winter approached and food needed to be stored for the cold months ahead. Each week, there was time for making homemade cheese. And there was always time for family stories and singing, for woodwork by my grandma's wooden stove, and for making "ciasto", a delicious sweet cake covered with fruit or jam. The ciasto was always available in case anyone visited us. We have a saying in Polish: When a visitor (*gosc* in Polish) is in your house, God is in your house. People did not schedule visits; they came when the time felt right to visit.

I lived with my grandparents and parents until my grandparents died, and when my dad remodeled our house, he made sure there would be enough room for my older sister and me, even when we got married and started our own families. The northeast corner of the house was dedicated to natural storage, as it was the coldest part. We harvested our own potatoes, apples, hazelnuts, lettuce, and cabbage; and we grew our own flowers and herbs. My maternal grandmother was the local "consultant" for treating illness with herbs. From chamomile, to sage, to caraway seeds, my grandmother passed on to us time-honored traditions. My grandmother never had an electric or gas stove. When my dad attempted to install one to modernize the house, she said, "What for?" and told him he was getting sucked in to new ways. As long as my grandmother lived, the wood-burning stove stayed.

I asked my grandmother tons of questions, and her answers drove me nuts. I would say, "Grandmother, how do you know when the food is done and needs to come out of the stove?" She would say, "When it feels right. You need to trust it." Isn't that similar to the answer we give to questions regarding the group process? We need to trust it.

Southern Poland, where I grew up, with all its natural beauty, was stained with the bloodshed of senseless power struggles. People used to say that even the flowers in Poland grew red because drank more blood than water. At about the same time as America was "discovered" by Europeans Poland started to receive frequent visits from Germans, Russians, Prussians, Austrians, Swedes, and Austro-Hungarian people, who decided that Poland should belong to them. To make a long story short, for more than 200 years, many people were killed or forced to take on another identity. Their land was taken away, and families were broken apart. The two world wars in the 20th century brought even more oppression to the lives of the Polish people. For many Polish people, it was very painful to give up their identity. When Polish people arrived in the United States, they felt forced to change their names, so once again their Polish identity was stripped away. Many well-known individuals were Polish but their Polish identity is unknown (e.g., Copernicus was really named Kopernik, Marie-Curie's Polish name was Sklodowski, and Chopin was originally Szopen).

My mother was born in a bunker, and my grandmother was in hiding before and after birth in order to avoid bombs. My paternal grandmother never knew her parents because she was taken from her poor peasant family by wealthy landlords, and there was nothing the family could do about it. She was never allowed to go to school and had to work for the wealthy family from sunrise to sunset. How was her life different from that of slaves?

My paternal grandmother had four children, one of whom died. Her oldest son, my uncle Frank, was kidnapped by Nazi soldiers. They showed up one day with rifles and, holding my grandfather at gunpoint, told the family, "You either give us your son, or we kill your family." They took my uncle and forced him to join the German army to fight against the Polish people. My uncle was only 14 years old at the time, but being brave and compassionate, he ran away from the German army and escaped to France, then to England, and finally to

Ireland. He was not allowed to come back to Poland, and the many letters he wrote home were confiscated by government officials, so my grandmother gave up hope and assumed her son was dead. My uncle, however, survived the labor camps (i.e., concentration camps) and came back to Poland after the war for a surprise visit. His mother almost passed out. He also came with his Irish wife and two beautiful boys, which shocked my grandmother as much as seeing him alive. He was the first to marry a non-Polish person, but my grandmother merely said, "At least she is not German." In Poland, marrying someone German was considered marrying outside of one's race. Even now many Polish people resent being mistaken for Germans.

While my uncle was forced out of Poland during the war, my dad, who was only about 9, was assigned farming and domestic chores at home. He lived in fear, as Poland was then occupied by Germany. Suddenly, the street names changed, and he and his friends would get physically punished for speaking Polish. Among his childhood memories is the memory of Jewish people being gathered at cemeteries and shot, one by one.

When the war was over, people celebrated the rebirth of Poland. My parents, both of whom loved life and the celebration of life, met when they were assigned to be dance partners as part of a folkloric dance group. As they took their first steps in dance together, their path to over 35 years of marriage unfolded. Meanwhile, however, Poland was grappling with communism. My parents were very brave. They participated in the Polish underground system of people supporting each other and trying to fight communism. My father became more and more serious and whispered a lot. Once I heard him say something about going to America, but my grandmother was worried and did not approve of the idea, and I never heard my parents speak of moving away again until after she died.

While I was playing in the mountains and taking dance lessons, the adults were getting more serious and something did not feel right. My grandmother would say, "Bogusia, what you learn at home, you must keep at home; what you learn at school, don't question it or challenge it, but don't believe it either. You will need to learn not to say everything you know from home, and you will need to learn not to see everything you see. Otherwise, your family could get hurt." I was shocked, confused, worried, and mad. One day a Polish government leader was driving through our town and all the schoolchildren were expected to greet him. I did not wave my hand because I had heard at home that he was not a good leader and was willing to sacrifice Polish culture and the safety of the Polish people. One of the teachers told me to wave my hand, and I said no; I tended to be pretty stubborn. Before I got home from school, my grandmother and parents knew what I had done. They were accused of raising an unpatriotic child, and the school staff told me that if I did not obey, I would end up in reformatory school. I was shocked and in tears, but my grandmother understood. She hugged me and told me to remember not to say what I learned at home. Then, one day, she died.

After my grandmother had died, I came home one day to find my mom in tears. She said, "Honey, we need to go. Please, do not say anything to anyone;

we must leave as soon as it gets dark." One of father's friends drove us to the airport in Warsaw, about eight hours north of where we lived. I was in shock, feeling like trees probably do when they get ripped from their soil by the winds of a hurricane and relocated to a place where they do not seem to belong and are not necessarily welcome.

At the airport, our belongings were confiscated. My parents' savings were taken, and they were allowed to keep only a $20 allowance per person. My older sister chose to stay in Poland. My parents were heartbroken, but they also tried to understand. When I was on the plane—14 years old, with tears rolling down my face—I told myself this was a nightmare and I would wake up soon. I thought my parents had lost their minds! We were going to the United States, to some big city called St. Louis, with no mountains nearby. And what was worse, I did not speak a word of English, so the only folks I could talk with would be my parents. I was really mad at them. The plane was not turning around, and I was not waking up from a dream. My dad tried to comfort me. He taught me how to order soda in English. He told me about Kennedy and many other brave people in the United States who decided to get together and form a new way of life. He said that someday I would know what it is like to live in a democratic system, something he never experienced as a kid. I said, "Does that mean democracy will start at home? If so, if I will have my rights, I want my rights to include going back to Poland." He just smiled and looked away.

During the plane trip to America, I decided that as soon as we arrived, I would get a job, any job, and save enough money to go back to Poland on a one-way ticket. Well, 22 years later, I still live here. I am a proud Polish immigrant and a proud American. I attended a wonderful all-girls school in St. Louis that emphasized social justice. Although my first year was rough, I learned to accept my new life. I was lucky to meet a friend, who is still my dearest friend, a sister to me. She is of Native-American and Irish descent. We connected and, without words, understood each other. Meanwhile, I attended English classes at night with people from all over the world. For the first time, I experienced the importance of universality. We laughed together, cried together, and recognized that although we came from so many different parts of the planet, we shared the values of wanting to maintain strong family ties, recognize the richness of our cultures, and belong to our new communities. Once again, one of my grandma's lessons helped me cope: "If you do not have what you like, then you might as well like what you have."

My parents had a baby not long after we moved to the states. At 16, I was starting to get a bit "Americanized" and was in shock. I told my mom, "You and dad still . . . Mom, I thought you were going through menopause." She blushed and said, "Yeah, me too." My parents also experienced for the first time what is it like to be discriminated against in a country with a supposedly democratic foundation. My dad's company shut down, but he was hired elsewhere right away; and he was glad to be away from his former coworkers who told Polish jokes and make the assumption that if one is Polish, one is not intelligent. To this day, I dislike ethnic jokes.

At this time, the borders to Poland had been shut down, and my family was not allowed to go back, even to visit. My parents were heartbroken when my older sister got married in Poland and they were not allowed to go there. But my parents were lucky. They met other Polish families in St. Louis and formed a strong Polish organization. A church where services were offered in Polish was established, along with a school where children could learn Polish. Although we were raised Catholic, the Polish Catholic Church was unique in many ways. In Poland, the Catholic Church was the voice of the oppressed. Many priests and nuns gave their lives in the fight for freedom. The Church helped to organize strikes and protests, and the sermons were about social justice.

Maintaining Polish identity was very important to my family. My younger sister, although raised in St. Louis, did not speak English until she went to pre-school. Now she speaks both Polish and English beautifully. As I was approaching graduation from high school, I wanted to maintain strong family and cultural roots and also open my wings a bit. So, I went to Southern Illinois University at Carbondale where I earned all my degrees, and with excitement studied psychology and counselor education.

My passion for and understanding of group leadership and group work grew. On weekends, I went home to my Polish community. I was thrilled when my godmother from Poland mailed me a Polish costume. I was so happy to go to the Polish Club and dance the night away with my parents and friends. I got upset when some of my Polish friends said I was no longer Polish, because I went away to college. Can one be Polish and actively involved with the community, and still live and work away from it? I would like to think so.

In college, I met a young man whose eyes reminded me of the deep caring look that was always present in my grandmother's eyes. I thought to myself, he must be Polish. Not only was he Polish, but he was from the same mountain region as I was, and he even knew the dialect spoken in southern Poland. I asked him if he knew the traditional Polish dances, and he did. As Andy and I took our first dance steps, we tought that our path to being "happy ever after" was unfolding. We organized a Polish-American club and were involved together in many cultural events. When we decided to get married, we got our families together and held the traditional engagement ritual. Then we returned to our respective colleges. A few hours later, however, I received one of the most painful phone calls in my life. The police called to report that he had been murdered by a drunk driver. I felt like my life had been shredded to pieces. What had started as the most beautiful day of my life had turned into nightmare.

I had a wonderful friend from Brazil, and she helped me through Andy's death. Then I decided to go to Brazil. I stayed with my "uncle," a dear family friend who was a liberal missionary priest. He taught me the value of helping others without perpetuating the cycle of oppression. He almost got kicked out of the Church because he was outspoken and disagreed with other missionaries; he thought they were disrespectful toward the Brazilian culture. In the church where he worked, I was honored to be allowed to partake in one of the traditional healing ceremonies. I put school on hold for a bit and stayed in

Brazil, thinking I could run from the pain. What a mistaken belief that was. Yet, I was so touched by the compassion of the Brazilian people and by my uncle's dedication that living in Brazil became one of the most enriching experiences in my life.

After I returned to the United States, I was strongly encouraged to attend school, but I did not want to be away from home. Home to me was Carbondale, home to me was St. Louis, but most of all home was the feeling of love, acceptance, and being able to be together with people from all walks of life. So, instead, I worked full-time at a residential program for teenagers who experienced numerous challenges, and I studied at night. Then, one day I met a person with beautiful deep dark eyes, curly hair, and a gentle smile that reminded me of my grandma's, but I did not think he could be Polish. I was correct; he was Honduran. He said he was going to be a priest. I told him, "You do not have to be a priest to be a father." I shocked myself when I said that, and he blushed. We became friends, and eventually took the path of marriage—an intercultural marriage.

When I was ready for my family to meet him, I wrote to my uncle Frank, since he had also married a non-Polish person. He and my aunt came all the way from Ireland to talk to my family, and after some family group meetings and confrontation, my dad and mom helped us have the most beautiful wedding ceremony one could imagine. We incorporated both the Polish rituals of breaking bread and salt and the Honduran blessing given by my husband's mother. My mom was fighting melanoma at the time and had a wish that she would see a grandchild before she died. A year later, Emily was born, taking her first breath almost as my mother took her last—but at least my mom got to see her grandchild.

My husband and I now have two wonderful children, Emily who is 9, and Christopher who is 4. Sometimes they ask, "Am I Spanish? Am I Polish? Am I American?" I say, "You are Latin, you are Honduran, you are Polish, and you are American. But most importantly by, you are the child of this universe, and just like us, you are a global visitor, passing in time and place." With joy I see my children singing in Polish, Spanish, and English. With joy I see their welcoming hearts wanting to embrace the cultural ways of both of their parents.

So, I am a granddaughter of people of the land, a daughter of brave people who gave up their motherland in the hopes of a better future for their children, a wife, and a mother of children whose experiences are influenced by a Polish and Honduran mosaic throughout the multiple layers of human interaction. I also am a counselor educator with a passion for group work who believes that learning is a process of shared meaning-making. That process can be helpful only when it is facilitated in a democratic spirit, which allows us to have culture vision. As Mary Catherine Bateson (1994) said, "What would it be like to have not only color vision but culture vision, the ability to see the multiple worlds of others?" (p. 53). I hope to keep expanding my culture vision, with my heart, soul, and mind. And I hope that my children, too, will have a culture vision that will allow them to celebrate their diversity while they honor unity among people.

DAYA SANDHU

I guess, I am approximately 58 years old. I was born in a small rural village in Sarhali, now in Pakistan, and all official records, including birthday records, were destroyed when the partition of India took place on August 15, 1947. An Indian holocaust took place when the British finally decided to leave India, and communal riots broke out among Hindus, Moslems, and the Sikhs.

It was not a tradition in those days to celebrate the birthdays of children in our community. My parents knew about my birthday, but only in terms of the indige nous calendar, called Bikrami era, which runs about 57 years ahead of the Christian calendar. Since public schools used the British system of education in India, on my first day of school, the registering teacher arbitrarily recorded my birth date as March 3, 1943. I will never know the exact date of my birth, however.

What race do I really belong to? It is an interesting question that I have not been able to resolve. While in India, I never had to address the question of race. However, according to Hindu belief, Indian society is divided into four castes, called *varna*. These varnas are ranked into four categories: Brahmins, Kshatriyas, Vaishyas, and the Sudras in the descending order of purity and respect. I belong to the third group, the Vaishyas (farmers).

The first time I confronted the question of race was while completing an application for a driver's license. Since I don't perceive myself as a Negroid, Caucasoid, Mongoloid, or Australoid, I categorized myself first as an Aryan, but soon changed to using "other," as I did not want to be associated with Hitler. I agree with Calloway and Harris (1977) that "The myth of human races constitutes one of man's most damnable masses of misinformation" (p. 7). Presently, I perceive myself as an Asian Indian.

Other than having a lazy left eye, I am fortunate for not having any physical disabilities, though I am conscious of the fact that as humans we are temporarily abled beings. I have a heterosexual orientation; I am very strongly attracted to women. As ethnicity is usually identified by cultural practices that include "language, accent, religion, customs, beliefs, and styles of living" (Axelson, 1993, p. 153), I will describe my background in the text that follows under these categories respectively.

My mother tongue is Punjabi, a language of the Punjab state where I was born. *Punjab* is a Persian word meaning five rivers. Punjab is a delta of five rivers, of which now there are two of them (Sutlej and Beas) in India and three of them (Ravi, Jhanan, and Jhelum) in Pakistan. More than 70 million people speak Punjabi worldwide. Punjabi is a rich and colorful language.

In addition, I can read, write, and speak Hindi as our national language and English as the international language. Each region of India has its own language that embodies unique cultural mores and unique ways of life. There are 16 major languages and many hundreds of dialects across the country. I also learned some Urdu and the classic language Sanskrit, a sister language to Latin and Greek.

Even after 30 years residing in the United States, I have not been able to change my accent. I studied English as a second language in India where more emphasis was placed on reading and writing than on speaking. Teachers taught us English through translation and retranslation methods. Many times we were not sure about the correct pronunciation and enunciation of English words. Since many of us speak English with a Punjabi accent; I call it Pink English. I was encouraged to read George Bernard Shaw's comments about English pronunciation that there is no one standard that can be followed. In sum, I speak kind of funny.

I was born in a Sikh family. Even though Sikhism is the youngest religion in the world, it ranks fifth in the world in number of its adherents. There are more than 20 million followers of Guru Nanak's religion residing in more than 20 countries. A large majority of the Sikhs live in the Punjab state of India. The famous Golden Temple in Amritsar is one of our holiest shrines.

Sikhism believes in only one God, called Wahe Guru, The Wonderful Supreme Being, and emphasizes Nam Japna (Worship His Name), Kirt Karna (Hard Work), and Vand Shakna (Sharing with the Others). It condemns Kam (lust), Krodh (anger), Lobh (avarice), Moh (worldly attachments), and Hauinkar (haughtiness). The Guru Granth Sahib, the Holy Book of the Sikhs, contains very inspirational and spiritual gospel of the Gurus couched in most moving and musical verses. The message of universalism and appreciation of diversity is the very essence of Guru Nanak's teachings. Not words, but deeds, are important. Baba Nanak preached "Truth is high, but higher still is truthful living." Historical errors are hard to rectify. Just as Columbus got confused, I am a case of a mistaken identity. Many Americans mislabel me as an Indian or a Native American. Actually, I was never called an Indian in India. *Bharti* or *Hindustani* is a preferable word. Since usage of these words is rare outside of Bharat/Hindustan, I perceive myself as neither an Indian nor an American, so I prefer to be called an Asian Indian to differentiate from a wide variety of Indians.

I believe that it is important to distinguish between internal and external identity here. I consider an internal identity to be more important, in terms of being that through which cultural messages are received, processed, and acted upon. It is the internal ethnic identity that creates our worldviews, which in turn determine our values, priorities, and actions. My internal ethnic identity has been primarily Asian Indian, deeply rooted in Punjabi culture. On the other hand, my children, with an external ethnic identity as Asian Indians, are full-blooded Asian Americans.

I was born and raised in India in an extended family. Unfortunately, my grandparents died when I was just 3 years old, depriving me of their love and warmth. Generally, grandparents live in the same house with their children and grandchildren, providing a strong support and safety network. They serve as surrogate parents, with only one big difference—they love their grandchildren more than their own children. Like most other families in India, my family of origin was patriarchal; my father served as the head of the household, a breadwinner, and protector of the family from external threats—a warrior indeed.

Mother was a pious household lady who prepared meals and kept the house. My father's authority is absolute even now when he is 83 years old. I have only one younger brother, about 11 years younger than me. Communication patterns have always been vertical, from the top to the bottom. As children, we seldom talked back to our parents or refused to do what we were asked to do. Even at the age of 58, I have not dared to confront my father. As a rule, I have always avoided my father when he is in the company of his friends.

Our family patterns in the United States changed dramatically. Our family became nuclear, and family communication patterns became circular. As a father, I don't have the same vertical authority that my father has. Most of the decisions are made at the dining room table. Input from all family members is invited and valued. I have rarely made any decision alone without discussing it first with my wife and children. This is a long-term process, and traditional authority as father and the head of the household is compromised. Not only family patterns, but also family configurations, changed. My parents belonged to the same caste and religion, and had similar social and economic status. My present wife and I belong to different religions and castes. She is a Hindu, and I am a Sikh. She belongs to the Kshatriyas (warrior) caste, and I come from the Vaishyas (farmer) varna. Since my first wife got killed an automobile accident, leaving behind a daughter and son, I have fathered a blended family.

I am a mild-mannered male who does not necessarily appreciate macho attitudes. I am a feminist who is deeply influenced by Guru Nanak who questioned, "So kiu manda akhye jit jamme rajan?" "Why to demean women who gave birth to kings and prophets?" (Sri Guru Granth, p. 473. Translated by Gopal Singh, 1978).

I migrated to the United States in 1969 with $8 in my pocket. Due to lack of foreign currency availability, the Reserve Bank of India would not allow emigrants to take more money. Now this limit has been raised to $20. Thanks to the great opportunities in the United States, my family belongs to the middle-class now.

I rate myself a little above average in intelligence, but I have never taken any intelligence test. I earned my bachelor of arts, bachelor of teaching degree, and master's degree in English from Punjab University in India before migrating to the United States. I came to the United States as an international student to complete my master's degree in education. I became a naturalized citizen of the United States in 1980. I also earned my specialist's degree in English and doctorate of counselor education from the University of Mississippi and Mississippi State, respectively.

From time to time in my academic and professional life, I have received numerous rewards. My most recent awards include: Alumnus of the Year Award (2000) from Mississippi State, Multicultural Research Award (2000), and Multicultural Teaching Award (2000) from the University of Louisville. I am also the recipient of the Fulbright Research Award (2001) for India and the Outstanding Research Award (2001) from the University of Louisville. On March 22, 2001, the president of the University of Louisville named me the Distinguished Professor of Research.

I see myself as a unique individual from several perspectives. First and foremost, I consider myself a Sikh, even though I am clean-shaven and do not wear the beard, turban, sword, and all other symbols required by Sikhism. My worldviews, values, priorities, goals, and purposes in life are directed, driven, and motivated by the ideals and teachings of the Ten Spiritual Masters called Sikh Gurus. Sadly, the word *guru* has been corrupted in the Western world. We hold the word *guru* (one who illuminates and removes spiritual ignorance) in highest esteem. Guru is the Divine Preceptor.

My cultural background, deeply rooted in India's rich cultural heritage, provides guidance, encouragement, solace, and satisfaction even in the most difficult and trying times. I believe that both of my very successful and satisfying marriages were determined by my unique cultural and ancestral traditions and practices, which are grounded in Indian or Punjabi culture. My background in the Jat Sikh family has given me a different set of values, including hard work, broad a mindedness, an open attitude toward life, and take-life-as-it-is and face-difficulties-bravely approach.

In sum, I am a unique individual with a psychospiritual personality profile of a Sikh and hard-working ethics. I am a sincere and caring person who believes in the brotherhood and sisterhood of mankind. I am not only a God-believing but also a God-fearing person. My external identity is fully that of an Asian Indian, but my internal identity is now becoming bicultural. This bicultural identity consists of various internalizations, a conglomerate of Eastern and Western values.

I strongly believe that we all have multiple internal identities. These identities are dynamic in nature. In the face of life's challenges, different internal identities become salient at different times. Simply put, in some situations, I may behave like an Indian, in others as an American, and in still others, I may act as a pure Punjabi Jat (a rustic farmer).

My cultural background makes group work a natural phenomenon. Indian culture in general, and Punjabi culture in particular, is a collectivist culture. More than 80% of India's population resides in small villages. These villages are like one close-knit family. In the center of each village (called *Chowks*), men get together daily to meet and discuss personal, family, national, and international matters of interest. This practice is similar to group work, where people share their problems and seek one another's help. Generally, elders' guidance and encouragement are appreciated. Women also get together frequently, but not in Chowks; they may meet at someone's house or discuss matters with each other in the streets or on their ways to fields when fetching dinners for their working spouses and children. Generally discussions in these groups are quite open, with the exception of those issues that might bring shame to the family.

I perceive myself as a bicultural counselor with a strong background in both Eastern and Western cultures and religions, and I strongly believe that my biculturalism is an asset and not a limitation. It has expanded my worldviews and broadened my outlook on life as a cosmopolitan. As a bicultural counselor, I believe that all humans are on a journey with special physical, social, and spiritual needs. Everyone is struggling for the better, and my role as a counselor is to facilitate that process.

As my life experiences are rooted in diverse cultures, religions, and languages, the topic of diversity interests me the most. As a Sikh, I value diversity and strongly condemn oppression against the weak and downtrodden. As a writer, I am one of the pioneering group that would like to employ counseling knowledge, skills, and strategies to address the social ills of our time, such as prejudice, violence, and racial and gender inequities. In sum, I believe that I bring sensitivity, flexibility, openness, and awareness as strengths to group work. I should be seen as a transformer leader who would like to empower the group members. From the contextual point of view, I have extensive experience in issues relating to acculturation, cross-cultural and intercultural issues, issues relating to cultural and bicultural identity, and spirituality.

In my group counseling approaches, I strongly agree with DeLucia-Waack (1996) that counselors must modify group theories and techniques that are culture-specific or have cultural relevance. I apply group counseling strategies that are congruent with the beliefs and behaviors of the various cultures from which clients come. As a bicultural counselor, it may take me longer to establish a relationship with my clients. Generally, issues relating to trust and expertness can emerge and become barriers. In addition, my Punjabi accent can be a problem for couple of sessions until members get used to it. Over the years, I have learned to understand many slang words, but not all of them. I sometimes have to ask clients to explain what they mean when they use slang words.

MUHYIDDIN SHAKOOR

My age is 56, and I have served 30 of those years in academic settings as a counselor and counselor educator. I have 17 years of experience as a family therapist in private practice, and I also have significant training and experience in the field of small groups and organizational change. I am an African-American male who is presently in good health; and I am a heterosexual who has been married for 23 years and has two college-age children. My ethnic identity is African, and my personhood has evolved through a historically Afrocentric family and community-oriented cultural background, an important and unique aspect of which heritage has been the inherent but broadly diverse spirituality of African and African-American cultures in combination with my personal Islamic faith.

I was born and raised in Cleveland, Ohio. I grew up in the urban village streets of the Lower East Side in a four-family apartment building. That building, its tenants, and the next-door neighbors, together with the families and community around our building, were my entire world until I left home at 18. I was the eldest of three children in a close-knit family that was sometimes seen as unique because two parents were present in it. But my mother was always the driving force of our family and often the ombudswoman for our street. Both she and my father worked at full-time jobs, but mother was the glue in terms of emotional support, training, teaching, and simply being there. Father was emotionally detached, but he provided for us as best he could. On behalf of our futures, he sacrificed the best years of his life doing blue-collar work in a factory.

My sister, brother, and I always stood out because of how we were raised. We were poor in terms of dollars rich inside ourselves. We were always clean and cared for and told that any one of us could be the pride of the entire nation of black people or even of the entire human race. The years when I moved from childhood into adulthood were characterized by extraordinary change. There was community solidarity and a sense of extended family with neighbors. There was renewed racial pride and social protest. I lived through the eras of Muhammad Ali, Dr. Martin Luther King, Malcolm X, John F. Kennedy and Robert Kennedy, hippies and love children, Afro hair styles, and Vietnam. I was a graduate student at Kent State on the day that three protesting students were shot. Music of the Beatles, Elvis, Miles Davis, John Coltrane, Ella Fitzgerald, Sarah Vaughn, Duke Ellington, Count Basie, Sly and the Family Stone, Isaac Hayes, Curtis Mayfield, and others provided the soundtrack for those years of my life.

I consider my worldview to be universal, transpersonal, and transcultural. By *universal*, I mean a view that relates to the world as one, in spite of and through all of its varied manifestations. It is similar to the nondominant conceptual view described by Meyers (1988) as *optimal*. The optimal view, like the universal, emphasizes human and spiritual interconnection and holds self-knowledge to be the basis of all knowledge and the key to humanity's achievement of its goals. The optimal perspective is directly antithetical to the more widely prevalent *suboptimal* worldview, which holds that the spiritual and material aspects of life are separate from each other. It is my personal belief that life is a unity and that every person, class, and category is a part of the whole. My affirmation of the *transpersonal* viewpoint includes the humanistic paradigm. When I speak of transpersonal, I mean a point of view that complements a universal worldview, that affirms the practical value of a nonfragmented, unified view of matter, spirit, and the interrelatedness of all things. By *transcultural*, I mean a transcendent multicultural point of view that spans, embraces, honors, and respects the different philosophies of life, beliefs, and values of different human communities and their cultures. This perspective is a multidimensional acknowledgment of peoples, races, lifestyles, religions, and their unique orientations, characteristics, and contributions.

Taken together in synthesis, the universal, transpersonal, and transcultural ways of perceiving life constitute a dynamic worldview for me that emphasizes the integration of ideas and experience, human potential, empowerment, heart, fairness, openness to personal process, interdependence, cooperation, and mutual support. When applied to education and learning, this view gives major emphasis to the learner's freedom, value, worth, dignity, and integrity. With regard to my educational background, I am a highly motivated achiever who earned a Ph.D in counselor education at age 29 after completing a master of education degree in rehabilitation counseling and a bachelor of arts degree in psychology. I regard myself as a highly intuitive, creative, intellectually curious, compassionate, spirit-centered being. My socioeconomic status is middle class.

With regard to my sense of uniqueness as an individual, I believe that the urban Afrocentric family and social context into which I was born during the middle 1940s contributed greatly to the person I presently am. I was a child during the 1950s and a young adult during the 1960s. As an adolescent, it seemed odd to me that the optimal worldview prevailed among the people, families, and community of my youth but not beyond our perimeters. I grew up with the idea that I could be anything I wanted to be in life. I was always encouraged to be proud to be black and to remember the millions who died in the bowels of ships during that "bitter passage" from Africa. Throughout my life, from childhood into manhood, my mother consistently reassured me that there is spectacular beauty in blackness. However, she also taught me that who I am as a being and what substance I have as a person is more a function of my heart, faith, intelligence, and service to mankind than a function of my skin color. My mother and a large segment of my community recognized the unity of life and that one's value and worth as an individual is more a function of *being* than one of *having*. I was taught that each human being is unique, worthy, and gifted with her own special capacities independent of her ethnic, cultural, or family background.

When I went beyond the security and familiar boundaries of the predominantly black community that was home, I was astounded that racism, oppression, discrimination, prejudice, and suboptimal thinking were so prevalent in the world-at-large. Entering it, I gained a glimpse through personal experience into why my community elders reminded youth of the African diaspora horrors. Malcolm X spoke aptly of the plight of blacks in America: "We didn't land on Plymouth Rock," he said. "It landed on us." In the world-at-large, I had yet to grapple with bitter remnants of ships that were no longer on the oceans but which sailed nonetheless through my life. Now and then, from time to time, their bleak massive sails still unfold and rustle in the winds of my mind.

The most valuable and enduring contribution of my background to my view of groups has been the rich, sustained, dynamic, colorful, and nontheoretical experience of living with other people in groups of various kinds throughout my life. I grew up in a community experience that was characterized by a powerful sense of group loyalty, with high tolerance for differences of opinion, moral ideas, and ethnic origin. Relationships, communication, and interactions with others were essential to the survival of the entire neighborhood. The first and most influential of these groups was my own family, which included my parents, two younger siblings, and frequently live-in extended family members like maternal or paternal grandparents, uncles, aunts, and cousins. We even considered some people as family who were not blood relations and often gave them honorary titles of Aunt, Uncle, Granny, Mama, or Pappa. These people were usually long-standing friends of my parents or neighbors who were highly respected. Other groups included softball teams, baseball clubs, track-and-field teams, and basketball teams from middle school through junior and senior high.

Within my community, from my birth through early adulthood, many interesting, lively groups and subgroups were a part of the fabric of my life. Besides those already mentioned, these included Jamaican and Caribbean folk, including some Latinos; immigrated blacks from the deep south; the gangster crowd; artists, including musicians, dancers, and painters; and others. Cooks, chefs, and restaurateurs formed an essential core together with religious groups. Many denominations were represented from among the Protestant Christian sects, including Baptists, Methodists, Pentecostals, Seventh-day Adventists, and Episcopalians. Other groups such as Orthodox Muslims, Catholics, Black Jews, Black Muslims, Rastafarians, and Moorish Sciences Brotherhood were also present. In addition, there were Masonic lodges, Elks, Eastern Stars, Black Nationalists, Black Panthers, and proponents of voodoo, snake medicine, dream reading, and fortune telling. While living this experience, I learned the lesson of how humans truly are one, though they appear to be many. Here, I had my first dealings with the challenges of listening to feedback and hearing what others think of me. I learned about managing conflict, and about love and connection. I learned about differences in power and personal influence. I learned what it is to feel horrifying fear because of threats of an antagonist group, and about the sense of refuge, relief, and safety that comes from a group offering friendship and protection.

My primary strength is my personhood. I believe that my experience and evolution as a being help me most in my work as an educator and group leader. The experience of a supportive family and proud community gave me a sense of what value and power exists within the group. From the urban tribal groups of my youth, I gained the strength and confidence to grapple with challenges of the world beyond my family and neighborhood. Tempered in fires of racism and discrimination, beaten on anvils of poverty and prejudice, my warrior heart was nonetheless sustained. Nurtured by the vibrant Afrocentric feeling of community and the spiritual grounding of my early years, my sense of personal worth was consolidated and affirmed. This vital support helped me to escape the limitations of my own lack of confidence and my secretly held self-doubt.

One aspect remains a challenge in terms of limitations. Part of my dilemma now is that I no longer think of human beings in terms of limitations. I have come to see that humans have challenges, blocks, and ways of resisting, all of which can be summed up as fear. If these things are faced, nothing remains except love and unlimited possibility. I see myself as a work in progress. I am still slaying my own inner dragons. One of the challenges I see that could be a limitation if I acknowledged it as such is this: I tend to be too critical of myself. I believe I have been given a lot, and I feel responsible to *be* as much as I can be and *do* more than I presently do. I am learning more and uncovering more than I ever imagined. In this process, I notice little anxieties and fears coming to the surface . . . fears about obligations that may accompany being more. I do realize that these are "out there" fears. When I am *here* and when I am *now*, I am courageous and full of hope. When I live in this place, I know that everything will work out for the best.

At this time in my life, I feel myself as a man who is carrying the entire universe within himself. I am striving to remain free of self-limiting thinking and free of doubt, so as to have no fear of being all that I can possibly be. I am striving to relate to those whom I meet in my journey with love, compassion, and light.

ZIPORA SHECHTMAN

My name is Zipora (Zippi) Shechtman. I am married and the mother of four grown-up children, and I am a professor in counseling education at a university in Israel. I hold an M.A. degree from the University of Dayton, Dayton, Ohio, and a Ph.D in counseling and student development from the American University in Washington, DC. I have been involved in group counseling since 1975, working mainly with students and teachers. I have also been supervising graduate students on their work in counseling children's groups. My main area of research is child group counseling and psychotherapy, where I study outcomes and processes. Recently, I also have become involved in studying the treatment of aggression, to a large extent also in groups.

I was born in Russia during World War II, the second child in a hard-working Jewish family. My parents were refugees from Poland who had managed to escape just the day before the Nazis entered their city. My father was straightaway mobilized into the Russian military, which left my mother with her parents and some other relatives struggling to survive the war. I was born in a small rural village into extreme poverty, with no home and little or no food or clothing. My mother was working in the fields for some bread or potatoes; hence, I spent the first three years of my childhood with her and my sister, who is five years older, largely in the fields. From the stories my mother told with pride about this part of our family history, I have learned that women are smart, strong, independent, and self-sufficient. I also have learned that life can be tough but at the same time also challenging, and that persistency and hard work may help overcome existential difficulties.

When the war was over, we returned as refugees to Poland, but not to our home. We were settled in an unknown former German city, and started a new life with little social support. Anti-Semitism was obvious in Poland at that time. I remember going to a Jewish school and often being bullied by the Polish children. It was one of the reasons why my parents decided that Israel is the solution for the Jewish people. After several unsuccessful attempts, we managed to leave Poland for Israel, without any of our properties, once again starting life all over in poverty. This meant living in an extremely disadvantaged neighborhood, socializing with children who were poorly motivated for academic achievement, and working for my tuition. But at the same time, it offered me a chance to discover that I could stand out and be highly appreciated not only by teachers, but also by parents of other children, as I soon became a private teacher for many kids who had learning difficulties. It was here that I learned the basic principles of quality teaching and began to

understand the potential for destructive relationships in families of low socioeconomic status.

For my parents, it was too late to build a new life based on self-fulfillment.
They were both too busy simply trying to make a living and support their three
children, having no chance to learn a new language or gain a profession. Very
early in my life, parent-child roles were switched around: We, the children,
could read the language and settle administrative problems better than our parents. We also took care of the house while they were working. I felt sorry for my
parents for the rough life they had, and I became the "good girl" who would do
anything to make things a bit easier for them. This included making sure I
excelled in school, doing all kinds of chores for them, and trying to make them
happy through small gestures (e.g., insisting on celebrating their birthdays).

I realized that education was the way out of poverty, a realization that was
reinforced by my own academic achievements and the positive feedback of my
teachers. I went through all educational levels. The background I have
sketched here had helped me become so persistent (and, I would say, industri-
ous) that I managed to make it through school while working full-time and
raising four children—on the whole, under quite difficult conditions. But I
remained optimistic throughout, with a sense of self-efficacy, and enjoyed the
journey very much. I have always been proud of the way I have balanced the
needs of my family with my own, so that my self-fulfillment has never come at
the expense of others. I am very happy with my own career and am glad to see
my daughters following a similar pattern; I am very proud of them, too.

My family background taught me a great deal about human suffering. I
have become sensitive to the suffering of other people and aware of their need
to be acknowledged and supported. I also learned to be persistent in my work
and not to give in to difficult people or situations that are put in my way. Finally,
I have become sensitive to peoples' taking advantage of others, using force or
social power against those who are weak. This has led me to try and help people under stress and, in case of violence, provide treatment to the aggressor and
victim alike. To me, groups are the ultimate answer to such needs.

I arrived in Israel when I was 7 years old, young enough to be still influenced by Israeli culture. I have experienced my life in Israel as highly stressful
in many ways: war situations, much interpersonal aggression, harsh economic
conditions, and high levels of competition. All have had their impact on my
life. Interpersonal interaction is often characterized as aggressively straightforward and direct, but also as sincere and naturalistic. Both solidarity and con-
formism play a large role in Israeli culture. These characteristics are manifest
in an active, nondefensive, often critical and judgmental method of communication, prompted by values and sociocultural processes that represent the so-
called "sabra" culture of the young. Coming from a different culture, I was
never able to absorb the sabra values and actually have become quite critical
of them. They are incongruent with the nonjudgmental family climate I grew
up in and with the high level of empathy I have always felt toward others. This
resistance to the Israeli sabra culture was reinforced by the frequent traveling
I did to the United States.

Overall, I guess I have absorbed aspects from each of the cultures I have been exposed to. From my early childhood, I took the motivation and assertiveness for self-growth, a strong sense of self-reliance, and sensitivity toward the suffering and the poor. From Israeli culture, I took the intimacy and sense of closeness on the one hand, and the ability to be assertive and confrontive on the other, though I also developed a personal aversion to criticism and roughness. From American culture, I took the value of people adhering to correctness in interpersonal relationships and the skills one needs to maintain such relationships.

As a result, in the type of groups that I conduct, I strive to build on a person's positive aspects. Group climate is the most important goal for me in establishing and maintaining a group. Self-expressiveness and support are highly cherished, and interpretives are used with care and reservations. The leader appears as a human being, always equal in status, sharing honestly the emotions that emerge and, when appropriate, private experiences. In my 25 years of running groups, I have constantly sought further training and learned to overcome my own vulnerability, or need to be loved, and permit group members to experience resistance with much freedom, something I had to work hard to achieve myself.

To summarize, my personal characteristics and my long, successful experience in leading groups, have taught me to trust the group process. In leading groups I expect the unexpected and look for challenges. I rarely get discouraged when difficulties come up. I am sensitive to the difficulties participants display and know how to engage the members in the group process. As a result, the groups I lead are characterized as warm and cohesive, and often members speak up for the first time in a group. On the other hand, I tend to take too much responsibility for the group process. When something goes wrong, I first look at my own behavior and mistakes, and find it difficult to let go even when it obviously was not my fault.

SUMMARY/ANALYSIS OF RESPONDENTS' AUTOBIOGRAPHIES

The autobiographies of our eleven experts each tell a story that is peculiar to the respondent's own acculturation experiences. We are made ever mindful of the influences such experiences have on the development of individual personalities and character. We also are made aware of how migration and acculturation experiences affect both the conscious and subconscious levels as one engages in interpersonal relationships—and more specifically, how such experiences may influence the way leaders lead groups.

Even though we have eleven persons of different cultural backgrounds, none of them claim to be representative of their whole culture. Each individual is a mix and a blend of migration and acculturation experiences that makes him most unique. Consider Muhyiddin Shakoor's view that he certainly does not consider himself representative of all African Americans, much less of all

African-American males, or Zipora Shechtman's experience of being at once a Jewish immigrant to Israel and yet an Israeli who at times experiences an internal struggle between the two cultures of which she is a part. Consider also that we have three experts who can claim Jewish heritage, yet whose own stories of migration and acculturation dare readers to claim that to know one is to know them all. And so as you undertake the reading of the next part of the book, we ask that you try to be very aware of each expert's story so that you have a context from which to hear and understand the how and why of each expert's responses to the various situations presented in the vignettes.

Responses to Multicultural Group Work Vignettes

In the following eight chapters, our experts face a variety of critical incidents that occur in groups. They were asked to respond first as a member, and then as a leader. As you read their responses to the guideline questions, we ask that you recall their autobiographical sketches from Part II so you will have a full context from which to understand how their personal stories of acculturation may have influenced the way they responded to the incidents. Please recognize that the group vignettes you are about to read may not be typical of the multicultural groups you have encountered or will encounter in your future counseling practice. We have amplified the cultural and ethnic diversity of our group members in an attempt to illustrate the importance of examining individual group members' worldviews and their impact on the group process. We also ask that you try to be aware of your own story of acculturation and the degree to which it may influence the way you listen to our experts.

Two or three experts responded to each group work vignette, and the vignettes provide different emphases: task/work, psychoeducational/guidance, and counseling/therapy. Following are the directions and questions we provided to our experts to guide them in writing their responses, first as a member and then as a leader of each group. We asked them to read the vignette first, and them to think about how they would view this group as a member and to answer the following questions:

1. Identify the multicultural issues that need to be taken into consideration for you as a member.
2. Explain how your ethnic and cultural background affected the way you would respond as a member.
3. Explain how your ethnic and cultural background may or may not inhibit the way you respond to the situation as a member.
4. Explain how your ethnic and cultural background may have influenced your choice of the response you made over any other that you may have been considering as a member.
5. As a result of the response you chose, identify the consequences you might anticipate as a member.
6. From your position as a member, explain what the most glaring or outstanding aspect was of the situation that impacted you from your ethnic and cultural orientation.

Then the experts were asked to read the vignette again and think about how they would view this group as a leader. They responded to the following questions based on being a leader of this group:

1. If this type of incident would not occur in your group, explain why it would not.
2. Identify the multicultural issues that need to be taken into consideration for you as a leader.
3. Explain how your ethnic and cultural background affected the way you would respond as a leader.
4. Explain how your ethnic and cultural background may or may not inhibit the way you respond to the situation as a leader.
5. Explain how your ethnic and cultural background may have influenced your choice of the response you made over any other that you may have been considering as a leader.
6. As a result of the response you chose, identify the consequences you might anticipate as a leader.
7. From your position as a leader, explain what the most glaring or outstanding aspect was of the situation which impacted you from your ethnic and cultural orientation.
8. Based on the composition of this group, what multicultural issues (etic and emic) need to be taken into consideration as the incident is addressed in group?

Keep in mind, as you read our group work experts' responses as both group leaders and members, that we asked them to really stretch themselves—to very critically examine their personal reactions and where they came from. Sometimes it was difficult for our experts to imagine themselves as members of particular groups, and yet as you read their answers, you will gain some very important insights into what it feels like to be different from other members of the group, how potential biases may affect group member behavior and participation, and how people try to connect with others whom they perceive to be different from themselves.

Also keep in mind the complexity of the influences on group member and group leader responses. Our experts worked incredibly hard to decipher how and when their cultural and ethnic backgrounds influenced their personal reactions, perceptions of group events, and choices of group work interventions. And yet, you will notice that even for experts, it is sometimes difficult to determine exactly what influence their cultural and ethnic backgrounds have had on their theoretical orientations as counselors and on who they are as people.

4 CHAPTER | **Task Group Vignette #1**

The First Meeting and Group Impasse

You have been appointed chair of a professional organization's national conference planning committee. The committee consists of six members and you. The president-elect of the organization appointed all the committee members.

- Dara is 42, and she has immigrated from Pakistan. She came to the attention of the president-elect when they both served together as members of the human rights committee. You have been informed that she is a hard worker.
- Emile is 38. His parents left Venezuela 10 years ago because of political strife in the country. They had to leave most of their wealth behind. He is very articulate and is an associate professor of psychology. He has been an active member on a number of the organization's committees.
- Suzanne is 37. She has been active in the organization's gay and lesbian rights division. She and her partner have two adopted children. She is the human resources department head for a Fortune 500 corporation.
- David is 35. He is a psychotherapist in the outpatient department of a large hospital. He is paralyzed from the waist down due to a skiing accident when he was 16. He uses a wheelchair. He is married. He has been a very active campaigner for making certain that the organization is accessible for persons with disabilities and

that its national programs have presentations whose content addresses the needs of people with disabilities.

- Zabelle is 27. She recently immigrated to the United Sates from Israel. Her Ph.D is in counseling psychology, and she is an assistant professor in the psychology department of a small midwestern university. She has shown a keen desire to strengthen the organization's international division, specifically to help build ties to the Middle East.
- Martin is 41. He is a marriage and family therapist in private practice in New York City. He is the fifth child of an African-American family. He has long advocated for the organization to provide pro bono work to the less fortunate. His activism caught the attention of the president-elect, and thus he was appointed to the committee.

The group was meeting for the first time. After a brief warm-up activity, where members had the opportunity to meet each other and learn about each others' special interests, you presented them with the group's task, which was to develop a national conference that would reflect the president-elect's theme. You expected that the group would get off to a swift start, given the profile of its members. You were not prepared for what you were about to face.

David spoke up first. In a warm, even tone of voice, he stated that he was flattered to have been selected for the committee by the president-elect. However, he saw the process by which the committee was selected as a reflection of how the organization was not making itself accessible to all. He added that while he was willing to serve on the committee, he felt there could not be any movement forward until this matter was addressed.

While David spoke, the others listened attentively. He had just finished speaking when Martin spoke up. Martin's tone of voice was more intense. He said he related to David's statement and felt the organization had been turning a deaf ear to his efforts to provide pro bono work to the poor. As far as he was concerned, he saw his primary role in the group as an advocate to ensure that the national conference would reflect his concerns.

When Martin finished speaking, Suzanne spoke. In a firm voice, she stated that she respected David's and Martin's concerns; however, she disagreed with them on two counts. First, she conveyed how during her years as an active member of the gay and lesbian division, she always felt the strong support of the organization and therefore disagreed with the two group members that the organization was insensitive to concerns such as theirs. Secondly, she argued that she did not see this group's task as having to provide a forum for its members' own special interests.

As this strong interaction ended, you noticed the effect it had on the group. Zabelle, who had been leaning forward early on, was sitting back with her hands clasped together in front of her. Emile kept looking at you, as if he were expecting the next remarks to flow from your lips. Dara had a look of puzzlement on her face as though she had not anticipated this kind of a beginning to the group. After all, she was accustomed to being given a task and setting about to get it done. As your eyes and ears absorbed all that happened, you contemplated your next move.

BEVERLY BROWN'S REACTION AS A MEMBER OF THIS TASK GROUP

Identify the multicultural issues that need to be taken into consideration for you as a member.

I need for a group climate to develop with respect for all members of the group and for the organization they are serving. It would be important that communication and influence be distributed across genders and members with differing communication patterns. Also, members have different values and experiences, and time may be needed to enhance understanding of one another as well as the goal of the group. In order for the group to focus on its task, members need to be encouraged to express any needs they have that are related to being in the group. For example, David would need flexibility to sit in the group where he chooses because he uses a wheelchair, and he might have other special need requests as well. Also, three of the members are from other countries, and it is unclear whether they have difficulty with the English language. If needed, arrangements could be made to ensure understanding in the flow of communication. An interpreter might be needed for all members' contributions to be understood. Furthermore, I would want members to have sufficient clarity about the group's goal so the variety of occupational roles they represent can come together to strengthen planning.

Explain how your ethnic and cultural background affected the way you would respond as a member.

My initial reaction would be lack of comfort with conflict, especially so early in the group, and awareness of discomfort by Zabella, Emile, and Dara. I would be likely to react as if I were a young person lacking experience in how conflict functions in a group. Is this discomfort due to lack of exposure to conflict as a child, or are other aspects of my early environment influencing me? I expect the latter is true. When I was young, women in my environment were expected to be polite, proper, and quiet. During social gatherings, the women often met in the kitchen to talk about children and cooking while the men gathered in a separate room to discuss politics, finance, and work-related matters. Women were expected to stay home, care for children, and find their identity through the success of their husbands. Thus, when many women, including myself, were placed in a situation where they needed to articulate a controversial position or mediate different points of view, they were unable to do so because of their lack of experience.

In addition to feelings about conflict, my experience with social issues would help me understand the possible validity of David's concern about accessibility of the organization to all members and Martin's concern about pro bono work with poor people. Suzanne's comment about feeling support from the organization when she was an active member of the gay and lesbian division suggests a contrast of perceptions about the association's response to social issues. The optimist part of who I am would be encouraged by the comment and would hope committee members could find common ground and proceed with the committee's work. If, indeed, the association could improve its position on pro bono work and procedures for accessibility of all members to committee work, I am confident this committee could make recommendations that would be heard by the full leadership without offending the president-elect.

Explain how your ethnic and cultural background may or may not inhibit the way you respond to the situation as a member.

While initially I would feel a desire to withdraw from the conflict, I would monitor the response given by the leader and then comment in a way I hoped would help the group move forward. My cultural background includes the need to stand up for what one believes, which is stronger than my desire to avoid conflict. Indeed, caring for others often requires the use of conflict communication skills. This is why I have worked over the years at learning to approach conflict rather than avoid it. Other influencing values include the desire to support others and the responsibility to proceed with a task and do the best job possible under the circumstances. The person I am today would choose to approach the outspoken members as well as the quiet ones.

Explain how your ethnic and cultural background may have influenced your choice of the response you made over any other that you may have been considering as a member.

Even though I am not acting in the leader role, my experience and training as a group leader would have a very strong influence on my chosen response. I would participate by acknowledging the concerns that were spoken and suggest that there might be a way to bring each person's concern into the planning process. Perhaps we could consider the way committee members are selected and the need for pro bono work as part of our agenda. My goal would be to build an agenda rather than letting one concern dominate communication in the group. When Suzanne's concern about addressing members' special interests was stated, I would encourage the group to see if exploring special interests might even strengthen the conference. I might also verbally wonder about the thoughts held by quiet members on things to consider as we planned our conference. A group is not likely to be productive unless all its members find their place in the group and feel their contributions are heard and respected. My response would strive to be consistent with my views on the value of all members, the desire to care for others, and the importance of giving full effort to completing the task. In order to keep my value of cooperation in mind, I would select a response that would support the leader of the group. The alternative of sitting back and letting outspoken members settle their own disputes does not appeal to me. I would prefer to see the group as a whole participate and so would distribute responsibility for the direction of its work.

As a result of the response you chose, identify the consequences you might anticipate as a member.

Reactions to my comments would depend on many factors: the intervention made by the leader, the ability of members to suspend their concerns and hear from other members, and the legitimacy of concerns expressed in the situation. For example, if motives included a bid for leadership, different response might be needed. However, if acknowledging outspoken members' concerns and hearing from quiet members would help to establish a pattern of communication, the group might be ready to establish norms and clarify the goal of the group. Also, the original concerns addressed need not be forgotten.

From your position as a member, explain what the most glaring or outstanding aspect was of the situation which impacted you from your ethnic and cultural orientation.

The early presence of conflict in the group was an outstanding aspect of the situation. The risk of people rejecting one another and the possibility of quiet members withdrawing from the group seemed evident. Different styles of communication could prevent the group from developing norms, learning to work together, and accomplishing its task. If this were to occur, important social interest concerns would not be addressed, and the group's goal of planning the association's conference would not get met.

BEVERLY BROWN'S REACTION AS LEADER OF THIS TASK GROUP

If this type of incident would not occur in your group, explain why it would not.

I would like to say that if additional attention were given to pregroup planning and early group formation processes, this incident would not occur. However, I believe this type of incident could easily occur in all types of groups. Members bring their unique passions and concerns, as well as a range of other characteristics including differences in communication style. At times the passions and communication styles of members lead to very early conflict.

Identify the multicultural issues that need to be taken into consideration for you as a leader.

There are three types of issues that would be important to me as a leader. First, I would want members to feel comfortable expressing any needs they have in order to be contributing members (i.e., disability or communication needs). Second, I would want to build a climate in the group that values diversity and allows each member to have influence in the group, regardless of gender, sexual orientation, ethnicity, cultural background, presence of a disability, and occupational setting. Valuing diversity would include respect for those with different communication patterns, even if that includes members who are not fluent with English. The soft-spoken as well as outspoken members would learn to work together in a way that respects the other. I recognize that the group would need to develop over time as members increased their understanding of one another and learned to work together. The third type of issue relates to the goal of the group. I would like to see diversity as an important part of the conference within the context of the president-elect's theme.

Explain how your ethnic and cultural background affected the way you would respond as a leader.

As a young woman, I was fearful of conflict and often felt left out of communication within groups. I also have watched those with disabilities be ignored due to differences in communication, and I have watched those willing to initiate leadership be criticized and rejected for assuming leadership roles. I have come to believe that facilitation of diverse communication styles and other, related issues are essential for understanding and respecting those different from ourselves. Thus, in the situation described, I would provide a summary that acknowledged the comments made in the group and included process observations about communication. I would suggest that those who had not yet commented might also have concerns or ideas related to conference planning: "I wonder if there might be some way to use your concerns in our planning. Let's take a few minutes and brainstorm all of your concerns and ideas so that we can consider addressing them in our planning." I would pull out a sheet of newsprint, write down all the comments, and refer back to the list frequently during the work of the group. If successful, this activity would help establish a pattern of communication by all members toward a common purpose and provide a positive experience that might serve as the basis for the initial processing of the work together and the creation of group norms.

Explain how your ethnic and cultural background may or may not inhibit the way you respond to the situation as a leader.

Although valuing diversity is a deeply rooted value in my life, comfort with different communication styles has been achieved only with great effort. If my first reaction served as the basis of my response, I might inhibit the expression of negative feelings because of my discomfort. I might change the subject or ask the group to focus on the task of the group without acknowledging the negative feelings being expressed. However, I would rather acknowledge negative feelings, be open to working through the issues as needed, and understand when the time is right to redirect the energy of the group toward building working relationships and the goal of the group. The brainstorming activity described in the previous section might help redirect the energy toward the goal of the group. When processing the activity, members might be willing to recognize how each of their concerns/ideas brings a different perspective to planning and helps in developing a better conference.

Explain how your ethnic and cultural background may have influenced your choice of the response you made over any other that you may have been considering as a leader.

I could have chosen to process the conflict immediately or ask the group to stay with the task of planning the conference. However, since this was so early in the group, I wanted to focus on establishing communication patterns to support inclusion with the task of planning the conference in mind. As the task group leader, I would want to balance process considerations with the task of planning. My experience supports the importance of tasks being completed and done well, but it has also taught me that this is unlikely without attention to relationships and learning to work together.

As a result of the response you chose, identify the consequences you might anticipate as a leader.

If all goes well, the verbal members will feel that their concerns have been acknowledged and that they have an important place in the work of the group. Also, the less verbal members may begin to feel they are an important part of the group and are valued for their input. However, David may be unwilling to move forward until his concern is more fully addressed. He may be serving in a blocking role or he may need a channel to express a legitimate concern, but in either case I would volunteer to obtain further information about procedures used to select conference planning committee members and report back at the next meeting. Also, quiet members may be unwilling to participate in a meaningful way. Another possibility is that conflict across genders or personality issues may be present. In this case, alternative strategies may be needed.

From your position as a leader, explain what the most glaring or outstanding aspect was of the situation which impacted you from your ethnic and cultural orientation.

The president-elect of the organization seems to have deliberately selected a diverse group of people to plan the national conference—a group of people with differing passions and experience, a breadth of resources for this task group. While sometimes the heterogeneity of a group is so great members have difficulty developing working relationships, I do not think that is the case in this situation. Considering the president-elect's selection of members, it is likely the conference theme would support addressing social issues such as inclusion and valuing diversity in the planning process as well as at the conference itself.

Based on the composition of this group, what multicultural issues (etic and emic) need to be taken into consideration as the incident is addressed in group?

Recognizing the diversity and energy being brought to the group, the group needs to find a way to channel its resources into planning a conference—a conference that values diversity and the variety of needs held by the membership. While there is value in recognizing resources brought by the more active members, attention needs to be given to the quiet members so they might find their place in the group and also be able to influence planning. Having said that, David's concern about the manner in which committee members are selected may influence the very success of the conference. If the process of committee member selection is perceived as biased by subgroups within the association, they may not be willing to attend the conference. The situation could be serious enough for some individuals to drop their membership to the association. Therefore, even if the selection of members is unbiased, the perception of bias could be enough for some members to feel disenfranchised. Attention would need to be given to the matter in either case. The committee is fortunate to have members that can view the association convention needs from so many different perspectives, so I would value their international heritage and inquire about their perspectives on the diverse needs of the organization.

THOMAS HERNANDEZ'S REACTION AS A MEMBER OF THIS TASK GROUP

As the member of a professional organization, being asked to serve on a conference planning committee sends numerous thoughts racing through my mind. I experience the feeling of honor that the president-elect has recognized my abilities: It is always an honor to be appointed to a committee as important as this one by a leader such as this. On the other hand, any additional work I might be required to do as part of this group may be difficult to complete given my already taxed workload. I am also feeling somewhat overwhelmed.

Identify the multicultural issues that need to be taken into consideration for you as a member.

As a Latino, I recognize the authority of the group leader and anticipate the task he will be presenting to us as a group. While working in groups can be awkward for me, my cultural background has provided me with the sense that working as a community toward a mutually beneficial end is a valuable exercise. It is for this reason that when the group leader suggests a "get to know you" ice-breaking activity, I at once feel uncomfortable with the newness of the faces and appreciative of the importance of us getting to know one another and our individual interests so that we can begin to work together effectively. At the same time, however, I was as surprised as the group leader by the intensity of the emotions expressed as other group members talked about their primary concerns with the organization. Because of my satisfaction with the organization and its leadership, I say few words and look to the group leader for leadership and guidance, in much the same way that I notice Emile is doing. In many ways, I look for the group leader to refocus us on our stated task to begin to "get the job done." On the other hand, I am looking to the group leader to address these concerns so that we can attempt to work together in open harmony, rather than in discord. As a Latino, I tend to be passionate about my opinions, but I also want us to be able to respect one another and respect the authority of the group leader. Without this respect for and understanding of the group's hierarchy, there would be far too much infighting.

Explain how your ethnic and cultural background affected the way you would respond as a member.

As I ponder the direction we might take as a group, I recognize some important concerns about our differences and our similarities from my perspective as a Latino group member. While I know that Emile and I were raised in Latin cultures, I am conscious of the fact that our experiences are dramatically different. This is certainly the case for all Latinos. That is, different national origins and socioeconomic experiences within those borders help to create different worldviews, and thus the potential for different expectations within task groups. In fact, the misconception that all Latino individuals share the same cultural values, norms, and experiences is an overgeneralization. Rather, Latinos have many different cultural experiences. For instance, not all Latinos speak Spanish, and the Spanish they do speak differs linguistically across the great geography of Latin America. I view others as having distinct experiences and perceptions of those experiences from me, whether Latino or not. That is, I look for the similarities and the differences people bring and respect and appreciate both. Knowing that Dara, Emile, Zabelle, and Martin bring different cultural experiences to our group affects how I react to this situation and how I understand them as group members.

As I look to the group leader for direction at the beginning of our task group encounter, I am conscious of the differences Suzanne and David bring to the group as well. Suzanne's homosexuality and David's experiences as a person with a disability provide important lenses through which they view the world. As a Latino, I respect the passion they have for their opinions, beliefs, and feelings. While I see that their differences have the potential to be divisive within the group, I also appreciate that they have strong feelings and should be allowed to express them openly. It is my experience of feeling marginalized at times that serves as the impetus to ensure that others not feel oppressed. Thus, their distinct experiences and worldviews will certainly contribute to the group.

Perhaps my view of group members' contributions leads me to talk about our similarities. First, we have all been appointed for our specific interests and presumably because of our skill and ability. However, we are also similar in that we are all members of marginalized groups. Because of this, many of the group members have been vocal regarding their concerns about the task to which we have been set. Clearly the group leader was not prepared for this openly hostile interaction. As I think about the intense feelings and opinions that are brought to the table, I wonder about two things. First, will others voices be heard, respected, and, in a more practical way, taken into consideration in the task that we have at hand? Clearly there is a multitude of agendas present, and it will be difficult to bring the group together with so many different and opposing points of view. Second, will my voice be heard, and recognized, and will my concerns be addressed? As a member of a cultural group that traditionally is underrepresented in professional groups, I have had to struggle to have my thoughts "count" in the process. So I wonder, what does this silence and these "puzzled looks" mean?

Explain how your ethnic and cultural background may or may not inhibit the way you respond to the situation as a member.

Inhibit is a strong word to use. It is clear that who we are and how we view the world affects what we do. I view the world through the lens of a male Latino who was raised in the United States during a specific historical period, and this context affects the way in which I respond to a group situation. Because of the values I was inculcated with and the overwhelming sense that I should respect the authority of a group leader (especially when working to accomplish a task) I may remain fairly quiet in regard to my thoughts about the group's task until the group leader lends permission to the group to address personal opinions. This does not mean that I would remain utterly silent. I would most certainly express my views. However, the group leader's authority must be prized. Because of this value, if I felt the need to share my ideas or concerns, I might ask first if this was the appropriate time to do so, and when given clearance to pursue my opinions, I would. In this way, my cultural values might be seen as inhibiting my response to the group. As a Latino, I would not see this as inhibition. Rather, I would see this as following an important tenet of group interaction: respect of and for the group leader and her authority.

Explain how your ethnic and cultural background may have influenced your choice of the response you made over any other that you may have been considering as a member.

As a member of the group, my first reaction to this situation would be one of surprise and disappointment. As stated, an important value with which I was raised as a Latino was to respect the leader of the group. The group leader has been given a charge by an individual wielding significant power—the president-elect—and therefore in many ways is acting on his behalf. While I may have strong feelings, I would respectfully present these to the group in a fashion that would be deemed appropriate by the group leader. In this way, I would acknowledge the authority of the group leader and my own opinions at the same time. As a Latino, I know that this is not an easy balance to strike, given that my cultural nature is to be "fiery" and passionate about my beliefs. So, although my initial thoughts might be to concur with some of the feelings expressed by David, Martin, and the others, I would temper this desire with a strong need to recognize the authority of the group leader, and look for a more appropriate and respectful opportunity to present my opinions.

As a result of the response you chose, identify the consequences you might anticipate as a member.

Because I would have remained quiet until the leader opened the group up for discussion of individual concerns, I would expect that people would be curious about my stance on these issues. The consequences for the group are clear: The group would not have a sense of my opinion until I expressed it. In some regards I might see this as a distinct advantage, somewhat analogous to not showing cards too soon in a game of poker. In some ways, this is a dis-advantage, as some in the group might make assumptions about my silence. In either case, the ultimate consequence for this Latino group member is that the group might pursue a course of action by which my opinion would come to light, placing everyone's "cards" on the table for all to see.

From your position as a member, explain what the most glaring or outstanding aspect was of the situation which impacted you from your ethnic and cultural orientation.

Perhaps the most significant aspect of this situation that must be considered is the differences that we all bring. As a Latino, I am conscious of my desire to be heard and my fear that this may not happen—after all, I have been ignored before. I am also conscious of the fact that while differences can enrich a group, my cultural experience indicates that keeping likeminded people together fosters more effective teamwork. It is for that reason that I look for our similarities first: similar cultural experiences, ideals, values, goals, or objectives. When I see the differences and recognize the chasms between us, I become disheartened that this process may not work as effectively as I had hoped and that my voice may not be heard.

So, I have chosen to remain silent, all the while looking to the group leader for a sense of leadership and empowerment. The choice to react in this way as a group member is in large part due to my cultural beliefs, values, and experiences: who I am.

THOMAS HERNÁNDEZ'S REACTION AS A LEADER OF THIS TASK GROUP

If this incident would not occur in your group, explain why it would not.

As the leader of this group, my frustration would be centered around the need to both complete the task we have been given and address the obvious concerns of the group members. I would see it as important to allow the voices of the individual members to be heard, so I would allow them to share as they have in this vignette. I would indicate to the members that clearly there is a need to share opinions before beginning the work at hand, and would open the floor to this. However, I would also share my own thoughts as the leader by indicating that we only have a limited amount of time to complete our task and need to begin our work in earnest. With that in mind, I would tell the group that I might need to cut our open discussion short if I think it might hinder our progress to our goal.

Identify the multicultural issues that need to be taken into consideration for you as a leader.

As mentioned earlier, being selected to this group is a great honor. To be selected chair of this group is an even greater mark of distinction. As the group leader, prior to the meeting, it tells me that my voice is valued, my skills and abilities are trusted, and the perspective I bring as a Latino is prized. While this is true for me as group leader, there are some important concerns that need to be taken into consideration as this group takes shape: (1) my culture and ethnicity as a factor in our discussions (my agenda); (2) the multitude of agendas present based on the multiplicity of cultural worldviews; and (3) the task itself as a political and cultural issue.

Explain how your ethnic and cultural background affected the way you would respond as a leader.

I might have begun this group in a different way. In an effort to ensure the effectiveness of this task group, rather than beginning the meeting by emphasizing those ways in which we are different, I would probably set the tone by emphasizing the task: the way in which we are similar. That is, we all have a common task. Our differences may take us individually on different paths in the achievement of this goal, but ultimately, we must produce a product. Thus, by starting with our common objective, I emphasize our collaborative and collective work together, an important cultural value of mine. It is also important for me to recognize individual differences, and thus I would follow that with an opportunity to get to know one another and the distinct perspectives and experiences we bring to the accomplishment of this task. Thus, my cultural background has a profound effect on the way this group might be shaped and on the process of the group itself.

Explain how your ethnic and cultural background may or may not inhibit the way you respond to the situation as a leader.

Any time a group of individuals is assembled in a somewhat artificial way, the perspectives of each individual affect how the assigned task ultimately is accomplished. The perspectives that come into play could include a multitude of variables: experience, position in the organization, or perceived power in the organization. The latter refers to those people in the organization who may not have an official capacity, but by virtue of their visibility or association with others are given referent power or authority. Additionally, a person's cultural viewpoint, gendered experience, ability, education level, and even physical attributes and the experiences they have had with those may affect the group's process. These perspectives are present within me, as I have suggested, and thus affect the group as well. So, to suggest that an incident like this one might not happen in the future would be preposterous. Groups by their very nature and definition are made up of individuals and are a system in action. Each of the members who spoke up—David, Martin, and Suzanne—expressed his worldview, and his concerns and perspectives at the inception of the group. By the same token, Zabelle, Emile, and Dara each expressed their cultural norms about task group participation by remaining silent. Although no words were spoken, their actions spoke loudly.

As the group leader, I recognized that each member was expressing who she was in the context of this task group in her own way. As the leader, it would be essential for me to acknowledge their views and recognize their contributions. By the same token, I also see this as a "make or break" point in the group's development. It is culturally important for me as the Latino group leader to bring the assembled members back to task so that we can begin to work collectively on a common goal. If the members continued to focus exclusively on their own ideas and intense emotions, the group could become deeply divided and not accomplish the goal of planning this professional organization's national conference. It is clear that my response to this situation would be critical in determining the degree to which the group was facilitated or inhibited.

Explain how your ethnic and cultural background may have influenced your choice of the response you made over any other that you may have been considering as a leader.

Once I had absorbed all that was said during the first few minutes of this planning committee meeting, a number of options were at my disposal. I could have: (1) ignored the interchange and moved on to the task at hand; (2) dismissed the interchange as something outside the purview of the committee and asked the committee members to come to order so that we could begin the task at hand; (3) recognized the volatility of the issues being raised and allowed the focus of the meeting to change entirely so that the group could address the concerns being presented; or (4) acknowledged the importance of the issues being raised while at the same time clearly stating the group's task. In this case, I could have allowed some discussion to continue so that all voices would be heard, especially on issues related to the task at hand, and then moved to address the task itself.

The first and second options, as seen through my cultural lens, would have silenced the voices of the group members and placed me in a despotic position. Such options would not have strengthened my role as facilitator, nor would they have allowed the individual members of the group to feel heard or valued. Hence, these were not options for me at all. The third option, on the other hand, would have encouraged and prized the voices of each of the group members. As a Latino group leader, such an action would have been facilitative, as it would have granted (I say grant because of the position of authority in which I have been placed) each member of the group permission to share his opinions and ideas. However, such an action also would have detracted from the group's ability to complete the task, in which case my effectiveness as a group leader might have been called into question by the authority who gave me the charge to complete this task with the group in the first place. My only real option, then, was option four. By taking such action, I allowed members to share their views and have their voices be heard, and at the same time provided some degree of direction for the group in completing the task set before us.

As a result of the response you chose, identify the consequences you might anticipate as a leader.

By providing each member with an opportunity to share her opinions and then acknowledging the differing points of view in the context of the task at hand, the group would have an opportunity to begin working together effectively. Everybody's concerns would have been presented, so the task would then have a context that would allow the group to move forward.

From your position as a leader, explain what the most glaring or outstanding aspect was of the situation which impacted you from your ethnic and cultural orientation.

Culturally speaking, the most important aspect of this vignette is the fact that the differing points of view presented by the group members could affect the ability of the group to complete the task effectively. Therefore (and as a Latino), I saw it as essential that each and every voice be heard. This allowed the members of the group to get to know each other in the context of the task and their various worldviews. If I silenced one or more members of the group, my oppressive action would hinder the group's ability to plan a professionally useful conference. Further, given that the conference will be a national conference involving people with diverse experiences and points of view, our failure as a group to coalesce around the task while still recognizing our differences could mean that our conference would be doomed from the outset.

Based on the composition of this group, what multicultural issues (etic and emic) need to be taken into consideration as the incident is addressed in group?

This task is a highly political issue with significant ramifications for the individual groups we all represent. Using this conference as a way to give voice to each of our expressed causes and opinions highly charges the room. I sense that in the voices of those who speak. I also sense it in me as I hear their voices and experience my voice and those of others as silent. It is essential to me that I recognize the political nature of this task in some way to ensure that all members of the group feel that they have a place to express their thoughts and feelings.

Had I not initiated the group as I suggested I would, and had this group begun as described in this case vignette, my choice of response could be understood on two levels: (1) as a response to nonverbal cues, and (2) as a response to verbal cues. Zabelle, Emile, and Dara say nothing but share their expectation that as the leader, I need to respond. I think I need to acknowledge them in some way, and do so by restating our cause and the need for us to work together, and work effectively. Dara may feel some degree of comfort in this, since she is accustomed to "getting the job done." Emile looks to me as the group leader, deferring to my expertise, and would hopefully hear an expression of group leadership in my voice. Zabelle might hear the same, but also hear the importance of working together.

On the other hand, my response to the flurry of powerful words and thoughts expressed through the first portion of this meeting needs to now acknowledge each of the strongly expressed views while reinforcing the collective nature of our task. That is, it is important that these strongly stated opinions and feelings not divide the group. Rather, as group leader, it is important that I help to refocus the group on our collaborative efforts and emphasize our working together.

Several responses can be anticipated to my approach with this very open group. The quiet members probably will appreciate the emphasis on the task, and it is likely to meet their needs in different ways. For instance, Emile will appreciate my approach, as he is deferring to my authority in the group and is comfortable with the hierarchy of the group as it was defined. Dara, being task-oriented, wants to complete the task and will hear that in my response. On the other hand, it is possible that David, Suzanne, and Martin may feel dismissed by my task orientation and may continue to express their frustration with the organization until we address their concerns further. In such a case, we may need to address these issues in the context of our work together and our task before we can set about planning the conference.

Thus, from my cultural viewpoint, the etic and the emic of this situation are both critical in determining the best response to an incident. It is important to recognize and understand the universality of the task we must accomplish—the commonality we all have in this experience. However, as a group leader, it is also imperative that I recognize that each group member brings his own set of values, experiences, thoughts, and feelings to the table as we begin this work. To be an effective group leader, I must help the group understand that both the etic and emic are part of our process and that both can further our work on our assigned task, but we must not allow these issues to inextricably divide us.

SUMMARY/ANALYSIS OF RESPONSES

As Members of This Task Group

Identify the multicultural issues that need to be taken into consideration for you as a member.

We find in Brown's response her acknowledgment of David's handicap and his need to have the flexibility to sit where he chooses, as well as recognition of the fact that he may have other special needs requiring accommodation. Brown identifies three members who may need assistance with the English language. She also cites cross-gender issues related to communication and influence as being areas that need to be considered.

As a Latino, Hernández recognizes the authority of the group leader. He offers us a Latino's perspective by informing us that his cultural background provided him with the sense that working as a community toward beneficial ends is valuable. He observes that his passion for his views is drawn from his cultural heritage; in addition, his background promotes his view that members need to have respect for one another and for the leader as the authority figure. He also perceives that attention needs to be given to the fact that the group members will hold many different worldviews due to the diversity of the group's membership.

Explain how your ethnic and cultural background affected the way you would respond as a member.

We hear from Brown that her gender and age, as well as early life experiences, played a significant role in how she responded to this situation. She informs us that as a young woman of her generation, she was expected to be "polite, proper, and quiet." Therefore, her initial reaction is one of discomfort with the group conflict. She also draws on her life experiences with social issues to offer empathy and understanding to David's concerns regarding accessibility and to Martin's concerns for providing pro bono service to the poor.

Once again, Hernández reminds us of the significance of authority in the Latino culture. He also draws upon his background when we learn of his commitment to building community through respecting the passion of the other members for their beliefs, opinions, and feelings. We learn that his experiences as a marginalized person have served as an impetus for him to see that others not feel oppressed. He notes that his background also encourages him to seek the similarities among the members and himself. In addition, he ponders whether his own voice will be heard, especially since many agendas have been presented by the members.

Explain how your ethnic and cultural background may or may not inhibit the way you respond to the situation as a member.

Althrough Brown's first inclination, as discussed previously, is to withdraw from conflict whenever she is faced with it, we learn that there is another side to her. Her cultural background would not allow her to retreat, and so she would take a stand for what she believes. Her background would not inhibit her in this situation. Hernández tells us that his ethnic and cultural background would not inhibit him either, due to its respect for authority and thus the leader, but that he would remain quiet until the leader opened the group for discussion.

Explain how your ethnic and cultural background may have influenced your choice of the response you made over any other that you may have been considering as a member.

According to Brown, her cultural background taught her to value all members of the group, to care for others, to complete assigned tasks, and to be cooperative; therefore, she chose to support the leader rather than sit back and allow the outspoken members to settle their conflict. From her response, we can understand the reason for her empathic acknowledgment of David's special needs, her concern for those members who may need assistance with the English language, and her support of Martin's concerns about providing pro bono service to the poor.

Hernández informs us that he was both surprised and disappointed by the early conflict in the group, as his background would not have him respond as the others did. Out of respect for authority and the leader, he would have waited to speak until the leader opened the discussion, even though his initial thoughts were in agreement with David, Martin, and the others.

As a result of the response you chose, identify the consequences you might anticipate as a member.

Brown's approach to this question introduces a dimension that we have not faced before. For her, the consequences to her response are dependent upon how the leader chooses to manage the situation and the members' ability to hear each other. She adds that if acknowledging vocal members as well as quiet members becomes the pattern of communication, then she expects that the group will be ready to establish norms and clarify the goal of the group.

Given that Hernández opted to remain quiet until the leader opened the group for dialogue, he believes the members will be curious about his stance on the issues that have been presented. He also sees the group moving on without him, but that he will ultimately be drawn in during whatever course of action the members take.

From your position as a member, explain what the most glaring or outstanding aspect was of the situation which impacted you from your ethnic and cultural orientation.

Brown informs us that the early presence of conflict is the first outstanding aspect of the situation. She sees that there is a risk of members rejecting each other, and a possible risk that quiet members will withdraw. She also notes that different communication styles could prevent norms from developing, collaboration from occurring, and the task from being achieved. The most glaring aspect of the situation for Hernández regards the group's diversity among its members, which may be too great for the group to become cohesive and work cooperatively.

As Leaders of This Task Group

If this incident would not occur in your group, explain why it would not.

Both of our respondents did not mince words with their answers to this question, albeit they each saw the situation differently. Brown tells us that she would try to prevent such incidents from occurring by using pregroup planning and attending to early group processes. We can infer that she would have spent time meeting with members and orienting them to the purposes of the group prior to the first group meeting and that she would have spent time in the early stage of the group attending to and building group culture and norms.

Hernández simply states that because of the diversity among the group's members, such an incident is likely to happen. We can infer from his response that it would be the norm to expect differences of view to be expressed, especially given the makeup of the group. His response also implies that as a Latino leader, he might be more tolerant of the expression of conflict such diverse views would generate.

Identify the multicultural issues that need to be taken into consideration for you as a leader.

Even though our respondents' responses were different, there are similarities in the issues they emphasized in their answers. Brown continues to be sensitive to the special needs of tpeople with disabilities and to the need to respect members who have different communication patterns. She also sees as an issue the need to establish a climate that values diversity and allows members to have influence regardless of gender, sexual orientation, ethnicity, cultural background, and disability. She believes that the group's goal should be to promote diversity as part of planning the conference.

Hernández's response demonstrates sensitivity to his own cultural and ethnic background and the role it plays in the group. He relates that it is an honor to be selected by the president-elect to serve on the committee, and an added distinction to be asked to chair the committee. This attitude reflects the Latino acknowledgment of those in positions of authority. Additionally, he cites as a concern the multitude of agendas due to the great diversity in the group's membership. Like Brown, he sees the group's task as addressing political and cultural issues.

Explain how your ethnic and cultural background affected the way you would respond as a leader.

Once again Brown demonstrates how her early life experiences led to her be especially sensitive to persons with disabilities and aware of the need to be attentive to group members' different communication styles. Moreover, she reintroduces gender as a cultural concern when she informs us of her fear of conflict as a young woman and describes how that fear often led her to feel left out of interpersonal communication within groups. We can infer that these experiences would influence the interventions she would make in the group.

A Latino cultural value that Hernández feels would influence his response to the situation emphasizes collaboration and collectively working together. Such an outcome could be achieved because he would emphasize the similarities more than the differences among members; by doing so, the members would see the commonality of their task. Hernández hastens to add that although efforts would be made to identify similarities, that would not be done at the expense of losing individual differences.

Explain how your ethnic and cultural background may or may not inhibit the way you respond to the situation as a leader.

As discussed earlier, Brown's early background influences how she responds to moments of conflict. She informs us that she has spent a great deal of effort to become comfortable with different communication styles; therefore, she could feel inhibited in regard to communicating negative feelings because she would find it uncomfortable to do so.

Hernández reiterates for us that it is culturally important for him as a Latino to bring the group back to task. The process through which that would be achieved is also culturally derived: He would strive to get the members to begin working collaboratively and collectively on the common goal. Consequently, he tells us that his ethnic and cultural background would not inhibit him from responding to the situation.

Explain how your ethnic and cultural background may have influenced your choice of the response you made over any other that you may have been considering as a leader.

As we read the answers from each of our leaders to this question, we find that their backgrounds, though different, have brought them to the same place. Brown relates that initially her background would have her focus on (1) establishing communication patterns to support the inclusion of all group members, and (2) the task of planning the conference. Brown's focus on communication patterns includes building relationships and encouraging members to work together.

Hernández informed us earlier of the cultural significance of building collaborative and cooperative relationships, which are necessary in order to achieve the group's common task. We learn that focusing on the task also has strong cultural roots for Hernández: As a Latino, he is obligated to meet the expectations of the authority (the president-elect) who appointed him leader. Therefore, he identifies his primary goal as a leader as accomplishment of the task, while simultaneously acknowledging and respecting the needs of individual members.

As a result of the response you chose, identify the consequences you might anticipate as a leader.

Brown identifies a number of possible consequences. Her concern that communication be facilitated might make the more vocal members feel that their concerns have been acknowledged and valued while simultaneously making the less vocal members feel important and that their input is valued. Her sensitivity for people with disabilities makes her aware of the possibility that David may be either in a blocking role or in need of a channel to express a legitimate concern. She also sees that quiet members may be unwilling to participate in a meaningful way and that gender issues could arise.

For Hernández, the consequence is more focused. He anticipates the members would have an opportunity to share their views, therby clearing the way for the group to focus on completing the task.

From your position as a leader, explain what the most glaring or outstanding aspect was of the situation which impacted you from your ethnic and cultural orientation.

Both leaders cited the diversity of the group's members as the most glaring aspect of this situation. Brown appears to have been affected not only by the diversity of the group's members, but also by the president-elect's deliberate selection of the mix for this group. She sees that because of the group's diversity, the members will present different passions and experiences. We can infer that she would be challenged to strike the balance in communication styles that she has informed us must be achieved in order for the group to work cohesively.

Hernández's response to this question is strikingly similar to Brown's. He not only cites the diversity of the group, but also sees in its diversity that the expression of so many differing points of view could negatively affect the group's ability to accomplish its task. Hernández reminds us of the commitment he makes as a Latino leader to building member collaboration and cooperation; and consequently, due to the diversity of voices in this group, he would need to make certain that each member was heard.

Based on the composition of this group, what multicultural issues (etic and emic) need to be taken into consideration as the incident is addressed in the group?

Brown identified two etic issues: (1) the diversity of the group will require it to find a way to focus its resources into planning the conference; and (2) attention needs to be given to the less vocal members so they feel included and feel they have influence in the group. The emic issues she considered centered on the fact that David's concern regarding how members were selected to the committee could affect the success of the conference, and the possibility that perceived bias might prevent some subgroups from attending the conference.

The single etic issue for Hernández regards universality, or the group's common concern, which is to accomplish its task. The most pronounced emic issues for him are the values, experiences, thoughts, and feelings that each member brings to the group. He notes that he would strive to help group members understand that both are important in the group process.

5 CHAPTER | Task Group Vignette #2

*The Fourth Meeting
and Silence before the Storm*

You are to lead a group of community volunteers whose task is to raise funds for rehabilitating an old firehouse and turning it into a facility that will become the community playhouse. Your committee consists of seven members plus yourself.

- Ernie is 41. He is a paraplegic. He invested his family's fortune wisely and is now in a position to engage in many philanthropic and community service activities.
- Tomika is 49. She is a professor of dance at the local college. She is a social activist who is known for her support of the gay and lesbian community.
- Joaquin is 68. He is a respected spokesperson for the Hispanic community. A successful industrialist, he frequently takes an active role in civic causes.
- Nathaniel (Nate) is 59 and is president of a start-up airline. A former lieutenant general in the air force, he was among the highest-ranking African Americans in the armed forces at the time of his retirement at age 55.
- Cisely is 53 and president of the largest residential and commercial real estate firm in the county. She has been hearing-impaired since birth. She can read lips as well as sign. She also speaks fluently.

- Ransis is 57. He arrived here from Egypt at age 12. He is now chief executive officer (CEO) of a telecommunications corporation that he founded which grosses over $200,000,000 annually.
- Amy is 48. She is a local artist. Drawing upon her Native-American heritage, she has produced works that have received international recognition.

This is the fourth meeting of the group. The first session included a warm-up segment where all the members became acquainted with each other, the group's goals were established, and dates and times for meetings were set. The second session got underway a little late because Nate came from a labor relations meeting with his airline pilots. Your agenda was quite full, and you were unable to get through it all before time ran out. The third session began on time. However, Cisely had to excuse herself three quarters of the way into the session because she had to close a large real estate deal. As she rose to leave, Tomika announced that she also had to leave momentarily because she had to attend a meeting between the college president and the gay and lesbian students' association. Their early departures disrupted the group enough that, once again, the agenda was not completed.

The fourth session began with everyone present. You were conscious of the way the past three sessions had gone and were about to comment on it when Ernie introduced the topic by stating how frustrated he felt with the way the three previous sessions went. Before he could continue, Joaquin spoke up and, in a soft but firm voice, stated that he felt the group was floating aimlessly like a ship without a rudder and that unless something was done quickly, the group's mission would fall by the wayside. Tomika did not wait for Joaquin's words to settle on the group before stating flatly that if anyone had anything to say to her about what was happening, she wished they would speak to her directly. Nate, who was level-headed during the first three sessions and actually made a number of helpful suggestions, for the first time appeared impatient and was about to say something when Cisely expressed how she felt invested in the group's mission, but she also felt that if she led her real estate firm the way this group was being led, she would have been out of business long ago.

Amy, having taken everything in, spoke in a calm voice that caught everyone's attention, and observed that perhaps the fault was not with the group's leadership but with all seven of the members; she suggested that perhaps the late arrivals and early departures, and the group's tolerance of them, was a statement they all were trying to make collectively. Her words had the same effect that splashing cold water on the group might have had. All the members seemed to be transfixed, and silence hung in the air like a heavy cloud. You were as taken aback by her words as the others; however, you also knew that this moment would not last long before the members would recover from the effect of Amy's words.

BEVERLY BROWN'S REACTION AS A MEMBER OF THIS TASK GROUP

Identify the multicultural issues that need to be taken into consideration for you as a member.

The situation brings to mind a common dilemma in groups. Does responsibility for the situation rest with the leader, specific members, or the group as a whole? I would want the group to seriously consider this question, and I would want the group as a whole to own responsibility for the group. I would like for members to view the group as a system and to explore whether it would be possible for the group to move forward with fluctuating membership. I would also like the group to explore what might be behind member decisions to arrive late or depart early. If some members had concerns that prevented them from following established norms, it would be important for those concerns to be addressed and resolved, if possible. Also, the group would need to respect member differences and value the variety of resources available because of their different experiences. I would want Ernie to be able to sit where he wishes and not be limited by his use of a wheelchair, and Cisely would need to feel comfortable asking members to speak directly to the group in a manner that would allow her to read their lips. We would need to ensure that accommodation needs were met in order to support member communication. Finally, we would need to find a way to focus on our task and make progress.

Explain how your ethnic and cultural background affected the way you would respond as a member.

I would probably respond by saying, "Amy, I hear you encouraging us to look beyond the leader to understand our work together. I would like to support that idea. I'm wondering if it wouldn't be helpful for us to look at our group as a whole and explore what is happening, rather than looking at specific people. Although it appears that having several people arrive late or leave early might be the problem, I'm wondering if there might be something else causing the difficulty." I have a very strong value for completing a task, but I am also uncomfortable when member behaviors are not respectful toward others (i.e., late arrival and early departure). That being said, I know the process of allowing all members to find their place in the group would be essential if we were to make progress toward our goal.

Explain how your ethnic and cultural background may or may not inhibit the way you respond to the situation as a member.

Although I do not like conflict, I really do not like seeing a scapegoat blamed for difficulties in a group—it is just not fair. The leader or specific members may contribute to the problem, but we all need to own and understand our part in it. I would encourage the group to follow up on Amy's comment and explore the group process. What are we all doing to contribute to the problem? Do late arrivals and early departures have another level of meaning we need to understand? How might we increase our progress toward our goal? What do each of you need to be a productive member?

Explain how your ethnic and cultural background may have influenced your choice of the response you made over any other that you may have been considering as a member.

I could have interpreted the situation to mean that some group members felt the work of the group was unimportant and were expressing this directly during the group interaction or indirectly by arriving late or leaving early. However, this interpretation would be in direct conflict with my value to be present and to complete tasks when I make a commitment. I also could have confronted the group for not staying on task and for being disrespectful to the leader and other members. However, these responses would seem to be of little value until the group explores and resolves the source of the problem. My value of caring for others would influence me to focus on the process of the group and the exploration of interpersonal relations, as needed, prior to refocusing on the group task.

As a result of the response you chose, identify the consequences you might anticipate as a member.

As I select a response encouraging members to focus on group process and share ownership for the manner in which they are working, I am aware that some members may not see this as a productive direction for the group. Some members may have values that focus heavily on task without looking at working relationships or group process. Also, all people do not view time commitments in the same manner. Indeed, some members may see the situation as one related to time commitments and be unwilling to explore more personal concerns. If the issue were related to member differences, perhaps exploration of the process would bring forth this information so that greater understanding might emerge and group development could continue. If the issue were related to the members trying to find their place in the group, a discussion of group process and shared responsibility should foster movement in group development.

From your position as a member, explain what the most glaring or outstanding aspect was of the situation which impacted you from your ethnic and cultural orientation.

I would be immediately aware of the diverse membership of the committee. I seldom have an opportunity to work with such an interesting variety of people. The committee even has two people with disabilities. Yet, there appears to be some type of resistance preventing us as a group from making solid progress in our planning. The pattern of late arrival and early departure seems very disrespectful of the leader as well as other members. My group work training, however, would encourage me to look beyond a lack of respect and consider other reasons why the process might be difficult. Perhaps the situation is due to having such a heterogeneous group membership, although my hunch is that the members of this group are accustomed to assuming leadership roles and that some members find it unusual to be in a member role. Thus, they may be expressing feelings of resistance by challenging the leader.

BEVERLY BROWN'S REACTION AS A LEADER OF THIS TASK GROUP

If this type of incident would not occur in your group, explain why it would not.

Once norms in a group are discussed and members make a commitment to them, we hope that all members will honor those norms; however, often this does not occur. Verbally stating a norm or even having members agree to abide by a norm does not ensure that the norm will become established in a group. I have more confidence in norms that I see actually operating within the group. Factors related to group development can be more important to members than norms. Especially during the transition stage of group development, factors operate that can compete with honoring norms—for example, power negotiation, resistance, and learning to manage conflict. Generally, once the group has successfully worked its way through the transition stage, members follow norms and have a stronger commitment to the group and its goal.

Identify the multicultural issues that need to be taken into consideration for you as a leader.

As a leader, the multicultural considerations that are important to me are much the same as when I am in the member role. I believe it is important to respect member differences, value the diverse experiences brought to the group, and accommodate member needs for full participation in the group. It seems the one thing members have in common with one another is their uniqueness—a theme that can be used to build universality. I also see members who are all successful in their own way and wonder how much experience each has in group work as a member—perhaps they are more accustomed to being leaders. Will sharing leadership in the group be a new experience for them? I am also concerned about financial differences. There may be a gap between the financial status of Tomika and that of Amy, and perhaps between other members as well. I would want to watch and see whether status might influence respect among members.

Explain how your ethnic and cultural background affected the way you would respond as a leader.

Because I value a variety of background experiences and believe these experiences can enhance the quality of a group's work, I would open the first session by commenting on the strength of the group's resources that comes from their wide variety of successful experiences. In this manner, I would hope to establish respect and a positive value toward diversity. I would also work to establish member comfort in making accommodation requests in order to enhance communication and members' work in the group. I would tell group members, "I hope you will all feel comfortable letting me or the group know how we can accommodate for any special need requests you might have." I like to give members the option of discussing special needs privately if they prefer, but if the members of the group were aware that Cisely is hearing-impaired, I would directly ask her during the group meeting if the use of cues would help her follow the communication flow for reading members' lips. I would also ask her if she had any accommodation requests, such as obtaining a sign language interpreter. I think it is important to establish effective communication in a group as soon as possible. Also, communicating respect for differences early in a group helps to shape the nature of conflict in the group.

Recognizing that there is likely to be a variety of communication styles, during norm formation I would encourage discussion of how members would like the group to manage differences of opinion when they occur. Thus, when conflict arose, as in the critical incident, the group would have previously established ground rules for communication about conflicts and a basis from which to evaluate their management of it. Having addressed such matters early in the group, my response in the situation described would be to first acknowledge members' concern about the group's progress. I would want members to know they were being heard. I would also want Tomika to feel supported; I would encourage her to help explore ways we could work together effectively. Then I would go on to say, "It may be helpful for us all to take responsibility for what is occurring. What ideas do you all have about ways we can work together more effectively and make progress toward our goal?" Hopefully, this question would encourage members to express their points of view, yet help them move in a positive direction toward preferred ways of working together. Perhaps the reason behind late arrivals and early departures would surface.

When bringing closure to the conflict, it would be important for the group to process their communication and reflect on their norm about managing differences. Is the norm working well for the group? If not, are changes needed to improve the norm? My experience suggests that a group will not become an effective working group until members learn to trust their ability to manage conflict and that discussing conflict as a normal and healthy part of the group's dialog during the early part of a group can normalize the management of diverse points of view.

Explain how your ethnic and cultural background may or may not inhibit the way you respond to the situation as a leader.

Although I still find it possible to respond to conflict in a laissez-faire manner or to get upset when I perceive a lack of respect, I have become more confident in the management of conflict. As a leader, responding in a laissez-faire manner would allow the group to follow Amy's suggestion that the members are at fault or perhaps return to the comment on the leader being at fault—neither of which is a helpful way to share responsibility. In my years of experience with teaching group leaders, I have found that many people who are accustomed to being in leadership roles are uncomfortable in the member role and will express resistance by challenging the leader. I once found such leadership challenges extremely difficult to deal with, but now see them as opportunities for sharing leadership and for helping the group learn to manage conflict.

Explain how your ethnic and cultural background may have influenced your choice of the response you made over any other that you may have been considering as a leader.

When leading a task group, it is important to help the group stay focused on the product expected from the group. Spending too much time on interpersonal relations can distract from the goal of the group. It would be natural to be concerned about the group's slow progress and to ask the group to stay focused on their task. Having a high value for task completion could easily influence the selection of this response. However, I have learned that a balance between task and process is needed. Understanding how group processes are related to interpersonal relationships and how members work together is essential for accomplishing the goals of a task group. By focusing on both the process and task, I can be true to my value of caring for others as well as my value for task completion.

As a result of the response you chose, identify the consequences you might anticipate as a leader.

If the process goes as hoped, members will share responsibility for the situation, openly share their concerns, and identify what they personally need to be effective group members. Issues the group might want to address include: Are there different values related to making time commitments? Do some members see the goal of the group as unimportant or their role in the group as not important? Is the goal of the group still unclear even though it was discussed in the first session? Was everyone included when the decision about meeting time was made? It would be important for the group to remain focused on concerns related to their work together and not shift the focus away from being a task group to becoming a support or therapy group.

From your position as a leader, explain what the most glaring or outstanding aspect was of the situation which impacted you from your ethnic and cultural orientation.

Leadership experience (i.e., these successful members are accustomed to being leaders) and financial status differences may be the most important multicultural aspects within this group. The group seems to be firmly in the transition stage of group development where trust, power, member roles, and norms are negotiated in a meaningful way.

Based on the composition of this group, what multicultural issues (etic and emic) need to be taken into consideration as the incident is addressed in group?

The unique multicultural characteristics of each member suggest the possibility of viewing uniqueness as a unifying similarity and a strength for the group. Their common success as individuals may suggest that members are unaccustomed to sharing leadership and are experiencing resistance to partic-ipation in the member role. The situation described presents an opportunity for the members as well as the leader to share ownership for and future lead-ership in the group. The question remains whether they can move away from blaming one person and take hold of this opportunity.

MICHAEL GARRETT'S REACTION AS A MEMBER OF THIS TASK GROUP

Identify the multicultural issues and explain how your ethnic and cultural background affected your response, inhibited your response, and influenced your choice of response. Identify the consequences you might anticipate as a result of your response, and explain what the most outstanding aspect of the situation was based on your ethnic and cultural orientation.

As a member, I am conscious of my feelings about whether or not I belong in this group. As I look around at those who are present, I wonder how con-nected with them I feel, and how much I trust them to understand my experi-ence and value what I have to offer. Many of the members appear to have a fair amount of educational, social, and economic status. Though I have achieved some of that status according to my current level of education and financial assets, I wonder to what extent my values, beliefs, and lifestyle are shared by other members of the group. It really comes down to trust; I gauge my level of sharing based on the amount of trust I feel. As a member, I would nonverbally "size up" the other members in the group before even saying a word, and I would be interested in seeing how accurate my perceptions at the beginning of the group turned out to be once I got to know the others.

As a member in the situation described, given what I would have perceived as lack of respect by several members for both the group and the leader, I probably would not have come back to the group, and would not have offered any explanation. My perception would have been that some of the members might be viewing the group as just another thing they have to do and that they might or might not consider it to be as important as the other things they have going on. I also would have perceived several members as thinking of them-selves first and foremost, with little regard for everyone else there. As a mem-ber, I would be likely to take this personally because of my cultural background and beliefs that when you are with people, being with the people and how you are being with them are most important, not the task at hand. Your word is your bond in Native culture. To leave early or to show up late when you have given your word to be prompt and attend meetings is not abid-ing by your word. Such behavior also tells the people there that they are not as important as other things that have to be done.

If I did stay in the group rather than bowing out quietly, I would be very guarded at this point. I might even shun the members that I perceived as hav-ing little regard for the group as a whole. That could well be interpreted as being defensive or closed, but could probably be interpreted more accurately as being tentative. Intent is the key to every social interaction in Native ways, and there are clearly defined ways of communicating one's intent in an appropriate and respectful manner, according to tribal social customs (which vary from tribe to tribe). It would be obvious to me that other people in the group might not be playing by the same cultural and social rules, so I would pull back, watch and wait, and consider what I needed to do as a member. I would ask myself: What do I have to contribute at this point? What am I willing to contribute at this point? Am I here because I really want to be here. Are others here for the same reason? The answers to these questions would dictate what I did or said next. I would probably show little eye contact, facial expression, or other nonverbal responsiveness as I tried to "feel" the group out in the silent realm of the heart.

The most outstanding aspect of the situation for me is the statement by Amy that focuses on the group as a whole, and on the movement, decisions, and energy of the group as a whole. If I stayed in the group, it would be because I had a hope that all of us together would begin to think as a group, and not as a collection of individuals who have to figure out a way to get along and get something done.

MICHAEL GARRETT'S REACTION AS A LEADER OF THIS TASK GROUP

If this type of incident would not occur in your group, explain why it would not. Identify the multicultural issues and explain how your ethnic and cultural background affected your response, inhibited your response, and influenced your choice of response. Identify the consequences you might anticipate as a result of your response, and explain what the most outstanding aspect of the situation was, based on your ethnic and cultural orientation.

Some of the same cultural issues that apply for me as a member would also apply for me as a leader—in particular, the issues of keeping good relations, maintaining respect, communicating with feeling and passion without losing compassion, finding common ground, using humor to build bridges (no matter how big or small), listening to silence as well as words, and approaching others with a sense of humility and openness to experiencing them. Some of these qualities and behaviors are a way of life for me and others in my culture who were raised similarly, and they are taken very seriously. People of many Native tribes believe that "whatever you put out there will come back to you seven times stronger." From that point of view, it is important to be sensitive about what you put out there in terms of your daily thoughts and actions, not from a sense of guilt or self-preservation, but more from a sense that you *are* connected with the things and people around you and should act with wisdom and humility in that recognition.

The current scenario could happen in a group with me as the leader, but it would not take so long to address it and would not be addressed in the same way. Even with a task group, I would use a Native talking circle format for conducting "business," just like it has always been used in Native nations across the United States as a way of not only addressing the issue at hand, but doing so in a way that maintains good relations. The expectations for a Native talking circle include the following:

1. Show respect when another person is talking.
2. Silence is acceptable, and sometimes necessary.
3. Each person speaks when he is ready to speak, and not always through the use of words.
4. Everyone is treated the same (equal status).

What is not included in this list is anything about time. The implication from a Native perspective has nothing to do with time, but more to do with speaking loudly and clearly through your actions. Even in a task group, where the apparent focus is on completion of a particular task, the main focus in a Native view is on proper relations as the means for completing the task in a harmonious way.

As a function of this focus on harmony and balance within the group, I would ask group members to request permission of the group before entering the actual space of the circle (and symbolically, before entering the physical or spiritual space of individual members), as well as when leaving the circle; I would ask for consensus on making this a normal part of the operation of the group. I would also ask that members speak when it is their time to speak (of course, speaking in terms of "I" rather than "you") and listen when it is their time to listen. I might introduce some form of "talking stick" or other sacred object with the idea of reinforcing through a physical reminder the importance of respect in the group. I also might introduce some form of ceremonial opening and/or closing of group sessions, and if I did, I might invite the group to lead these ceremonies, or create their own, through consensus.

Since the people in this group have multiple things going on in their lives that require their attention in addition to the group, it would be appropriate in the talking circle to address this as a possible future issue before it occurs. As leader, I might have brought this up in the first session or so and asked the group to discuss how the group wants to approach the issue of arriving late or leaving early for other obligations, and I would have sought consensus on that issue, as well as any other issues that could be foreseen with that particular group of people.

Given the current scenario where the fuse has already been lit, I might reaffirm several members' statements in the segment that just occurred, while focusing in on Amy's statement, which was the most outstanding aspect of the situation, as a way of summarizing one of the underlying issues and challenges of the group at this point: being together as a group and functioning as a group. I would not be looking to stifle any tension or conflict that might have already happened, but at the same time, like Amy, I would want to find a way to facilitate the group in examining what it will mean from that point forward to work (or play) as a group. Maybe this would be truly the first time as a group that we would grasp our essence as a circle.

As a part of my response at this point, I might highlight the passion and energy with which everyone is approaching the group at the moment, and wonder out loud how we could pull all of that energy together with a focus toward the completion of our task. I might ask: Do we need to address the issue of arriving late or leaving early at this point? Is that what the group needs? Do we need to reevaluate our goal(s) as a group? Do we need to check with individual members and resolve any hurt feelings or differences that have arisen now? I would be with the group in whatever the group needed and wanted at that point, but I would not allow useless exchange of disrespect in, what to me, is the sacred circle.

Given my choice of response as leader, I would anticipate that the group members would feel both challenged and supported. It would be interesting to see what we would decide to do with that together. I trust the process, and I trust the momentum of group members in the moment. Everyone is there, and everyone is charged in one way or another, it seems, so why not put it to work—on being or on doing?

Based on the composition of this group, what multicultural issues (etic and emic) need to be taken into consideration as the incident is addressed in group?

As a leader, I am conscious of the fact that the members fall into the age range of 41 to 68; they are male and female; they come from different cultural and ethnic backgrounds, probably with different ways of communicating, seeing the world, and interpreting their experiences; they all have a wide mix of talents and abilities; and they seem to be a part of the group because they really want to be part of the group or believe in its purpose. Even as I think about some of the differences between these group members, I am intrigued with the possible ways that each could complement the others in a synergetic movement as a sacred circle, of sorts. More importantly, I would ask myself what role I could play in helping them discover their own interrelation, which is like the ebb and flow of a river flowing steadily toward its destination and, yet, simultaneously back to its source, one and the same.

BOGUSIA MOLINA'S REACTION AS A MEMBER OF THIS TASK GROUP

Identify the multicultural issues that need to be taken into consideration for you as a member.

I would want to check with the group about how we would share and influence power distribution. If I were a member of this group, I would want to find a way to ensure that all the voices are heard, mine included. I would be taken aback by Cisely's remark. I would think to myself that she must have some very ambitious standards for herself and the group and that it must be hard to live up to them. I would be concerned that if we do not address the conflict and power within the group, confrontation could become destructive instead of conveying the message of "grace and caring" (Hulse-Killacky,

Killacky, & Donigian, 2001). Also, as a member I would be very impressed by the successes experienced by all the group members and would want to figure out how, as a group, we could weave a culturally rich mosaic consisting of our strengths. That mosaic could serve as the instrument for developing strategies conducive to reaching the goal-raising funds for the rehabilitation of the old firehouse that will function as the community playhouse.

Explain how your ethnic and cultural background affected the way you would respond as a member?

The persistent side in me, the warrior, would want to challenge Cisely's statement, as it implies that the group members do not know what they are doing and that ultimately we will fail. I would want to have a dialog about how we could create an environment conducive to reaching goals. I think, however, I would want to challenge Cisely and the group gently, as it seems that, as a group, we are operating under the assumption that we have to rush and quickly accomplish tasks, possibly at the risk of not developing relationships with each other. I would want to ask the group, whether we might be "wasting time here, or if time pressures were not the issue," how we would be spending our time in the group. My personal cultural lenses would be telling me that we as a group are at risk of getting sucked into macrosystemic pressures that invite us to rush, get things done, be efficient, even if it means giving up meaningful relationships.

I would be aware of the reaction I might have toward the statement made by Cisely, as I would experience anxiety and fear that once again I need to live up to someone's "shoulds." Those "shoulds" would stem from my family system. However, my family system has experienced a different set of "shoulds" as a result of acculturation pressures than the "shoulds" that I experienced in my culture when my grandmother was the family leader who passed on time-honored traditions. So, perhaps my response would be somewhat resisting. The resistance would probably stem from the concern that as a group we might be moving into a path of implied rules such as "be perfect, hurry up, constantly hurry, work constantly, hurry up, you will run out of time, live to complete your duties." I have been working hard to give myself permission to let go of these oppressive messages and reclaim the ones that my culture at one point emphasized, such as: give yourself permission to be you, life can be fun, working together can be fun, you can live your feelings and emotions.

So, I think the challenge for me and us as a group would be to determine what we hope to accomplish and how we could do that so our wishes would be attained. Perhaps focusing on who comes late or early seems safer than addressing what it is like for us to enter into an unknown territory of shared goal identification and shared decision-making process. I would want to check with the group about what solutions to the situation we were creating. Each member has important roles in the group and outside of the group. To me, it seems like we need a group norm on how to handle members' needing to leave early or come late so that the group goals will not be hindered. I would want the group and the leader to share responsibility for making such decisions.

Explain how your ethnic and cultural background may or may not inhibit the way you respond to the situation as a member.

My persistence can be an asset and a challenge. So, I would need to monitor closely my interactions with others to make sure that I do not come across as a bulldozer. However, speaking up for what I value in a gentle and caring way would be an asset. Thus, following in the steps of my grandmother and trusting the group process and the people who are involved would be a great asset.

Explain how your ethnic and cultural background may have influenced your choice of the response you made over any other that you may have been considering as a member.

In light of my cultural lenses, I would tune into Cisely's statement the most. Initially, the conflict could escalate. When what I value is at risk of being lost, I find it important to address the issue until a win-win solution can be identified. Amy's remark also seems consistent with my values, so it stood out for me as well. Fostering relationships with others is deeply valued within my culture, as I experienced it, so wanting to relate to everyone in the group would be "natural" for me.

As a result of the response you chose, identify the consequences you might anticipate as a member.

I would hope that as long as we stayed on focus, the group as a whole would benefit from addressing the issues at hand. Staying on focus, however, would be crucial. I would hope that sharing my views would be accepted by others and that they, too, would voice their opinions regarding our group's process. I would hope that Cisely and I would get closer as a result of the gentle and caring feedback exchange. And just as I was taken aback by her reply regarding the group, perhaps she would have some observations that I could learn from and use to modify my actions, so that she would also be able to gain more trust in the group's ability to accomplish its goals. I would not want to discount her frustrations. For me, the issues would revolve around how we could respectfully give feedback to each other.

From your position as a member, explain what the most glaring or outstanding aspect was of the situation which impacted you from your ethnic and cultural orientation.

The courage that Amy demonstrated in expressing her views regarding the group really impressed me. That involved a lot of risk and would give me courage to take risks as well. Cisely's remarks would be opportunities for growth, as they would help me become aware of my own weaknesses. I would perceive the group as feeling frustrated as a result of pressures to accomplish tasks quickly and I would want to find a way to respect the group members' need to efficiently manage time without sacrificing the relationships in the group. As a strong believer in group work, I would want to emphasize the fact that our collective strengths would give us the synergy to accomplish the tasks that otherwise could not be done. I believe it would be very important to have an open dialog about who we are as a diverse group and how we could convey respect for differences. Just as we would have to be sensitive to the obvious differences, we would need to convey respect for the not-so-obvious differences: A Jewish group member might be wondering if the group would really accept her; a gay man might be wondering if he would be respected and his contributions would be validated if the group knew his sexual orientation; a person with an invisible disability might be wondering if the group would find her to be a valuable group member. Thus, all the differences would need to be addressed.

BOGUSIA MOLINA'S REACTION AS A LEADER OF THIS TASK GROUP

If this type of incident would not occur in your group, explain why it would not.

I believe a process very similar to this incident could occur in one of my groups. Group work is a dynamic process embedded in art and science. Although each group experience is unique, like a melody, the processes are perhaps more like chords, that is, alike.

Identify the multicultural issues that need to be taken into consideration for you as a leader.

In terms of culture, I would want to discuss with group members how they grapple with power and decision making in light of their cultural backgrounds. I would invite the group members to share answers to the following three questions:

1. What kind of culturally embedded rules regarding accomplishing tasks do you live by?
2. How will your culturally embedded rules help us accomplish our tasks?
3. In the process of accomplishing tasks, how do you cope with the issue of power and decision making?

In addition, I would be asking myself how we could foster success. I would most likely use triads and then regroup to process. I would ask group members to discuss the three questions in small groups. Thus, power could be shared, each person's views could be heard, and we could maintain time efficiency.

In addition, I would want to check with the group about how we could share and influence power distribution and how we could strive for efficient use of time while still honoring the importance of relationship building. I would want to pay close attention to the process of how we as a group were communicating and working toward accomplishing our task. I would strive toward balance between content and process. I would stay with the suggestions offered by Donigian and Malnati (1997) as well as Hulse-Killacky et al. (2001), who emphasize the importance of balancing the process and content of group work in all systemic levels. So, first I would become aware and I would remind myself to pay close attention to the emerging dynamics. Second, I would want to process our frustrations and struggles by making here-and-now immediacy statements (Carroll & Wiggins, 1997). I might say, "I can sense a lot of frustration here. What makes this group difficult now?" I would work on linking concepts and people in order to foster universality and hope (Yalom, 1995). Perhaps the group is getting frustrated with the potential for wasting time and not accomplishing the task. As the group is experiencing conflict, recognizing diverse views while identifying unifying forces is imperative.

As a leader, I would want to find a way to ensure that all the voices would be heard. I would want to recognize the conflict and address it. I would pay attention to potential subgroupings that might occur. I would pay close attention to nonverbal communication as well as verbal communication. When Cisely shared her frustrations, I would pay attention to (a) who else seems to share those, (b) how others were affected by her statements, and (c) who might be wanting to join her and might also have a "good" reason for leaving. I would want to pay attention to potential communication breakdowns. The group seems to be shifting from the beginning stage (getting to know one another) to the action stage, and in the process is encountering conflict, which is to be anticipated.

The leader in me would say, on a cognitive level, this is good, this will give us a chance to work through conflict so we can get into action planning and continue working through conflict in smoother ways. In addition, on an affective level, I would be taking deep breaths, reminding myself I need to deal with my own discomfort and recognize this critical moment so we can address it. Furthermore, the career counseling background in me tells me that these individuals may be experiencing higher levels of conflict for two reasons: (a) their enterprising, competitive personalities, and (b) their shared value of wanting to be in charge. I would emphasize the unique attributes and talents that each member brings. In the process, each person's unique attributes could contribute to meeting the goal. I would probably make a process comment such as: "I sense that we want to be successful in accomplishing our task. Right now that seems to be difficult. I am aware that the leaving early and coming late seems to have become a pattern. What is that about?" I would ask the group, "How do we want to handle this dynamic as a group?" I would also ask the group, "What should we do about developing an agenda and proceeding with it?" Perhaps some of the frustration stems from group members not feeling like they had an input into the agenda. I would want to make sure that the group has an agenda that is truly the group's agenda. The here-and-now orientation would be very helpful, I think. I would ask group members, "How do our culturally embedded rules regarding accomplishing tasks influence our group dynamics?" Finally, if no one else brought it up, I would share an observation that it seems like the group does not think we are spending our time in a useful and productive fashion. I would then invite the group to brainstorm solutions that would help us become more useful and productive.

I might propose that we review the key elements to successful group work as identified by Hulse-Killacky et al. (2001, p. 6). After reading the key elements, I might invite the group to discuss to what extent we feel: listened to; accepted in our individuality; that we have a voice; that we are part of the climate in which leaders and members acknowledge and appreciate varied perspectives, needs, and concerns; that we understand and support the purpose of the group; and that we have the opportunity to contribute to the accomplishment of particular tasks. Based on the responses, I would invite the group to develop an action plan that would help us foster elements conducive to successful group work.

I might want to address the unique richness of the group by asking the group to engage in the *Weaving of the Web* activity. The Weaving of the Web would have a twofold purpose: (a) promote the importance of culture building and (b) identify an action plan for the goal of fundraising for the old firehouse that will be transformed into a playhouse. Here, from processing what the group as a whole is experiencing, I would shift the focus to: "How can each group member here enhance the accomplishment of our goals?" I would ask the group members to participate in the Weaving of the Web activity, which involves the following steps:

1. I take a ball of yarn and identify a cultural strength that I bring to the group and how this can help us attain our goal. Then, I toss the ball of yarn to another group member and let him know what kind of cultural strengths I identify in him.
2. The group member to whom I tossed the ball of yarn identifies another cultural strength he has and how this would help us attain the goal. Then he tosses the ball of yarn to someone else, sharing with that person the cultural strengths he identifies in that member.
3. The process continues until everyone in the group is linked.

Thus, the group members would be able to recognize each others' strengths and would be able to identify what the group needs to do in order to move toward goal accomplishment.

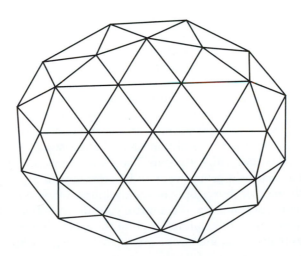

The web could become a symbol of the culturally rich mosaic consisting of our group members' strengths. That mosaic could serve as the instrument for developing strategies conducive to reaching the goal—raising funds for the rehabilitation of the old firehouse that will function as the community playhouse. As the activity is processed, I would emphasize the strengths and riches of diversity. I would also stress the importance of everyone's involvement; otherwise, the web loses strength and the goal accomplishment diminishes.

Finally, I might proceed with some leader-to-member interventions. Specifically, in order to validate Cisely's concerns I might say, "Cisely, I am aware of how important closing the deal is for you and how equally important this group is to you. Before you leave, let me quickly ask you, what did you gather from today's meeting, and what can you do to help us out by the next meeting time?" Thus, her other commitments would be recognized along with a concrete commitment to this group. I would want to emphasize the importance of fostering a collaborative environment.

Explain how your ethnic and cultural background affected the way you would respond as a leader.

As a leader, I would need to stay aware of the fact that I am perceiving the interactions through constructions embedded in my culture. The persistent side in me, the warrior, would want to challenge Cisely's statement, as it implies that there is a right way and a wrong way of leading groups and that her way is the right way. Through my cultural lenses, I might perceive her interactions as a symbol of valuing tasks or material goods more than relationships. So, part of me would want to protect the group, perhaps too much. I would need to monitor my "warrior energy." At the same time, a strong cultural value deeply embedded in me tells me to honor each person with whom we interact. So, combining the warrior energy with patience and honor would probably lead me to gently challenge Cisely and the group. I would probably say something like, "I am experiencing this dynamic as a message that in this group, we have to rush and quickly accomplish tasks, possibly at the risk of not developing relationships with each other." So, I am wondering, how can we be efficient with time without sacrificing relationships? I am curious, what is the rest of the group experiencing?" I would want to ask the group, if we were not "wasting time here, or if time pressures were not the issue," how would we be spending time here?

My personal cultural lenses would be telling me that, as a group, we are at risk of getting sucked into macrosystemic pressures that invite us to rush, get things done, and be efficient—even if that involves giving up meaningful relationships. So, my response would be somewhat resisting, perhaps. If so, I would honestly share that with the group. The resistance would probably stem from the concern that as a group we may be moving into a path of implied rules such as "be perfect, hurry up, constantly hurry, work constantly, hurry up, you will run out of time, live to complete your duties." I have been working hard to give myself permission to let go of these oppressive messages and reclaim the ones that my culture at one point emphasized, such as: give yourself permission to be you, life can be fun, working together can be fun, you can live your feelings and emotions. So, I think the challenge for me and us as a group would be to determine what we hope to accomplish and how we can do that. Perhaps focusing on who comes late or early seems safer than addressing what is it like for us to enter into an unknown territory of shared goal identification and a shared decision-making process. I would check with the group about what solutions to the situation we are creating. I would want the group and the leader to share responsibility for making such decisions.

Explain how your ethnic and cultural background may or may not inhibit the way you respond to the situation as a leader.

My persistence can be both an asset and a challenge, so I would need to closely monitor my interactions with others to make sure that I do not come across as a bulldozer. However, speaking up for what I value in a gentle and caring way would be an asset. I would want to make sure that I do not impose my values as the "right ones" to have. My culturally embedded values trigger strong responses to group dynamics when they seem to clash with values held by others in the group. However, I believe I need to take responsibility for being aware of my values and then be honest with the group about how my group experiences may be influenced by those values. At the same time, valuing relationships would help me stay patient and strive to find win-win solutions for everyone. I might say to Cisely, "Thank you for helping us stay on task. I may be drifting off too much at times, and I think that your strengths could really help us." So, my culturally embedded values would not inhibit the way I would respond to the situation as a leader.

Explain how your ethnic and cultural background may have influenced your choice of the response you made over any other that you may have been considering as a leader.

Groups are so rich in dynamics. Although my decisions regarding those dynamics that I notice and find it important to address are influenced by my cultural lenses, my selection of responses is also influenced by my training. In terms of my training, I ask myself about the dynamics, and I ask myself about the therapeutic factors.

Being aware of cultural background is so important. As a leader who values relationships, I might find it very important to address the dynamic that emerged with Cisely's comments, as I would be afraid that the group could be sucked into developing a group culture that values tasks more than relationships. Someone else, however, might find her interactions very helpful and significant in helping the group stay on task. That is the beauty of group work—constantly being aware of who I am, of my assets and potential liabilities, and of how those influence the group dynamic. Being open to feedback exchange is the most relevant part of group, along with recognizing the limits and strengths embedded in our cultural constructs. Some of the strengths that my cultural lenses bring include perseverance in honoring people. I would make sure that Cisely had been heard and understood. If this were not a value deeply embedded in my belief system, I might be tempted to quickly move on to agenda setting—perhaps too quickly. Then, the weaving of a culturally rich group could be hindered, and in the long run the quality of our accomplishments might not be as great.

As a result of the response you chose, identify the consequences you might anticipate as a leader.

Some group members might welcome the emphasis on relationship building. Others might find it somewhat frustrating. I would hope that as long as we stayed on focus, the group as a whole would benefit from addressing the issues at hand. Staying on focus, however, would be crucial. I would hope that the views I shared would be accepted by others and that they, too, would voice their opinions regarding our group's process. At the same time, some group members might view my focus on relationships as a sign that I am getting off track. Such members might experience frustration. Others, based on their cultural lenses, might think I am too structured. I would hope that through our dialogs, we would reach some win-win solutions.

Cisely and I might get closer as a result of the gentle and caring feedback exchange; I would hope that we would. Though I was taken aback by her reply regarding the group, I am aware that she could be making some observations that I need to learn from. I might need to modify my actions so that she too will be able to gain more trust in the group's ability to accomplish its goals. I would ask her to tell me what about me as a leader makes this a difficult group, and I would listen to her. I would not discount her frustrations. For me, the issues would revolve around how we could respectfully give feedback to each other.

From your position as a leader, explain what the most glaring or outstanding aspect was of the situation which impacted you from your ethnic and cultural orientation.

The courage Amy displayed in expressing her views regarding the group really impressed me. That involved a lot of risk and would give me courage to take risks as well. Cisely's remarks would be opportunities for growth, as they would help me become aware of my own weaknesses. I would perceive the group as feeling frustrated as a result of pressures to accomplish tasks quickly, and I would want to find a way to respect the group's need to efficiently manage time without sacrificing the relationships in it. As a strong believer in group work, I would emphasize the fact that our collective strengths would give us the synergy to accomplish tasks that otherwise could not be done. Perhaps I would also find Cisely to be very brave in responding as she did, since in my motherland, people who spoke up were often punished—and yet it was the courage of people who did not choose silence that instilled hope in those who were striving to live in peace.

Based on the composition of this group, what multicultural issues (etic and emic) need to be taken into consideration as the incident is addressed in group?

We have shared values of wanting to help our communities. We have shared struggles of figuring out how we can relate to each other and how we can accomplish our tasks. Those are universal themes, unifying all cultures. What may be different among members is how each person values relationships, time, power, communication patterns, gender issues, and priorities in life. For some individuals, financial health is a symbol of accomplishment, and sometimes the way one maintains cultural loyalty and pride. For others, financial health is irrelevant. As a group leader, I would be sensitive to the universal experiences as well as to the culture-specific experiences. Most importantly, perhaps, I would be sensitive to the meaning each person attributes to the culture-specific experiences.

SUMMARY/ANALYSIS OF RESPONSES

As Members of This Task Group

Identify the multicultural issues that need to be taken into consideration for you as a member.

For Brown, the multicultural issues are related to group process concerns. One issue relates to her identification with and sensitivity to members of the group with disabilities. She believes that because he is wheelchair-bound, Ernie should be permitted to sit wherever he wishes, and not be limited because of the wheelchair. Likewise, Cisely, who is hearing-impaired, should be able to position herself where she needs to in order to read members' lips. Brown also cites the need to accommodate the diversity in member communication styles. Other issues for her are the group's need to establish norms of respect for member differences and the need to value the great diversity within the group as a resource.

We can infer from Garrett's narrative that there are a number of multicultural issues related to his Native-American background. First, human relationships are more important than the task at hand. This must be considered when one is with people. It is both being with people and the way one is with people that are valued. Second, for Native Americans, giving one's word creates a bond, so Garrett views the comings and goings of group members during the first two sessions as members' not honoring their word, which conveys disrespect and disregard for other members. Third, Garrett says *intent* is the key to every Native-American social interaction and that tribal customs clearly define ways of communicating one's intent in an appropriate and respectful manner. It is clear to him that the other group members do not play by the same cultural and social rules as Native Americans do.

Molina views the issues somewhat differently than the other two respondents do. As a member, she experiences one issue to be about power—how it is managed, shared, and distributed among the various members in the group. Her Polish background emphasizes that she is to first listen to others, and not focus on herself. We also see some conflict within her between her Polish background, which would emphasize the building of relationships, and her personal desire to speak up and disagree with Cisely.

Explain how your ethnic and cultural background affected the way you would respond as a member.

Brown indicates that even though she has a strong value for task completion, she also values respect and therefore would address the conflict by asking the group to explore the issues involved in it. She points out that all members need to find their place in the group if the group is to make progress in completing its tasks.

Garrett's narrative demonstrates how his Native-American background affected the way he responded to this situation. He informs us that he would personalize the goings and comings of the other members and would view such behavior as being disrespectful and a sign that the other members are not honoring their word. As a Native American, he might shun members who behaved that way.

Molina's response to this question is that the warrior side of her Polish self would want to challenge Cisely's statement, particularly its message that the group should be task-focused and not attend to developing member relationships. For Molina, that is in direct conflict with her Polish-American background, which (like Garrett's Native-American background) emphasizes building relationships prior to addressing tasks.

Explain how your ethnic and cultural background may or may not inhibit the way you respond to the situation as a member.

We can surmise from Brown's biography that she would take a stand even though her background would discourage her from facing conflict and confrontation. Additionally, her background taught her to disapprove of scapegoating and to be responsible, so she would want to encourage members to explore how they each might be contributing to the problem.

We learn from Garrett that his background might inhibit the way he would respond to the situation. He offers two possible alternative responses. He would consider withdrawing and not returning to the group, since the group members were not being respectful and were not honoring their word. The other alternative he would consider is withholding vocal interaction; he would just sit, listen, and wait to see what the other members' *intentions* are.

Molina is clear in her response to this question. She would draw from her background, specifically her grandmother's influence, and trust the group process and the members' ability to work through the situation. Consequently, she tells us that her background would not inhibit how she would respond to the incident.

Explain how your ethnic and cultural background may have influenced your choice of the response you made over any other that you may have been considering as a member.

We know from Brown's autobiography and her responses to earlier questions that she might fear facing conflict and confrontation and that her first instinct might be to withdraw from it. However, the same background taught her to take a stand for those who are oppressed and disenfranchised. We can therefore infer that the late arrival and early leaving by some members would be in direct conflict with her values, and Brown informs us that she might confront the group for not staying on task and for being disrespectful to the leader and the other members of the group. She states, however, that she would also be guided by her value for caring for others, so she would focus on group process and interpersonal relationships.

Once again, Garrett offers us two alternative answers that he is contemplating. First, he tells us that he might not return because he views the members who arrived late and left early as behaving disrespectfully to him and the other members and as not keeping their word. As an alternative, he might stay but not speak; he would be guarded and would shun the members who were behaving disrespectfully. He reminds us that the intention behind one's social interaction is central in Native-American ways, so he might watch, wait, and "feel" the group out in the silent realm of his heart. Perhaps this might lead to discovering the intentions of the other members.

Molina's Polish background strongly encourages her to listen to members and to build relationships, and her tenacity and warrior heart are also drawn from her cultural heritage. So it is no surprise that her response to this situation includes her willingness to listen but also a challenge to Cisely's statement above all the others, since Cisely's statement conveys the value of being task-focused at the expense of building relationships. Molina adds, however, that she sees the ultimate outcome of her confrontation of Cisely as a win-win solution. Since fostering relationships is deeply valued by the Polish, another dimension of her response relates to supporting Amy's remarks.

As a result of the response you chose, identify the consequences you might anticipate as a member.

There are a number of splits in the consequences Brown anticipates as a result of her response to the situation. She thinks some members might view her focus on group process and her encouragement that members share ownership of the situation as not being productive. Focusing on building relationships could be perceived as being nonproductive by members who are more task-focused. Those who are concerned about time commitment might view the exploration of personal concerns as a waste of time. Yet, she believes that exploring and processing member differences leads to greater understanding and group development.

Garrett's narrative reveals that he would expect the other members to misinterpret his shunning of those who arrived late and left early, and to see him as being defensive, closed, or tentative. He does not think they would understand the intentions behind his behaviors.

Like the other two respondents, Molina would expect some consequences that would not be positive. She anticipates that the conflict could escalate in reaction to her voicing of her views and feelings, which would make her feel uncomfortable. Although some members might experience an easing of tension as a result of her response, she expects that she would be viewed as an annoyance by those who would like to see the group remain solely task-focused.

From your position as a member, explain what the most glaring or outstanding aspect was of the situation which impacted you from your ethnic and cultural orientation.

Brown sees three glaring aspects in this situation. Initially, the diversity of the group's members receives her attention. She reveals again her sensitivity toward those with disabilities by noting that two of the members have disabilities. Lastly, she cites the pattern of members arriving late and departing early as reflecting disrespect for the leader and the other members.

Garrett surprises us a little by not identifying the late arrival and early leaving of members as the most glaring aspect of the situation. Instead, Amy's statement is the most outstanding aspect for him because it focuses on the group as a whole. He regards the group's movement—the decisions and the energy of the group as a whole—as being another significant aspect of the situation.

Like Garrett, Molina found Amy's behavior to be a glaring aspect of the situation. Amy's statement required courage to make and involved risks; Molina felt she might draw courage from Amy's example and take more risks herself. Cisely's remarks were another glaring aspect of the situation for Molina, who saw them as helping her to become aware of her own weaknesses and thus stimulating her to grow. Another significant aspect for Molina, one that is in keeping with her Polish background, is the challenge to find ways to accomplish the task without sacrificing relationships.

As Leaders of This Task Group

If this type of incident would not occur in your group, explain why it would not.

All three of the leaders stated that the incident could occur in their groups. According to Brown and Garrett, it could be expected to happen even after the group had discussed group norms. Garrett, however, would have used the Native-American technique of the talking circle to not only address the incident sooner but also to deal with it differently. Molina attributes the incident to natural group processes and points out that regardless of the type of group or the composition of its membership, group processes remain the same.

Identify the multicultural issues that need to be taken into consideration for you as a leader.

Our respondents' combined answers identify a wide range of multicultural issues that need to be taken into consideration. Brown acknowledges the need to respect member differences and recognizes the need to value the diversity of member experiences. She continues to be sensitive to the special needs of the members who have disabilities, and she identifies economic disparity as a cultural issue to be addressed by citing the financial gap between Tomika and Amy. Finally, she sees a need to acknowledge member uniqueness and then to use it to build a sense of universality through which members can find their similarities.

Garrett recognizes the age range of members (41 to 68) and is also cognizant of gender concerns as well as the diversity in the members' cultural and ethnic backgrounds. He presents a number of Native-American issues to us in pointing out the need to:

- Keep good relations
- Maintain respect
- Communicate with feeling and passion without losing compassion
- Find common ground
- Use humor to build bridges
- Listen to silence as well as to the words
- Approach others with a sense of humility and an openness to experiencing them
- Believe that one is connected with the things and people around oneself

Molina takes a novel approach in answering this question. She identifies a separate holistic and unifying culture that is reflective of this group with its culturally and ethnically diverse members. She describes the group as a rich mosaic of successful individuals who represent a variety of diverse cultural groups but who share common experiences with higher levels of conflict because of their shared values of wanting to be in charge and their competitive personalities. This observation reveals two other value-laden cultural dimensions in this diverse group: the desire to be in power, and the urge to compete.

Explain how your ethnic and cultural background affected the way you would respond as a leader.

Brown's background makes seeking comfort and avoiding conflict important to her, but her background also prepared her to value diversity, to be sensitive to the special needs of persons with disabilities, and to be cognizant of the variety of communication styles that are presented by persons of diverse ethnic and cultural backgrounds. Therefore, we may infer that Brown would address all of these matters.

From his narrative, we can infer that Garrett would place importance on developing and maintaining good relations—more so than focusing on the completion of a particular task. Molina tells us that her Polish-warrior (persistent) side would want to challenge Cisely's position that there is only one right way to lead a group and that Cisely's way is the right way. Cisely's words also stirred the side of Molina's cultural background that would tell her not to give into oppressive issues such as time (hurry up, work constantly, etc.) and to allow herself to focus more on relationship building, to be herself, and to live her feelings and emotions.

Explain how your ethnic and cultural background may or may not inhibit the way you respond to the situation as a leader.

Brown does not believe her background would inhibit her. However, she does address how she had to learn to overcome the disabling effect that conflict can have on her. She adds that initially she might take a laissez-faire approach to managing the group conflict and that she would feel upset with the lack of respect shown to members and the leader.

From Garrett's response we can infer that his background would not inhibit him from intervening. He has stated that if the incident occurred in his group, he would not take so long to address it and he would not deal with it the way the leader in the scenario did. Instead, he would have followed the Native-American talking circle format that emphasizes building and maintaining good relations.

Molina tells us that her culturally embedded values would not inhibit her; however, she would need to monitor her "warrior" side carefully so she would not come across as a bulldozer.

Explain how your ethnic and cultural background may have influenced your choice of the response you made over any other that you may have been considering as a leader.

All three of the leaders' backgrounds encourage them to focus on building member relationships. Brown's background taught her to value caring for others as well as completing tasks. Both can be achieved by balancing the focus on member interpersonal relationships with that of task completion.

Although Garrett does not present an alternative response to the situation, we again learn that the Native-American approach emphasizes developing and maintaining good relations and completing the task in a harmonious way.

Like the other two leaders, Molina tells us her background would have her make certain that building relationships received primary attention. Therefore, she would ensure that Cisely's remarks would not lead members to focus on tasks at the expense of relationships. Molina hastens to add that her Polish background, which would have her consider Cisely as a guest in her house, would also help her to respect Cisely's views and to make certain that Cisely was heard.

As a result of the response you chose, identify the consequences you might anticipate as a leader.

Brown expects that the members would share responsibility for the situation. She would have the members openly share their concerns and identify their personal needs so that everyone would feel included and valued.

Garrett anticipates that the group members would feel both challenged and supported. He also anticipates that, as a result of employing the Native-American technique of the talking circle, the members would develop and maintain good relationships, thereby taking their charge (energy) and putting it to work.

Molina anticipates a number of consequences in her response. She believes some group members would welcome her emphasis on building relationships while others would experience frustration with it. Since Cisely has drawn her attention, Molina anticipates that the consequences from their encounter would lead to a closer relationship between Cisely and herself. In addition, she might modify her views after hearing Cisely's response to her intervention. Finally, Cisely might again trust in the group's ability to accomplish the task while maintaining a balance between content and process.

From your position as a leader, explain what the most glaring or outstanding aspect was of the situation which impacted you from your ethnic and cultural orientation.

Brown identifies three glaring points: (1) the diversity of the group, (2) the fact that most of the group members have been more accustomed to leading than to being members of groups, and (3) the financial status of the members. For Brown, the leadership experience and financial status of the group members may be the most important multicultural dimensions.

Garrett's narrative reinforces his view that the most outstanding aspect of the situation is being together as a group and functioning as a group. He found hope that this group could accomplish this in Amy's statement, which focused on the movement, decisions, and energy of the group as a whole.

Molina reminds us that being able to speak up in opposition to oppressive hierarchies is a privilege. Those who did so in Poland were punished; consequently, for Molina, speaking up rates high among the most glaring aspects of this situation. Another regards Amy's courage in expressing her views. Molina believes that seeing Amy take such risks would encourage her to follow Amy's example. Finally, she cites the group's frustration in its attempt to manage time without sacrificing relationships as yet another glaring aspect of the situation.

Based on the composition of this group, what multicultural issues (etic and emic) need to be taken into consideration as the incident is addressed in group?

For Brown, there is only one etic and one emic issue. The etic issue is the unique multicultural characteristics of all the members, which could serve as a unifying theme leading to group cohesiveness. The emic issue regards the fact that all the members are successful individuals, which might mean they are unaccustomed to sharing leadership and therefore might experience resistance in their role as members.

Garrett identifies a number of etic and emic issues. For him, the etic issues are:

- Age range of members (from 41 to 68)
- Gender (number of male and female members)
- Variety of forms and ways of communicating and expressing oneself in such a diverse group
- Need to build good relations
- Need to listen effectively (including listening to behaviors)
- Need for members to be treated as equals
- Need to accept silence
- Need for harmony and balance

He cites the emic issues as being:

- Need to address how the issue of arriving late and leaving early affects each member
- Reevaluating how members' behaviors reflect their views of the group's goal and members' personal commitment to achieving it
- Need to understand each member's way of viewing the world
- Need to understand the meanings in the way each member uses language

Molina's etic issues concern the need to have shared values in order to build communities, the need for members to share in their struggles as they attempt to relate to each other, and the need to know how to accomplish the task. She has but one emic issue. It is concerned with addressing how each person values relationships, time, power, communication patterns, and gender issues.

Psycho-educational Group Vignette #1

CHAPTER 6

The First Meeting and Group Silence

You are a counselor at an urban eastern university counseling center. You have formed a group for first-year students to help them make the adjustment to university life. Your group consists of eight members.

- Joelle is 18. She is the oldest of eight children. She is African American and is in school on an academic scholarship.
- Francine is 17. She is the youngest of four siblings from an Italian-American family. She graduated from high school a year ahead of her peers and is the first in her family to attend college.
- Jose is 19. He is the oldest of two boys. He and his parents arrived from Puerto Rico seven years ago. He transferred from a community college after one semester.
- Bob is 18. His parents are Native American. He was born and lived in the Southwest. Both of his parents were hesitant to have him leave the reservation and attend a university so far away.
- Jaime is 18½. His parents immigrated from Israel while his mother was three months pregnant with him. He excels in mathematics and has a full academic scholarship.
- Mary is 18½. Her parents are third-generation Asian Americans. Both of them are professors at the university. Mary is enrolled in the college of fine and performing arts.
- Bill is 22. He served four years in the air force. His father is African American, and he met and married Bill's mother while on an Oxford scholarship in England.

- Jim is 18. He is from Tupelo, Mississippi. His parents own a large farm. He traces his Irish heritage to when his great-great-grandparents escaped the potato famine to arrive in the United States. He is enrolled in the college of engineering.

This is the first session. The group members arrive and seat themselves. One chair remains empty. You arrived moments earlier to arrange the room and place the chairs in a circle, and you are writing a few outline notes on the blackboard as the students arrive. As is often the case, the students manage to seat themselves according to gender: women together and men together. They remain quiet. Some are thumbing through their notebooks, a couple are simply staring into space, and a few are looking at the blackboard as if they are planning to take notes. You finish your outline and notice that if you take the empty chair, you will be sitting among the male students. As you approach the group, an unrelaxed silence emanates from all eight members, and you can feel all the members' eyes set upon you expectantly.

THOMAS HERNÁNDEZ'S REACTION AS A MEMBER OF THIS PSYCHOEDUCATIONAL GROUP

As a member of a group consisting of eight first-year college students, I see a number of issues surrounding culture that need to be taken into consideration: (1) my response to the whole group; (2) my sense of connectedness to members of the group; and (3) my willingness to share with the group based on my personal set of cultural expectations.

Identify the multicultural issues that need to be taken into consideration for you as a member.
    The first issue is my reaction to the group itself. As a Latino, I might find it difficult to be part of a group situation if I did not have some degree of assurance that other members of the group would understand my situation. Because of this, I might have chosen to come to the group with a friend, such as Jose, whom I might have met through a mutual friend. It might be that someone had to convince me that attending this kind of group would be necessary, since I have a strong family and community network of support, and I might not view going outside that group as necessary. If I did not know Jose before this group experience, I would probably spend the early awkward moments of this group looking down and avoiding direct eye contact with other members and the group leader. I might also engage in some purposeful activity (e.g., looking through a notebook or textbook, or perhaps doodling on a notepad) while avoiding engaging with any other person in the room. On the other hand, if I did already know Jose, he and I might reduce each other's anxiety by talking to each other. This might help us feel connected to the group and increase our level of comfort with it.

Explain how your ethnic and cultural background affected the way you would respond as a member.

Group membership, along with connectedness to the group, is an important factor that needs to be considered. As a Latino student who is placed in what appears to me to be an artificially created group, I might feel inhibited in my responses to other members of the group. The group feels artificial because it is not a group that I usually consider as part of my cultural support system. This system or network in which I function includes subgroups such as my nuclear family, my extended family, close family friends, and my community. So, although I am accustomed to working and functioning in groups, I know that each group has clear expectations about the roles member are to play. My nuclear and extended family serves as my primary support system, for instance. If I have problems of any kind, they are the groups that I access for support. Not only am I expected to use them as my primary support, but it is also understood that if I step outside this cultural norm in search of support, I am sending (in some cases, inadvertently) a message that my family and I are incapable of solving the problem or resolving the issue. This is an affront to the family. Because of this, if I feel disconnected from the group or the group feels artificially created to me in any way, I might find it difficult to share and actively participate. Certainly my silence as the group leader comes to sit in the circle would serve as a reflection of my discomfort with being in a group of people I am not familiar with—a group that I do not consider to be my primary source of support.

Explain how your ethnic and cultural background may or may not inhibit the way you respond to the situation as a member.

The notion of sharing personal information, values, fears, difficulties, and the like would be very difficult for me. The reason is quite simple. As I mentioned, there are strong expectations that my personal support system always begins with my family; that is, mother, father, siblings, grandparents, aunts, uncles, and cousins are expected to provide all the support I need. In turn, I am expected to provide an equal amount of support to each individual member of my family and to the family as a whole extended unit. Given that none of the members of this psychoeducational group are family and that I would be expressing my own fears and shortcomings to them, my instinct would be to not share. Rather, I might find myself trying to be strong enough both physically and emotionally to be able to deal with any situation that came my way. This is an expectation provided to me by my family: I should always first share any difficulties I am having with the family and not seek support outside the family.

Explain how your ethnic and cultural background may have influenced your choice of the response you made over any other that you may have been considering as a member.

Placing myself squarely in the group of male students would be both a comfortable and uncomfortable position to be in. Culturally, I was raised to believe that sharing among males is preferable to revealing weaknesses to women. As a member of this group, I would find it far safer to sit among the men than with the women. Culturally, however, I also was raised to believe that revealing that revealing weaknesses or personal issues of any kind to those outside the family system is not appropriate. After all, my cultural self would argue, if I am having difficulty adjusting to university life, I should be relying on my family—my whole family—to provide me with the guidance that I need. I would be very conscious of the eyes fixed upon me as I approached the empty chair, primarily because attending such a group would be an admission that I am having difficulty and seeking support outside that body or system that is supposed to help me when I have the need—my family. The situation, therefore, would leave me feeling vulnerable and watched, since my limitations would be revealed to a group that I may not know at all.

As a result of the response you chose, identify the consequences you might anticipate as a member.

In many ways, the counselor or mental health professional is seen as a problem-solver. This is a person, as is a physician, who can provide a clear picture of what is "wrong" with me and what I can do to alleviate my "symptoms." I would expect nothing less of such a figure of authority. I see the counselor as an officer of the college or university, not as part of my immediate support system. This deeply hampers the ability of the counselor to reach me and of this group modality to help me.

An additional complicating factor is my view of the counselor in this process. The counselor is seen as an expert, an authority figure. She is someone who has the ability and power to provide me with significant ways to address my concerns. I would probably show a great deal of deference to the counselor and consider her words carefully before considering those of the other group members. As the group leader approaches the group, my contribution to the pregnant silence in the room comes from my discomfort in this group setting. Additionally, I would pay very close attention to the group leader, waiting for her to set the tone and present her expectations of me during this experience. This serves as a reflection of my expression of respect for an expert who is in a helping capacity.

An additional factor needs to be raised at this time. While in today's Latin-American countries the women's movement has changed the landscape of gender expectations for both men and women, many Latinos in the United States are raised in homes that are isolated from this movement. Therefore, many families continue to espouse gender role expectations of both men and women from the previous generation. The patriarchal system reflected in many (but certainly not all) Latino homes might lead me to see this female counselor as a maternal figure who might nurture me. On the other hand, I might just as easily accept my male gender role socialization and see her as less of an authority figure than a male counselor. Additionally, if feeling particularly threatened, I might see myself as more of an expert than this female counselor. Clearly, how I have been socialized and how I interpret such cultural gender role stereotypes in my own life depend a great deal on my personal experiences. As mentioned earlier, I would be more likely to understand the multiculturality of this situation and my culture of raising: Latino within mainstream American culture.

Because of these many factors, the following consequences can be anticipated. First, and perhaps most obviously, I would probably be very quiet and nonparticipative in the early stages of the group. I would probably share as little as possible. I might express my embarrassment at having to go outside of my family system for help by making little eye contact with other group members and giving short, vague answers to questions they posed. On the other hand, I would be likely to show deference to the group leader while still being uncomfortable about answering questions or sharing important information.

Second, and perhaps most important at this stage of group development, how I perceived the group leader might dramatically affect the perceptions I would have of the group as a whole, of the ability of this group to help me in my stated area of concern, and of my own ability to trust this groups and its individual members. Thus, what the group leader chooses to do, say, and how she chooses to behave may alter the course of the group for me as an individual. The group leader has already taken an enormous step in that direction by sitting among the male members of the group. Until then, I saw this group as being polarized by gender, but the leader's decision to sit with the males indicated that as a male, I would be heard as well and would be an important member of the group.

From your position as a member, explain what the most glaring or outstanding aspect was of the situation which impacted you from your ethnic and cultural orientation.

This group leader chose to remain silent as the group members filed in, and she wrote things on the blackboard instead of introducing herself to the members of the group. This serves to enhance my expectation that the group leader is an "expert" who will provide me with important pieces of information. If she chooses to involve me while allowing me to engage with the group at a pace that is comfortable for me, and allowing me to work through my own cultural expectations about groups in this new context, I can anticipate more active participation and a positive growth experience.

THOMAS HERNÁNDEZ'S REACTION AS A LEADER OF THIS PSYCHOEDUCATIONAL GROUP

Adjusting to college and university life is never easy. First-year college students often struggle with a multitude of transitional issues for which the group setting is perfectly suited. Students often feel as though they are the only members of their peer group experiencing the emotional difficulties associated with college transition. This may lead them to an overwhelming sense of aloneness and isolation that affects their academic work, their relationships, and their ability to become active participants in the campus community. Learning that other students have similar experiences, thoughts, and feelings, and may even have unique ways of addressing these difficulties, can be an eye-opening event.

If this type of incident would not occur in your group, explain why it would not.

As the leader of the group, I would see it as my role to help the students reduce their anxiety about attending a college adjustment group. In order to do this, I have to help them realize first that they have anxiety about being in the room to begin with, and then to know that my role is to support them as they make their adjustment to their new life as first-year students in this university. In order to accomplish this and build a sense of group, I would make certain that any notes that needed to be placed on the blackboard were placed there before the group members arrived. This would free me to greet the students as they arrived, to begin comfortable, safe conversation with them (e.g., a discussion about the university football game the night before); and to help the students find commonalities that would facilitate their communication with each other. I would not turn my back to the students, as this might set up a dynamic that would cause some of them from certain cultural backgrounds to see me more as a teacher than a facilitator—a role that could silence some students. I would be particularly aware of this for Jose, though Bob and Mary would never be far from my mind either. In short, I would address the unrelaxed silence and allow the students to begin talking with one another in order to commence a process of group bonding.

Identify the multicultural issues that need to be taken into consideration for you as a leader.

There are three vantage points from which to view this critical incident as the group leader. First, as the group leader, it is important to discuss my cultural background and its impact on the group process. Second, it is important to address the Latino student as viewed from the perspective of the group leader. Finally, and perhaps most critically, it is essential to view the group process as an integrative experience that requires an assimilation of both of the former perspectives into a context-driven way of understanding group process. That is, group leaders and group members both affect the group process, and their individual effects are profoundly influenced by their past experiences, current context, and perceptions of their future situations based on the former two.

Leading a group of first-year students struggling to adjust to their new life as college students can be a difficult task. These students may be experiencing a variety of emotions associated with being in a new situation for the first time: anxiety, fear, tentativeness, being overwhelmed, confusion, depression, and loneliness, to name just a few. The first few moments of contact with members of the group are therefore essential in creating an environment where all members feel welcome, important, and heard. All of the students coming to the college adjustment are already expressing overtly, through their willingness to attend such a group, that they are experiencing difficulties. Creating a climate where the students can feel safe is critical to having this group not become a casualty.

Explain how your ethnic and cultural background affected the way you would respond as a leader.

As the group leader, I find it extremely important to welcome the students as they come to this group. The students need to feel that they have made a good choice for themselves and not be given time for anxiety to build. This is clearly important to all members of the group. More importantly, as a Latino group leader, my own cultural experiences indicate to me that entering a group with the purpose of sharing my deepest, darkest secrets, fears, and weaknesses with someone other than a family member or traditional support person is frightening and challenging, to say the least. In my own empathic way, welcoming the students and attempting to create a climate of safety and acceptance reflects my desire to help and recognize their personhood at the same time.

As the group leader, I am conscious of the importance of addressing each member of the group "as they are," recognizing the uniqueness of each as an important piece of what they can contribute to the group. Therefore, I recognize that which I bring culturally and experientially to the group, and begin the task of recognizing that which each group member brings as well. This helps me to understand the group and our collective context. By virtue of this understanding of the group and its subsequent organic process, I become conscious of the uniquenesses of the individuals in the group and of our newly created whole.

Explain how your ethnic and cultural background may or may not inhibit the way you respond to the situation as a leader.

As a Latino group leader, I am conscious of the difficulties Latino students might have just presenting themselves to a group, so I will make every effort to listen to them both verbally and nonverbally as the group progresses. I will also make every effort to draw them into the group if they begin to withdraw from the process. For the female student, this also becomes paramount. I am conscious of the struggle female students might have in participating in the group. These students, by virtue of the fact that I am male, may react to the power afforded me in society because of my gender. I am keenly aware that the silence in which they sit and the expectant gaze they present with may reflect this power differential. This increases the importance of my seating position in the circle. I would make every effort not to physically align myself with the male group members by sitting with them.

Explain how your ethnic and cultural background may have influenced your choice of the response you made over any other that you may have been considering as a leader.

As a Latino, I have become keenly aware of the comfort level a client might have in a group counseling situation. Much of this awareness comes

from my own experience with the cultural values I was inculcated with surrounding the sharing of limitations, "weaknesses," and vulnerabilities. Because
of this, when considering a course of action, I find myself aware that in certain
situations, I might be more or less comfortable and responding in kind. In this
particular situation, my course of action emerged from a desire to help the students become aware of their anxieties and discomfort with the awkwardness of
the group, feel more connected to other group members and with me as the
group leader, and ultimately use this knowledge and experience therapeutically
to grow and adjust to uncomfortable situations. In many ways, how I choose to
react to the situation mirrors the purpose of this adjustment group.

*As a result of the response you chose, identify the consequences you might
anticipate as a leader.*

My sense is that, had I responded in the way I described, those students
who might have been somewhat reluctant to be present might be more willing
to share, more open to feedback, and more likely to participate in groups in
the future. As a Latino, it is important for me to know that the group I am in
is safe, that it values my presence, and that I feel connected to it in some way.
If, as a group leader, I can facilitate this, then I believe I am well on my way
to creating a therapeutically positive environment that is conducive to growth
for these individual students.

*From your position as a leader, explain what the most glaring or outstanding
aspect was of the situation which impacted you from your ethnic and cultural
orientation.*

As the group leader, the aspect of this vignette that stands out the most for
me is the word *expectantly*. The idea that the eight group members would wait
in silence and stare in expectation at my next action conjures a number of feelings for me as a Latino counseling practitioner. First is the sense that as the
group leader I am expected to have answers, solutions to the concerns the students bring to this group. Second is a sense of power and authority that I feel
as the group waits patiently for my next word. These two notions are power-
fully intertwined in the Latino cultural role of the counselor as educator and
an authority figure who should be given respect, in much the same way that
one might listen to a teacher: with deference. It does not surprise me, then, that
some of these students would wait quietly in anticipation of my words. As a
counselor, I know that other Latinos might see me as an expert who can, perhaps, provide much-needed guidance. For them, the guidance they expect
might not be so much in the form of facilitating personal growth as in the form
of value-laden advice ("this is the *right* way to address your situation; this is
the *wrong* way to address your concern").

It also strikes me that this unrelaxed silence and expectation that the
leader will problem-solve might come from individual students' discomfort
with taking a "personal" issue (difficulty with adjustment to college life) outside the student's natural support system: the family. However, this complex
mix of expectant behavior and silence, filled with hope for the right answers

and discomfort with revealing one's limitations, is the most fascinating aspect of the vignette for this Latino counselor.

Based on the composition of this group, what multicultural issues (etic and emic) need to be taken into consideration as the incident is addressed in group?

The composition of this group and the perspective I bring as a Latino group leader would suggest that while I acknowledge that there are certain qualities of the counseling relationship and group process that can be generalized across cultures (etic), it is equally important to acknowledge the individual cultural context of each group member as having a profound impact on the group process (emic). This does not suggest that there can only be culture-specific approaches to counseling but, rather, that the context of each member of the group must be understood. Thus, I am conscious that each member of this college adjustment counseling group has a compelling and moving life story. These students come from various cultural, familial, gender, academic, career, socioeconomic, and ability backgrounds and experiences. As I accept the role of group leader, it is essential that I recognize and honor all that is each group member.

CYNTHIA KALODNER'S REACTION AS A MEMBER OF THIS PSYCHOEDUCATIONAL GROUP

Identify the multicultural issues that need to be taken into consideration for you as a member.

I would be interested in knowing how the other members feel in new situations, and specifically what it is like to be the only person of their particular cultural or ethnic background in a new place. Perhaps an issue for me as a member would be that I am not a visible minority (VREG; visible racial/ethnic group, as coined by Helms & Cook, 1999), nor did I attend college in a different part of the country. It is difficult for me, given my positive experiences in college, to relate to the specific individuals in this group and to the concerns they expressed. However, when I have felt like an outsider, my comfort level has been increased by finding people like me in some way. Therefore, I think an issue of importance in this group would be to find commonalities among members of the group. As a member, I might try to connect with people by discussing topics such as classes, academic major, hobbies, or other interests.

Explain how your ethnic and cultural background affected the way you would respond as a member.

Of the members in the group, I might connect most easily with Francine, based on her Italian-American background, and because she is clearly a bright young woman. Many of my friends are of Italian background, perhaps because many of the family issues are so similar to those of Jewish families like mine. I am attracted to other bright and motivated individuals; in fact, this description would fit my closest friends. I might also feel a connection to

Jaime, based on his Israeli parents, but I think that might depend on his level of association with Jewish cultural values. As a member, I can easily imagine myself becoming impatient and frustrated with the other members as they struggle to adjust to college life, though I am not sure what aspect of my cultural background might lead me to this reaction.

Explain how your ethnic and cultural background may or may not inhibit the way you respond to the situation as a member.

Maybe the reason I think I would have a difficult time connecting to the issues in this group is that being Jewish is not clearly visible in any way. I do not look different, sound different, or seem like a member of a minority group. If I am not comfortable telling new friends I am Jewish, I can keep it to myself. I do not have to wear a Jewish star or say things to make others see me as different. Although college was not one of them, I have been in situations in which I did not feel comfortable letting those present know that I am Jewish, and I have kept my Jewishness to myself. It is worth noting that this is a very uncomfortable feeling, and when possible I stay away from such situations. The members of this group, however, are from minority groups in which most of them cannot keep their membership in these groups hidden.

Being a member of this group would be difficult for me. I would have a hard time connecting to the minority status that the other students feel. I would need to listen carefully as they expressed their feelings of isolation and be careful to not jump right in and tell them to just make friends and have some fun. I do not think that this is because I am a Jewish female, though I do think it comes from being in the majority and not really understanding what it is like to always be in the minority in a visible kind of way.

Explain how your ethnic and cultural background may have influenced your choice of the response you made over any other that you may have been considering as a member.

My behavior in this group would probably be to remain quiet during this initial meeting and not come back for future sessions. I would not know how to be helpful to the other members, since I would not share their presenting concerns.

As a result of the response you chose, identify the consequences you might anticipate as a member.

My lack of participation in the group might be seen by the other members as additional evidence that it is difficult to make new friends and fit into the college environment. This would be unfortunate, as it would not be my intention. I would not know, however, how I could (as a member) help the others to adjust better to this environment. It might be uncomfortable for me to talk about being okay in this new place while they are struggling to make the transition to college life.

From your position as a member, explain what the most glaring or outstanding aspect was of the situation which impacted you from your ethnic and cultural orientation.

The most critical issue in this situation is the visible versus nonvisible minority one. Being a member of an invisible minority group often makes me sensitive to ethnic/racial issues, but not quite acceptable to those who are visible members of a minority group.

CYNTHIA KALODNER'S REACTION AS A LEADER OF THIS PSYCHOEDUCATIONAL GROUP

If this type of incident would not occur in your group, explain why it would not.

I would not form a group with only "one of a kind" for this purpose. What I mean is that, if at all possible, I would form the group with more than one person of similar background (e.g., Native American, African American, or from a different part of the country). It would be best if the gender of these persons also matched (e.g., two African-American females). Since this is a group about making connections and adjusting to a new place, these familiarities could help a great deal. If it were impossible to form the group this way, I would attempt to unify the group through the common theme of isolation, and I would encourage the members to share their experiences and offer ideas about how they could begin to feel more connected.

In this group, all the members are members of a minority group as a function of either their ethnicity, educational background, or where they came from (or more than one of these). They might feel as if they do not fit in their classes, residence halls, or with roommates. They might miss their parents and siblings and long for news about home, as they struggle to figure out how to deal with this new place. They might feel they were misled by the college brochures with pictures of other members in their minority group. They could be isolated and intimidated. This universality in reaction could be an important way to connect the group members. I would capitalize on it in a structured exercise designed to foster universality.

The members of this psychoeducational group need more structure than that which would be needed in a counseling group. This group, unlike a counseling group, needs to be run with an agenda, structured activities, and resources. The members seem to expect that, and they may be in need of practical information that would greatly assist them in their adjustment to the college setting. I would provide weekly handouts, lists of resources on campus, guidelines on making new friends, exercises for use in the group, and homework assignments. For example, students could be provided with the names of student organizations and faculty members so they could begin to make some connections. I believe that if this group were run without the necessary structure, group members would feel different and unconnected during the group sessions, which are exactly the feelings they are struggling with outside the group.

Identify the multicultural issues that need to be taken into consideration for you as a leader.

One interesting cultural issue relates to gender. Although contact with home might be desired by both male and female members of the group, males may prefer to initiate telephone calls home, rather than to receive them. One male member of my class said that the last thing anyone wants is to have someone call down the hall to tell you, "Your mom is on the phone." None of the females felt that way. I was surprised by this gender difference, but obviously some male students are more uncomfortable than females with letting their peers know they are in close contact with mom and dad.

Explain how your ethnic and cultural background affected the way you would respond as a leader.

I am not sure how my ethnic and cultural background operates here, but my cognitive-behavioral theoretical view influences me to provide structure for this group. The students seem to be in need of information, an opportunity to practice friendship skills, and some reassurance that everything will be okay.

Explain how your ethnic and cultural background may or may not inhibit the way you respond to the situation as a leader.

I would begin this group with a structured exercise that would be a bit silly and fun so that members could begin to relax and allow themselves to get to know each other. I doubt that I would sit at all in the beginning, since I would have the members standing up to do the exercise. The first activity would involve people moving around, and could end with them sitting in different seats, so the gender distribution of seating before group began would not bother me.

In a psychoeducational group, there may be less attention to the effects of cultural and ethnic differences in the beginning sessions and more attention to adjustment issues that are common for all members. However, it is important to open the discussion of cultural and ethnic differences and how these differences make the students feel in the college environment. There are a variety of exercises that could be used to facilitate this process. One that I have used in groups with members from a variety of backgrounds is called the Insider/Outsider exercise. This exercise concerns the feelings associated with being purposefully ignored. Most of the members of the group become the insiders; they form a tight circle and are told not to let anyone join the circle, no matter what they say or do. One or two members become the outsiders and are told that it is very important that they get into this group, one way or another.

What happens during the Insider/Outsider exercise is that the insiders resist the entry of the two outsiders. I have seen outsiders use all kinds of strategies to get in, including tickling insiders and using force, bribery, begging, and verbal attacks. This exercise raises strong feelings about how it feels to be outside of a group and not accepted. Outsiders can discuss what it was like to try to get in and fail. They can relate this to other times in their lives when they experienced such feelings. At the same time, the insiders can discuss what it was like to exclude others. Had they ever done that before? How did they feel when the outsiders tried to get in? Who wanted to let them in? Why?

Other structured exercises could be used to raise topics that surface in the group as it progresses.

As a result of the response you chose, identify the consequences you might anticipate as a leader.

If the group were run as a psychoeducational group, I think the members would learn some skills that would enable them to make some connections and facilitate their adjustment to college. Additionally, the use of structured exercises would allow members to talk about cultural issues that are influencing their adjustment to college. The goal of this work is to help group members develop an awareness of the role of culture and ethnicity and how this relates to adjustment to college. With this understanding, and the opportunity to learn new skills in developing relationships with peers, the group members might have a better adjustment to college life.

From your position as a leader, explain what the most glaring or outstanding aspect was of the situation which impacted you from your ethnic and cultural orientation.

The profound issue was "being different" even in a group of other members of minority groups. For me as a leader, being a member of a nonvisible minority group would provide the greatest challenge to running this group effectively.

Based on the composition of this group, what multicultural issues (etic and emic) need to be taken into consideration as the incident is addressed in group?

The major issue is "being different" and not fitting in. Making connections and feeling a part of something are the issues facing the members, both in this psychoeducational group and in the college environment. Common feelings of isolation and reactions to adjustment could form the basis of a connection between group members.

MUHYIDDIN SHAKOOR'S REACTION AS A MEMBER OF THIS PSYCHOEDUCATIONAL GROUP

Identify the multicultural issues that need to be taken into consideration for you as a member.

Coming into this group as a member, my concern related to multicultural and ethnic issues is whether or not I can fit as a person. I am satisfied if people notice that I happen to be a man who is black; however, I do not want others who meet me to see me only in terms of my skin color. Also, I do not want others to expect that I represent the entire nation of black people. I think it is a general tendency of black youth to seek similarity upon entering a new group. Perhaps this is also true for persons of other cultural, ethnic, or gender orientations. The similarity might initially be based on ethnic appearance, or it might be based on gender. It also might be based on some other factor such as age, social circle, or athletic affiliation. I would notice that there are three young women, and I would probably notice that one is black, one is Asian or brown, and one is white. There are five young men. With me as the sixth, there are twice as many men as women. Observing the group members, I would probably be thinking to myself that one guy appears to be Latino, and another looks like a Native-American person. I am surprised that there is so much color and youth in this group. There is a white guy staring into space. I am not sure about what's happening with the guy in the old military jacket. He too could be Latino, or maybe he is a "light-skinned brother."

Were I to enter this group at my present age, with at least a 30-year difference in age between other group members and myself, I suspect that I would feel some initial discomfort and uncertainty. I would also think that these younger group members might wonder why I was there.

Explain how your ethnic and cultural background affected the way you would respond as a member.

My multicultural and ethnic orientation encourages me to meet people from the best place in myself. I notice that this is a diverse group of young people, and I would likely feel a sense of connection just based on that fact. I want to expect the best. My idealism is really in the forefront. I am thinking that this is the Urban East. This is a university. I am expecting the best, and I do not want to create those things by my negative expectations that I really hope will not happen. In the back of my mind, I hold open the possibility that things could go wrong here. I know that "stuff" happens—crazy stuff. Maybe the white guy has a problem with people of color, or maybe he is just feeling the same nervousness that I feel. Now that I look more closely, I see that the young guy who appears to be Native American seems to be analyzing patterns in the carpet. But all in all, these people look okay.

Everybody's eyes are glued on the counselor—my own included. I know why I am looking. I wonder if my coming here was the right choice. I heard that the counselor is cool—a good person. But college is not all it is cracked up to be. I miss my friends. Maybe I will make some new friends. I am old enough now to understand the truth of the song that states, "Everything must change," but I am not looking to become a whole new person (at least not today, anyway).

Friends back home in the neighborhood told me that college would change me (into what, they did not say). Some of them think that I will forget where I came from, while some old people think I will not make anything of myself without an education. My mentor, Uncle Bob, also stressed education. Regardless, I am here now. I guess I am making my own choice. I am only the second person in my family to make it to college. But I know that there are things I want to do. So here I am in this group. I am going to really check it out and just wait and see what happens.

Explain how your ethnic and cultural background may or may not inhibit the way you respond to the situation as a member.

I am uncertain whether it is because of my multicultural-ethnic background or simply my personality that I feel a moderate level of anxiety anytime I enter a new group. I am not immobilized. I do not feel an overwhelming sense of fear. Even though the setting and the people may be new, I know that I still have the ability to at least say hello. I know that I can introduce myself to others, or I might ask the leader what to expect. I know that I am the kind of person who wants to make discoveries and connections when relating to people, but I also want to know what to do in this group and how it is going to help me adjust to college life.

Explain how your ethnic and cultural background may have influenced your choice of the response you made over any other that you may have been considering as a member.

At this point, I am remaining open and hopeful. I am noticing as much as I can, and I am interested in making connections but not ready to say everything that I am thinking about these people whom I really know little about at this point. And like I said before, I want to fit. I want to be liked. I want to be cool with the guys and the young ladies. But I do not want to be talking like I have a motor mouth.

As a result of the response you chose, identify the consequences you might anticipate as a member.

As a consequence of my moderate initiative to be friendly without "gushing," cool but not superior or arrogant, easygoing and natural, I would expect a positive reception by others. I would expect them to say, "Hey, how's it going? My name is Joelle (or my name is Bob)." I am expecting the group to be friendly, and I definitely hope that the group leader welcomes me and helps us get to know each other.

From your position as a member, explain what the most glaring or outstanding aspect was of the situation which impacted you from your ethnic and cultural orientation.

What is most glaring in this situation is that the empty seat among the men really stands out for me. I might wonder whose chair it is. Is that my place next to the leader? I notice that there are three women and the men are all together. But still, the women are together too. I notice the intelligence in Joelle's face is as striking as her braided hair. The Asian woman moves with symphonic grace. The young white man is quiet. I wonder what he is thinking about me and about this group. After I was seated, I would likely notice the silence. By now, I have long since been aware that everyone is looking at the leader. I take that to mean that the leader is the person who will help us get started on addressing what it is that we came here for.

MUHYIDDAN SHAKOOR'S RESPONSE AS A LEADER OF THIS PSYCHOEDUCATIONAL GROUP

If this type of incident would not occur in your group, explain why it would not.

This type of incident could and has occurred in my group. I prefer that members sit in a circle, but I allow them to decide where to sit and whom to sit next to. I think it is common for members to seat themselves next to persons of the same gender, especially in situations where everyone is new.

Identify the multicultural issues that need to be taken into consideration for you as a leader.

The multicultural issues relate to my own sense of self, personal identity, and comfortableness with myself and with diverse peoples. I can relate to a wide variety of people in natural, genuine, down-to-earth ways. I have some knowledge and experience with diversity concerns. I am informed, but I also know that I am not perfect in what I am becoming or in what I know. I do not believe, however, that I must be perfect. I respect people and am open to discovering more about who they are. While I want to be appropriate, I am not overly focused on being politically correct to such an extent that I am totally lost to the person. I do not assume that because I belong to a particular group, I know who the other person is; I do not assume that all people of any gender or racial or ethnic identification are the same. Nor do I assume that my experience completely frames them as they truly are. For me, that is the potential of the mystery in the other people: the potential of discovery. This is an aspect that highlights the paradox of group work. One frames what unfolds in one's experience, and then unframes it and reframes it in a continuous process springing from what I call the "possibility view"—always learning more, discovering more, understanding more, and becoming more.

Explain how your ethnic and cultural background affected the way you would respond as a leader.

I do not see any effects from my ethnic and cultural background in how I would respond as a leader aside from my open-mindedness, interest to learn, and a sense of balance with not knowing all and everything in this moment. The people in this group are young men and women, and clearly the group is diverse, but aside from brief biographical data and an expression of interest in attending the group, I know very little about them and am looking forward to knowing more.

Explain how your ethnic and cultural background may or may not inhibit the way you respond to the situation as a leader.

I am looking at the situation now more from the perspective of an effective group leader than as a person with any particular ethnic and cultural history. My ethnicity is there. I will draw on what it has taught me. I do not perceive it as something separate, but more as a part of me, like a ray is a part of the sun. I am not surprised if others make assumptions about it, but I am hoping that my personhood and that who I am as a man and as a being will be most prevalent in the others' experience of me. If who I am as a being is not most prevalent in the others' experience of me because of *their* experience, their history, or their worldview, then I see the potential for an interesting group. Members can explore the extent to which they feel comfortable or not here and now, with how they relate to me, to the group, and to others. Should such an event occur, I would see it as a chance to have real life in the group.

Aside from this, I want to work to help the group members get oriented and express their expectations and what things led them into this group. I would like to know more about the silence that hovers above us. I would likely wonder about it out loud. I would notice how many pairs of eyes are on me and I might even talk about the colors of those eyes. If members were not initiating of their own accord, I would likely say aloud what I sense is the meaning of the eyes fixed on me. I might say to them how I could easily feel like a deer or moose in the headlights, and ask them how they are feeling.

Explain how your ethnic and cultural background may have influenced your choice of the response you made over any other that you may have been considering as a leader.

From the outset, in this particular group, in this particular session, I do not know that any factors in my ethnic and cultural background would influence any particular aspects of my response over others. My background does help me to be at ease with people who may have very different points of view and perspectives. I know that almost anything can happen in a group, but I do not expect the worst to happen. If it does, then I proceed moment by moment. In this group, I feel encouraged. Every member has given me eye contact. I notice that Bob is looking at the floor and Jim seems to be staring into space, but I have no real clue about why just yet. I realize that the group members are dealing with adjusting to college life within a very complex, potentially challenging urban environment. Even though their behavior might seem somewhat dependent and one or two of them may be distracted or even rebellious, my intuitive sense tells me they are all sincerely looking for help.

As a result of the response you chose, identify the consequences you might anticipate as a leader.

As a result of my response, I would anticipate a productive, useful first meeting to ensue. If other issues emerged, such as covert meanings related to seating arrangements, for example, or power-related challenges, or dominance and control issues, I would see them as adding potential and interest to the group. I would not expect a beginning group to pick up on issues like these and address them in a forthright manner, especially not in the first meeting of a psychoeducational group. But if to my surprise, they did react to any of these things, I would work to help group members use them as points of development and learning. I also know group members are checking me out, and I suspect they are noticing what my energy is like and how I move and speak. They see that I am older and probably wonder if I can relate to them. They may wonder if I can deliver, or if they came to the right place. Up until now, not much has been said, but a lot may be happening in the silence—and all of it is encouraging to me as a leader.

One aspect of the multicultural ethnic issue here is my suspicion that even though this group is very diverse, its participants are all *bicultural*. One of them is a third-generation Asian American and very likely relates to American ways with a sense of familiarity, if not with a level of ease. This young Asian woman, Mary, and the Native-American man, Bob, might not look so directly at an elder within their own family contexts, but here they look directly at me. I sense no challenge, however, nor do I sense any inappropriate deference. I only notice their interest in knowing how things will go and their curiosity about what I as the leader will do to help us get where we want to go.

From your position as a leader, explain what the most glaring or outstanding aspect was of the situation which impacted you from your ethnic and cultural orientation.

The most glaring or outstanding aspect of this group was what I felt when I looked back into the 16 eyes looking at me. The seating arrangements held some potential, but the silence and the eyes looking at me as the leader spoke volumes. In a moment like this, even though I might make a light-hearted remark, such as I did in commenting that I felt like a deer in headlights, in order to ease the tension a bit, I would not get too lost in analysis. I would not work too hard to make group members shift their glances away until I looked back into each one of those expectant faces with a glance of empathy and some words of welcome. I might say something like the following: "I'd like to welcome everyone to our group. I look at your faces, and I see a great group of people. And perhaps by now you've already noticed that there *are* some great faces here. But if by chance you haven't really looked, now could be a good time to do that, and to say hello to a neighbor and the group. I feel very optimistic that we have great potential to help each other here."

Based on the composition of this group, what multicultural issues (etic and emic) need to be taken into consideration as the incident is addressed in group?

The multicultural issues that need to be taken into consideration in this group are age, gender, ethnic identity, and family-related expectations, including boundary concerns. Initially, perhaps the most outstanding multicultural issue in the etic sense would be the apparent diversity among group members in terms of ethnic origins. This etic perspective most often views the raw data of an area of behavior without considering the significance of the data or its impact as it functions within its relevant system. Although something is lacking for me in this view, I consider it fundamentally important as a leader because it means that I think to notice how things are. I look at what is apparent without judging it, evaluating it, or projecting meaning onto it, and without distracting myself from looking at the person who is before me. If I am busy attempting to fathom the deeper regions of the other person's psyche, I may miss seeing more obvious but important things like a blank expression, tears, hand-wringing, or smiles. So, as I look into this group from the outside, I notice that it is a very diverse group of young men and women. Each of them had enough initiative to join a group that might help them adjust to university life. I believe it is fair to assume that some transition challenges are happening for all of them.

Beyond this, my considerations would take a more emic turn. The emic here would be that perspective which looks at significant units or aspects of behavior as they function *in contrast to* other units and aspects of behavior within a system. This perspective is essential for effective counselors, thera-peutic helpers, and group leaders because it points to the critical importance of context, which is easy to lose sight of, miss, or ignore. In Bob's case, under-standing that his family does not want him to be far from the reservation gives insight into what one might refer to as the emic aspects of his Native-American and intergenerational context within his family. Similarly, Jim has left a farm-ing family, which appears to have a strong Irish history, in order to pursue engineering. Hopefully, we will discover more about the circumstances of his leaving, how his transition into college is progressing, and whether or not returning to Tupelo is in his vision. Earlier, it was mentioned that Mary is a third-generation Asian American from a family in which both parents are pro-fessors at the university she attends. Joelle is a young African-American woman on scholarship who hails from a family in which she has seven younger siblings. Such contextual information would, over time, be increas-ingly uncovered for each member with the likely effect of changing members' perceptions of each other as well as members' perceptions of the group itself.

The incident to which I am responding places us in an early stage of the group's development. I expect that if I am successful in welcoming the members and providing them a sense that this is a safe place, then the possibility of get-ting to know each other and developing a sense of trust will be open. Another aspect of the behavior in this meeting has to do with psychological membership, something any effective group leader hopes that group members will achieve. Psychological membership is a function of attraction and acceptance (Shakoor & Rabinowicz, 1978). Members who have both a high sense of attraction to the group and a high sense of acceptance by the group are the most vested psycho-logical members. As we open this group, members are showing signs of interest to be in the group. My efforts to facilitate members' sustained interest to remain in the group and get to know each other have extraordinary meaning. Further, in this situation, I hope that members will see me as an older adult who is an ally to them. I hope they will see me as someone who is down-to-earth and accessible but also as someone who is wise. If I can be these things as a leader and, early on, simply establish an atmosphere of interest to be in this group, then transformational growth has a good chance to happen.

Multicultural and ethnic issues will flow into synthesis with knowledge and information issues. These in turn combine with the leader's understand-ing, experience, and what I think of as "essential empathic interest." This is a particular kind of interest in truly knowing oneself and truly knowing the other. Essential empathic interest helps one develop a capacity to understand

as if one lived within the other's experience. Simultaneously, as one understands the other "as if" one were within their experience, one also witnesses a
paradox. One sees and feels how it is to experience as if one is within the other,
yet remains outside as well. Such a way of relating and seeing is powerful in
my view. The ability to take such a perspective may be a powerful supportive
component of effective group work.

The etic and emic aspects of multicultural issues in group leadership have
everything to do with escaping the limiting, one-dimensional, and flat ways of
viewing ourselves and others. For me, group work is about the wonderful,
revealing path of multidimensional perspective. It is about the possibilities paradigm where it is okay to wonder what if this or what if that? Thinking and
being combine with knowledge, experience, and skill in the possibilities paradigm. The anticipated outcome is increased understanding, healing, and transformational growth.

SUMMARY/ANALYSIS OF RESPONSES

As Members of This Psychoeducational Group

*Identify the multicultural issues that need to be taken into consideration for
you as a member.*

Kalodner and Shakoor have identified an issue they share. Kalodner states
that her Jewish culture and family of origin experiences would have her seek
out commonalities she has with the other members, and she sees the issue of
group members needing to seek out their commonalities as the single most
important issue in this group. Shakoor also identifies this multicultural issue
when he informs us that black youth tend to seek out those with similarities
upon entering a new group.

Shakoor offers us other information from an African-American perspective. Personally he is concerned that other members not see him only as a black
man or as a representative of the entire nation of black people. Issues for the
group relate to the great diversity of cultures, the youth of the group, gender
issues, and the fact that males outnumber females.

Hernández informs us that from a Latino perspective, being part of such
a group would be seen as going outside the family and the Hispanic community for help—an action that would be considered unnecessary in his culture.
Consequently, he would need to be convinced that attending the group is necessary. He also relies on Jose, a fellow Latino, to accompany him as he enters
this new experience. In addition, Hernández touches on a communication
issue when he states that if Jose were not in the group, Hernandez would avoid
direct eye contact with the other members and the leader.

*Explain how your ethnic and cultural background affected the way you would
respond as a member.*

We are presented with an interesting mix of answers from our experts in
their responses to this question. Kalodner tells us that she is feeling impatient

and frustrated with the group members. While she attributes these feelings to her Jewish culture, she informs us that she cannot identify which aspect of it is responsible for her feeling as she does. Shakoor credits his multicultural and ethnic orientation for urging him to meet people from the best place within himself.

Hernández is more expansive in his responses to this question. We are reminded that because he is Latino, his family of origin, nuclear family, extended family, close family friends, and Latino community serve as his primary support systems. Therefore, if he were a step outside of these support systems, he would be conveying that neither he nor his family are capable of solving the problem. His joining the group would be an affront to the family. We learn that because of these cultural issues, the group would feel artificial to him and that Hernández would feel inhibited by them.

Explain how your ethnic and cultural background may or may not inhibit the way you respond to the situation as a member.

Hernández tells us that his Latino upbringing emphasizes that he turn to his family for help with personal problems. Therefore, he would hesitate to share personal problems with a group of strangers. Kalodner, on the other hand, informs us that she does not see being Jewish and female as placing her in a minority culture. To the contrary, she sees herself as part of the majority culture primarily, since being Jewish does not have any visible clues that the person is a member of a minority culture. However, she feels she would have difficulty fitting in with a group whose members more visibly convey that they represent different cultural and ethnic groups. Therefore, she might feel inhibited by her efforts to avoid being seen as impatient. Shakoor relates that his multicultural and ethnic background might lead him to feel a momentary anxiety; however, he would not let it immobilize him but would take the initiative to reach out to other members.

Explain how your ethnic and cultural background may have influenced your choice of the response you made over any other that you may have been considering as a member.

Once again, Hernández reminds us that because of his Latino background, admitting to persons other than family that he is having difficulty would not be easy for him to do, since it would violate cultural norms. However, he offers us a new twist to this familiar cultural issue. Culturally, sharing among men is preferable to sharing weaknesses with women. Consequently, Hernández might feel safer in a group of men than in one with women. To participate in this group would leave him feeling vulnerable and watched.

Kalodner is still struggling with being in this group. Being Jewish and from a family that encouraged individual development and self-reliance, she might feel impatient with the other group members. The other response she contemplated was to initially remain silent.

Shakoor is interested in making connections, fitting in, and being liked. Therefore, he would be careful to not be overly transparent.

As a result of the response you chose, identify the consequences you might anticipate as a member.

Hernández conveys that as a Latino male, he would in all likelihood remain quiet and not participate. He would convey his embarrassment about seeking help outside the family by engaging in little to no eye contact. Given that the leader is a woman and chose to sit among the male members, he expects he would respond favorably to her action. We are able to conclude, therefore, that he would eventually speak up, since he believes she will listen and regard him as being important. This would be in keeping with male/female roles in Latino culture.

Kalodner reminds us that she is not a member of a visible racial/ethnic group. Therefore, she feels her nonparticipation would be viewed by others as her being difficult to get to know, and she expects that the other members might not see her as one of them, given that she does not view the adjustment to college as being difficult.

Shakoor reiterates that his early life experiences prepared him to view the group experience as positive. Consequently, he expects the other members and the leader to receive him and react to him in a positive way.

From your position as a member, explain what the most glaring or outstanding aspect was of the situation which impacted you from your ethnic and cultural orientation.

We are treated to three very different responses to this question by our experts that reflect their diverse cultural backgrounds. What stands out most for Hernández about the situation is the leader's choice to remain silent and continue writing on the blackboard as the members file into the room. From a Latino perspective, such behavior by the leader might heighten his anxiety and encourage him to view the leader as the "expert."

Kalodner's perspective touches again on the issue of visibility. Her perception of the other members is that they represent visible racial or ethnic groups while she is from an invisible minority group. Kalodner points out that although her minority status makes her sensitive to the issues, she does not always feel accepted by those from more visible minority groups.

Shakoor makes no direct reference to how the issues he identified as being the most glaring relate to his background, but he does identify issues that would be relevant to him as a member of this group. He desires to be friendly, to be accepted, and to seek similarities between himself and others. It would follow, therefore, that he would probably notice the empty seat among the men, the way the members chose to sit according to gender, and the silence among the members as they waited for the group to begin.

As Leaders of This Psychoeducational Group

If this type of incident would not occur in your group, explain why it would not.

Hernández informs us that instead of ignoring the students as they enter, he would make sure to write all notes on the blackboard in advance so he would be free to greet the students and make them feel welcome, safe, and respected. He would address the silence and encourage the students to talk to each other to commence the process of group bonding.

Kalodner does not think it is likely that this incident would occur in her group because she would try to form such a group by including matching pairs of members, for example, pairs of the same gender or ethnic and cultural orientation. An alternative plan would be to use the unifying theme of isolation to help the students form bonds with each other.

In Shakoor's response, his experience as a group leader leads him to say that incidents like that in our scenario are quite common in groups and are to be expected. He has members sit in a circle in his groups but allows them to decide where to sit and with whom. He states that with a newly formed group, members often seat themselves by gender.

Identify the multicultural issues that need to be taken into consideration for you as a leader.

Hernández would address the Latino issues that are present. He would approach them by viewing the group process as an integrative experience that requires an assimilation of the perspective of his cultural background, his understanding of the Latino group member, and the perspectives of all group members in order to establish a context from which to work.

Gender issues stand out most for Kalodner, particularly the need to be sensitive to the different ways in which females and males approach problems. Female students generally approach problems initially from a more open and transparent position than male students do.

Shakoor takes a novel approach in answering this question. He sees the multicultural issues as being centered with him. They regard his own sense of self, personal identity, and comfortableness with himself and diverse groups of people. As a leader who is sensitive to multicultural and diversity issues, he is careful not to assume that he is all-knowing, especially with regard to persons from his own ethnic and cultural group. He stresses the importance of not assuming that any one individual in a group fully represents that particular group.

Explain how your ethnic and cultural background affected the way you would respond as a leader.

From his position as a Latino group leader, Hernández tells us that his own cultural experiences make the personal sharing of intimate matters outside the family both frightening and challenging. Therefore, he would offer empathy to group members, welcome them, and try to create a climate of safety and acceptance. His intention would be to convey to the members his desire to help them, along with a recognition of each member's personhood.

Kalodner is uncertain how her ethnic or cultural background applies to this question. In her autobiography, however, she describes her conservative Jewish upbringing and says that since the Jewish culture values interdependency and a sense of community, group modalities make sense to her. Therefore, she would try to help the members see what each of them brings to the group individually, and at the same time, she could begin to understand the collective context.

Shakoor believes that because he experiences the world from the position of a multicultural person, he has respect for people and an openness to others. Also, because he does not wish for others to view him solely as a black male, he does not view others from different cultures and ethnic backgrounds in stereotypical ways.

Explain how your ethnic and cultural background may or may not inhibit the way you respond to the situation as a leader.

None of our experts thought their background would inhibit the way they would respond in this situation. Hernández perceives that his background helps him to have empathy for the Latino student and to be sensitive to the gender issues in the group. Since he is a male leader, he realizes that female students may see his position as one of power and that this may in turn inhibit them from interacting freely. Consequently, he would not seat himself in the vacant seat among the male members.

Kalodner states that in a psychoeducational group, less attention may be given, at the beginning, to the effects of ethnic and cultural differences than to adjustment issues that are common to all members. She recommends opening the discussion of ethnic and cultural differences early on, however, possibly by using exercises with the group.

Shakoor responds to this question by telling us that he would draw on what his ethnicity has taught him as he helped members to open up and share their feelings and expectations with one another.

Explain how your ethnic and cultural background may have influenced your choice of the response you made over any other that you may have been considering as a leader.

Hernández informs us that he would draw upon his Latino background to provide comfort for each member. His background discourages him from publicly expressing limitations; therefore, he would encourage students to share with others in the group to find their commonalities and feel connected.

We can extrapolate from Kalodner's responses to earlier questions that she believes her background would influence her, although she might not be certain how it would. Perhaps her commitment to employing a cognitive-behavioral approach in this group is, itself, a result of background influences.

Like Kalodner, Shakoor is uncertain about how his ethnic and cultural background might have influenced his response to this question, but he does say that his background helps him to be at ease with people who have different points of view and perspectives.

As a result of the response you chose, identify the consequences you might anticipate as a leader.

All three of the leaders anticipated productive sessions. Hernández thought that students might become more willing to share, open to feedback, and willing to participate in future sessions. Kalodner foresaw members learning new skills that would enable them to make some connections. Shakoor also expected a productive, useful first session and viewed other issues that might arise during the session as simply adding potential and interest to the group.

Hernández and Shakoor offer additional culturally related outcomes from their interventions. As a Latino, Hernández tells us that his response would lead to his feeling safe, valued, and connected with the members. In addition, he believes it would help to establish a therapeutically positive environment that would be conducive to growth. Shakoor believes that because the group is newly formed, it is not ready to explore such matters as power, seating arrangements, and so on—but he also does not sense any challenge or inappropriate deference from the culturally diverse members, such as Mary (Asian) and Bob (Native American).

From your position as a leader, explain what the most glaring or outstanding aspect was of the situation which impacted you from your ethnic and cultural orientation.

We experience the diversity of the three leaders through the different approaches they each took in responding to this question. As a Latino, Hernández experiences the expectant looks from the members as placing him in the position of being an omniscient, all-powerful authority figure, since Latinos view educators in this way. Kalodner again refers to the issue of visibility; being different stands out most for her, even though the group is comprised of members from other minority groups, because her minority group is not a visible one. Shakoor describes his response to the expectant stares of the group members as being friendly, warm, welcoming, respectful, and accepting—which would contribute to building rapport and a sense of safety among the members.

Based on the composition of this group, what multicultural issues (etic and emic) need to be taken into consideration as the incident is addressed in group?

The etic (universal) issues for Hernández consist of meeting the safety needs of the group as a whole, providing respect and empathy, and listening effectively. In addition, he hints that attending to basic group processes remains the same regardless of the cultural complexion of the group. Kalodner identifies the etic issue as the ability of the members to relate to "being different." She would encourage the students to identify and share their common feelings, along with their reactions to adjusting to the college environment. Shakoor seems to have a similar view, as he also identifies the ethnic diversity of the members as the etic issue.

The emic (culturally specific) issue for Hernández begins with his awareness of the effect each member, working from her own cultural context, will have on group processes. Therefore, he acknowledges that members' cultural needs must be honored by him while he simultaneously helps members learn how to function effectively in the college environment. Kalodner identifies the emic issues as how to make connections with others and learning how to belong to something. Shakoor perceives the emic issues as being related to an understanding of each member's ethnic and cultural background, which can then bring understanding and meaning to the behaviors and actions of the members while they are in the group.

Psycho-educational Group Vignette #2

CHAPTER 7

Asian American Group—
To Disclose or Not to Disclose?

You are a counselor at a local mental health center. The Asian Community Center affiliated with a local university but serving the entire community has approached you about coleading a psychoeducational group for middle school students with the goal of increasing relationship skills. The director of the center has explained to you that the youth programs aimed at the middle school students have experienced some problems this year, specifically several incidents of name calling and one incident of pushing and shoving. She has decided that those youths involved in the incidents (10 in all) must participate in an intervention around conflict resolution and relationship skills in order to continue to participate in the center's programs. Parents of all the adolescents have agreed that the adolescents will participate. The center director has an Asian staff member who would like to cofacilitate the group because he knows the adolescents, but he does not have sufficient group work training and experience to lead the group by himself. You agree to lead the group with the understanding that it will meet for eight weeks for an hour and a half each week, with topics and activities to be determined by you. You and your coleader will also meet each week for an hour to plan and process the group sessions. Your members include:

- Debbie, whose given name is Yuan-Yu, is a 7th-grade female whose parents immigrated from Taiwan when she was 2. She has been the instigator of several incidents of name calling toward the two Korean group members.

- Ae-Jung, who goes by A.J., is an 8th-grade female whose parents have been doctoral students at the university here for several years. The family is from Korea. A.J. has been the victim of several verbal harassment incidents.
- Younn-Jung is an 8th-grade female whose parents immigrated from Korea two years ago. She has also been the victim of several verbal incidents.
- Joe is a second-generation, Chinese-American, 9th-grade male who is constantly teasing other community center members. Several times this has resulted in someone threatening to beat him up.
- Su-yen is a 6th-grade female whose parents are professors at the university. Her parents originally came from Taiwan, but she was born in this country. She has been one of the people who has been taunting others during the incidents initiated by Debbie.
- Kwan-Liem, who goes by Karl, is originally from Hong Kong and is a 7th grader. However, he was adopted and has been in the United States since shortly after his birth. Karl is one of the students who has attacked Joe as a result of his teasing.
- Meghan is an 8th-grade student who was born in mainland China but was adopted at 9 months old by an American family. Victoria, her younger sister, also was adopted at 9 months from mainland China. Community center staff have had to break up several screaming matches between the two of them over who their real parents are and what their nationality is.
- Eileen Liu, who recently has begun to spell her last name Lee, is a third-generation Chinese American. She, Debbie, and Su-yen have taken a team approach to taunting others.

You meet with your coleader to discuss goals for the group. Your coleader and the director of the community center are in agreement that these adolescents do not have much respect or tolerance for each other and need to learn those skills as well as some basic communication skills. You proceed with three sessions of communication skills, which go well. Members switch partners for each activity, and no verbal conflicts occur. You do not notice any nonverbal conflict either, which is a good sign.

Since it appears that all members are cooperating and cohesion is starting to develop, you and your coleader decide to use a Native-American technique called the Inner Circle/Outer Circle (Garrett, 2001) during the fourth, fifth, and sixth sessions. The goal of using this activity is twofold: (1) to increase sensitivity to other cultures and their traditions, and (2) to increase empathy and respect between members of this group. The technique requires self-disclosure of a painful or difficult experience and the forming of circles to indicate support for each other. At the end of the third session, you explain what you will be doing for the next three sessions. Members respond by saying that the activity sounds interesting and that it will be okay.

During the next week, however, three of the members of the group approach your coleader and tell him that they will not be coming to group anymore if they have to do this activity. Their reasons include: "I don't want to disclose in front of these other people," "This isn't a cultural tradition that I am comfortable with," "Members have been talking outside of group about me," and "I can't talk about my problems in front of this group because my family would be hurt or upset." Your coleader feels comfortable sharing with you the reasons, but not the names of the members who talked with him. Your coleader has assured the members that they will not be made to participate in this activity if they come back to group. When you arrive at the fourth group session, all the members are already there and are sitting quietly.

RITA CHI-YING CHUNG'S REACTION AS A MEMBER OF THIS PSYCHOEDUCATIONAL GROUP

Identify the multicultural issues that need to be taken into consideration for you as a member.

The two major issues are the use of the Inner Circle/Outer Circle and the dynamics occurring between group members. The first issue is the use of the Inner Circle/Outer Circle technique. Group leaders must acknowledge that this technique is in the Native-American tradition and not culturally appropriate for this group comprised of Asian Americans, since Asian cultures emphasize shame and loss of face. Furthermore, the interrelationship between family and individuals creates a concern for Asian-American group members in terms of disclosure and the issue of confidentiality. Since individual actions and behaviors are tied to family, the disclosure of issues is not just an individual matter but has implications for the entire family. Group members approached the coleader who is Asian, rather than the group leader who is not Asian, strongly suggesting that the group members assume that the Asian coleader is aware and understands cultural issues. This highlights the importance of having group leaders who are culturally aware and sensitive.

The second issue relates to the dynamics between group members and reflects the differences between U.S.-born and foreign-born Asian Americans. Not all Asians are alike; there are differences between individuals and subsequent intraethnic relationship issues, such as those that occur in this group. When group leaders put Asian group members together, they need to be aware of this and acknowledge the potential conflicts that may occur because of inter- and intragroup conflicts. For example, past and current historical and political situations between Asian countries such as Taiwan and China can affect the attitudes, behavior, and interaction of group members from these countries. Furthermore U.S.-born Asian Americans may view foreign-born Asian Americans as a symbolic reminder of the painful discrimination, struggles, and challenges Asian Americans have had to overcome in the United States. The phrase "fresh off the boat" is used in the Asian-American community to describe foreign-born Asian Americans who have recently arrived in the United States. The term implies that these people lack language skills, knowledge, and acculturation to the U.S. culture. Therefore, group leaders need knowledge about the process of acculturation; levels of acculturation; the development of ethnic identity; and intergenerational, historical, and political issues within and between Asian groups. These are important multicultural issues that need to be taken into account.

Explain how your ethnic and cultural background affected the way you would respond as a member.

I would find it difficult to participate in the Native-American technique, given the strong cultural emphasis on shame and loss of face in the Asian-American community. This exercise could result in participants sharing little or nothing about themselves, especially in light of the already-established negative group dynamics. The environment is not safe for discussing personal issues, and imposing a technique from another culture is highly inappropriate. Furthermore, as a group member, if I believed that the others were talking outside of the group about me, I would worry about whether the group members had said anything about me to their parents and others not involved in the group. Asian communities are close-knit communities, so I would be afraid that others in the community might know about my problems. This may relate to concepts inherent in a collectivistic culture, whereby confidentiality is viewed differently. It would be only natural for one to share problems with family and close friends, since they are the core foundation of the social network, not the psychoeducational group. Hence, I would probably be reluctant to participate in this technique, as I would want to avoid the shame and loss of face to my family that we could experience if other community members had access to such personal information.

Another issue is the group dynamics. Given my background as first generation and brought up in a traditional Chinese family and therefore being bicultural, I can understand the views of those in the group who are doing the teasing and the potential reasons why they exhibit such behaviors. Although I can understand the source of such behavior, the behaviors are still disturbing and uncomfortable for me. The confrontation, taunting, and name calling are behaviors that are countercultural in light of traditional Asian values. Furthermore, being first generation and with English as my second language, I also can identify with those who are being taunted, having experienced similar situations. In addition, in traditional Asian culture, women are seen as the ones who establish balance and harmony in the environment. Therefore, as a group member, I would try to establish peace within the group and explore our similarities and not our differences. I would try to draw on the strengths of Kwan-Liem, who seems to be protecting those who are being teased, while addressing his attacks on Joe. I would also approach the Asian coleader privately to reveal my discomfort and concern with the group dynamics and ask him to work with us to resolve the negative behavior and build cohesion to the group. Working with the Asian coleader and Kwan-Liem, I would hope to achieve understanding and sensitivity to the group members. Once the group has established cohesion, it would be important to assist Meghan and Victoria in resolving their issues of ethnic identity.

Explain how your ethnic and cultural background may or may not inhibit the way you respond to the situation as a member.

My cultural background would definitely influence the way I would respond to both situations as a group member. As explained earlier, coming from a face culture I would be hesitant, reluctant, and possibly resistant to participating in any technique that would create loss of face and bring shame to self and family. The approach I would take in confronting group members with regard to their teasing also would be influenced by my cultural background. I would approach the situation from a collectivistic viewpoint, focusing on group similarities and experiences, with a focus on being Asian American rather than on the inter- and intragroup differences between U.S.-born and foreign-born Asians or on levels of acculturation. Within this discussion, an important exploration would be about how "we" fit into the broader U.S. society that perceives us as an ethnic minority group and the subsequent challenges we face as a ethnic minority group.

Explain how your ethnic and cultural background may have influenced your choice of the response you made over any other that you may have been considering as a member.

This question has already been discussed.

As a result of the response you chose, identity the consequences you might anticipate as a member.

In regard to the use of the Inner Circle/Outer Circle technique, I would be concerned that the group leaders would be upset about my refusal to participate. Given the age of the group members and the assumption that the coleaders are adults, the cultural view is that respect be given to adults/elders and authority figures. The group coleaders would be viewed in this manner, and therefore by refusing to participate in the technique, I would be going against my cultural values of respect and obedience to the adults/authority figures. I would be afraid that my parents would be told of my disobedience and, therefore, shame and loss of face would be brought to my family. Another concern would relate to the possibility that the coleaders might insist that we, the group members, take more responsibility in working out the group dynamic issues, relegating their authority to us. This would make me feel alienated and estranged, without the active support of authority figures, and cause me to rethink whether I should suppress my behaviors, since there could be harmful retribution if the group should "turn on me." My concern would be that if I took a stand and tried to diffuse the negative behavior, group members might turn against me and see me as a traitor. The consequences could involve myself being teased and alienated from the group. Thus, I could feel alienated, withdrawn, and secretive in the group.

From your position as a member, explain what the most glaring or outstanding aspect was of the situation which impacted you from your ethnic and cultural orientation.

The Inner Circle/Outer Circle exercise was the most significant aspect of the group situation for me because of the degree of cultural inappropriateness in using this techniques. The group dynamics in terms of U.S.-born versus foreign-born members and their levels of acculturation is a topic that is and will always be an issue within the Asian-American community. This issue is not a new situation for Asian Americans, and therefore it is not surprising to see these dynamics emerge within this group.

RITA CHI-YING CHUNG'S REACTION AS A LEADER OF THIS PSYCHOEDUCATIONAL GROUP

If this type of incident would not occur in your group, explain why it would not.

There are actually two incidents here: the use of the Native-American Inner Circle/Outer Circle technique and the group dynamics. The first incident would not occur because, as an Asian-American group leader facilitating a group that consists of only Asian-American members, I would be aware of the group cultural values and would not employ a technique that is culturally inappropriate and hence ineffective. The second incident is expected due to the long-standing sociopolitical history among Asian Americans.

One method that could be utilized to address the intercultural group conflict would be for the group leader to emphasize to group members the similarities or commonalities of being Asian. This includes the challenges and racism encountered by Asians in the United States. The group leader could lead a discussion on the sociopolitical and historical aspects of racism encountered by Asians, as well as current experiences. To establish a sense of cohesiveness, the group leader could encourage members to share experiences regarding instances of racism, discrimination, and challenges in being an Asian American. This exercise, if done properly, could produce a sense of unity among group members and therefore facilitate understanding and appreciation of differences. If there were still residual intergroup conflicts, the group leader could explore the cultural concepts of shame and guilt in discussing the conflict within the group and examine the cultural concepts of loyalty and shame/losing face.

Identify the multicultural issues that need to be taken into consideration for you as a leader.

As an Asian group leader facilitating a group with all Asian members, I would need to consider: Asian cultural values of loss of face, shame, respect for adults or authority figures, and obedience and compliance. The importance of the interrelationship between the individual and family—that is, the impact of individual actions and behavior on the family—must also be acknowledged, since this would inhibit individuals from disclosing information for fear of bringing shame and loss of face to the family. Therefore, confidentiality is an important issue.

Another issue that needs to be taken into consideration is the inter- and intraethnic group relations—that is, the perception and attitudes of Asian Americans regarding the different Asian groups, as well as the attitudes within each group. For example, an intergroup issue would be how the Japanese and Chinese view each other given the history of war between the two groups, which an intragroup example would be the perceptions of the different subgroups of Chinese Americans, that is, Mainland Chinese versus Hong Kong Chinese versus Taiwanese and so on. The issue is complicated by the cultural attitudes about U.S.-born versus foreign-born Asians, levels of acculturation, and intergenerational issues. Although from an outside viewpoint there seems to be homogeneity in a group consisting of all Asians, in fact, due to the differences between and within the Asian-Americans groups, this group is extremely diverse, and cultural considerations on multiple levels need to be taken into account. Furthermore, understanding the historical and sociopolitical experiences of the different Asian-American groups is also important, as well as recognizing the cultural dynamics between and within Asian-American groups and in their interactions with mainstream society.

Explain how your ethnic and cultural background affected the way you would respond as a leader.
   Because of my cultural background as a first-generation Chinese person, a child of immigrant parents, who was brought up in a traditional Chinese household, I have a deep understanding of all the cultural issues. Therefore, as a group leader, I would respond in a culturally sensitive manner, using appropriate methods of interacting that are culturally responsive to social interactions in Asian cultures. Being a product of an Asian community, I am aware of the tension between U.S.-born versus foreign-born Asians, and I would sensitively assist the group to work to understand tension and misunderstanding by focusing on the cultural similarities and similar experiences. Having the ability to empathize with both the U.S.-born and foreign-born members would be an asset. Regarding issues of acculturation, for example, the fact that Kwan-Liem goes by Karl and Eileen recently has begun to spell her last name as Lee strongly suggests issues of acculturation and wanting to be accepted and fit into the mainstream culture. Coming from an immigrant background, I have experienced similar struggles and challenges. Also, the tension between Meghan and her sister Victoria suggests issues of ethnic identity, which is not necessarily an adoptee issue but an issue encountered by Asian Americans and other people of color in the United States because of living in a prominently white ethnocentric society.
   Since the issue of confidentiality is critical in working with Asian Americans, it is crucial to establish trust, a safe environment, and counselor credibility before group members can disclose information. As a group leader, I would disclose personal information, since this is a cultural technique for establishing trust as someone who has also experienced acculturation challenges, and therefore establishing ascribed credibility and demonstrating an understanding about group members' worldviews and experiences.

Explain how your ethnic and cultural background may or may not inhibit the way you respond to the situation as a leader.
   My cultural background might inhibit the way I would respond as a leader. Because Asian culture emphasizes maintaining balance and harmony, I might be inhibited in being confrontational and direct with group members.

For face-saving purposes, those in Asian cultures oftentimes relate in a non-direct circular manner, therefore being less direct and less focused on problem solving. Interventions used, therefore, would need to be focused on understanding the social context and relationship of the person rather than on resolving the immediate situation. By communicating in such a culturally congruent manner, especially for those members in the group who are acculturated, this method of communication may not be productive. In addition, for Asian clients to feel safe and comfortable, the leader would need to disclose personal information in a way that might not be acceptable in mainstream group work.

Explain how your ethnic and cultural background may have influenced your choice of the response you made over any other that you may have been considering as a leader.
   This question has already been discussed.

As a result of the response you chose, identify the consequences you might anticipate as a leader.
   As an Asian adult who has had experiences similar to those of the group members, being the elder in the group and identified as the authority figure would have great significance. Transference might be heightened, given the cultural respect for authority. Group members might not deal with the issue/situation but instead respond to me as the elder in an attempt to gain approval. Also, out of respect, group members might not raise issues or confront each other, not wanting to offend me. Furthermore, given my cultural background, group members might be reluctant to attack each other in terms of intragroup differences in case they might offend me, trying to save me from embarrassment or shame as the authority figure. Finally, they might be inhibited in what they share, since they might be wary of my connections to their families and communities.

From your position as a leader, explain what the most glaring or outstanding aspect was of the situation which impacted you from your ethnic and cultural orientation.
   The most glaring aspect of the situation was the employment of the wrong intervention technique (i.e., the Inner Circle/Outer Circle). One cannot assume that a multicultural technique applicable for one population can be generalized to all ethnic groups.

Based on the composition of this group, what multicultural issues (etic and emic) need to be taken into consideration as the incident is addressed in group?
   This has already been discussed.

DAYA SANDHU'S REACTION AS A MEMBER OF THIS PSYCHOEDUCATIONAL GROUP

Identify the multicultural issues that need to be taken into consideration for you as a member.

If I were a member of this group, a number of multicultural issues would have to be considered. As a matter of fact, most of my personal cultural variables should be taken into consideration. All human problems are basically problems of developing relationships. Unfortunately, cross-cultural variables can become deterrent factors. For example, my age, race, religious preference, ethnicity, gender, and intellectual ability would play a negative part. Issues of multicultural transference and countertransference would become salient. As a part of this group, I would be seen as a stranger and as different.

As most of the other members belong to Chinese and Korean ancestry, my joining of this group as Asian Indian would change the psychodynamics of this group due to issues relating to ethnocentrism. Age would also make a difference because of life experiences and worldviews. My unique accent would be noticed by other members of this group and could cause some communication difficulties.

Different surnames, skin color, unique physical features, and other cultural ornaments all play a significant role, both consciously and unconsciously, in developing meaningful relationships. In addition, interethnic relations, historical hostilities, racial prejudice, and so on might become important issues.

Despite all these differences, I believe that there are some universals in all cultures. These universals (etic variables) prevail over the cultural distinctions (emic variables).

Explain how your ethnic and cultural background affected the way you would respond as a member.

Since I come from Asian-Indian ancestry and do not have enough knowledge about Chinese and Korean cultures, I would experience anxiety or uneasy feelings about actively participating in this group. As a member of this group, I might respond with less certainty, and I would lack self-confidence. There is a real danger that a person with my type of ethnic and cultural background might resort to such negative strategies as intellectualizing, ignoring, or detaching myself from the group. Since I am trained in the counseling field, I would personally be conscious of these things and engage in open listening and discussions to combat my anxieties.

Explain how your ethnic and cultural background may or may not inhibit the way you respond to the situation as a member.

I believe that my ethnic and cultural background would be an asset, not a limitation, in responding to this situation. Issues relating to racial and ethnic intolerance, ethnocentrism, cultural mistrust, cultural paranoia, and cultural encapsulation are not new to me. Since childhood I have witnessed and experienced the pains of bigotry, discrimination, and prejudice due to the caste system in India. Religious intolerance has torn the great nation of India into three parts. Hardly a month or year goes by when my native country does not suffer the flames of racial and religious fires. Religious riots are commonplace. Having Hindus set against Sikhs, Christians, and Muslims (minority groups) is the order of the day in India, even now.

The vignette presented about this group clearly contains an example of ethnic and cultural prejudice and hatred. Debbie's (Yuan-Yu's) name calling of Korean group members can be attributed to ethnic prejudice. As defined by Allport (1954), this type of prejudice is "thinking ill of others without sufficient warrant" (p. 7). Most likely, this prejudice has been presented to Debbie by her parent's cultural heritage through stereotypes and discriminatory attitudes.

Most of the prevalent multicultural counseling literature has studied between group differences. Unfortunately, information about within-group differences has been overlooked. For instance, scant information is available about interethnic issues within Asian-American groups. Chinese, Korean, and Japanese people are generally lumped together without any discussion of ethnic differences among them. The same is true of Asian Indians, Pakistanis, Sri Lankans, and Bangladeshi when they are considered as one group, called South Asians, and no ethnic differences are delineated.

As a result, I believe that the field of multicultural counseling is misdirected, pitching all ethnic groups together against the whites, called European Americans. Even European Americans have several intergroup differences. Consider the differences among Appalachian Americans, French Acadian Americans (Cajuns), Italian Americans, and so on. There seems to be a real void in knowledge about many ethnic groups.

I believe that the multicultural counseling field is now at a crossroads and needs a new direction. This new direction might be a paradigm shift from multicultural counseling to intercultural counseling.

Explain how your ethnic and cultural background may have influenced your choice of the response you made over any other that you may have been considering as a member.

From the perspectives of my own cultural experiences with ethnic prejudice and religious differences while growing up in a caste system, I believe I am equipped to understand Debbie's bias and hatred toward the Korean students. In essence, my background is an asset here, not a limitation. My experiences can be easily transferred to this vignette. I also can easily empathize with the Korean students who are being teased or threatened.

Based on my ethnic and cultural background, I would consider the historical hostilities in my responses. I would also pay attention the sociopolitical realities of these students' families of origin. Since most Asian-American families are patriarchal, I would seriously consider consulting these students' parents to resolve the conflicts.

As a result of the response you chose, identify the consequences you might anticipate as a member.

Most likely, I would become the victim of xenophobia in this particular group. Cultural dynamics demand that I would be singled out as a target of hate, fear., and alienation, since I would be unique to all other members of the group. Prejudice generally is driven by either disdain or fear. If I were the only Asian-Indian person in this group, I would be subject to both disdain and fear. My belonging to an outer group would create disdain, and my being older than other members would make me an object of fear. I might also become an object of ridicule because of my different accent, and a danger exists that because of my cultural background, other members of the group might behave indifferently toward to me.

From your position as a member, explain what the most glaring or outstanding aspect was of the situation which impacted you from your ethnic and cultural orientation.

The main glaring aspect of this situation is the awareness that my cultural and ethnic background would be a restricting factor in developing close working relationships with the others. It is interesting that even second-generation students in this group harbor negative feelings toward other group members whose parents migrated from other national origin and cultural and ethnic backgrounds. It seems that the legacy of hate and fear continues for a long time. Parental injunctions about cultures seem to be passed on to children through a series of generations. This has a negative impact on me; it makes me feel pessimistic in the area of race relations, and it distresses me to see the pervasiveness and magnitude of interethnic hatred.

DAYA SANDHU'S REACTION AS A LEADER OF THIS PSYCHOEDUCATIONAL GROUP

If this type of incident would not occur in your group, explain why it would not.

I see here two main incidents: (1) lack of respect/tolerance among the adolescents, and (2) the students' refusal to disclose family matters in front of other group members. Regarding the first instance: Unfortunately, ethnic and racial prejudice permeates all ethnic groups, so this situation seems probable regardless of who is leading a group. We are basically prejudiced beings, but we practice either positive prejudice or negative prejudice. In this case, negative prejudice is the culprit and a major reason for concern and resolution.

The second situation (students' refusal to disclose in group) might not happen if I were the group leader. Belonging to an Asian culture myself, I am sensitive to this special consideration while leading groups. Children are raised with strong parental instructions not to disclose family matters to strangers, especially when they bring shame. I believe that more positive outcomes could be achieved with these Asian-American children through pregroup planning, with the input from their parents.

Identify the multicultural issues that need to be taken into consideration for you as a leader.

Multicultural literature has mainly focused on all minority groups together versus European Americans. There is clearly a void in the literature when it comes to interethnic and intraethnic relationships among and within minority groups such as Asian Americans, Native Americans, and Latin Americans.

As an Asian group leader, most likely I would meet resistance from the group members. To begin with, they would not disclose themselves and might not openly participate in the group. Issues of trust, expertness, and confidentiality might dominate.

I would also have to examine my own beliefs, thoughts, and feelings about Chinese and Korean Americans. There has been strong political propaganda in both India and China against one another since both countries fought against each other in 1962. The political, social, and cultural hostilities have negatively affected many, including myself when I was growing up in India. Unfortunately, too many cultural mislabels prevalent among Chinese and Indians have been generalized. For this reason, I have to continually monitor my own feelings and thoughts about cultural stereotypes and become more sensitive to individual differences. I would also need to reexamine my own cultural values, biases, and assumptions so that these would not negatively affect the group processes.

Explain how your ethnic and cultural background affected the way you would respond as a leader.

Being an Asian Indian, I share several values with these group members. For instance, I can appreciate these students' reluctance to share family matters with strangers. In general, in Asian cultures, counseling means just academic and career counseling. There is no place for personal counseling. Personal matters such as interrelationships are left to the parents to manage. I might be more successful if I met with the parents individually during the pregroup sessions, before meeting with their children.

I might share my own family experiences with these children to get them involved in group activities. Because Asiatic cultures place a great deal of emphasis on didactics, as a group leader, I would use both types of activities, didactic and experiential.

Explain how your ethnic and cultural background may or may not inhibit the way you respond to the situation as a leader.

My ethnic and cultural background might not inhibit the way I responded to the situation as a leader. As an Asian American myself, I would be able to understand these students' values, worldviews, and respect for authority. I could also be quite effective with their parents. In addition to experiential exercises, I believe these students would benefit from psychodidactics.

Explain how your ethnic and cultural background may have influenced your choice of the response you made over any other that you may have been considering as a leader.

My decision to use psychodidactics, to involve parents during pregroup activities, and to discuss matters of relationships individually (before discussing them in the group) all arise from my own cultural and ethnic background. Since separation of sexes before marriage is practiced and highly recommended in Asian cultures, I might be concerned about mingling boys and girls in one group. Having a coleader who is an Asian staff member is a great idea, although I would prefer a woman rather than another man. The female students might be more open with a female coleader than with me. As a matter of fact, Asian parents would prefer this arrangement.

As a result of the response you chose, identify the consequences you might anticipate as a leader.

With my ethnic and cultural background, I would be concerned about the strategies and processes used to conduct these groups. If appropriate strategies are used, better outcomes can be achieved. It would be extremely important during the preplanning phase to see each student individually first, before bringing all students together in the group. These students' parents also must be notified, and preferably a consulting session would be held with them.

Asian parents place a higher value on the education of their children than on their social development. A group leader might have to explain how these students' misbehaviors negatively affect their academic achievement to enhance parents' active involvement. I anticipate that psychodidactics would have positive effects.

From your position as a leader, explain what the most glaring or outstanding aspect was of the situation which impacted you from your ethnic and cultural orientation.

As a leader, I am shocked to read about the acting-out behaviors of these students. This is the not the norm for the Asian children. Generally, Asian children's behaviors in classrooms are rarely rude. Asian children generally are more obedient, conforming, cooperative, and have a greater respect for the authority. They usually do not express their impulses, as they are taught to control themselves and to first discuss matters of grave concern with their parents at home. Also, Asian children generally are more introverted and quite cautious about expressing their anger at others openly.

Based on the composition of this group, what multicultural issues (etic and emic) need to be taken into consideration as the incident is addressed in group?

Emic here refers to what is specific to a culture, while etic means what is universal in all cultures. From an emic point of view, these children have an

Asian cultural heritage. Most likely, their parents speak other languages at home in addition to English. They may also be practicing different religions and have different social traditions and marriage ceremonies. They might have a preference for Chinese and Korean foods, and their dress may differ from that of mainstream American culture. Preferences for music and other arts could also vary.

Parents from Asian cultures generally have different expectations for their children than parents in some other cultures. Many Asian parents prefer boys to girls, and they have different academic and career plans for their daughters and sons. They also restrict social activities of their children. From an etic point of view, however, like all other children, these students need to love and be loved. They have the same academic, emotional, and social needs as children from all other ethnic and cultural groups.

ZIPORA SHECHTMAN'S REACTION AS A MEMBER OF THIS PSYCHOEDUCATIONAL GROUP

I would feel uncomfortable in this group. It includes a subgroup, composed of Debbie, Su-yen, and Eileen Liu, who take advantage of the two Korean group members. Then there is Joe, whose bullying of the others adds to the threat some of the group members must feel. I would not like these students or the way they treat one another. Kwan-Liem is not unable to protect the group's "victims"; I would like to help him, but I would not know how. I would feel kind of helpless and angry. The group would not seem to be a safe place for me either, and I would not trust the group members enough to share any private information with them.

Some of the group members feel close to the Asian coleader, but I would not trust either leader. The American group leader smiles too much; I would not trust that smile. Besides, she did not protect me when group members called the Israelis "aggressors." She does not seem to like me, perhaps because I am Jewish or Israeli.

But suppose I am forced to participate in this group of troubled kids. I would not have chosen to be there, and they would not change me! If only I could select what group members I could be with; but here I would be stuck with Chinese and Korean people—and they are different "creatures." They even look different, smell different. The Korean girls are too submissive. I would feel sorry for them, but would not be able to identify with them. They are also very close to each other, and I do not know if they would like me to get closer to them. I would hate the bullying that goes on against them but would not know how to help them. I appreciate Kwan-Liem's efforts to stop it, but as he is male, I would not feel comfortable getting close to him. The two sisters are a mystery to me, too; they are too withdrawn and depressive—there would be no chance for me to get close to them.

The next session, we have been told, will require some serious self-disclosure. Some of the members have threatened to leave the group. I was thinking about it, too, but this would not be like me at all; I never give up on any task I have started, and I would feel like a loser for chickening out. I am also curious to see how the group will evolve, and would like to understand the "victims" in this group a bit better. Someone has to help them to stand up for their rights; perhaps I can. I would particularly hope that we could hear the two sisters speak. Perhaps if they shared their big secret, they would be happier, too. Finally, I would hope that the bullies would be stopped somehow; perhaps they should disclose their "secrets" first. I would hope that the two group leaders could handle the situation properly.

Here they are, the two leaders, coming together into the room where the group is already present, all of us waiting silently for their instructions. I would be hoping I would not be called into the inner circle. I do not really know what I can share with the group of my culture. I would be confused, as I would not know which culture I should share—that of my early childhood, that of my life in Israel, or the one of my present life in the United States? All three are so different from each other. I think that sharing my past secrets would be too risky and embarrassing at this point, but perhaps I could share with the other members the feelings I had during the Gulf War. How frightening it was getting up in the middle of night to the sound of sirens, the whole family being locked in a small sealed room, waiting helplessly to hear where the missle came down and whether it carried a nuclear head. I think the children might be interested in this.

Now that I have decided what I will share, I would no longer mind being called into the inner circle. This might serve as an opportunity to make some friends. As an Israeli, I like being in a group, and I am interested in other children of my age. Actually, I had expected to make American friends, but it did not work out that well. The American classmates do not easily open to me; actually, my only friend here is of Chinese origin. As I myself was an immigrant to Israel, I can identify with many of the difficulties these kids have gone through. Actually, I am curious to hear how they and their parents have made it in America.

I also would choose to take part in the inner circle because I always tend to take responsibility in social situations. The silence in the group would make me feel restless, nervous, and helpless—feelings that I would prefer to avoid. I would like to help the group move on, and I feel I have the capacity to do so. I believe the group would respond well to my story. Once the members got to know me and like me, I might be able to confront them with the bullying that goes on in the group, which I hate. But I would not confront the bullies directly. If they responded to my story of the Gulf War with empathy, I might be able to share other feelings related to situations in which I was victimized. This might help the withdrawn group members join me and speak up. They, too, make me feel helpless and unsuccessful with our group task, and I generally hate to fail.

ZIPORA SHECHTMAN'S REACTION AS A LEADER OF THIS PSYCHOEDUCATIONAL GROUP

I am quite an experienced leader, usually feeling safe in and with the group I am leading. I trust the group process, as I have seen adolescents participating effectively in groups. In this particular group, I would feel a bit different, as I am not familiar with most of the participants' cultural background. I would be pleased to have a coleader who could fill me in on cultural issues that I am ignorant of. When he told me the fears the group members had and how some had threatened to leave the group, I was quite surprised. Following the first three sessions, I had thought that my plan was reasonable, as no one had rejected it in any overt or covert way. On the contrary, they had all agreed with the plan I had set out for the next several sessions. I have learned something very important about this group: They are not ready to disclose their here-and-now feelings, they avoid open confrontations, and rather than being assertive, they choose to avoid conflict, ready to give up the group. I also have learned that some cultural experiences may be too difficult for children to share; they may think them not interesting to the others, too personal, or associated with shame or guilt. At this point in the group development asking for such self-disclosure might be inappropriate; rather than helping members to achieve respect for each other, it might lead to conflict and rejection.

I need to reduce the threat on these kids. We need to work on group cohesiveness, and their anxiety needs to be properly addressed. I need to help them verbalize their fears and resistance. In my early childhood, I was raised to behave very much like them: obey adults, shy away from confrontation, be good, act mature. Later, in Israel, in a culture of overriding straightfor-wardness, I learned to deal with conflicts more openly and to be more assertive. At the same time, I learned to accept responsibility as a group leader and to try my utmost to achieve the group's goals without causing too much embarrassment.

As this is a short-term psychoeducational group, high levels of self-disclosure would be inappropriate. Asking group members to disclose painful family issues might be especially difficult for children from "collectivistic" societies, as most of these children are. Therefore, I might reconsider my plan. I would encourage them to express what they think regarding the suggested activity, and reassure them that whatever opinion they have will be accepted. I think it would be important to help them be constructively assertive, as many of their acting-out and withdrawal behaviors reflect this lack of assertiveness. I would share with them my personal difficulties as a child, and sometimes as an adult, in facing authoritative figures and resisting the demands they make on us. I would introduce a therapeutic game to help them express their here-and-now feelings honestly. For example, they could complete the sentence, "I would prefer not to share private information because. . . ." Or, we could play the "I guess" game, in which group members have to guess why others might be resisting self-disclosure at this point in the group. Such activities would legitimize the members' resistance and help them move to the next stage.

To achieve the goals for this group—that is, mutual understanding and respect—I would use an indirect method of intervention, such as bibliotherapy, art therapy, a film, or pictures. All of these methods can be used to present information about different cultures and their unique difficulties without having to disclose personal secrets. Usually, following the presentation of such material and subsequent therapeutic discussion, children will identify with the content or figures, and can more easily choose to share some private piece of information with the group.

Changing your plan if you are the group leader is not easy, but it can be done if you see yourself as being in equal relationships with others. Thus, even as a leader, I believe I should respect the children's need of privacy. I also think that a great part of their misbehavior results from never having gotten this kind of respect, and that because of this they ended up as either submissive victims or aggressors. As I personally dislike both types of behavior, I would find it important to help them be more assertive.

As many other experienced group leaders know, resistance at the fourth session can be expected, and it should be openly discussed. However, in this particular group, the silent resistance or avoidance the members show has much to do with their culture. Part of me knows this feeling from my own early years; disobeying meant being "bad," or imposing more difficulties and suffering on others. But another part of me has matured in a culture that cherishes directness in relationships. This part feels good, and I would want to forward that to the group participants. I trust the children would be happy to express their difficulties through the structured activities, and the goals of the group would be better achieved through use of the special techniques I have discussed.

In sum, despite my long experience in counseling groups of children and adolescents in an immigrating country, such an incident could occur in my group if I failed to take cultural aspects in consideration. These group members were misleading in their response, and thus it was easy to ignore the hidden agenda. However, I should have been aware of the restrictive culture of the group members, been more sensitive to their fear of self-disclosure, and particularly I should have taken into consideration their difficulty with expressing their resistance overtly and with being assertive. Once I learned about their resistance, I had no problem with changing my agenda. I guess my past experience has helped me to find the way out of conflict, and provided me with appropriate strategies for helping these group members out as well. I trust that the structured activities and the use of the arts in therapy would lead to group participation, as well as to enhanced understanding and respect of each other's culture.

Interestingly, I could identify with the children's reaction because as a child or adolescent, I would have reacted very much like they did. This reaction would have been associated with my childhood culture. However, as a mature group leader, influenced by Israeli culture, I would strive assertively but skillfully for open communication and for more mutual understanding. Although the two cultures seem to be conflicting with each other, they are at the same time also complementing each other, and both are helpful in performing the group leadership role.

SUMMARY/ANALYSIS OF RESPONSES

As Members of This Psychoeducational Group

Identify the multicultural issues that need to be taken into consideration for you as a member.

We are given a good deal of information regarding the Asian culture in Chung's response to this question. She offers much for our consideration. She immediately challenges the use of the Inner Circle/Outer Circle technique. It is a Native American technique, and she informs us that it is inappropriate for a group comprised of Asian Americans, especially since Asian Americans would lose face and feel shame. We are made aware that disclosure is a concern for Asian Americans, since it means breaching family confidentiality in front of individuals who are not family. Disclosure is not viewed as an individual matter, since it has implications for the entire family. Chung enlightens us further by explaining that there are differences between U.S.-born and foreign-born Asian Americans, which creates a peculiar dynamic. Furthermore, she tells us that all Asians are not alike. There are differences and intraethnic relationship issues present in this group. An example she offers relates to the acculturation issues that are created between U.S.-born and foreign-born Asian Americans as evidenced by the lack of language skill knowledge and acculturation to U.S. culture by foreign-born Asians. She sees the need for the group leaders to consider the process of acculturation, the level of acculturation, the development of ethnic identity, and intergenerational, historical, and political issues within and between Asian groups.

We are given yet another Asian's perspective of the multicultural issues in the group by Sandhu, who alerts us to the ethnocentric issues that may exist as a result of the group being comprised of members of Chinese and Korean ancestry. This could mean that as an Asian Indian, he would be seen as a stranger. He also notes that interethnic Asian relations have a long history of hostilities and racial prejudice, which we are led to infer could affect this group. As a member, Sandhu is aware that issues related to his age, race, religious preference, ethnicity, gender, and intellectual ability also enter into the mix, as do the processes of multicultural transference and countertransference.

Shechtman's very approach to this question (i.e., a narrative) could be a reflection of her own culture. She reveals that she feels the ethnocentricity of the group, as she is the only Israeli member. She introduces the issue of distrust by relating it to the smile that the American coleaders wears as she greets the members, and she conveys that she just has a general lack of trust in regard to both of the coleaders.

Explain how your ethnic and cultural background affected the way you would respond as a member.

The responses to this question are as diverse as our respondents. Chung reiterates how the Inner Circle/Outer Circle technique is Native American and is culturally inappropriate for these Asian-American students. If she were to participate in this group, the technique would cause her to lose face and be shamed. She also considers the possibility that members might share outside the group with persons in the Asian-American community. Consequently, she fears others might find out about her problems, leading to her being accused of having violated Asian custom against sharing her problems with outsiders.

Chung introduces us to additional dimensions of Asian culture that affected the way she would respond. She informs us that the group members' behaviors of confrontation, taunting, and name calling are countercultural to traditional Asian values. She adds that being a first-generation Asian with English as a second language, she would identify with those who were being taunted.

Another significant aspect of Asian culture to which Chung introduces us is the tradition of viewing women as those who establish balance and harmony in the environment. As a result, she would see her role as being the one who establishes peace and explores similarities as opposed to differences among the members.

Sandhu's response to this question emphasizes the existence of intercultural differences between Asian cultures. He says that because of his Asian-Indian ancestry and unfamiliarity with Chinese and Korean cultures, he might respond with less certainty and a lack of confidence. He also believes that due to his cultural background, he might resort to intellectualizing, ignoring, or detaching from the group.

Shechtman conveys that she feels uncomfortable and that she does not like Joe's bullying nor the way the Chinese girls take advantage of the two Korean members. Perhaps her feeling for the oppressed and her dislike of aggressors is due to her own background. For her, the Korean girls are too submissive, and although she cannot identify with them, she does not feel sorry for them. Perhaps this is a reflection of her Israeli background, which taught her to be assertive. Since she views herself as one who takes responsibility, she would choose to participate in the inner circle. She says that as an Israeli, she likes being in a group, and she has expected to make American friends. Because of her Israeli background, she would be likely to take responsibility in this social situation; nevertheless, the group silence makes her feel restless, nervous, and helpless—feelings she prefers to avoid.

Explain how your ethnic and cultural background may or may not inhibit the way you respond to the situation as a member.

Chung tells us that because she is from a face-saving culture, she would be hesitant, reluctant, and resistant to any technique (i.e., Inner Circle/Outer Circle) that would lead to loss of face and bring shame to self and family. Sandhu's response to this question indicates that although he would experience anxiety or uneasy feelings about actively participating in this group (as indicated in his answer to question two), he would not be inhibited, for he believes his ethnic and cultural background would be an asset, not a limitation, in responding to this situation.

Shechtman feels confused by the situation. Her uncertainty is based on not knowing which of her cultures to share, since each is so different from the other. However, because of her Israeli background, she likes being in groups. She would choose to take part in the inner circle.

Explain how your ethnic and cultural background may have influenced your choice of the response you made over any other that you may have been considering as a member.

Chung reminds us once more that in order to save face for herself and avoid bringing shame to herself and her family, she would not join in the Inner Circle/Outer Circle technique or any exercise that would require her to disclose herself and her family to outsiders. Therefore, she would choose to meet the Asian coleader privately. She would also try to establish peace within the group and explore member similarities, not differences, as this is often the role ascribed to Asian women.

Sandhu's background experiences included the anguish of ethnic prejudice while growing up in a caste system with religious differences. Consequently, he feels an empathy both for the Korean students and for Debbie with her bias and hatred toward them.

From Shechtman's narrative, we learn that she was contemplating leaving the group. However, to do so would not be like her, since she never gives up on any task that she has started. She does not want to feel like a loser for chickening out. Perhaps this stems from her Israeli background, which taught her to be assertive and responsible. Therefore, she would join the circle; as an Israeli, she likes being in a group and being with other people.

As a result of the response you chose, identify the consequences you might anticipate as a member.

We are treated to three very illuminating answers to this question. Two of our experts anticipate negative responses, which the third is more optimistic about the consequences of her choices. Chung expects her response to place her in a double bind. In refusing to participate, she would be disrespecting her elders and authority figures as represented by the coleaders. Therefore, she would be going against her cultural values, and she would be afraid that her parents would be told of her disobedience, which would bring shame and loss of face to her family. Conversely, if she were to participate, she would again be in noncompliance with Asian customs, and the consequences would be the same.

Chung also expects that the leaders would be upset about her refusal to participate in the Inner Circle/Outer Circle technique. However, should the leaders turn the responsibility for working through group issues over to the members, thereby giving authority to the members, she projects that she would have to rethink her behaviors for fear that the members would turn on her, especially if she had tried to diffuse the negative behavior of the other members. She foresees the negative behaviors taking the form of teasing her and sees herself being alienated from the group, which would lead to her becoming more withdrawn and secretive.

The consequences Sandhu anticipates are no more optimistic than Chung's. He sees himself becoming a victim of xenophobia because he is the only Asian-

Indian person in the group. He also expects prejudice to be present and that he will be singled out as a target due to the nature of the group's cultural dynamics. Sandhu introduces the issues of age (he is older), accent, and his being from an outer group as reasons why the other members might have fear and disdain for him. Furthermore, he thinks it is possible that the other members might behave indifferently toward him due to his cultural background.

Shechtman is more optimistic about the anticipated consequences to her responses than either Chung or Sandhu. Shechtman believes that her participation in the inner circle might lead to making some friends. In addition, she believes the members would respond well to her story about the Gulf War, and through her telling of the story, they would get to know and like her. Telling the story would enable her to share her feelings related to when she was victimized. As another consequence of sharing, the withdrawn members might be encouraged to join her and to speak up. She hopes all this would lead to her being in a position to confront the members about the bullying.

From your position as a member, explain what the most glaring or outstanding aspect was of the situation which impacted you from your ethnic and cultural orientation.

Chung cites the Inner Circle/Outer Circle technique as the most significant aspect of the situation because of its cultural inappropriateness. Another outstanding aspect for Chung is the group dynamics of U.S.-born versus foreign-born Asian Americans, as well as the ever-present issues regarding the levels of acculturation within the Asian-American community.

Sandhu highlights that his cultural and ethnic background would be a restricting factor in his developing close or working relationships with the others in this group. Another glaring aspect of this situation for him is the fact that the second-generation students harbor negative feelings against other members whose parents emigrated from other cultures; thus, for him the legacy of hate and fear continues.

The most glaring aspect of this situation for Shechtman regards her being an Israeli and Jewish in a group comprised predominantly of Asian Americans. She describes how others refer to the Israeli as "aggressors," which is what led her to that conclusion.

As Leaders of This Psychoeducational Group

If this incident would not occur in your group, explain why it would not.

Each of our leaders gave reasons why the incident might occur and why it might not. Chung first explains why it would not occur in her group. She would not use the Native-American Inner Circle/Outer Circle technique in a group that consists only of Asian Americans, since it would be culturally inappropriate to do so. On the other hand, she believes the situation could happen due to the long-standing sociopolitical history of Asian Americans.

Sandhu sees that this incident could occur due to the lack of respect or tolerance among adolescents for ethnic and racial differences (diversity). In his view, all persons practice either positive or negative prejudice. In this situation, the prejudice is negative. Sandhu, however, would not expect the students to disclose family matters in front of group members. As an Asian, he understands that disclosing family matters in public can bring shame to family members.

From Shechtman we learn that she might avoid such an incident in her group because she would not ask members to self-disclose at this stage of the group's development (she sees that as being inappropriate), especially when personal disclosure might be associated with shame or guilt. She would first work to establish group cohesiveness and to establish a feeling of safety. Shechtman does see the possibility that this incident could occur if she failed to consider the cultural diversity of the members.

Identify the multicultural issues that need to be taken into consideration for you as a leader.

Here Chung discusses a number of multicultural issues related to Asian Americans: (1) values regarding self-disclosure and possible shame and loss of face; (2) respect for adults or authority figures, and accompanying obedience and compliance; and (3) importance of the interrelationship between the individual and the family (i.e., the impact the individual's behavior has on the family). These issues could inhibit individuals from disclosing information for fear of bringing shame and loss of face to the family.

Chung also discusses the the inter- and intraethnic group relations issues that could exist among the members, offering a number of examples that reflect these issues. Some of the perceptions and attitudes of Asian Americans toward different Asian groups relate to their sociopolitical and historical experiences; for instance, Japanese and Chinese people have views of each other based on the history of war between these two groups. Because the various Asian American groups are so diverse, cultural considerations on multiple levels need to be taken into account. An intragroup dimension, for example, includes the need to be sensitive to the differences between mainland Chinese, Hong Kong Chinese, Taiwanese Chinese, and so on. Likewise, there are issues surrounding cultural attitudes related to U.S.-born versus foreign-born Asian Americans and their levels of acculturation, as well as intergenerational issues.

Sandhu also points to historical and sociopolitical factors that are significant from his perspective as an Asian American. His response reinforces Chung's comments about the importance of these factors. One multicultural issue he would anticipate being present in this group is resistance from the Asian members due to his being an Asian Indian. He is candid in stating that he, too, would have to guard against being adversely influenced by his own thoughts, beliefs, and feelings toward Chinese and Korean people, since he was raised in India where political propaganda about these groups has been widespread since India and China fought each other in 1962.

Reading through Shechtman's narrative, we find she has identified a number of multicultural issues in this situation. She cites that it is important to recognize that the members are from collectivistic societies and to be sensitive to the values and norms by which they are guided. Another important issue regards self-disclosure. Given the cultural makeup of the group (i.e., that members are from restrictive cultures), it would be culturally insensitive (inappropriate) to expect members to self-disclose. Finally, because she comes from a Jewish-Israeli background, she is not familiar with all the ethnic and cultural issues presented by Asian Americans; therefore, she would take cues from her Asian coleader.

Explain how your ethnic and cultural background affected the way you would respond as a leader.

Chung believes that because of her experiences as a first-generation child of immigrant parents who was raised in a traditional Chinese household, she has a deep understanding of all the Asian cultural issues in the group. She offers examples of the issues that influenced the way she would intervene as a leader. First is the tension between U.S.-born and foreign-born Asians, which would lead her to focus on the students' cultural similarities and similar experiences. There are also issues of acculturation; the students want to be accepted and to fit into the mainstream culture. Tensions between Meghan and her sister, Victoria, suggest issues of ethnic identity for Asian Americans for living in a white ethnocentric society. The issue of confidentiality is another issue that is critical to Asian Americans. Finally, Chung realizes the significance for Asians of honoring elders and respecting authority, as well as the need to save face. Therefore, she would establish her credibility as a counselor by disclosing first in order to help the members feel safe and to encourage them to follow her lead.

Again we find parallels between Sandhu's response to this question and Chung's. Sandhu informs us that as an Asian Indian, he shares several values with the Asian members of the group. Foremost is the reluctance to share family matters with strangers. Realizing, as does Chung, that Asians are part of a face-saving culture, he would disclose his own family experiences first in order to help the Asian members get involved in the group process.

Shechtman recognizes that a lack of cultural sensitivity could lead to an incident such as this one. Because she comes from a Jewish-Israeli background, she is grateful for her Asian-American coleader, who can help her become more culturally aware.

Explain how your ethnic and cultural background may or may not inhibit the way you respond to the situation as a leader.

Asian culture emphasizes maintaining balance and harmony. Therefore, given the existing situation in the group, Chung believes she would be inhibited from being confrontational and direct. However, from her response to question three, we know she would establish her credibility as a counselor by being first to disclose and would rely on her experiences as an Asian to help her bring about harmony and balance in the group.

Sandhu, on the other hand, does not see himself being inhibited by his background. Instead, he expects that his Asian-American background would be an asset. He believes it would help him understand the students' world-views, values, and respect for authority.

Shechtman discusses her Israeli culture supports being straightforward and assertive, and how she has learned to deal with conflicts more openly. She acknowledges that this approach is different from that of the Asian culture. Additionally, she owns that she is not all that familiar with the participants' cultural background; consequently, leading this group would be a bit different from her experiences of leading other adolescent groups.

Explain how your ethnic and cultural background may have influenced your choice of the response you made over any other that you may have been considering as a leader.

As an Asian American, Chung quickly eliminates being confrontational and direct from her consideration of possible responses to the situation. Since her culture supports maintaining balance and harmony, her interventions would be focused on understanding the social context and relationships of the students rather than on solving the immediate problem. She would be the first to disclose personal information in order to help the Asian members feel safe and comfortable with her as a leader.

Like Chung, Sandhu relies on his background as an Asian American in determining how he would address this situation as a leader. He also would avoid being direct and confrontational. He would use interventions that would allow members to save face and avoid shaming self and family. Additionally, he would do some pregroup consulting with parents.

Although Shechtman's Israeli background would make her inclined at first to intervene in a direct manner and to have the members self-disclose, she rejects that intervention and opts to defer to what she learned from her early childhood experiences. These experiences taught her to obey adults, shy away from confrontation, and be good and act mature. Armed with the sensitivity gleaned from her early experiences as a child in a Jewish family, Shechtman says she would respect the members' Asian cultural background and employ a less confrontational intervention in this situation.

As a result of the response you chose, identify the consequences you might anticipate as a leader.

Chung offers us a host of possible consequences, beginning with the possibility that transference could be heightened due to cultural respect for her authority. She expects that the group members would not deal with the situation directly, but would respond to her as the elder in order to gain approval. Out of respect for her, they might not raise issues or confront each other for fear of offending her or causing her embarrassment or shame as an Asian authority figure. She also notes the possibility that members could be inhibited about sharing because they would be wary of her connections to their families and communities.

Sandhu is succinct in his response to this question. He expects positive effects to come from his presession meetings with members and pregroup consultation sessions with the students' parents.

Shechtman forecasts that as a result of using indirect methods such as bibliotherapy and art therapy, members might feels like they can share without having to disclose personal secrets. These experiences might eventually lead members to share more intimate information about themselves.

From your position as a leader, explain what the most glaring or outstanding aspect was of the situation which impacted you from your ethnic and cultural orientation.

Chung's response to this question as a leader is the same as her response as a member. The most glaring aspect of the situation for her was the employment of the culturally inappropriate Inner Circle/Outer Circle Native-American technique.

Sandhu reacts to the acting-out behaviors of the children. Such behaviors are not the norm for Asian children, nor is openly expressing anger typical. Asian children generally are more introverted and cautious.

Shechtman sees the most glaring aspects of this situation as being the differences between the two cultures—Asian and Israeli. As an Israeli leader, she would make necessary adjustments in order to accommodate the students' need for an indirect approach to self-disclosure.

Based on the composition of this group, what multicultural issues (etic and emic) need to be taken into consideration as the incident is addressed in group?

Chung identifies the etic issues as being related to the need to establish trust and a safe environment, and to ensure confidentiality. Sandu identifies the etic issue as the members' need to love and to feel loved. Shechtman's narrative implies that she would agree with these two Asian-American leaders about the etic issues that are present.

The emic issues that exist in the group for Chung revolve around the Asian-American cultural value of saving face and not bringing shame to self and family. She also considers the need to avoid open and direct conflict. Sandhu agrees with Chung that the emic issue relates to the Asian-American cultural need to save face and not shame self or family, but he also includes his own Asian-Indian issues with regard to the Chinese, and vice versa. Shechtman, too, identifies the emic issues as being specific to Asian culture, including the fear of self-disclosure, the reluctance to express resistance overtly and to be assertive, and the avoidance of open conflict. Shechtman identifies additional issues as well: the students' need for mutual respect and unconditional acceptance, and their need for a safe environment in which to express themselves freely.

Counseling/ Therapy Group Vignette #1

The Assertiveness Group and the Bomb

You are a counselor in private practice. You have brought together a group of eight men and women who responded to your notice that you were forming a group that will help them become more assertive.

- Christina is 32. She was born in Greece and immigrated to the United States with her family when she was 3. She is single and lives with her aging parents. She has four siblings, all of whom are married and do not live nearby.

- Cho is 25. He immigrated from Vietnam after his parents died. He is a waiter and he attends college part-time. He is single.

- Sam is 29. He is engaged to the vice president of a successful cosmetics company that manufactures products for African-American women. Six months ago he became a casualty of a corporate downsizing.

- Malik is 33. He and his family immigrated to the United States from Saudi Arabia. He has fallen in love with a woman whom his parents do not approve of and he feels torn.

- Sophia is 27. She is a second-generation Polish American. On the eve of her wedding, her fiancé revealed that he was gay and could not marry her.

- Joelle is 31. She is married and has three children. You are the only person who is aware that she has fallen in love with a woman she met in her aerobics class.

- Chloe is 23. She has fallen in love with her boss who came to the United States from Turkey. She knows that the only way she can marry him is to convert from Catholicism to the Islamic faith. She per-ceives that she has nowhere to turn for help. Her brother is a Catholic priest and her parents are very devoted to their faith.

- Sohe is 31. She has a Ph.D in computer technology from a university in India. She is single. She arrived in the United States alone with a position in an established computer technology firm. She never dated while she was in India unless she was chaperoned. Now she has had a number of offers to date, but she has felt too uneasy to accept them.

This is the third session. In the first two sessions, most of the group members' efforts were spent simply getting acquainted. During the second session, Cho spoke mostly about how he felt after he arrived in the United States and how much effort it has taken him to learn the American way of life. Sam revealed how hard it was to be engaged to his fiancé while he is still out of work. He feels he has fallen into the stereotype of black males and he hates it. Christina related to Sam's feelings as she expressed how she felt about the guilt she harbored for wanting to leave her parents and have her own life. After all, she was the last child to be living at home, and she feels she must follow custom, which is to tend after her aging parents. These disclosures marked the tone of the second session. As the session came to a close, you noted to yourself how Malik, Chloe, and Joelle had remained quiet and kept to themselves. They appeared to be listening to the others, but did not share themselves as openly.

As the third session gets underway, the three who were most verbal in the previous session appear to be withdrawn. Christina is looking down into the palms of her hands, Sam is fumbling with his watch, and Cho is sitting with his legs crossed at the ankles and is staring off into space. The others are engaged in superficial chatter with the exception of Chloe, who appears to be ready to burst. Before you can make any intervention, she blurts out how she feels the group is just like her family. With a strong and high-pitched voice, she recalls how session two went. She states that three persons shared important and meaningful "stuff"; that the rest of the group did nothing to support them; that this is precisely how she feels in her family; and that they all knew how much she loved her boss and how torn she was, yet none of them reached out to her or tried to help! Chloe's outburst has the affect of an atomic bomb. All the members appear to be stunned. You are left to deal with the effects her outcry has had upon the group.

BOGUSIA MOLINA'S REACTION AS A MEMBER OF THIS COUNSELING/THERAPY GROUP

Identify the multicultural issues that need to be taken into consideration for you as a member.

It seems like we are grappling with trust and acculturation issues. The acculturation issues seem to be embedded in the experiences of isolation, loss, and disapproval. It seems that the group members are wondering: (a) Is it safe here to address feelings and thoughts that our cultures have taught us to be

silent about? and (b) How do we cope with acculturation—on one hand wanting to maintain the deeply seeded roots of our culture while at the same time
wanting to open the wings and explore the new endings to stories?

Here are some questions that would come to my mind: When I become
more assertive, what impact will that have on my family? Will I still be perceived as a Polish-American woman, or will I be categorized as
"Americanized"? As a member, I would be asking myself: What is my part in
the concern expressed by Chloe regarding not feeling heard and supported? I
would also ask myself: Did you listen to others enough? I would want to check
that out and make sure that while we honor our differences, we have a strong
group rule that emphasizes listening to each other so that disagreements will
not become contests, where problems go unresolved. As a woman, it would be
very important for me to address issues of oppression, especially the gender
oppression that most of the group members seem to have experienced.

As a group member, I could relate to the struggles shared by other group
members. I would hope that being able to relate to others would help us as a
group to offer support to each other. For example:

- *Christina,* I would think, must be feeling lonely and guilty. On the one
  hand, she wants to take care of her parents, but she also wants to open up
  her wings, fly away from the nest, and explore the world. In my culture,
  children are expected to take care of their parents as well. When children
  move away, families have ways of "teaching" adult children about the
  mistake they have made. The mistake could be considered the decision to
  move away and, as a result, not taking care of parents daily. The "teaching" techniques may include forgetting to invite adult children to family
  events like weddings, not keeping in touch, and so on, yet being angry at
  the adult children for not partaking actively in the family events. To me,
  Christina needs support. As a member, I would want to reach out to her.
  I would want to say something like: "Christina, I can relate to your struggles. I experience you as someone who so deeply cares for your family,
  does not want to lose them, and at the same time wants to take care of
  your own needs."

- *Cho,* an immigrant who is working as a waiter, probably feels lonely, isolated, and disconnected from his relatives. I would wonder if he has family here in the states, or friends who can help him regain the sense of
  kinship. I could relate to his experience, as my family suddenly moved to
  the United States. I felt like a tree whose roots were ripped off and
  smashed into a totally different soil. Cho may feel like a man with no place
  to call home. Here in the states, he may be ostracized, but going back
  home to Vietnam may not be safe. His life has been rained on with a lot
  of pain. I would want to find a way to relate to him and find a way to celebrate his successes. I would do so by saying something like: "Cho, I
  admire you for the courage you have in learning a new language, attending school, and working, in spite of all the obstacles that came your way."

- *Sam* seems to be dealing with a loss as well. I recall when we first moved
  here and we barely spoke English. My mom was pregnant and my dad

suddenly was laid off. He was horrified at the possibility of not getting hired again due to his ethnic background and age. I would want to find a way to connect with Sam and let him know how painful and scary his situation must be. I would want to be supercautious with relating to Sam. I would not want to underestimate the challenges experienced by African Americans, who by skin appearance are an obvious minority, while I am not (not until I speak). I would relate to him by saying something like: "I admire your courage to share the painful experience of job loss with us. Such oppressive events can invite depression into our lives. Although I can relate to your challenges, I have no idea how painful it must be to grapple with oppression experienced by African-American males. I am impressed by your willingness to talk with us about your experiences, and I am wondering how I can help you."

- *Malik*, too, is dealing with family pressures. The pain he is experiencing must be enormous—it is like he is stuck between choosing his family and the girlfriend whom he loves. I would be thinking he and his girlfriend might have a bumpy road to follow in their intercultural relationship. Yet, this could be such a growth-promoting opportunity. I could relate to him, as my husband is from a different cultural background than I am and I recall vividly how difficult it has been to cope with family and community pressures. I would respond to him by saying something like: "You seem to feel trapped because you love your family and a woman who may not be welcomed by them."

- *Sophia*—I could relate to her struggles. Most likely we come from the same culture. Although I would want to know more about her, I come from the mountains; I am a proud Cieszynianka (a region in the Beskidy mountains of Poland, with a unique dialect and customs). If she is from an urban community like Warsaw and part of the "noble blood," she may be very stoic and under a lot of pressure to keep the pain and sadness under control. Her experiences may be very different from the ones experienced in my region where, for centuries, time-honored dedication to the land prevailed. After all, we were Polanie, a tribal group, meaning people of the land. As a result of oppression experienced from the surrounding kingdoms, many of the traditions died out. My heart goes out to her, because regardless of her cultural experiences, an overall unified Polish tradition regarding weddings prevails. Weddings are not only about couples but involve families, extended relatives, neighbors, and villages, and they last two to three days. Even Polish Americans usually find a way to celebrate for a couple of days. Weddings are carefully planned and take a major ritualistic and financial commitment. Her family might remember that forever and could blame her for the losses. Polish families tend to be community-oriented to the point that the image of the family presented to the whole community seems to be more important than the individual family member. I catch myself recalling Polish phrases, like *ale wstyd* (what a shame)—a phrase that her family might fervently use. I would want to respond to her by providing support and assurance that it is not her fault that the wedding did not take place. I would want to say: "To nie jest twoja wina" (it is not your fault). I would want to convey empathy and say something like: "You feel so hurt because what seemed to have a promising takeoff, suddenly crashed."

- *Joelle* is dealing with losses, too, I think. She may have experienced identity losses stemming from not being safe, and perhaps in not being openly gay. She takes on a hidden identity like many Polish people who have felt forced to change their names and to hide their "Polishness." I would want to make sure that, as a group, we have established a norm that respect for diversity will be conveyed, including respecting gay people. I would hope that such a norm would give her hope in disclosing her struggles. I would respond to her indirectly, I think, by saying: "Being gay in our society is still so unsafe. I hope our group will be the exception where everyone will feel they have permission to be who they are without feeling like their identity must be sacrificed. I want to make sure that our group has norms of respect for diversity—both hidden and obvious.

- *Chloe* might be feeling sad and angry about having to give up a major part of who she is, to marry someone of a different religion. I would want to know where the pressures are stemming from: Are they coming from her boss and a lover, his family, or all parts of the system? That would be a tough one for me, as I am aware that my feminist bones would shiver. I would want to tell her: "If he is pressuring you to change religion, and it does not feel right to you, maybe it is not meant to be. How is that going to affect you and your life together with him when you will be sucked into the cycle of oppression?"

- *Sohe*—I think she would be my hero, and I would feel a strong connection to her. I would admire her accomplishments, while I could relate to her regarding dating. I remember the shock my parents survived when I told them I was dating someone they had not met, and the mixed feelings I had: On one hand, I felt empowered for making my own choices, but then the guilt trip kicked in. I would want to say to her: "I can sense you wavering. Entering a new territory of relationships can be exciting and scary."

Explain how your ethnic and cultural background affected the way you would respond as a member.

I am aware that the connections I would feel toward other members stem from different yet shared experiences of losses, some real, some potential. I am also aware that it would be important for me to connect and be there for others—a value deeply embedded in my culture. We have a saying, "When a visitor is in your house, God is in your house." My grandmother deeply fostered in me this belief. Each group member then becomes the visitor, a Godlike individual who needs to be treated with dignity and generosity. Yet, I am also aware that the being there for others, according to my family cultural background, would mean bringing in good homemade food and cheering people up—laugh, sing, dance, maybe even cry a little—but do not talk about the real feelings of loss. However, living in a relatively democratic society and attending high school with a commitment to feminism, fighting oppression, and the theology of liberation, along with my training as a counselor, has helped me become more comfortable with the discomfort of dealing with painful feelings. My culture is very group-oriented, so as a group member, I feel like a fish in water. I am aware that what I consider as my Polish culture may not be representative of experiences of other Polish people. First, I have a strong loyalty and pride of coming from the mountain region that has strong folkloric roots and identity referred to as Cieszynianie. Although most of us speak standard Polish, the Cieszynian dialect is very unique. We have unique rituals, songs, dances, and even traditional clothing through which one can identify us. For hundreds of years we maintained time-honored traditions that emerged from the Polanie tribe. As a result, my cultural experiences were enriched. For example, growing up with these experiences allows me to connect to others without worrying about time. So, if other group members feel like sharing stories and using songs and music, I am very comfortable with it and can easily lose my sense of time. It is the relationships that matter. However, the general Polish norms focus more on structure, awareness of time, and completing tasks in orderly fashion. So, planning ahead and maintaining structure are second nature to me. I can see myself taking time to relate to each member, regardless of how much time it takes.

Explain how your ethnic and cultural background may or may not inhibit the way you respond to the situation as a member.

I think wanting to connect with others could be very helpful, yet I would also want to be cautious, as some members may feel like I do not understand their unique struggles. In addition, I would experience quite a bit of anxiety, stemming from a strong history of more modern Polish cultural norms that do not promote dialogues based on win-win solutions for men and women, as they are embedded in oppressive hierarchies. As an individual, I can be very persistent (or more honestly put, stubborn), and I would need to watch that in my interactions with others. Stubbornness has helped Poles overcome numerous challenges in life—after all, we maintained our language for over 200 years, although we were forbidden to use it. So the richness of cultural ways can also be my weakness. However, my responses would also be a reflection of my personality. I could imagine myself asking the group: It does not seem like we feel safe here; what do we need to do to feel safe? I would focus on sharing with the group what I need to feel safe, and on sharing with the group what I could do to help the group feel safe.

Explain how your ethnic and cultural background may have influenced your choice of the response you made over any other that you may have been considering as a member.

I think that understanding my cultural experiences would help me understand the struggles of the Polish-American woman. If one did not know that a Polish wedding is a three-day ritual, one might minimize the loss that Sophia and her family may be experiencing at numerous levels. So, I might be very sensitive to her situation. However, she may have a different reaction. Although Poland now covers a small geographic region, there are many regional differences, so I am not sure if Sophia would want to connect with me. My cultural background has taught me to be sensitive to the suffering of other individuals. So, tuning into one's experiences is a natural process. As I reflect on the responses I might have, I notice that I tend to tune into experiences of loss and find it so important to validate those experiences. Furthermore, I would want to be very sensitive to other invisible dynamics regarding diversity. For example, would someone with a disability feel safe enough in the group? I would wonder the same thing about religious and sexual orientations. Once again, I attribute my values to my grandmother who often said, "People follow different paths while searching for God." A person with culture understands that and respects that. So, in my culture, even the term *culture* implies respecting the ways of others. She was one of the best multicultural teachers I had. So, chances are, in my interactions with others, I would want to make sure that everyone feels respected.

As a result of the response you chose, identify the consequences you might anticipate as a member.

I think some group members might like to focus on trust and might feel relieved that their losses are not a "hidden" topic. I would hope that the shared experiences would allow for the universality to emerge, thus leading to more trust. Others may feel taken aback that I might be violating my cultural norms and inviting them to do the same with their cultural norms. I think it would also depend on how well the group members were prepared for group participation. I get a feeling that we as a group would connect more and feel more relieved once we would give ourselves permission to deal with the losses and the challenges of grappling with intercultural relations. In the process, we would start weaving a supportive community where the stories of "happily ever after" could be reconstructed.

I can also anticipate some potential tension regarding gender issues. It would be a growth-promoting event for all the members. To me, it seems that we need to start the weaving of different endings to stories of oppression of women that often get camouflaged by culture. An example of a cultural camouflage is depicted in the following hypothetical case. Assume a woman named Kasia cooks traditional meals and takes care of her children while her husband, Juan, shows to his male relatives around town. Juan has assured her they will be back in time to start cooking together, but Juan does not show up. Kasia is angry. Juan arrives several hours late, assuming dinner is ready, and tells Kasia, "Sorry I am a couple hours late, but I am Hispanic." So, in this group, I would anticipate that we would grapple with the challenges of gender issues camouflaged by our cultures.

From your position as a member, explain what the most glaring or outstanding aspect was of the situation which impacted you from your ethnic and cultural orientation.

I can imagine that my heart would be beating fast as Chloe was fervently sharing her feelings. I would think about times when I felt like that in my family, when I or my relatives felt unheard, and times when my friends from various cultures have experienced similar struggles. I would be worried, however, if the focus was on blame without looking at the responsibility that each one of us has for making sure it is a safe group. I would want to address it in a form of a dialogue. My culture, I guess, and my personality would kick in, as I would not want to let go of the topic of trust and creating a safe environment. I can imagine saying something like: "The norms of silence and being unheard are toxic for everyone; we all need to take responsibility for creating a safe group." I would think to myself, "Why does there have to be so much pain when a person wants to be assertive and kind-hearted, when a woman wants to be loving yet not subservient? There have been enough tears of sadness; we must do something differently. Our invisible strands from the past weave our web of life now. I am just a strand in it, wishing we could foster the strengths of our cultural past while changing some of the history." I would admire Chloe for her courage to speak up, and I would share that with her. I would also ask her whether she felt she was heard and understood, and what we as a group could do. This could really help us move to a deeper level. How the group leader handled the situation would play a major role in my feeling that the group could work through this versus a feeling that this group will be like so many families where disagreements become contests, problems are left with no solutions, and resentments become the secrets that everyone senses yet tiptoes around. I would trust that although we might stumble through and our rhythm might not be pretty, we would find a way of creating a different ending to the discouraged stories. I am aware that, even as a member, I might sound like a leader at times.

BOGUSIA MOLINA'S REACTION AS A LEADER OF THIS COUNSELING/THERAPY GROUP

If this type of incident would not occur in your group, explain why it would not.

I believe a similar incident could occur. Group work is a dynamic process embedded in art and science. Although each group experience is unique, like a melody, the process is perhaps like chords, pretty much the same each time.

Identify the multicultural issues that need to be taken into consideration for you as a leader.

As a leader, I would be thinking about the group stages and how cultural issues influence the rhythm of the stages. Understanding the group stages would help me understand the group dynamics. This group seems to be moving out of the forming stage and will soon be embracing the challenges of storming. Storming (Gladding, 1999), which is frequently characterized by increased conflict, has arrived at the group's doorstep. The conflict may be magnified, as the group members seem to have learned that it may not be safe to trust others. The group members may be wondering if it will really be safe to share their thoughts and feelings. The conflict, I think, would need to be addressed, and negotiations leading to win-win outcomes for everyone in the group would need to emerge.

In addition to the group stage information, my theoretical orientation influences how I perceive the multicultural dynamics of this group. I am a systemic person who values an integrated approach to counseling. So, as I ponder the issues of this group, Donigian and Malnati's (1997) questions echo in my mind: Who are we as a group? Who are the members? Who am I as a leader? As a group, we seem to be grappling with acculturation issues and trust issues. Each person in this group seems to have experienced isolation, oppression, and rejection. Each person brings unique strengths and perspectives along with unique multicultural experiences. Those experiences seem to weave a mosaic throughout the multiple layers of human interactions. The weaving process may be rocky until the conflict is addressed. We are just strands in the weaving of the web of life, yet what we choose to do affects us, our group, and our families. The group members may also be grappling with acculturation challenges. For example, they may be revisiting and renegotiating boundaries and expectations defined by their cultural lenses. Their own cultures, perhaps, have taught them to be silent about their painful and difficult experiences. For women, especially, this message might have been delivered very fervently. In addition, the "macro" culture that they are a part of might have plagued their hopes and silenced their concerns.

In addition to the systemic perspective, I tend to focus on the constructivist, Adlerian, Gestalt, and psychodrama orientations. So I see the issues as normal struggles of individuals who have been perhaps discouraged as a result of unhealthy systems. The discouragement might have invited anxiety, oppression, loneliness, and depression into the group members' lives. In the process, their voices were silenced. As a leader, I would be asking myself: What is my part in Chloe's feelings of not being heard? Did I listen to her and others enough? I would want to check this out with her and others. First, however, I would ask myself: How will the intervention influence the members, the group, and me as the leader? (Hulse-Killacky, Killacky, & Donigian, 2001).

I can relate to each group member, but as a leader I would provide sporadic examples of how I can relate to each person. However, I would ask group members to identify which members they could relate to, so we could develop a supportive web and decrease their feelings of isolation. I would hope that the group members would experience universality and instillation of hope (Yalom, 1985), and in the process, the search for rediscovery of their skills, talents, and strengths would emerge. It appears to me that all the group members are grappling with challenges of rejection, alienation, and oppression. Techniques associated with psychodrama and Gestalt might be helpful in providing members with an opportunity to address them. I am in the process of learning more about the Cherokee healing Inner/Outer Circle (Garrett, Garrett, & Brotherton, 2001) and believe that the Inner/Outer Circle would be an excellent technique that would allow the members an opportunity to experience community support. In the process, the talents that each group member brings would foster the healing experiences of all the group members.

As a leader, I would want to be aware of issues that individuals are grappling with, as well as how the group as a system can assist in addressing those issues. I would ask our group: How did isolation and feeling not heard arrive at our group's doorstep? This approach could help group members feel liberated from the systemic challenges without negative labels. Then we could focus as a group on solutions. How, as a group, do we invite connectedness? How do we help each other discover paths that lead to harmony while grappling with the richness and challenges of multicultural relationships? Those are some of the questions that the constructivist views would prompt me to ask.

In addition, there are some intercultural issues that group members might find it helpful to address. Following are some of the possibilities for each of the group members.

- *Christina*, I would think, must be feeling lonely and guilty. On one hand, she wants to take care of her parents, but she also wants to open up her wings, fly away from the nest, and explore the world. To me, Christina needs support. As a leader, I would want to reach out to her. I would want to say something like: "Christina, I get a feeling that this group can relate to your struggles. I experience you as someone who deeply cares for your family, does not want to lose them, and at the same time wants to take care of your own needs. The *philotino* (love of honor) flows deeply within you." I would be thinking to myself how hard it must be for a woman who most likely experienced a life designed by patriarchal rules emphasizing the good of the family. However, the "good" is defined only by men, and women have no voice (Moskos, 1989). I would want to make sure that in this group, she would have a voice and she would be able to rexperience primary family dynamics and macrosystemic dynamics by deconstructing the dominant messages of oppression (Semmler & Williams, 2000).
- *Cho*, an immigrant who is working as a waiter, probably feels lonely, isolated, and disconnected from his relatives. I would wonder if he has family here in the states, or friends who can help him regain the sense of kinship. Cho may feel like a man with no place to call home. Here in the states, he may be ostracized, but going back home to Vietnam may not be safe. He might have been revictimized by the forced exodus and the potential racism that he will experience in the United States. His life has been rained on with a lot of pain. I would want to find a way to relate to him and find a way to celebrate his successes. Encouragement (Adler, as cited by Corey, 1996) could be so empowering for him, I think. I would encourage him by saying something like: "Cho, I admire you for the courage you have in learning a new language, attending school, and working in spite of all the obstacles that came your way." I would also ask the other group members to share ways in which they have experienced Cho's courage in our group. In addition, I would explore with him his potential value of

worshipping his ancestors (Leung & Boehnlein, 1996). I would invite him to share with the group stories about his ancestors. The group could become the "audience" for the worshipping. In this case, the psychodrama techniques might be helpful to Cho and the group members, who would have an opportunity to make contributions to others, in accordance with a value shared by all the members.

- *Sam* seems to be dealing with a loss as well. I would want to find a way to connect with Sam and let him know how painful and scary his situation must be. I would want to be supercautious in relating to Sam. I would not want to underestimate the challenges experienced by African Americans (Baldwin, 1980), who by skin appearance are an obvious minority, while I am not (until I speak). I would relate to him by saying something like: "I admire your courage to share the painful experience of job loss with us." Such oppressive events can invite depression into our lives. Although I can relate to your challenges, I have no idea how painful it must be to grapple with the oppression experienced by African-American males. I am impressed by your willingness to talk with us about your experiences." Guided imagery, associated with Gestalt techniques (Latner, 1973), might be an activity I would try with Sam's and the group's permission. For exam- ple, he could imagine walking and having "trashy" massages thrown at him. He might be asked to share with the group how he was inducted into feeling unworthy. Next, he would be asked to use a firm voice and act out "throwing out the garbage." The group could become the chorus, chant- ing, "Don't catch this trash; you are capable, productive, and will find a way to make meaningful contributions to our society."

- *Malik,* too, is dealing with family pressures. The pain he is experiencing must be enormous—it is like he is stranded between choosing his family and the girlfriend whom he loves. I would be thinking he and his girlfriend might have a bumpy road to follow in their intercultural relationship. Yet, this could be such a growth-promoting opportunity. I would respond to him by saying something like: "You seem to feel trapped because you love your family and a woman of whom they do not approve. That is a heavy load to carry." I would convey a lot of empathy for him and would be very cautious in moving toward action. I might ask him, "How did isolation arrive at your doorstep?" I would invite him to externalize his problem by identifying the challenges of oppression within the systems, rather than pathology within himself (Semmler & Williams, 2000). Being aware of the communication styles among Arab families as described by Sharabi (1988), I am aware that the hierarchical instead of horizontal patterns might be deeply embedded in his family system. I would delicately invite him to share with the group the wishes he might have for being heard and understood.

- *Sophia's* struggles—We come from the same culture, most likely. Although I would want to know more about her, I come from the mountains; I am a proud Cieszynianka (a region in the Beskidy mountains of Poland, with a unique dialect and customs). If she is from an urban community like

Warsaw and part of the "noble blood," she may be very stoic and under a lot of pressure to keep the pain and sadness under control. She may not even perceive me as a real Polish person due to my roots. My heart goes out to her, especially if she comes from a traditional Polish background where weddings are not only about couples, but involve families, extended relatives, neighbors, and villages, and last for two to three days. Weddings are carefully planned and require a major financial commitment. Her family might remember that forever and could blame her for the losses. Holding grudges is not uncommon (Folwarski & Morganoff, 1996). I catch myself recalling Polish phrases like *ale wstyd* (what a shame)—a phrase that her family might fervently use. I would want to respond to her by providing support and assurance that it is not her fault that the wedding did not take place. I would want to say *to nie jest twoja wina* (it is not your fault). I would want to convey empathy and say something like: "You feel so hurt because what seemed to have a promising takeoff suddenly crashed." Some of the Gestalt techniques might be helpful in identifying a person with whom she feels comfortable. She could then tell that person whatever she would like to tell her fiancé and her family (Latner, 1973).

- *Joelle* is dealing with losses, too, I think. She may have experienced identity losses stemming from not being safe, and perhaps in not being openly gay. She takes on a hidden identity like many Polish people who have felt forced to change their names to hide their "Polishness." I would want to make sure that as a group, we have established a norm that respect of diversity will be conveyed, including respecting gay people. Hopefully, that would eventually give her hope in disclosing her struggles. I would respond to her indirectly, I think, by saying, "Being gay in our society is still so unsafe. I hope our group will be the exception where everyone will feel they have permission to be who they are without feeling like their identity must be sacrificed." I would want to make sure that this was a strong norm, leading to an increased trust level. I would hope. I would want to dialogue with the group about invisible differences and the importance of making sure that when we really know we are, we will continue to honor each other.

- *Chloe* might be feeling sad angry about having to give up a major part of who she is to marry someone of a differenct religion. I would want to know where the pressures are stemming from: Are they coming from her boss and a lover, his family, or all parts of the system? That would be a tough one for me, as I am aware that my feminist bones would shiver. I would need to monitor my energy, and I would pay close attention to my nonverbals and hers. I might say, "I can sense a lot of pain. If your eyes and ears could talk, what would they say?" I would hope that this would give her permission to address issues otherwise hidden and ignored by her family system.

- *Sohe* seems to be wavering as well. I might say, "I can sense you wavering. Entering a new territory of relationships can be exciting and scary." I might ask her to share with the group stories of success—times when she felt confident, competent, and happy. The group members could function as the audience of her success, giving witness to her accomplishments and the strengths she brings to her family. Finally, I would ask her how she can utilize her talents to decide what to do about dating. Awareness of feminist views may be stressful to Indian families (Dhruvarajan, 1993). So, gently I would invite Sohe to explore how macrolevel oppression of women has invited isolation into her life.

Explain how your ethnic and cultural background affected the way you would respond as a leader.

I am aware that the connections I would feel toward other members stem from different yet shared experiences of loss—some real, some potential. I am also aware that it would be important for me to connect and be there for others—a value deeply embedded in my culture. We have a saying, "When a visitor is in your house, God is in your house." My grandmother deeply fostered this belief in me. Each group member then becomes the visitor, a Godlike individual who needs to be treated with dignity and generosity. Since creative arts are deeply rooted in my culture, I tend to find experiential, creative techniques very interesting. My culture is very group-oriented, so as a leader, I feel very comfortable as long as the leadership is shared. I am aware that what I consider as my Polish culture may not be representative of experiences of other Polish people. First, I have a strong loyalty and pride of coming from the mountain region that has strong folkloric roots and an identity referred to as Cieszynianie. Although most of us speak standard Polish, the Cieszynian dialect is very unique. We have unique rituals, songs, dances, and even traditional clothing through which one can identify us. The songs, dances, and rituals are very spiritual and emphasize unity with God-creator, and thus with nature. Growing up with these experiences allows me to connect to others without worrying about time. So, if other group members feel like sharing stories, using songs and music, I am very comfortable with it and can easily "lose" sense of time. It is the relationships that matter. However, the general Polish norms focus more on structure, awareness of time, and completing tasks in orderly fashion. So, planning ahead and maintaining structure are second nature to me. I can see myself taking time to relate to each member, regardless of how much time it takes.

Explain how your ethnic and cultural background may or may not inhibit the way you respond to the situation as a leader.

I think wanting to connect with others could be very helpful. Yet, I would also want to be cautious, as some members may feel like I do not understand their unique struggles. In addition, I would experience quite a bit of anxiety, stemming from a strong history of cultural norms that do not promote dialogues based on win-win solutions for men and women as they are embedded in oppressive hierarchies. As an individual, I can be very persistent (or more honestly put, stubborn), and I would need to watch that in my interactions with others. Stubbornness has helped Poles overcome numerous challenges in life—after all, we maintained our language for over 200 years, although we were forbidden to use it. So the richness of cultural ways can be very helpful. Yet, at times, it can also be my weakness. My responses would also be a reflection of my personality. I could imagine myself asking the group: "It does not seem like we feel safe here; what do we need to do to feel safe?" This could be helpful, yet perhaps the group would want to go in a different direction, and I would need to respect that. In my cultural experiences, there was a lot of anxiety. I need to be aware and let anxiety be my teacher.

I am aware that although I identify myself as Polish, I also see myself as a Polish American. As a woman, I was lucky to attend a very liberal girl's high school in the Midwest where girls had a voice. Growing up in the Midwest was a cultural experience in itself. As I reflect on this question, I realize that my life in the Midwest was very unique, as the neighborhood where I lived was a true microcosm of our globe. My first true American friend, and my best friend still, is a woman with a Cherokee Indian background. When we met, I did not speak a word of English. She knew a way of just being there for me. She taught me what my grandmother instilled in me—the importance of honoring each other and being. My other friends and my neighbors came from all over the world. However, as a Midwesterner, I also learned that if one looks and talks differently, one may never be allowed to be a member of the community. I was lucky to have faculty who respected diversity. And yet, even at the school I attended, I recall being asked at graduation, "So, when are you going back home?" I had no home to go back to. I have learned that I am just a global visitor, passing in time and place. I was also lucky to meet a woman who has become like a grandmother to me and who "adopted" all the kids in the community who had no home. Grandma Mary still is one of the best teachers; she models the richness of diverse communities. Those experiences helped me to be sensitive to the struggles that others experience when they feel like they do not have a place to call home and people to call family.

Explain how your ethnic and cultural background may have influenced your choice of the response you made over any other that you may have been considering as a leader.

I think that the cultural piece for me would assist in fostering a sense of community and belonging. I would want to make sure that the struggles experienced by all the individuals are recognized and validated. Specifically, I could relate to Sophia from a cultural context that is familiar to me. However, I would not assume that I understand her better just because we both are Polish. Being a spiritual woman, a mother, a wife, a family member, a friend, a professional, and balancing those roles has helped me reexperience the importance of validating the challenges experienced by women. In my responses, I would anticipate a feminist flare. However, some Polish individuals may share totally different perspectives on issues experienced by women. So, this is a very thought-provoking question. While the cultural piece helps me validate and support individuals, I find it very important to address gender issues as well.

As a result of the response you chose, identify the consequences you might anticipate as a leader.

I think some group members might like to focus on trust and feel relieved that their losses are not a "hidden" topic. I would hope that the shared experiences would allow for the universality to emerge, thus leading to more trust. I would hope that the variety of techniques would match the group members' needs. If they did not, then it would be my role to modify what we do and how. I think it would also depend on how well the group members were prepared for group participation. I get a feeling that we as a group would connect more and feel more relieved once we would give ourselves permission to deal with our losses and the challenges of grappling with intercultural relations. In the process, we would start weaving a supportive community where the stories of "happily ever after" could be reconstructed. Some group members may be taken aback by my views regarding oppression of women and me find me unwomanly. I can also anticipate some potential tension regarding gender issues. It would be a growth-promoting event for all the members. To me, it seems that we need to start the weaving of different endings to stories of oppression of women that often get camouflaged by culture. So, in this group I would anticipate that we would grapple with the challenges of gender issues and culture. The group member preparation would be very important in how those dynamics are addressed. The guidelines offered by DeLucia-Waack (1997) would be very helpful. Without sufficient pregroup preparation, this group could be hindered.

From your position as a leader, explain what the most glaring or outstanding aspect was of the situation which impacted you from your ethnic and cultural orientation.

I can imagine that my heart would be beating fast as Chloe was fervently sharing her feelings. I would think about times when I felt like that in my family, when I or my relatives felt unheard, when my friends from various cultures have experienced similar struggles. I would be worried, however, if the focus was on blame without looking at the responsibility that each one of us has for making sure it is a safe group. I would want to address shared responsibility for safety in the form of a dialogue. The culture, I guess, and my personality would kick in, as I would not want to let go of the topic of trust and creating a safe environment. I can imagine saying something like: "The norms of silence and being unheard are toxic for everyone; we all need to take responsibility for creating a safe group." I would think to myself, "Why does there have to be so much pain when a person wants to be assertive and kind-hearted, when a woman wants to be loving yet not subservient? There have been enough tears of sadness; we must do something differently. Our invisible strands from the past weave our web of life now. I am just a strand in it, wishing we could foster the strengths of our cultural past while changing some of the history." I would admire Chloe for her courage to speak up, and I would share that with her. I would also ask her if she felt she was heard and understood, and what we as a group could do. This could really help us move to a deeper level. I would be asking myself questions offered by Donigian and Malnati (1997) such as: Why do some members seem so angry while others seem so withdrawn? What makes this group seem so tight? How are we going to handle power so that win-win solutions can be achieved for everyone? I would trust that although we may stumble through and our rhythm might not be pretty initially, we would find a way of creating different endings to the stories of discouragement.

Based on the composition of this group, what multicultural issues (etic and emic) need to be taken into consideration as the incident is addressed in group?

Once again, I think it is imperative to unify the group members in their shared struggles. The universal experiences of grappling with existential issues need to be illuminated. I am a strong believer in the importance of understanding the therapeutic factors identified by Yalom (1985). At the same time, equally important, I think, is tuning into the individual experiences. In case of Sophia, for example, recognizing that a wedding is a family and community event can help in understanding her struggles. Another example would be a Native American person talking about having to cut his hair when he entered a boarding school. A leader needs to be sensitive and respectful to the meaning that a person, within a cultural context, attributes to an event. If a leader did not understand and respect the symbolic meaning of hair, that leader might perpetuate the cycle of oppression by minimizing how painful the experience of being forced to cut one's hair could be for a Native American. This is an excellent question, and one that I think as leaders we need to explore with group members during the screening and preparation for the group process. I would want to ask each group member, before she joined the group, about her values, beliefs and events that would be considered difficult and painful. I would want to ask each person questions such as: "When you feel respected by others, what do others do? When you feel disrespected by others, what do they do?"

MUHYIDDIN SHAKOOR'S REACTION AS A MEMBER OF THIS COUNSELING/THERAPY GROUP

Identify the multicultural issues that need to be taken into consideration for you as a member.

As a member of this group, I would want some help from the leader in terms of orientation. I would be thinking that I came to the group looking for some help in being more assertive. In those first two sessions, I would want to have gained some sense of what others had come for. I would be looking for the leader to help me discover that, and I would be curious to know where other members were in this regard. As a member, I feel certain that by the third session I would have made several disclosures in the group as to what brought me there and what I hoped for. I might gently express my sincere interest to get to know the hopes of others. I might be a member who would risk saying that he was struggling even now in sharing these things because he usually feels some anxiety on first entering a new group, in spite of the fact that he likes people very much.

Aside from orientation, acceptance would be an issue for me. I see immediately that there are five women in this group and three other men. I would probably look cool and calm, but I would be thinking all kinds of thoughts. I want to be liked, and I want to be accepted, I am wondering if these women will like me—if they will see me as attractive, mature, nonsexist, nonchauvinistic, and intelligent. I would be hoping that I would not be boxed in or be seen only as a color. No one in this group knows that I came from a family and community of matriarchs. My mother, whom I love immensely, has been a major force in shaping my views of people in general, but especially my views of women. I wonder about the other men. One is black, the other two appear to be brown. I wonder where they will be with me. I want to be equal with them, not competing but also not skimming the surface or doing "whaz-ups" and high-fives like we are the only ones in the room, or like we are leading a mating ritual in hopes for one of the women. Deep down, I am hoping for a sense of real fraternity and connection. Coming from a matriarchy, I always gave special value to positive connections that I had with men. For many years, I did not have them with my father, and when good men of substance entered my life, it always increased my confidence in striving to know what it is to truly be a man.

A side aspect of the issue of acceptance for me is vulnerability. I want to feel safe. I expect that if I am going to gain anything from a group that I self-selected into in order to learn to be more assertive, I will likely have to take a risk. But I am not expecting combat training. I would have chosen a therapist who had a good reputation, and from a multicultural and ethnic point of view, I would have pointedly asked about his or her sensitivity to diversity issues and minority concerns. I would come expecting that this therapist is someone who knows for sure how to relate to people. This is a big issue in my book. It leads to my considerations about leadership from a member's perspective. I do not expect the leader to hold my hand at every step or tell me everything, but I do not want to be overpowered either. I can see specialized challenges I might have with a leader I perceived to be overcontrolling, dominating, or too highly structured, regardless of whether the leader was a man or a woman. I have my own unique challenges and historical experiences, both good and not so good, with matriarchs and powerful men.

Explain how your ethnic and cultural background affected the way you would respond as a member.

I would hope that more mutual sharing would have occurred. I feel certain that I would have related to all of the men and to at least two or three of the women. I can identify with Sam as a black man. I know his story and his fears from similar experiences in my own family. Even in a matriarchy, men were expected to work and be providers. Somehow, for many of them, ideas and feelings about their personal worth often became intertwined with having work. A menial job could make the difference between being a man or being "lazy, trifling, and shiftless." In the community of my youth, when a man courted a woman and her family and friends reviewed him, the first questions about him would likely be these: Does he have a job, what does he do, and does he have an education? In the paradigm of my mother and a few wise elders, the steps to personal worth and power were to first *be* then *do*. Somewhere along the way, suboptimal thinking crept into our urban village, and the "do first, then you will be" paradigm became very prominent. It is my opinion that this prevailing paradigm in combination with digitalization, the advent of hip-hop (a culture within itself), and professional sports (to name just a few influences) has brought major challenges to the survival of African-American youth. I can also relate with empathy because I have probably known someone like Sam's fiancée. My family and the community context in which I grew up had many highly competent women. Personally, I believe that competent women have been the mainstay and lifeblood of African-American communities, families, and men.

I can relate to Malik, who is very likely a Muslim if he has immigrated from Saudi Arabia, although he is not necessarily an Arab. It is possible that he is from Pakistan (Sri Lanka), Egypt, or some other place in the world. I can relate to him from the perspective of Islamic culture because I just happen to be a Muslim. I have also spent time in Saudi Arabia. I have some knowledge of the language and sociocultural mores, and religious ideas as well. Malik would likely recognize my name immediately because it is derived from Arabic. Whether or not he and I would have a deep and powerful connection would depend on what happened when we interacted, in similar ways as hold for my connection with the other members, but Malik and I do have a unique reference point in common.

I feel optimistic for myself in this group because I see the possibilities for relating to others in this group in meaningful, deeply relevant ways. I relate to Cho because I was in the Army during the start of the Vietnam era. Having spent time outside of the United States and having grappled with the challenge of adjusting to life in another culture, I feel empathy for his struggle with transition. I am sure that I could describe how I might respond were I to say something here about my reaction to each woman in the group. However, since I have disclosed what I believe to be the single most influential factor in terms of my own family and women, I will move on to discuss the next question.

Explain how your ethnic and cultural background may or may not inhibit the way you respond to the situation as a member.

Chloe's outburst has thrown me directly into my family history. She is sounding exactly like one of my siblings, a sister who is two years younger than me and who constantly complained that my younger brother and I "ganged up on her" (she was always the one who was blamed and misunderstood). I am much older now, so I can also hear that Chloe is hurt and that she is in love with her boss. Through the first two meetings, she was a little quiet and I wondered what was happening with her. I had considered reaching out to her and Joelle. But I could not seem to engage Chloe. There may have been an opportunity before or after the group, but I would have been hesitant. I was struck by what was shared in the second session, and I would probably have been one of those who shared. Now, as Chloe is erupting, I feel sympathy for her problem, and I am surprised at how forceful she is. My mother can be like that. I also see that Cho is totally out of it and Sam is inspecting his Rolex. I wonder if they think I failed to support them. I hear Chloe telling me that I failed her. I have some multicultural and ethnic issues here with Chloe related to how I deal with conflict, guilt, and blame. Historical family feelings are emerging, as well as issues of relationship, gender, and power. I want to be liked; I want to be seen as a good person, a good man—but I do not want to be misunderstood. I see that Chloe is edgy, and I do not want her to think I am pushy. I am wondering what the other women think. Maybe Malik will judge me in terms of religion or Sam will say I am more sympathetic to this frantic white woman than I am to him as a brother. Maybe Sam and Cho will align themselves with Chloe. I might be thinking any one of these things, or they might all pass through my mind.

Explain how your ethnic and cultural background may have influenced your choice of the response you made over any other that you may have been considering as a member.

In terms of multicultural and ethnic influences on what response I finally chose, I suspect the moral influences would be most prevalent, that is: "Be honest, and before you go off on a tangent, try to understand where the other person is coming from." These were the words of my childhood mentor, Uncle Bob. I can hear his voice ringing in my ears and resonating inside myself. I would likely put the thoughts I have described out into the open. I believe that I would try. I would attempt to let Chloe know that I had noticed her and that I heard her complaint about some of our group members not responding to powerful "stuff" shared by Sam, Cho, and Christina. I would say something about my fears of being vulnerable, of possibly being misunderstood, and of my hesitancy when it comes to conflict. If it seemed to me that members were really listening and interested in what I was putting out in response to Chloe, I might share about my family or my mother, or my sister. I might share my feelings about Sam, Cho, and Christina. I might also say something about my deferring to the leader and how I noticed that I did not like that tendency in myself. In fact, dealing with that puzzling thing in myself that prevents me from asserting myself more is why I came to this group.

As a result of the response you chose, identify the consequences you might anticipate as a member.

Consequences I might anticipate as a member would include hopes that Chloe would receive some affirmation, and that Sam, Christina, and Cho would know that they did have some impact. I would want them to know that what they shared in the second session had some meaning for me. I would also hope that my initiative might draw some positive response from Malik, Joelle, and Sohe who still appear to be looking on. I hope the leader will give us some feedback or say something that will let us know whether or not what was going on was what was supposed to be happening in our group.

From your position as a member, explain what the most glaring or outstanding aspect was of the situation which impacted you from your ethnic and cultural orientation.

What affected me most was Chloe's empathy. Even though it seemed that she dropped a bomb, she was disclosing that she had pain and that even though she had been silent in the second session, she actually related to what others had shared. She saw her own pain, she saw her own dilemma, and she gave the group a clue. Chloe's initiative might also give me the idea that Malik, Christina, and Sohe were affected like Chloe was, but had not or could not find the wherewithal just yet to risk sharing their personal stories. I would also want to know more of Chloe's story. Additionally, if the word were used, I might mention that Muslims do not like to be referred to as *Mohammedans;* the religion is known as *Islam.* I might also be able to share with Chloe that it is a point of Islamic faith that a Muslim man can marry a woman of the Catholic faith and she is entitled to keep her faith. There are, of course, other challenges with regard to her family and its power to force Chloe to conform. Then there is Malik, who has a story, and Joelle and Sohe. Perhaps the leader will do something to help Chloe and the rest of the group.

MUHYIDDIN SHAKOOR'S REACTIONS AS A LEADER OF THIS COUNSELING/THERAPY GROUP

If this type of incident would not occur in your group, explain why it would not.

I cannot say that this incident would absolutely not happen in my group. One of the things I find most amazing is that even though certain aspects of groups are fairly predictable, laws of chaos do exist, and some areas of group movement remain completely unpredictable. Beyond groups, it is almost entirely impossible to predict what any single human being will do. Personally, I find this unpredictable characteristic of humans to be a large part of the joy as well as the heartache found in working in a helping or therapeutic context with others. Thinking about the incident and the members of the group, I would like to think that I am the kind of group leader who would be working throughout the first and second sessions to bring members into interaction with each other. I do not hesitate to let group members know about the sense of hope I have for them. I do not hesitate to be with them and honestly welcome them. I want them to feel the real me—who I am as a person. I smile and I allow group members plenty of room to try things and make something happen. I think that if I were the leader and we had drawn near the end of the second session with Malik, Chloe, and Joelle remaining quiet, I do not think I could have ended without wondering out loud what might be happening in their silence. I might share some of my reactions to the things presented in the group, or I might share how I might struggle if I were a new person to a group as Joelle, Chloe, Malik, and the other members are. I might also attempt to support the silent members by helping them just to notice more. Perhaps I could help them see how it is possible to consciously decide where one directs one's own attention and that one can *choose to notice* what goes on in the life of one's own thoughts, feelings, and body. No one would be forced, but certainly everyone would be invited to look into herself. Based on one's own sense of readiness, one might share some part of what one notices in any area of oneself with any other person or with the group as a whole. I am going to assure people that it is my commitment to work to ensure that this group is a place where it is safe to risk being known. I might even say before closing that if people are not ready to share specific pieces of their story or dilemma, it is okay. If they cannot do this, it may help them and the group if they can simply share any part of what they think prevents them in this moment, in this group or in their minds. This would not be a lecture, but it would be an acknowledgment of the presence and the silence of those particular members. It would be honoring their personal process, and it would be an invitation to every member to consider the workings of his own inner self. After all, the members chose to come and said they were interested in learning how to assert themselves more. Consciously choosing in the sense of actively *deciding to notice* one's thoughts and one's feelings in this moment is only one small step for the process, but it could easily be one giant leap for the person.

Identify the multicultural issues that need to be taken into consideration for you as a leader.

For me, the multicultural and ethnic issues that need to be considered have to do with understanding that this is a diverse group. There is a man from Saudi Arabia, a woman from India, an African-American man, a Greek-American woman who is possibly enmeshed in her first-generation parental unit, a Polish-American woman, and two other women whose family origins are not yet known. There is yet another man who has no living parents and who immigrated to the United States from Vietnam. It is a complex interpersonal system with members who literally cross cultures from opposite sides of the planet. They are all interested in learning to assert themselves more, but they have idiosyncratic cultural styles of communicating, of using eye contact, of relating to members of the same or opposite sex, of eye contact while speaking or listening to someone older or younger. These members have unique ways of dealing with fears, conflict, friendship, sexual attraction, pain, and power yet to be discovered by the group. Apparently, a few members ventured out in the second session. Chloe is grappling with her own personal difficulties. Ironically, they have to do with her being in love with a man from a largely non-Western culture whose religion, if not completely alien, is very likely unacceptable to her family members, whom she also loves. She is torn. Probably without any recognition of the complex personality of her group in multicultural terms, she projects her perceptions onto their silence. She stuns the group with the power of her outburst. The pain is apparent in the high-pitched strain of her tone, and even though she is vague about herself, it is evident that she wants her problem to be known.

Explain how your ethnic and cultural background affected the way you would respond as a leader.

My ethnic and cultural background would affect my response in terms of expanding my awareness of the complexity of my group's context. As we proceed, I am remembering my own history while members interact actively or even with caution and hesitation. I am thinking about them as a group, and I see Chloe as a part of them and as a part of us. I feel a sense of empathy for Chloe's pain as much as I feel a sense of empathy for all of the members. I see that they have made the step to get themselves into a therapy group with all of the connotations such a choice might have relative to their own unique cultural, community, or family-related circumstances. I see what is going on in the group. I am feeling present and connected. I feel hopeful. Members are stunned, yes, but the group is not dead.

Explain how your ethnic and cultural background may or may not inhibit the way you respond to the situation as a leader.

My ethnic and cultural background would serve as an asset. I cannot see it inhibiting how I respond. Perhaps, if I am overidentified with myself as a black man, I will respond differently from how I might if I am overidentified as a Muslim, or as a veteran or group theorist. In this moment, I feel myself as one being with many possibilities. I would use any part of who I am as much as I could, as genuinely, honestly, respectfully, empathetically, intuitively, nonjudgmentally, lovingly, challengingly, and confrontingly as I could, as a person who truly loves people. I attempt to be all of these things as someone who believes in the power of group process to assist group members to realize and reclaim their own potential.

Explain how your ethnic and cultural background may have influenced your choice of the response you made over any other that you may have been considering as a leader.

At this point, I have made a choice, and what I do is respond with empathy to Chloe and reflect what I am hearing from her: "It sounds like you are feeling, here in this moment, much like you feel in your family. I get the sense that the feeling is painful and hurts you immensely. You are in need. You are in love. You are torn between the love of your family and the love of a man, but you are not helped. Your family knows your situation, but none of them reach out." I would be looking to see if Chloe nodded or signaled any affirmation that she is being understood. I am honest. I am completely myself, and I know that if how I am being is real and true, Chloe and I can only resonate like opposite prongs of a tuning fork. Other members of the group will resonate together with what flows between Chloe and I. As this happens, I will notice the atmosphere. I will notice the warmth or coolness. I will notice any of those barometric energy shifts that guide us in groups. I will notice the members' faces and what their energy and feeling quality are like. I will say to Chloe that I suspect that other members feel a sense of what she is feeling even if they are silent. I will wonder out loud if Chloe remembers that she remained silent throughout the second session while members shared their "stuff." Members whom she chided today are as she had been before. I might wonder if she could be now in this moment as she felt in her silence and share that with us. I would say to Chloe that even though she seems to be scolding the group, she also seems to be one of the best to help us all understand how much can be happening inside of someone, even when they are silent.

As a result of the response you chose, identify the consequences you might anticipate as a leader.

I anticipate that Chloe might weep. I would expect that some quiet members might be drawn out of their silences as Chloe "hooked" them by casting blame and assuming their lack of support. As members saw Chloe gaining insight into her own process, and into her projection and transference of family-related feelings onto the group, they would likely be affected. Yalom (1995) identifies this dynamic insight as recapitulation of the primary family experience. Members would likely feel a sense of connection and, in some odd way, a sense of empathic feeling with Chloe. She is so much in the grip of her desperation that she has completely forgotten that earlier, while those people were putting out their stories, she did nothing apparent to provide them with support. Nonetheless, she felt connected with them, and perhaps thought about them after the meeting ended and came ready today to set the group straight. I feel hopeful for this group, and I do not see it as dead. I would anticipate that the love-related dilemma Chloe awkwardly and rather indirectly disclosed might reverberate throughout the group. Sam, Sophia, Joelle, and Chloe are all dealing with relationship and love-focused concerns. Even though neither Christina nor Sohe have spoken about relationships, I would not be surprised if Christina later revealed her own hopes to marry or that some person has now attracted her. Something like this might raise feelings of conflict or turmoil in Christina that would be similar to what Chloe is feeling, but with a slightly different dynamic. Christina's family is dependent whereas Chloe's appears to be controlling and religiously demanding. Sohe has been asked out on dates, but she has declined because in her culture dates are chaperoned. Her presence appears to indicate that she is possibly at a crossroads. Malik and Joelle, who may perceive themselves as the most different or most likely to be misunderstood in their family systems and in the group, might come to trust the group enough to share their dilemmas and personal plights.

I anticipate a powerful potential for personal insight into honesty with one's self, with how one mediates between the rule and the heart, between looming existential challenges of balancing life's challenges of responsibility and freedom. A spectacular opportunity presents itself. The group members have a chance to ride atop the sweet cresting wave of universality. The ride is all the more awe-inspiring because members probably never imagined that they could rise up on a wave from such a stormy sea of complex differences of family, culture, religion, sexuality, gender, and race. How beautiful!

And what consequences might be anticipated expressly *for* the leader? I anticipate that there is simple exquisite joy for the leader who succeeds in this way, who is allowed into the lives and journeys of others. It is a way that is so rich, so chock-full of surprise, discovery, mutual transformational growth, healing, heart, renewwal, and expansion. To succeed in this way is pure delight. To miss it is nagging regret, and a little taste of hell. But evolution in group work includes both the bitter and the sweet. The haunting poet Bruce Boehlen (2000) says. "And these . . . these are the words of the lesson."

From your position as a leader, explain what the most glaring or outstanding aspect was of the situation which impacted you from your ethnic and cultural orientation.

The thing that affected me most from my ethnic and cultural orientation was how different the members thought they were from each other. Poignantly Chloe, however, holds the possibility to gain insight into what seems to be an impossible dilemma and to be pivotal in helping other members to be and do the same.

Based on the composition of this group, what multicultural issues (etic and emic) need to be taken into consideration as the incident is addressed in group?

I have addressed this question in part in my answers to questions two and six. The multicultural issues (etic and emic) that need to be considered as the incident is addressed are age, gender, ethnic and cultural identity, and the intergenerational family system. The most evident multicultural issue in the *etic* sense is the scope of diversity among group members in terms of sex, race, and gender. The etic perspective relates to the raw data connected to an event or behavior without consideration of the data's meaning, significance, or relevance within its system. Looking from this angle of vision, we simply take notice of what is obvious or apparent. In this group, it is a powerful picture. There are five women. One is Greek American, and another is Indian. One woman is Italian American, another is second-generation Polish American. One woman is married with three children and has fallen in love with another woman. There is a man from Saudia Arabia, a man from Vietnam, and an African American. As simple as this perspective may seem, it is fundamentally important for the reason that I am helped and encouraged to remember to *choose* to look, in which case my consciousness shifts and somehow I see more.

From the *emic* perspective, one is looking at the obvious behavior or data toward the end of obtaining a sense of that behavior's contrast within the system. We learn a great deal in a multicultural system at the level of the etic, but we gain increased understanding as we make discovery into the emic where meaning resides. Multicultural and ethnic issues flow into synthesis with knowledge and information issues. These combine with the leader's understanding, experience, and essential empathic interest. Group leaders who develop and incorporate the ability to see and relate from multiple perspectives bring unique power to the small group setting. The challenge and the interest are to turn, explore, relate, and feel empathy for members and for the group as a whole. It is to see many, and at the same time to see one. If one is interested, the secrets will show themselves. The characteristic of heliotropism in plants causes them to incline toward the sun. It is helpful to remember that, likewise, it is characteristic of the sun to incline toward plants.

SUMMARY/ANALYSIS OF RESPONSES

As Members of This Counseling/Therapy Group

Identify the multicultural issues that need to be taken into consideration for you as a member.

Molina identifies the primary issues as those of acculturation and trust. The acculturation issues she notes are isolation, loss, and disapproval. In order for members to disclose those feelings and thoughts that their cultures "taught" them to be silent about, members need to feel safe. Acculturation also creates conflict between maintaining one's cultural roots while being receptive to the dominant culture. Molina also identifies gender concerns. As a woman, she believes it is important to address issues of gender oppression. In addition, she points out issues of language, given the diversity of the group's membership, and intracultural differences between herself and the other Polish member.

Shakoor sees acceptance as a primary issue. Certainly embedded within that are matters of safety, inclusion, approval, and so forth. He, too, identifies the presence of gender issues. He notes that the group has more women members and discloses concern about how the women will relate to him (i.e., whether his gender will be an issue). he also illuminates the possible intracultural issues that may be present between himself and the three male members who appear black and brown to him; he wants to be considered equal to them, which means that more than cultural identity is at issue. Another gender issue Shakoor points out is the acceptance of male vulnerability. He adds that, in order to feel safe and understood, members need to have a leader who is culturally sensitive.

Explain how your ethnic and cultural background affected the way you would respond as a member.

Molina tells us that she would draw upon her own shared experiences of loss and their accompanying growth potential in this group. Part of her culture is placing value on connecting with and being there for others. She is reminded of the Polish saying, "When a visitor is in your house, God is in your house." Thus, Molina would be inclined to treat each member as a visitor, with dignity and respect. She strongly believes that connecting with others (i.e., building relationships) is a priority and should take precedence over meeting time deadlines.

Shakoor grew up in a matriarchal family. His mother had a profound influence on him, and the community in which he was raised customarily had competent and strong women. Consequently, how he would relate to members of the group would be drawn largely from those early life experiences. He believes he can rely on those experiences to provide him with the sensitivity to relate to the female members in the group. In addition, he thinks he can relate to Sam not only as a fellow black man but also as one who understands Sam's story from a gender position. Shakoor sees his Islamic background as being helpful in reaching out to Malik, and his military experience at the dawn of the Vietnam era as being helpful in finding commonality with Cho.

Explain how your ethnic and cultural background may or may not inhibit the way you respond to the situation as a member.

Both Molina and Shakoor had mixed reactions to this situation. Molina experienced conflict between herself (a feminist) and contemporary Polish norms that do not promote win-win relationships for men and women, given that the current norms are immersed in an oppressive hierarchy. She admits that her behavior could be viewed as too forceful. She would be inclined, however, to want to reach out and build relationships and to help the group establish norms that would provide a safe climate for sharing.

Shakoor also identifies conflict between himself as he is presently and the cultural norms with which he grew up. He admits to having multicultural and ethnic issues with Chloe that are related to how he deals with conflict, guilt, and blame. Historical family feelings also emerge in relation to issues of relationship, gender, and power. He wants to be liked—to be seen as a good person and as a good man—and not be misunderstood by the members of the group. Like Molina, Shakoor would be inclined to reach out to the others in order to build relationships, but he might hesitate due to a fear of being misunderstood by others, leading to his not being liked and accepted. Therefore, he would want to first make certain that he would not be misunderstood.

Explain how your ethnic and cultural background may have influenced your choice of the response you made over any other that you may have been considering as a member.

Molina's Polish background has had a deep influence upon her. Her inclination is to reach out to the Polish-American member first and to convey to Sophia empathy regarding her loss. Simultaneously, she could illuminate for the other members an element of Polish culture that they, in all probability, are not aware of. Her early life experiences helped to sensitize her to the suffering of others; thus, tuning into those experiences is a natural process. Molina would offer respect to the other members as a natural extension of what her early background taught her to do.

Shakoor would also respond to the situation on the basis of moral influences drawn from his culture. He cites his uncle, who taught him to "Be honest, and before you go off on a tangent, try to understand where the other person is coming from."

As a result of the response you chose, identify the consequences you might anticipate as a member.

Molina emphasis that she would break with her cultural norms through her transparency; by doing so, she might help some members focus on trust and feel relief in sharing their losses openly as well. Through such sharing, members would realize the universality of their experiences, and seeing their similarities would help them become more trusting of one another. Molina anticipates that some members would recoil from her disclosing, believing she has violated her cultural norms through her sharing and is asking them to do the same. She also expects there will be gender issues that will cause tension in the group, yet she anticipates that this tension would lead to member growth. She foresees that the cultural stories of oppressed women would raise other gender issues as well.

Shakoor anticipates a number of facilitative consequences resulting from his response. He believes that Chloe would feel affirmed; that Sam, Christina, and Cho would realize that their presence has an impact in the group; and that Malik, Joelle, and Sohe would begin to offer positive responses.

From your position as a member, explain what the most glaring or outstanding aspect was of the situation which impacted you from your ethnic and cultural orientation.

Both of our respondents identified Chloe's disclosure as being the most glaring aspect of the situation. For Molina, the disclosure raises her sensitivity to her own cultural orientation as it relates to women and gender roles. She views Chloe as being courageous because Molina's cultural heritage views women who speak up and do not remain silent in the face of an oppressive hierarchy as being courageous.

Shakoor regards Chloe's action as an empathic act and quite powerful. In spite of the fact that she seems to have "dropped a bomb," he sees the sharing of her pain as a means of conveying that although she was silent during the second session, she was listening and not only heard all that the others who shared had to say but also related to them. From his cultural position, Shakoor sees Chloe's action as creating an opportunity for him to clarify that Muslims refer to their faith as Islam; furthermore, he would explain how the Islamic faith is very tolerant of and open to interfaith marriages—meaning that, should Chloe marry a Muslim man, she would be entitled to keep her Catholic faith.

As Leaders of This Counseling/Therapy Group

If this type of incident would not occur in your group, explain why it would not.

Both Molina and Shakoor address the nature of group processes in their answers. Molina tells us that a process very similar to this incident could occur in her group because group processes are very much the same, regardless of their purpose. Along the same lines, Shakoor believes that there are some areas of group movement that remain unpredictable, just as it is not possible to predict what any single human being will do.

Identify the multicultural issues that need to be taken into consideration for you as a leader.

Both leaders identified acculturation issues as the most pronounced concern. Molina adds the issue of trust to the mix of acculturation issues. She observes that as members revisit and negotiate the boundaries and expectations defined by their cultural lenses (e.g., they have been taught to remain silent regarding painful experiences), they are experiencing varying degrees of isolation, oppression, and rejection. In addition, each member brings a unique set of strengths and a unique personality to the group, as well as different multicultural experiences, all of which need to be taken into consideration. She believes that the issues stem from unhealthy systems that generate anxiety, oppression, loneliness, and depression, which ultimately silences those who live with such systems.

The diversity of the group is what captures Skakoor's attention first. He acknowledges the idiosyncratic cultural styles of communication, relating to members of the same or opposite sex, and of eye contact while speaking or listening to someone older or younger and states that all these factors need to be taken into consideration by the leader. These factors can all be viewed as issues of acculturation.

Explain how your ethnic and cultural background affected the way you would respond as a leader.

Both of the leaders demonstrate that their cultural and ethnic backgrounds have prepared them to have empathy for each of the group members. Molina's Polish background contains experiences with loss, both real and potential. Her deeply embedded cultural value of connecting with and being there for others emerges in the Polish saying, "When a visitor is in your house, God is in your house." She translates that to mean that each member is like a visitor— Godlike, and worthy of being treated with dignity and respect. The creative arts (songs, dances, and rituals that unite human beings with God and nature) are equally embedded in her culture, so she would be likely to employ creative techniques as she works with this group. Although her culture stresses completing tasks in a timely and orderly fashion, Molina is also aware of her culture's emphasis on how building relationships is more important than time, so she would take time to listen to the members and trust that tasks would be completed on time. Shakoor, much like Molina, sees his cultural and ethnic background as having prepared him to manage the diversity and complexity of the group because it has expanded his level of awareness and given him a sense of empathy for each member.

Explain how your ethnic and cultural background may or may not inhibit the way you respond to the situation as a leader.

Both leaders believe their backgrounds would not inhibit the way they respond to this situation, although Molina states that in following her cultural norm of connecting with others, she would need to be careful not to impose on those members who might not want to connect at the moment. She also might experience anxiety due to strong cultural norms that do not promote dialogue based on win-win solutions for men and women, given that traditional Polish culture is based in oppressive hierarchies. Such oppression, however, has also fostered persistence (stubbornness) in her, which she sees as both a strength and a limitation. An additional influence comes from her experiences while living in the Midwest, which added another layer to her background that has served to make her sensitive to the struggles of those who have been displaced.

Shakoor also sees his multicultural background as an asset and does not think it would inhibit his response in this situation. The diversity of his background—the melding of race, culture, religion, and professional experiences in his life—contributes to his being able to respond without reservation completely and fully as a human being in an empathic way to others.

Explain how your ethnic and cultural background may have influenced your choice of the response you made over any other that you may have been considering as a leader.

Molina's Polish background has contributed to her focus on building relationships. Her initial intention here would be to foster a sense of belonging and community. In addition, she would validate and recognize the struggles of each member. Molina also refers to the continuing theme of gender issues, especially as they relate to the struggle of women. She would be particularly attentive to the concerns of the Polish female member.

Shakoor's response to this question seems to be a reflection of his early childhood cultural experiences. His mother's strength and the community of competent women in which he grew up helped him to become sensitive to women's issues. He also credits his multicultural background as having contributed to his developing into a complex person who can have empathy for others. The only response he considered was to offer empathy to Chloe and reflect what he heard her say. In order to do so, he realizes he would need to be completely himself.

As a result of the response you chose, identify the consequences you might anticipate as a leader.

Both leaders expect positive growth experiences for all the members. Molina foresees that some members may desire to focus on trust and will experience relief that their losses no longer are a hidden topic. Through the sharing of their differences, she anticipates that members will discover their similarities and thus will begin to trust one another, resulting in the building of relationships and community. Through this supportive community, stories of "happily ever after" can be reconstructed. She also anticipates that some members may be startled by her strong views of the oppression of women and may not at first find her to be very womanly. Such experiences could lead to tension related to gender issues. She remains optimistic, however, since such tension can lead to personal growth.

Shakoor anticipates group tension as well. He sees it as being generated by Chloe's weeping, which he anticipates as a response to his reaching out to her.

The tension generated by her weeping, he expects, will lead to responses from the quiet members who experienced her earlier castigation of them, for they will have been affected by her disclosures and insights. He believes this will lead members to feel a connection with and empathy for Chloe. He also believes that her disclosures will resonate throughout the rest of the members and will lead them to start sharing. Shakoor predicts that through these disclosures, trust will develop. He projects a climate that will foster discussion of the following: powerful personal insight and honesty with one's self, how one mediates between the rule and the heart, and meeting the existential issues of balancing life's challenges of responsibility and freedom. Like Molina, he forecasts that universality of experience will evolve as a result of members coming to realize that through expressing their differences, they will find their commonality. Shakoor expects, as the leader, to feel the "exquisite joy" that comes as a result of being allowed to enter the lives and journeys of the members.

From your position as a leader, explain what the most glaring or outstanding aspect was of the situation which impacted you from your ethnic and cultural orientation.

Chloe's disclosures are perceived as the most glaring aspect of the situation by both leaders. Drawing from her cultural background, Molina sees the concerns being generated by Chloe's pronouncements as being related to member safety, trust, and member responsibility for making the group a safe place. Molina also identifies her concern that a dialogue develop among male and female members leading to win-win solutions. Shakoor cites the members' view of themselves as being different from each other as another profound aspect of this situation.

Based on the composition of this group, what multicultural issues (etic and emic) need to be taken into consideration as the incident is addressed in group?

Molina identifies the etic issues as being the need to unify the group through their shared struggles, the need to address the universal existential issues with which members are grappling, and the need to establish mutual respect. The emic issues relate to understanding the symbolic meaning attendant with cultural backgrounds. She cites as examples the meaning of weddings in the Polish culture and the symbolic meaning hair holds for Native Americans.

Shakoor cites the etic issues as being related to age, gender, ethnic and cultural identity, the intergenerational family system, and the scope of diversity among the group members. For him, the emic issues relate to such matters as the meaning behind Chloe's behaviors, the reason members emphasize their ethnic and cultural differences, and the need for him as a leader to develop and incorporate understanding and empathy for each member, since all of them come from their own cultural contexts. He adds that the members need to learn to do the same for each other.

Counseling/ Therapy Group Vignette #2

An Adolescent Boys' Group and the Missing Member

You are a counselor in a counseling center at a mental health clinic. You have formed a group for adolescents who have been referred to the clinic. They have been referred for a variety of reasons ranging from school adjustment problems to leaving home. Your group has nine members.

- Eduardo is 15 and a sophomore. He is Mexican American. He is the middle child of five. He has been referred to the clinic because he has been skipping school again. He skipped school 25 times last year. Prior to his freshman year, he was a model student.
- Michael is 16. He is a sophomore and a fraternal twin. His sister is on the varsity track team and is an A student. Born in Jamaica, he and his sister along with his parents arrived in the United States eight years ago. His mother has been diagnosed with cancer. She has been receiving treatment for a year. Michael has been exhibiting impulsive and rageful behavior. Most recently, he assaulted a teacher so severely that the teacher had to be hospitalized.
- Jamal is 17. He is repeating his sophomore year. His father is a professional boxer who converted to Islam when Jamal was 5. Jamal has been withdrawn, and his school grades have gone from passing to nearly failing. When he meets with his school coun-

selor, he only shrugs his shoulders and says he has no explanation for the dip in his grades.

- Richard is 16. His only sibling, a brother, an honor student and an outstanding athlete, was killed in a car crash last year. His brother's death traumatized his parents to the extent that his mother, a schoolteacher, has been on a medical leave of absence. Richard has become noncompliant at home and at school. He recently acquired a tattoo that is a skull and crossbones with a knife plunged through an eye socket. His grandparents immigrated from Israel 40 years ago.

- Jason is 17. He is a junior. A robust boy, he was active in school athletics until two months ago when, without warning he withdrew from the basketball team and his grades plummeted. His school counselor has been unable to draw any explanation from Jason for these dramatic changes. His parents report that he has been unusually quiet and withdrawn of late, which is totally unlike him.

- Steven is 16. He is Asian American. Recently he ran away from home and was spotted by an off-duty police officer while riding on the subway. Steven had run away before but had always returned home within a day or two. This last incident was unlike the others. His parents had to file a missing person's report because he was gone for more than a week.

- Gary is 15. He is a freshman. His parents are Native American. He has been suspended three times this year for fighting. He has a history of fighting throughout grade school. His counselor believes that Gary could benefit from more intensive counseling than that which can be offered at school. Gary's parents wholeheartedly support his referral to you.

- Sammy is 16. He is a junior. He was classified as gifted when he was in grade school, was passed rapidly through each grade, and was given advanced placement to the 6th grade when he completed 4th grade. Both of his parents are physicians who arrived in the United States 20 years ago from India. Recently, he has demonstrated defiant behavior at home and at school. He has also "taken up" with a group of kids who are known drug users and who are described as being noncompliant.

This is the fifth session. Since the boys were referred, this is not a volunteer group. You realized this and accommodated for that fact when you began the first session. The group went through the predictable behaviors for the early stages of group development. The first two sessions were marked with limited interactive behaviors. The members responded with few words and much jostling for position. Trust and safety issues were of primary concern, and you focused on building a culture that would develop them. There was conflict and confrontation in session four. The boys who were most vocal were Michael, Jamal, Richard, Gary, and Sammy. Eduardo, Steven, and especially Jason remained quiet. Whenever he was confronted by any of the others, Jason would respond with one or two words; then he would quickly withdraw into himself. It seemed that the more he responded in that manner, the more the subgroup of five were drawn to confronting him. Their words were cutting. They referred to him as a *faggot* and *queer,* at which time you intervened and had them explore not only what they understood those terms to mean but also what about Jason drew such venomous tones from them. That discussion led to an exploration of issues regarding gender orientation—what it means to be a "man," homophobia, and so on. All during this segment of the session, Jason remained quiet. Eventually, time ran out, and you terminated the session by saying that the group would pick up where it left off in the next session.

As you arrive for the fifth session, you find the boys busily talking among themselves. You quickly realize, however, that Jason is missing.

BETH FIRESTEIN'S REACTION AS A MEMBER OF THIS COUNSELING/THERAPY GROUP

Identify the multicultural issues that need to be taken into consideration for you as a member.

Wow! What an interesting place to find myself. Here I am, a 17-year-old senior high school girl, and through an odd set of circumstances, I find myself in this therapy group with a group of rough-and-tumble, attractive, sexy, troublemaking teenage boys. Well, they aren't *all* attractive and sexy, of course, but most boys look that way to me these days. How did I get here? After all, I've been a poster child for "Good Girl" virtually all of my life—well, at least until the very recent past when I started trying pot and getting more sexually active with boys. (Don't get me wrong; I'm still technically a virgin.) And more recently, I've begun creating opportunities to explore being sexual with a couple of girls, too—but I'm not a lesbian. I'm just sexually curious. Adventurous, I guess. I'm a sexually adventurous heterosexual girl, I suppose. I really like sex—but I want the first time for intercourse to be really special, so I don't do that with the boys, and I won't until I'm married, or maybe until I'm really, really in love.

I really don't care much for alcohol, and I've only drunk a lot one time. Boy, did I wake up with a headache. I don't even know if I like pot, but it's an interesting experience. I've done it once or twice. I find things that change my consciousness and awareness levels to be very interesting.

I've only skipped one class in my whole life. I don't even dislike school. I really like it, actually. The teachers always like me, and I make almost all As. I'm finding out that I don't have to be perfect or always be the "good girl" to make good grades. My grades haven't dropped at all since I started experimenting with not being perfect. I've always been "perfect"—the perfect daughter, the perfect student, the perfect citizen in my school. Well, I'm not perfect, but I do try to be. I try to be good and do right and be the best person I can be. I just skipped this one class this year, just to see what it's like, and wouldn't you know? I felt so guilty about skipping out on the class that I decided to sneak back into the class, and that's when I got "caught skipping class." I've never been a good liar. After a long talk with the school counselor, in which I confessed more than I should have, I got sent to this therapy group at the mental health center and put in this group with these teenage boys. Talk about overkill! It's kind of like putting a little lark in the same cage with a bunch of hawks and eagles. I really think they made a mistake, but I'm here, so I guess I'll make the best of it.

As usual, I'm the only Jewish one in the group. Well, I guess there's Richard. Richard said something about his grandparents immigrating from Israel 40 years ago, so I guess he's Jewish, but he really doesn't talk about it. Of course, neither do I. These days, most of the time my Judaism is really about the farthest thing from my mind. I mean, I did get confirmed when I was 15, but my Dad, who is a rabbi, really discouraged me from having a Bat Mitzvah (the female version of a Bar Mitzvah) at 13 and I really, really wanted one. I guess it must have been the fact that I'm a girl and my dad was raised Orthodox Jewish. Orthodox Jews don't let girls get Bat Mitzvahed. Now my dad is Reform Jewish, but he must still believe that girls aren't supposed to have Bat Mitzvahs because you would think that if *any* girl would get to be Bat Mitzvahed, it would be me, the oldest daughter of a rabbi. I guess my Judaism hasn't meant the same thing to me ever since I didn't get my Bat Mitzvah. I believe in equal rights for girls and women, no matter what. There is absolutely no reason a girl should not be allowed and encouraged to be Bat Mitzvahed. Other girls in our congregation have been. I was crushed, but I never really told my Dad that. I just accepted his discouraging words as the final answer, but I really wish I hadn't. I am still angry about it, and that was four years ago now.

Anyway, being Jewish isn't a problem for me in this group. I just don't talk about it. I never have much. What's the point? No one at school really understands anything about Judaism, anyway. I guess I sort of pretend that I'm not Jewish most of the time. It really doesn't matter to me that much, anyway.

Explain how your ethnic and cultural background affected the way you would respond as a member.

The guys in the group mostly seem like really scary people to me. They're like delinquents and troublemakers, and I've never, ever hung around with that crowd in school, and I've never really wanted to either. They are the bad kids who skip school and run away from home, and I've always looked down on those kinds of people because I'm not like that at all. I come from a good family. We follow the rules and try to do things right. And I know my parents love me. At least I felt that way until a couple of years ago, when I started getting interested in boys. Then my mom didn't know what to do with me, how to talk to me—anything! It really hurt. And my dad started pulling away from me when I was about 12—I guess because I started developing into a woman, but I'm not really sure why he pulled away. He didn't explain it or anything. But still, I know I'm a good kid—not like these boys in this group.

Explain how your ethnic and cultural background may or may not inhibit the way you respond to the situation as a member. Explain how your ethnic and cultural background may have influenced your choice of the response you made over any other that you may have been considering as a member.

These questions are discussed within responses to other questions. See also the "Summary/Analysis of Responses" section at the end of this chapter.

As a result of the response you chose, identify the consequences you might anticipate as a member.

I was really upset that Jason didn't come back to the group today, but I'm not surprised. I almost didn't come back myself. But that would be going against the leader's expectations that I am supposed to attend, and I would never break the rules like that for no good reason. We talked some about why Jason might not have come back, but the boys who had been taunting him were pretty defensive. Steven and Eduardo did say some things in Jason's defense and expressed some anger at how he had been treated. I remained fairly quiet, but eventually I joined in with some of Eduardo's comments on behalf of Jason and the whole issue of fairness. I guess that indirectly I was also standing up for myself because I am an open-minded person and I don't have anything against gays. I've gone to gay nightclubs before to go dancing with a guy I was dating, and I thought it was interesting. But, of course, I would never share anything about my experiences with this bigoted group of boys.

Maybe I would talk to Jason if it was away from group and I thought it was safe to tell him. All through the group today I thought about Jason. We're from the same school, and I know where he lives. I decided that after group I'm going to call him and just see if he's okay. I don't know if he'll ever come back to the group, and I at least want to tell him that I think he's a good person and be able to say good-bye. I don't know if I will tell the other group members about talking to Jason. I might and I might not. I don't know if they would understand, but I'm really not too worried about what they would think of me. I'm not a boy, so I know they won't think I'm a "fag," and because I do date boys, I think the secret of my own sexual experimentation will remain safe.

I think the overall effect of the experience of being a member of this group is mainly just to make me trust these boys even less than I did at the beginning, and I doubt I will open up about myself here in any important way. I can always confide in my friends instead; that certainly feels much, much safer. I'll just complete my time here, and this will all be in the past.

From your position as a member, explain what the most glaring or outstanding aspect was of the situation which impacted you from your ethnic and cultural orientation.

The boys I'm most scared of are Michael, the Jamaican guy, Gary, who is an American Indian, and Richard, who has a scary tattoo on his arm. These boys are in trouble for fighting with other people and for being violent. I hate violence. I was picked on and teased quite a bit when I was younger. A bully on the school bus in 7th grade picked on me, and he acted a lot like these guys in group—all macho and everything. I don't know why that boy chose to pick on *me*. He even got physically pushy with me, but I told my mom and she called that boy's mother who then made him apologize to me. But I was still always scared of him after that incident. When I think of the boys in this group, I do feel sorry for Michael because his mom has cancer and she might not live very much longer. That must be really awful. I couldn't imagine losing my mom! And I guess I feel sorry for Richard, too, because of his brother being killed in the car wreck last year. I had his brother in a couple of my honors classes. He was a nice guy. It's really too bad for Richard and his family.

I wasn't scared of Sammy or Jamal before, but after the last session, I'm really feeling scared of them, too. They all ganged up on Jason and were picking on him, taunting him and calling him a "fag" and "sissy" and "queer." The whole thing really freaked me out. For one thing, I thought Jason was one of the coolest guys in the group—maybe *the* coolest one. He's an athlete, he makes good grades, and he's good-looking. I would love to date someone like him, but he'd never ask me out because I'm not one of the popular girls. Anyway, Gary, Sammy, Richard, Michael, and Jamal were really being mean and starting to get loud and call Jason names. I *hate* that kind of thing. It's so unnecessary! I don't understand why people do it. It reminds me of when my parents fight at home and all the tension that fills the house when that happens.

I don't know why they ganged up on Jason. After all, he wasn't the only quiet one that day. Eduardo and Steven were pretty quiet, too. And, of course, I did my best to make myself totally invisible. I didn't want to be there. I felt like I was in the wrong place for sure because I don't like being with people who are mean to other people just because they are different. I hated those boys for making Jason a scapegoat, and I really wished that the nice boys—Steven and Eduardo—had stood up for Jason. I don't know why they didn't, although once the leader had us talk about gender roles and sexual orientation and stuff, I sort of understood better why Eduardo and Steven wouldn't speak up for Jason. I think it's mainly because then the other boys would think they were gay, too. Jason was so quiet during that part of the session that it did make me wonder if maybe some of those accusations were hitting home for him—maybe he does struggle with his sexuality, or maybe he's been experimental like me. But he doesn't *seem* gay. After all, he's a big-shot basketball player and one of the most popular boys in the school.

BETH FIRESTEIN'S REACTIONS AS A LEADER OF THIS COUNSELING/THERAPY GROUP

If this type of incident would not occur in your group, explain why it would not.

A therapy group consisting of high school aged teens who have been mandated to counseling certainly has to be one of the most difficult groups in the world to lead effectively. Issues of trust and safety are compromised from the outset by the conditions of the referral, and it is really difficult to engage teens that do not want to be engaged. Certainly that is the case in this therapy group. I do not think that this type of incident would be something I could effectively prevent in a group of this type. The cultural narrative of the adolescent male is pervaded by themes of competition, dominance, and juggling for position, and that is exactly what is unfolding in the group at this juncture. Gender roles, defining one's masculinity, and the equation of a lack of masculinity with homosexuality seem to be themes with a strong cross-cultural presence. In this group, the more aggressive members scapegoat Jason by challenging his masculinity and consciously or unconsciously pushing him to fight or flee. I really doubt that any action I might have taken as a group leader could have completely prevented this from occurring.

Identify the multicultural issues that need to be taken into consideration for you as a leader. Based on the composition of this group, what multicultural issues (etic and emic) need to be taken into consideration as the incident is addressed in group?

This is clearly a challenging group to lead from a multicultural perspective. It consists of boys ranging in age from 15 to 17, most of whom have experienced significant trauma, either private and internal trauma or as a result of external events. Their ethnicity, their cultures of origin, and their degree of acculturation all mediate their responses to these traumatic events and internal crises. At this juncture, I actually know very little about the reasons for the dramatic changes in behavior that I am observing in several of these boys. The primary themes manifesting in these boys' recent behavior are confrontation, withdrawal, avoidance, and flight. Given the ethnic diversity of this group of boys, it may be more difficult for them to bond with each other if they are already strongly bonded to their ethnic group or culture of origin.

As a broad cultural example, there have been long-standing issues of distrust between Jews and blacks, and between Jews and members of Islamic cultures. To the extent that Richard identifies culturally with his grandparent's Israeli heritage, this could affect his ability to form close emotional bonds with Jamal, and possibly with Michael as well, though I am not certain how strongly anti-Semitic themes run in the Jamaican subculture. Of course, anti-Semitism is not confined to these specific subcultures but exists in both subtle and more obvious ways in our dominant Christian-American culture as well.

Virtually every boy in this group has been subject to prejudice and discrimination in one form or another. Eduardo, Michael, Jamal, Steven, Gary, and Sammy are all members of underrepresented groups in the United States, subject to prejudicial treatment and stereotyped perceptions. These experiences of discrimination inevitably interact with their budding explorations of gender roles and sexual orientation. This can create a confusing and sometimes aggressive mix of influences on these boys' present functioning and behavior. However, to the degree that these boys have been attending school with boys from a number of other cultures over a period of years, some of the strain of cross-cultural relating may have eased. It is impossible to determine this from the amount of information presented in this vignette.

From an emic perspective, the boys in this group come from cultures that are diverse with respect to their specific definitions of masculinity and their expectations of boys. Each subculture has implicit and explicit standards for the rite of passage from male adolescence into male adulthood. I would have to weigh the impact of any intervention I might make to "protect" a member against the emic imperatives of competition and establishment of a hierarchy of dominance that would be natural to this type of group of boys. From an etic perspective, to the extent that this vying for position took the form of emotional and verbal abuse of one or more of the members, I would tend to view that process as unhealthy and one that needs to be interrupted and redirected. My fear is that the emic cultural imperatives would be significantly more powerful than the more "civilized" interaction into which I would hope to redirect their exchange.

Explain how your ethnic and cultural background affected the way you would respond as a leader.

This question is discussed within responses to other questions. See also the "Summary/Analysis of Responses" section at the end of this chapter.

Explain how your ethnic and cultural background may or may not inhibit the way you respond to the situation as a leader.

The critical incident portrayed in this vignette involves a situation in which several members of the therapy group accost another member. Jason's fairly passive and withdrawn response style seemed to elicit increasing amounts of aggression, criticism, and ridicule from the five boys who were attacking him. My ethnic and cultural background as a Jewish, bisexual, female psychologist would inevitably shape my responses to this group in general and to this incident in particular. For example, I had a fairly traditional gender role orientation during my growing up years and grew up primarily with two sisters close to me in age. One product of my upbringing is that I lack an understanding of what motivates the violent and aggressive behavior that boys seem so ready to direct toward one another.

I find these boys' verbal, emotional, and physical aggression to be very disturbing and the motivations for that behavior difficult to relate to and understand. Whether this is a product of my gender, my ethnicity, our family's levels of educational attainment, or my own personality and temperament would be difficult to tease out. My background would lead me to struggle to some extent with issues of feeling intimidated and angry in the face of an incident like the one described in this vignette. I would struggle with questions of when and how to intervene. My tendency would be to take a proactive approach to provide appropriate conditions of emotional and physical safety for the boy under attack by the group, and to interrupt the destructive dynamic and try to redirect it into a more productive and balanced interaction between the boys.

I think I would also struggle with some feelings of helplessness and power-lessness in the face of the boys' aggression because I know such dynamics are rather ubiquitous in groups of teenage boys and there is probably little that I can really do to effectively prevent emotional harm to Jason. As a leader, I know I would also have to control my countertransference reactions to the boys who were being aggressive and control my potential overidentification with Jason, the victim of the aggression.

Explain how your ethnic and cultural background may have influenced your choice of the response you made over any other that you may have been considering as a leader.

In this vignette, the leader responds by helping the boys explore what they understand to be the various possible meanings of the homophobic epithets they hurled at Jason. The leader tries to help the boys explore both the meaning of those words and issues regarding gender roles, for example, what it means to be a "man" and homophobia. I probably would have taken much the same approach.

When Jason failed to return to the next group session, there are a number of responses I would have considered. The primary traditions I associate with my Jewish heritage are traditions of intellectualism, education, fairness, and standing up for those who are unable to stand up for themselves. These values would have influenced my choice of response. These elements of my ethnic and cultural background would probably lead me in a couple of directions in this group. Taking into account the emic considerations relating to adolescent male rites of passage, though these may be manifested differently in various subcultures, I would try to move the boys into an exploration of larger issues relating to their behavior toward Jason. I would ask them to explore their concepts of honor, of honorable conflict, and what it means to be a man. I would invite them to talk about who in last week's group they felt acted most like a man, whose behavior they felt was most worthy of respect, and I would push them to make explicit what element went into their definition of manhood. I would ask them whom they felt acted in the least honorable way and what definition of honor they were using.

In other words, I would probably keep most of the focus on the boys who were present and how they evaluated their own behavior from an emic perspective rather than create further opportunity to verbally bash Jason in his absence. If this process went well, I might shift to an attempt to have them develop empathy for Jason's position by having each of them reflect on a time when they had been on the outside of a group rather than on the inside. I would ask the boys who had been quieter about a time when they may have played a more dominating role in such an interaction, thereby hoping to help all of the boys understand roles, cultural expectations, and personality as separate but intermingling elements of their lives and experiences.

As a result of the response you chose, identify the consequences you might anticipate as a leader.

I'm really not certain what the result of this approach might be. My hope would be that I would successfully avoid being perceived as having a bias against the boys who were being aggressive and that I would be successful in inviting the conversation to move to a deeper and more interesting level for all of the boys in the therapy group. I do not think it is productive to assign blame or to focus on "who did what to whom." Rather, I believe that the most important thing is to get these boys to become conscious of their motivations and to begin to critically examine the messages they have adopted. I believe it is important to invite these boys to think about what it means to be honorable, what it means to be a man, and to begin to make conscious choices about how they wish to embody their beliefs and values in the world.

From your position as a leader, explain what the most glaring or outstanding aspect was of the situation which impacted you from your ethnic and cultural orientation.

The most significant aspect of this situation from my perspective is the complex interplay between rites of passage, gender roles, and sexuality. It is startling to realize that boys, even whole cultures, feel so threatened by deviations from traditional gender expression that they will resort to heart-numbing degrees of physical and emotional violence to enforce these supposedly "natural" cultural mandates. If traditional roles were, in fact, so "natural," they would not need to be enforced with such venomous intensity. I believe that my position in this culture as a Jewish-American, bisexual, female psychologist allows me to move beyond majority perspectives within the dominant culture and create alternative visions for how we might define even our most basic notions of adulthood and masculinity. I facilitate groups from a position of open-minded questioning consistent with my Judaism and the fluidity of my sexuality, and this allows me to create the space for others to find their own unique path of cultural integration and self-expression.

MICHAEL GARRETT'S REACTIONS AS A MEMBER OF THIS COUNSELING/THERAPY GROUP

Identify the multicultural issues and explain how your ethnic and cultural background affected your response, inhibited your response, and influenced your choice of response. Identify the consequences you might anticipate as a result of your response, and explain what the most outstanding aspect of the situation was based on your ethnic and cultural orientation.

One of the first issues that stands out for me as a member is the fact that the group is not voluntary. On a positive note, I am likely to come because I am curious about what happens or is going to happen in the group. I am also curious to hear the stories of others who are different from me, or maybe very similar. However, though the intent and purpose of the group may be good, the fact that I am forced to go creates a scenario where I am less likely to actively participate because my choice is not being respected. For me, that does not necessarily mean doing anything to actively disrupt the group, but it might mean that I will be more withdrawn.

In my culture, disrespecting a person's choice may be met with that person being subtly elusive or outright shunning of the person or people who are doing the disrespecting. Interference is "bad medicine" and not taken lightly. As a result of my being withdrawn, I am likely to connect more readily with the other more withdrawn, less verbal members of the group, at least nonverbally, if not otherwise. Any dynamic of connection or trust between myself and the leader(s) may deteriorate quickly if I begin to feel like I am being pushed in any way rather than invited to participate.

Another glaring issue for me as a member is the way in which conflict and confrontation are allowed to happen in the group, and how these things are dealt with in the group, not only by members but also by the leader(s). By allowing the other members to confront Jason in a very aggressive way, the message that gets sent to me is, "Hey, you could be next!" Why? Because Jason may have been doing exactly what I would be doing as a member: being quiet, observing the interaction, choosing my words carefully so as not to disrespect anyone else in the group, possibly speaking a little more slowly and a little more softly, and limiting my eye contact (again, out of respect and a desire to not be pushed).

Either way, the issue of safety is called into question for me at that point. Would I stand up for Jason when the others begin to come down on him? I do not know, but I would probably be identifying strongly with him at that point. If I stand up for Jason, I am likely to incur the same wrath from the other members and, at the same time, make Jason lose face by not letting him deal with it himself. If I do not stand up for Jason, however, then I am not being true to myself and the principles of relation in which I believe.

In my culture, two or more people may have a disagreement, but one never causes another person to lose face, especially in a social situation. This can sometimes be especially true for men. Losing face is a form of harming someone's spirit and is considered worse than harming that person physically. Even in times of disagreement, one must not harm the relation. Proper ways of communicating must be used to address the issue without hurting or disrespecting the person. "Being right" or "being mad" never gives one the right to disrespect someone else; that is putting oneself in bad relations and, in some cases, can be considered a form of "witchcraft."

As for Jason's choice about "should I stay or should I go," given a choice, I would probably not want to come back either. It seems like a no-win situation. I might want to participate, but I would wonder: If I say things that offer up my essence, will they be respected or will they be criticized and used against me? Yet, if I choose not to come to the group, that will work against me, too, as I do not have that choice without other consequences. The experience of the group may begin to seem a lot like my experience of being Native American in a mainstream world: Sometimes you win, and sometimes you lose; overall, you just hope you can go home at the end of the day.

MICHAEL GARRETT'S REACTIONS AS A LEADER OF THIS COUNSELING/THERAPY GROUP

If this type of incident would not occur in your group, explain why it would not. Identify the multicultural issues and explain how your ethnic and cultural background affected your response, inhibited your response, and influenced your choice of response. Identify the consequences you might anticipate as a result of your response and explain what the most outstanding aspect of the situation was based on your ethnic and cultural orientation.

Some of the same cultural issues that apply for me as a member would also apply for me as a leader. In particular, the issues of keeping in good relations, maintaining respect, communicating with feeling and passion without losing compassion, finding common ground, using humor to build bridges no matter how big or small, listening to the silence as well as the words, approaching others with a sense of humility and openness to experiencing them—these are but a few. Some of the qualities or behaviors that I mention here are a way of life for me and others in my culture raised similarly, and they are taken very seriously. There is a belief among people of my tribe, and many other tribes that I know of, that "whatever you put out there will come back to you seven times stronger." When you look at things from that point of view, it becomes more important to be sensitive to what you put out there in terms of your daily thoughts and actions, not out of a sense of guilt or self-preservation, but more out of a sense that you *are* connected with things and people around you, and you are acting with wisdom and humility in that recognition.

It is not a certainty, but the incident that occurred in the group with a number of members ganging up on Jason would not be likely to happen if I were the leader. I would like to say that it would not happen because of my outstanding skills as a group leader, but it would probably be more attributable to the attention I would give to the group setup. I would set up the format for this group based on the Native talking circle. Moreover, I am careful from the beginning of every group to be very clear about my expectations of what is to happen or not happen in group, while making sure to clearly listen to the expectations of group members. Part of the setup for a talking circle includes the following:

1. Show respect when another person is talking.
2. Silence is acceptable, and sometimes necessary.
3. Each person speaks when she is ready to speak, and not always through the use of words.
4. Everyone is treated the same (equal status).

In using the talking circle, I ask group members to request permission of the group before they enter the actual space of the circle (and symbolically, before they enter the physical or spiritual space of individual members), as well as when they leave the circle. I also ask for consensus that we make this a normal part of the way we run the group. I ask that members speak when it is their time to speak (in terms of "I" rather than "you") and listen when it is their time to listen. I might introduce some form of "talking stick" or other sacred object with the idea of reinforcing, through a physical reminder, the importance of respect in the group. I also might introduce some form of ceremonial opening and/or closing of group sessions, and I might invite the group to lead these, or create their own, through consensus.

With this group, I would likely have talked from a traditional Native perspective about both the concept and the act of respect in a group setting. I might say, for example, "Everyone here has his own purpose for being here, and his own unique contribution to the group that may be made in many ways besides words." I might ask that we, as members of the group, seek to "speak from the heart, but also listen with our senses."

I want to sensitize group members to the energy of the group, and their own place within that flow. To further the notion of respect and the practice of interference versus noninterference, I might talk about my perception of the sacredness of space, both inner space (mind/spirit) and outer space (physical/environmental). A brief demonstration of this concept might involve asking for one volunteer, processing what happens when I just walk right into that person's "space" without permission, showing the proper way to approach the person, and asking for the person's reaction to the contrast between the two different approaches. Following this, I would likely talk about the idea of "connect/disconnect" as a way of beginning to have members be sensitive to what they are experiencing in the group at any given moment, and sensing what that means for them before they react (offensively or defensively). I also would be likely to talk about the concept of *nuwati* or medicine (essence) from my perspective as a Cherokee, and have them relate that concept to themselves as a way of understanding their own experiences and the experiences of others.

I might have done all this in a mere 15 minutes (do you really believe that?) or over a period of several sessions, as a way of beginning to build a strong sense of community within the group that is consistent with my cultural background. As an elder once said to me, "Without community, a group is just a bunch of people sitting around talking, but not really hearing anything."

Specifically, I would wonder whether some of the things occurring in the group beyond what was said might indicate that sexual identity is an issue for one or more of the group members. If so, I would ask myself how I could create therapeutic benefit for those members while at the same time being conscious of the need to protect them from harm in the current group context.

Generally, I am conscious that this group consists of members who fall into the age range from 15 to 17; they are all males; they may or may not all be heterosexual; they come from different cultural and ethnic backgrounds, probably with different ways of communicating, seeing the world, and interpreting their experiences; and they are all present in the group as a result of referral by someone else and for difficulties related to school or home. Some of the questions that run through my mind, as I consider the experiences of these young men from their perspective, are the following:

- Who am I?
- Where do I belong?
- Where is my source of power?
- Who is trying to take my power away, and how do I deal with that?
- How have I dealt with oppression, and how do I deal with it now?
- How do I deal with pain, discouragement, sadness, and anger?
- What does it mean to be a man?
- What does it mean to be successful, and how important is that to me?
- What makes me happy?
- Where do I come from; where am I going?
- Why bother?

These are all important questions for the group members to consider.

MICHAEL HUTCHINS'S REACTIONS AS A MEMBER OF THIS COUNSELING/THERAPY GROUP

Identify the multicultural issues that need to be taken into consideration for you as a group member.

The primary issue for me as a group member is that of safety. As I look around the group, I have difficulty identifying with the other group members. Jason appears to be the group member who is most like me. If I am an adolescent sorting through issues of sexual orientation, I need to know that my peers are not going to be abusive and that it is safe for me to discuss my attraction to other males. In the previous session, the words *faggot* and *queer* were used. This hurt, and I felt angry. However, other group members are really angry, and I need to know that they will not attack me with their anger. I believe that I could be a target of such attacks in the future.

Related to the issue of safety, I need to know that I am going to be respected. I need to know that my peers and the counselor are going to listen to me and that they are going to make attempts to understand me. The use of abusive language in the previous session does not feel like respect. I want to be able to talk about how I feel. The discussion about "being a man" and "homophobia" was nice, but it did not address feelings, and I felt excluded and isolated.

As a member, I want to know what the rules are in the group about anger. Are group members allowed to attack other group members? Does anyone here know what it is like to be attracted to other males? How do these guys who are very different from me feel about being in the group with me? How do I feel about being in the group with them? I do not like it. Everyone here seems really different from me. I think a couple of these guys might be gay, too, but it is not safe to say that.

I am not sure what it means to be attracted to other males. I wonder if the others in the group do. I wonder what their families think about gay people and the people in their neighborhoods. I suspect that most of these guys are not comfortable with their sexuality. Do people here know the difference between being afraid of sexuality and being afraid of being gay? Some things that are called "homophobia" should be identified as fear of anything sexual.

I wonder if everyone here feels as different as I feel. Some of these guys have had difficulty in school Maybe they believe they are not accepted either. Some of these guys do not talk much. I understand that. Maybe talking is a way to keep out of trouble. I know these guys look really different from me. They cannot hide what makes them different. I can hide the fact that I am attracted to other guys. When I do that, I feel lonely and afraid. Sometimes it feels like it would just be easier to run away from all of this. Hmmm, I wonder if the other guys get as depressed as I do.

Explain how your ethnic and cultural background affected the way you would respond as a member.

Having grown up in a blue-collar, Catholic, Irish-American family, I was taught not to discuss religion, sex, or politics. In my family, we talked about Catholicism a lot. We were not supposed to know about other religions. We never talked about sexuality. As a result, issues of sexual orientation were kept secret. Additionally, there was little understanding of different ethnic and cultural groups. With that family history, I would be very quiet and would withdraw if conflict seemed possible. My family members would not understand the differences in the group; they either would not say anything or would quietly make disparaging remarks. Fighting and arguing directly were not rewarded. As a result, I would have withdrawn, as did Jason.

If I were one of the other group members, I would wonder about Jason. How did he get to be in this group? If he is gay, I do not think I could feel comfortable around him. What if he is attracted to me? What would that say about me? It is not safe having him in here. It would be easier if he just did not come to group anymore.

Explain how your ethnic and cultural background may or may not inhibit the way you respond to the situation as a member.

My parents, particularly my father, had a great deal of "respect for authority." If I followed his belief system, I would have deferred to the counselor and expected her to resolve any conflicts that arose in the group. To engage in an argument or fight would have been seen as disrespectful to the entire group.

My family did not address issues of sexuality in the family. It was not considered appropriate to do so. Additionally, there was little or no understanding of homosexuality. The introduction of discussion about sexuality and homosexuality would have offended my parents. They would have held closely to the teachings of the Roman Catholic Church. No questioning of papal authority or teaching would have been acceptable.

Additionally, direct expression of anger was considered disrespectful and "beneath us." The norm in the family was to work hard to be part of middle-class, white America. Any behavior that did not approach that norm was quietly discouraged. Open expression of anger was not permitted. When the group members became more vocal and "venomous," I would have wanted the group to become more peaceful to follow along with the cultural norm with which I was raised.

If I were to follow "family rules," I would have withdrawn from the discussion, answered any questions in a minimal way, and not returned to the group. Jason's behavior was very much in keeping with the norms with which I was raised.

Explain how your ethnic and cultural background may have influenced your choice of the response you made over any other that you may have been considering as a member.

Respect for authority and the importance of safety would have been cultural driving forces for me. Additionally, avoidance of anger and conflict would have had their impact. As a result, the decision to address inequality, abuse, and anger would have been hampered by the sense of needing to "create security" at all costs. Additionally, the prohibitions concerning discussion of sexuality are very strong. Fear of sexuality inhibits much of the discussion. The acceptance of traditional Catholic teaching would have influenced my decision making as a youth. Again, the cultural norm would have been to quietly endure, not confront, and not return for another session.

As a result of the response you chose, identify the consequences you might anticipate as a member.

The decision to quietly endure, not confront, and not return would have created safety. However, it would not have helped in self-discovery, growth, and personal change. Perhaps if I had been quiet for long enough, the group would have moved on to other issues. However, at this stage in group development, I might have become the scapegoat for group anger.

From your position as a member, explain what the most glaring or outstanding aspect was of the situation which impacted you from your ethnic and cultural orientation.

The most outstanding aspect of the situation is the anger, oppression, and misunderstanding about sexual orientation. As the group jostled for position and a culture was built, Jason was left on the outside of the group. The anger of already-angry peers was building and predictable. While each of the group members was also a member of a nondominant group, none was identified as being from a sexual minority. Often, members of the gay, lesbian, bisexual, and transgendered community are invisible. While other group members were mostly identifiable as belonging to a specific cultural or ethnic minority, Jason may not have been. This invisibility creates special concerns and may also make a person a target for angry, uninformed discrimination.

MICHAEL HUTCHINS'S REACTIONS AS A LEADER OF THIS COUNSELING/THERAPY GROUP

If this type of incident would not occur in your group, explain why it would not.

I would like to believe that this type of incident would not occur in a group that I was leading for several reasons. First, the group would be clear about norms for confronting dissonance and difference. Early in group, I would teach group members a model for identifying feelings, thoughts, and behaviors. Additionally, they would learn a confrontation format that taught ownership of their responses and accountability. This would allow members to have different worldviews and would encourage acceptance of differences.

In working with young men, I would build community in the early stages of the group by having the group involved in a community-building experience, which is different from verbal, insight-oriented group work. We would have been involved in a problem-solving activity that encouraged collaborative decision making and trust building. Additionally, the group would have had the opportunity to discuss what the group norms would be concerning discussion of sexuality, creating safety, showing respect for one another, and addressing differences.

Identify the multicultural issues that need to be taken into consideration for you as a leader.

The issues that need to be accounted for are the diversity of the young men who are in the group. Several have been identified as being angry. It is important to know how their anger is expressed and supported in their families and greater community. It is also important for me to recognize that it is necessary for each of the group members to feel safe. I believe that safety comes from sharing a common experience and developing understanding of each other's worldviews. In reviewing the brief descriptions of the young men, I wonder about the relationships they have with their fathers or father figures. Men are expected to play a number of culturally defined roles. I wonder what roles these young men are learning to play and how they have learned about these roles. I would want to explore these questions with the young men and would chose to do so with experiential, perhaps adventure-based, activities designed to address gender roles.

It would be important for me to recognize that alternatives to verbal, insight-oriented psychotherapy might be more appropriate for the young men in this group. It is quite likely that young men from diverse backgrounds could work collaboratively at a nonverbal task. In a task group, they would re-create the way they behave in their worlds and might then be able to pull together some conclusions as a group.

Additionally, it would be important for me to know that young men who are beginning to explore who they are as men may have fears, shame, anger, and hurt surrounding sexual identity development. When experiencing such affective states, they can move into culturally sanctioned defensive positions.

Explain how your ethnic and cultural background affected the way you would respond as a leader.

As a result of having grown up as a gay man in a family that does not recognize issues of sexuality, I learned to read my environment very carefully. The world was not as safe as it appeared to others. The norm was to keep secrets and not discuss personal issues. A high value was placed on respect and security. As a result, I believe that it is important for a group leader to create an environment where group members can build safe, respectful communities.

My experience in having lived in different cultural settings and working in a variety of work settings has increased my ability to tap into diverse cultural norms. This life experience assists me in recognizing that I do not always recognize diverse worldviews, even when I am most committed to doing so. As a result, I consistently check with group members and invite them to share their observations of what is occurring. Sometimes, group members will not share verbally but will share in other ways. Hopefully, I encourage such sharing by working with group members to create an atmosphere of safety and respect.

Explain how your ethnic and cultural background may or may not inhibit the way you respond to the situation as a leader.

At times, as a white male, I assume that group members may have access to power when they know that they do not have such access. It is important for me to check out the perceptions of group members. Also, it is important for me to acknowledge that, even if they have definite views, they may not share such views with me. Some of the assumptions about white privilege are a part of who I am.

Additionally, having grown up in the time in history that I have, I must acknowledge my own prejudices. My assumptions and prejudices can, and do, interfere with how I see, hear, and experience the world. I must be willing to be confronted and to confront such prejudices in the least defensive way possible. Otherwise, these prejudices can interfere with my effectiveness as a group leader.

Explain how your ethnic and cultural background may have influenced your choice of the response you made over any other that you may have been considering as a leader.

As a result of having lived with several different cultural groups, I am more aware of differences in worldviews than some people with more limited backgrounds. In my family of origin, there was little tolerance for differences. Much of this lack of tolerance came from the need to work together to ensure that family members had basic needs met. As a result, I consistently explore ways for the group to express differences in a manner that will enhance group safety and respect, even when the task confronting the group is to address dissonance among group members.

As a result of the response you chose, identify the consequences you might anticipate as a leader.

As a result of the way I would structure the group, I would like to believe that Michael, Jamal, Richard, Gary, and Sammy would have learned skills that would allow them to express their anger in ways that would be safe and respectful for all group members. Additionally, by using experiential group activities early in the group sessions, I would hope that group members would have developed a respect for themselves and each other that would transcend the anger and fear around sexuality.

If the norms for safety and diversity had been appropriately integrated, Jason might have felt safer in exploring issues of sexual identity within the group. This might have invited other group members to do so as well. Additionally, a change in norms might have encouraged Eduardo and Steven to express themselves more assertively.

From your position as a leader, explain what the most glaring or outstanding aspect was of the situation which impacted you from your ethnic and cultural orientation.

The most glaring dynamics are the differences and similarities between the young men. There is the presence of anger, the lack of healthy male role models, the presence of trauma, and the adolescent acting-out behaviors. It seems that each of the young men is struggling for definition, and that these young men may be caught in the dynamics of changing cultural values. Additionally, I suspect an underlying loneliness and isolation. Group members appear to be disconnected from the norms of the dominant culture. They may be very connected to the norms of the nondominant culture with which they more closely identify. I suspect the group is acting out the tension of the culture in which they live. The dominant culture has a changing set of norms, and nondominant groups, feeling the tension, often act out these stresses within their own groups and families.

Based on the composition of this group, what multicultural issues (etic and emic) need to be taken into consideration as the incident is addressed in group?

The most significant incident, at this point, appears to be Jason's absence. As the group leader, I would want to engage the young men in a reflective discussion of the previous session. Perhaps I would work with the young men to look at how they express anger and frustration. I would also want to explore differences and similarities in ways different families and groups think, feel, and behave when they are feeling excluded or unsafe. The exploration of differences and similarities might lead to productive work for each of the young men.

I would want to engage the group in an experiential session after we had come to a greater understanding of where each individual is, what their relationships with each other are, and what we can say about the group as a unit. After that discussion, we would explore ways to invite Jason back into the group. As the group leader, I would contact Jason, and would probably see him in an individual session. Clearly, the fourth group session was not a safe one for Jason. If he would be willing to speak with me, I would help him to express that lack of safety. I would also explore ways to make the group safer for him.

It is critical to understand the potential difficulties that young men with sexual identity concerns have with their peers. While the dominant culture may be more willing to openly discuss issues of sexual orientation, many young people are not prepared to openly discuss the issues in their own lives. Stereotypes about gay people are still predominantly negative and often misunderstood. Although more attention is being paid to issues of sexual identity development, young people still experience the pain of discrimination.

Many resources are available to these young men. The Internet is changing the lives of many young gay men and women. Jason may or may not know this. Much caution, however, should be observed when exploring Internet resources. Not all of the information is helpful to healthy identity development.

It is important to consider the pace of change in contemporary culture. While some changes are happening rapidly in the dominant culture, these changes may not be conducive to understanding and security. It would be most helpful to assist the young men in this group in exploring change and seeing how it plays out in their lives and the lives of their families. It also might be helpful to work with the schools and other organizations with which these young men identify. Group members could learn how to support and advocate for each other outside of this particular group setting, but in order for that to happen, the leader must help the group reconnect and become a safe place for all members.

There has been an increase in youth violence recently. In the past several years, young men have begun to act out their anger more openly. It would be critical to assist the young men in this group in exploring culturally appropriate expression of anger. With the rise in violence in youth culture, counselors need to be aware of the potential for danger for young men. It would seem *most* appropriate to work collaboratively with these group members to develop ground rules for respectfully disagreeing with each other. Respect is an important dynamic in the world of young adult males, and creating a respectful environment is key to working with these young men.

SUMMARY/ANALYSIS OF RESPONSES

As Members of This Counseling/Therapy Group

Identify the multicultural issues that need to be taken into consideration for you as a member.

Both Firestein and Garrett identified issues of gender and sexual orientation. Garrett points out that from a Native-American perspective, the group members did not respect (i.e., showed disrespect for) a person's right to choose when they treated Jason as they did. Issues related to age (developmental stage of members) were also identified by both respondents.

Another issue raised by Firestein, Garrett, and Hutchins is the issue of respect and safety. Garrett speaks of the Native-American view that forced membership shows disrespect for a member's right to choose and that the boys were disrespectful in their confrontation of Jason. He questions whether he should take a stand for Jason; if he does, Jason could lose face, but if he does not, then he would not be true to himself. Hutchins would like, as a member, to know what the group rules are for handling anger.

Garrett views Jason's choosing to not return to the group as a no-win situation. Had Jason opted to participate and share with the group, he might have opened himself to criticism. However, to not participate works against him, too, since he loses an opportunity for growth.

Explain how your ethnic and cultural background affected the way you would respond as a member.

Firestein, Garrett, and Hutchins all come from families in which fighting, conflict, and open hostile disagreement are not tolerated. In addition, Garrett tells us that from a Native-American perspective, public display of disagreement leads to loss of face, and Hutchins refers to the reluctance of his family of origin to discuss mattes of sexuality. For all respondents, their early life experiences would influence how they would respond as a member of this group.

Explain how your ethnic and cultural background may or may not inhibit the way you respond to the situation as a member.

Garrett and Hutchins both refer to the disrespect shown to Jason as central concerns. Garrett tells us his respect for authority would have him defer to the counselor to deal with the conflict, since his Native-American culture considers it disrespectful to engage in open arguing and fighting. As a member, he would talk softly and slowly, with limited eye contact in order to show respect and a desire not to be pushed. Firestein would probably offer Jason support but not disclose her own sexual orientation. All the respondents come from backgrounds where sexual matters were not openly discussed, which would make this situation difficult for them as members.

Explain how your ethnic and cultural background may have influenced your choice of the response you made over any other that you may have been considering as a member.

Both Firestein and Garrett would be concerned about safety issues as members; therefore, they would keep their involvement in the group rather minimal. Firestein's Jewish background, with its emphasis on respect and fairness, might influence her to break her silence in order to offer words of support for Jason, but basically would bide her time in the group and then move on. Garrett's Native-American background would influence him to help Jason save face, but he would maintain a low profile to avoid injuring Jason's spirit. His background taught him to convey respect and to avoid harming relationships. Likewise, Hutchins's Catholic background would make him reluctant to express anger or be involved in conflict, and that, combined with his concern for safety issues, would probably lead him to drop out of the group.

As a result of the response you chose, identify the consequences you might anticipate as a member.

Firestein would not expect to get much from the group, since the safety issue would make her reluctant to open up in this group. She might, however, try to talk to Jason away from the group. Garrett believes his response would help the group to establish respect, not harm members' spirits or relationships, and help others save face. Hutchins anticipates that he would either lose a growth opportunity by dropping out of the group, be left behind by the group when it moves on to other issues, or become a scapegoat for group anger.

From your position as a member, explain what the most glaring or outstanding aspect was of the situation which impacted you from your ethnic and cultural orientation.

Firestein presents four glaring aspects in this incident. The first relates to the theme of violence, which she finds uncomfortable. She presents loss as another. One member is about to lose his mother to cancer, and another lost a brother. A third aspect addresses scapegoating. Firestein underscores how much she hates the way the boys picked on and taunted Jason just because he was different. The fourth regards sexual orientation, particularly as it relates to the struggle of adolescents.

For Garrett, disrespect, aggressiveness, the lack of safety, and the loss of face were the most glaring aspects of the situation. Hutchins identifies anger, oppression, and misunderstanding of sexual orientation as the aspects that stood out most for him.

As Leaders of This Counseling/Therapy Group

If this type of incident would not occur in your group, explain why it would not.

Firestein anticipates that the incident could occur in a group she was leading due to a number of variables. The group is comprised of adolescent males who are mandated to attend it. Firestein sees one consequence of forming such a group under those conditions as loss of trust and safety. She also identifies the cultural issues of adolescent males (competition, dominance, juggling for position, and sexuality) as factors to be addressed, along with the relationship between masculinity and homosexuality.

Hutchins and Garrett, on the other hand, do not think that this incident would occur in the group if they were leaders. Hutchins explains that he would have established clear norms early in the group regarding such matters as confrontation, dissonance, and difference; sexuality; and safety and respect. In addition, he would teach members to identify feelings, thoughts, and behaviors. He also places emphasis on building community early in the life of the group with experiential activities related to problem solving through collaboration and trust building.

Garrett, like Hutchins, would have established norms early in the group related to identifying what members can expect will happen or will not happen. Other norms Garrett would have built would be related to respect and allowing for silences. He would have members view silence as being necessary, although they would be free to speak when they felt ready. He would help members understand that communication can take nonverbal forms and that all members are equal. Similar to Hutchins, Garrett would employ an experiential approach to establishing these group (community) norms, in this case, the Native-American technique of the talking circle. Members would request permission to enter and leave the space of the circle and before entering the physical or spiritual space of others. Garrett would seek consensus of the group members, however, before employing this technique.

Identify the multicultural issues that need to be taken into consideration for you as a leader.

All three respondents are in agreement that given the diversity of the membership, an accounting has to be made for the different worldviews that are present in this group. Firestein points out that this is a group comprised of adolescent males and because of their ethnic diversity, they will find it hard to bond with each other. She sees issues of ethnic and cultural origin and degree of acculturation present in this group and raises the possibility that there will be distrust based on age-old issues between Jewish and black members and Jewish and Islamic members.

Garrett and Hutchins identify sexuality as an issue and the need to establish respect and safety so that gay members can be free from harm. Garrett adds that due to cultural and ethnic diversity, the group members will have different ways of communicating and interpreting their experiences.

Explain how your ethnic and cultural background affected the way you would respond as a leader.

Because she is a Jewish, bisexual female psychologist, Firestein finds it disturbing and difficult to relate to verbal, emotional, and physical aggression. Her family of origin context also had traditional gender roles, and there were no aggressive or violent male behaviors, since both of her siblings are female.

According to Garrett, Native Americans must be sensitive to what one "puts out there" in thought and deed, but without a sense of guilt or self-preservation—rather, one needs to show respect based on a sense of being connected with all things and people. Additionally, one needs to act with humility and wisdom. In sum, these are all related to conveying respect and feelings of passion and compassion.

Hutchins states that as a gay male, he has learned to read environments carefully. His family of origin did not acknowledge issues of sexuality. Therefore, he emphasizes creating a group environment where members can build a safe and respectful community.

Explain how your ethnic and cultural background may or may not inhibit the way you respond to the situation as a leader.

Of the three respondents, Garrett seems to be the least inhibited, perhaps due to his Native-American worldview. He informs us about many qualities and behaviors that are a way of life for him. He would be guided by the Native-American belief that "whatever you put out there will come back to you seven times stronger."

Firestein and Hutchins both claimed that their backgrounds would inhibit them. Firestein would struggle with male verbal, emotional, and physical aggression. She would also struggle with her own feelings of helplessness and powerlessness in the face of the boys' aggression. She acknowledges a need to control her countertransference toward aggressive boys and her overidentification with Jason as a victim. Hutchins relates that he would need to be conscious of and control his assumptions based on white male privilege. He acknowledges that being a while male, these assumptions and prejudices could interfere with how he sees, hears, and experiences the world.

Explain how your ethnic and cultural background may have influenced your choice of the response you made over any other that you may have been considering as a leader.

Firestein identifies that her Jewish heritage and traditions related to intellectualism, education, fairness, and advocating for the helpless directed her choice of response. Garrett's Native-American background is strongly in evidence when he lists the issues of keeping good relationships, maintaining respect, communicating with feeling and passion without losing compassion, finding common ground, using humor, approaching others with humility, and maintaining openness to receiving others. Hutchins explains that his family of origin did not tolerate differences; consequently, he explores ways to encourage group expression of tolerance for differences and to establish norms of safety and respect.

As a result of the response you chose, identify the consequences you might anticipate as a leader.

All three respondents anticipated that members would develop self-respect and respect for others. Firestein expects that the boys will know what it is to be honorable and a man. Both Garrett and Hutchins anticipate that the members will show respect to one another. Hutchins believes that once that is achieved, the members would be able to transcend their feelings of fear and anger with regard to sexuality. Garrett sees the members developing the Native-American sense of *nuwati* (essence), which is a form of empathy. Firestein adds that once the conversation reaches a deeper level, she expects the boys to learn to make conscious choices about how to embody their beliefs and values in the world, and to become more conscious of their motivations.

In addition, Hutchins anticipates that the group members will become more willing to explore sexual identity issues and that Eduardo and Steven will learn to express themselves more assertively. Garrett foresees the members learning to express feelings and passion. He also believes the members will learn to accept silence and view one another as equals, develop a sense of humility, and learn to work from consensus. He would discuss with members the sacredness of inner space (mind/spirit) and of outer space (physical/environmental). The members, he believes, would learn the difference between interference and noninterference in human relationships.

From your position as a leader, explain what the most glaring or outstanding aspect was of the situation which impacted you from your ethnic and cultural orientation.

Firestein highlights the complex interplay between rites of passage, gender roles, and sexuality. Her Judaism would direct her to lead this group in a manner that would address the group's issues in an open-minded, questioning way. She also believes that the fluidity of her sexuality and her Judaism would allow her to create space that would encourage others to find their own unique paths of cultural integration.

Hutchins's response parallels Firestein's in some ways. The most outstanding aspects of the incident for him include adolescent acting out, the struggle for definition and changing cultural values, disconnection from norms of the dominant culture, and conflict between the members' nondominant cultures and the dominant culture's changing norms. Garrett refers to the dominant issue as being sexuality. He also sees ethnic and cultural influences as having a significant impact. Hutchins suggests further that, as a leader, the members might see in him a healthy role model that could be lacking in the rest of their lives. He also illuminates the existence of anger, trauma, and the differences and similarities between the young men in the group.

Based on the composition of the group, what multicultural issues (etic and emic) need to be taken into consideration as the incident is addressed in group?

On the emic side of the question, sexuality and sexual orientation were identified as primary issues by all three respondents. Firestein notes that group members are from different cultures that define masculinity and expectations of boys in different ways. Garrett also notes the differences that exist between members, and Hutchins mentions the importance of examining stereotypes of gay people. Hutchins also adds to the list of emic issues the expression of anger, attention to Jason's absence, expression of frustration, the pace of change in contemporary culture, and the violence that is found in youth culture.

The respondents identified the following etic issues: gender roles, sexual orientation, differences in cultural groups, and gender and chronological age of members. Firestein notes that six members are from underrepresented groups, which has probably led to experiences of discrimination that interact with the issues of gender roles and sexual orientation. Given the diversity of the group, Garrett perceives there will be different ways of communicating and interpreting member experiences. Both Garrett and Hutchins, however, point out that the members are all boys between the ages of 15 and 17. Hutchins notes a further member similarity in that they are all adolescent males struggling with sexual identity. Finally, as Garrett points out, all the members have been referred to the group (i.e., they are not there voluntarily) and have home or school difficulties. This would be another issue related to safety and respect in this group.

10 CHAPTER

Counseling/ Therapy Group Vignette #3

A Gender Orientation Group— Where Do We Fit?

You are a counselor in a counseling center at a major university. Over the years you have developed a reputation for being exceptionally sensitive in your work with students who are struggling with issues of gender identity and sexual orientation. You have written extensively and conducted seminars on the subject. Recently you decided to offer group counseling to a number of lesbian clients. Your sessions are running for 12 weeks during the spring semester. Your group consists of the following eight members.

- Sonny is a junior. She is a psychology major. She has two older brothers and one younger sister. She traces her ancestry back to the arrival of the Mayflower. You first met her when she was a sophomore. She came to you because she had heard of you through a "friend." At that first meeting, she presented as being quite anxious and uncertain. She stated that she was feeling very uneasy about a recent experience she had had with her roommate. As her story continued to unfold, she disclosed that while she and her roommate were "fooling around," she experienced herself becoming sexually aroused. She said that she had not revealed that to her roommate at the time. However, she added that the experience only heightened her curiosity. By the time she came to you, she had had a sexual experience with another woman. It was her first, but she found it to be pleasurable. She had sexual intercourse with a boy while in high school, but it was an unpleasant experience, totally unlike her recent experience with this woman. Wondering and confused about her sexual orientation, she came to you

- Jesse is a sophomore and a fine arts major. Her maternal grandparents are Orthodox Jews. Her mother married an Asian American. The marriage lasted until Jesse was 7 years old. Jesse's mother has not actively practiced her faith since she was a junior in college. Jesse "knew" she was different from the other girls since she was 12 years old when the other girls were interested in boys. She "came out" when she was a junior in high school. Ever since then, however, she has felt her relationships have been shallow and unfulfilling.

- Tikki is a senior and a political science major. She is African American. She has been in a relationship with one of her women professors whose identity she will not reveal. However, as Tikki is now in her final semester, her college professor said that they are going to have to end their relationship. Emotionally distraught by the prospect, Tikki has sought help from you.

- Ashara is a junior and a business major. Her family is very prominent in the Muslim community in her hometown. She has felt great conflict and anxiety since "discovering" her preference for women. She has stated that should her "secret" be discovered, it would bring great shame to her family. She realizes that she may no longer be able to avoid disclosing her secret. She came to you to help her with her dilemma.

- Star is a junior and a criminal justice major. She is Native American. Her partner of two years has asked to end their relationship, revealing that she has fallen in love with a man.

- Carla is a junior majoring in computer science. She is Hispanic American. She sought you out recently because she believed she was developing an interest in one of her male friends. He is straight. She has been with her partner for the past year and a half. She stated that for as long as she can remember, she has never experienced such feelings toward a male. Confused, anxious, and unable to sleep, she is uncertain about what to do with these newly discovered and unexpected feelings.

- Rosalie is a senior. She is an education major with an emphasis in early childhood and elementary education. Her parents are first-generation Polish Americans and devout Roman Catholics. With graduation nearing, she and her partner, who is also a senior, are planning to be married by her partner's Episcopalian priest who has blessed such relationships many times before. Rosalie has not come out to her parents. She and her partner want to celebrate their marriage with their respective families and friends. She has expressed concern that making such a desire known to her parents might have dire consequences. For that reason, she approached you to get some direction as what to do.

- Indira is a sophomore. Her major is communications. Her parents immigrated from India and have developed a very successful computer business. When you first saw Indira, she said she had attended a meeting of gay and lesbian students at the invitation of her friend. Shortly thereafter, she had her first lesbian relationship which she acknowledged as being pleasurable and personally fulfilling. However, since that experience, she has found herself feeling restless, on edge and avoiding, whenever possible, invitations to socialize with her friend who had introduced her to the gay and lesbian community. She states that she is torn from within and unable to bring resolution to her conflict because to do so would mean she would have to publicly admit to her sexual orientation. Just the thought of doing so causes her to feel panic.

This is the seventh session. The first two sessions followed expected group development processes for the first stage. Group goals were clarified, and codes of conduct were established. The emotional climate at first was tense, awkward, and ambiguous. Toward the latter moments of the second session, it seemed that the members realized they had permission to confront one another and they could set aside their concern for maintaining a "proper" public image. Sessions three through five saw members confronting one another directly, frequently challenging each others' incongruent statements and behaviors. It was also evident that members were dealing with dominance and control issues, and vying for positions of power during these sessions. Everyone seemed to weather the "storms" of these sessions, and by the end of the fifth session and all through the sixth session, an emotional closeness/intimacy among the members took the place of members seemingly rigidly holding onto their individual boundaries. There was clear evidence of emotional cohesion in the group as the group entered the seventh session.

The session began with Rosalie disclosing how anxious she was feeling. She reflected that they were now past the midpoint in the group, and she still had not figured out how she was going to address her parents, especially with an impending marriage only a few months away. The tone of her voice was filled with an intensity congruent with how she stated she was feeling. Ashara immediately stated how strongly she was affected by Rosalie's situation and how closely it related to her own circumstances; thus, she, too, felt a similar powerlessness. Tikki, upon hearing the word *powerlessness,* joined in by stating that she also feels powerless with the prospect of her relationship with her professor ending when she graduates. As these three members continued to engage with one another, the other five sat back, their demeanor conveying their uncertainty about their place in the transaction occurring between Rosalie, Ashara, and Tikki. Realizing that this is a significant moment in the group, you know you need to capitalize on it before it is lost.

CYNTHIA KALODNER'S REACTION AS A MEMBER OF THIS COUNSELING/THERAPY GROUP

Identify the multicultural issues that need to be taken into consideration for you as a member.

The multicultural issue that has most importance for me as a member of this group is the value of family in my cultural world. In Jewish families, the choices that individuals make have major significance for other members of the family. It would not be easy to "go against the family" by doing something that is not supported by my mother and father. If I were in this group, I would think about the parallel between the lesbian relationship and intermarriage. I could connect with Rosalie based on her situation, but I doubt that I would have any answers for her. I can imagine that someone in the group might tell Rosalie, "In my family, when I told my parents about my partner, it was awful at first. They didn't talk to me for almost a year. But, it got better, and now it is okay." I can imagine that this might make Rosalie (and me) feel better. If another member questioned whether Rosalie had checked out her suppositions with her parents, I think that Rosalie would see this as ridiculous, since she is sure how her parents will respond to this news. I understand this as well, since I knew that my parents would respond badly to the news of my plans to marry a non-Jew. I didn't need to check it out, and I knew that Rosalie didn't have to do so either. Rosalie said that she had been very careful to be sure that her parents didn't know about her partner. This is easy in a Jewish family as a function of "Jewish denial," which is the ability to ignore news that is not desired until it is impossible to ignore it any longer. As a member, I think that I would be able to connect with Rosalie and understand her strong desire not to alienate her family, but also her need to do what is right for herself in her life. Issues that recur in this group are parental acceptance, acceptance of self, internalized oppression, external oppression, and living an honest life.

Explain how your ethnic and cultural background affected the way you would respond as a member.

If I were a member, I might be inclined to try to explain the parallel between intermarriage and coming out as a lesbian. Maybe this would be helpful, since it could allow Rosalie and others in the same situation to know that others have survived similar disclosures to parents. I think this might open the topic a bit and allow others to share their stories about making painful decisions and the effects of those decisions on their lives. This could be used to encourage other members to participate in the discussion.

Explain how your ethnic and cultural background may or may not inhibit the way you respond to the situation as a member.

I can imagine that members of the group who are not sure about their sexual identity might react to this session by feeling like life would be much easier if they could be in a relationship with a man. Several members might say that it sounds like telling Rosalie's parents will be too stressful, and they want to rethink their sexual orientation. Sonny, Star, and Carla could develop an alignment around their desire to try again with men, which could create a subgroup. The subgroup issue of "Should I really be a lesbian, or can I be heterosexual somehow?" could be a culturally based issue for individuals with a cultural or religious response to lesbian or gay relationships. There is no universal Jewish response to gay relationships; the response depends in part of the type of Judaism (Orthodox Jews would have the greatest difficulty with lesbian relationships, but most Conservative and Reform Jews would not have a religious reaction to gay relationships). I was not raised to believe that it is wrong to have a partner of the same sex, so this is not a cultural issue for me. However, I would be aware that this may have an effect on the members of the group.

Explain how your ethnic and cultural background may have influenced your choice of the response you made over any that you may have been considering as a member.

My cultural background might influence me in that I understand the desire to keep secrets from parents when the secrets consist of something that parents will not like. If there were someone in the group who said, "Just tell them. If they don't understand, it is their problem," I would know why that is not useful advice. Someone who does not understand the importance of family may not be able to connect with Rosalie. My ability to relate to the situation, though, may not help me to move Rosalie out of her "stuck" spot.

As a result of the response you chose, identify the consequences you might anticipate as a member.

If I talked about my intermarriage, I expect the others would wonder how this situation is related to Rosalie's life. In fact, I am not sure that the other members would understand that the issue might not be a lesbian lifestyle issue, but rather an issue of parental acceptance and personal life choices.

From your position as a member, explain what the most glaring or outstanding aspect was of the situation which impacted you from your ethnic and cultural orientation.

Again, the profound issue is the centrality and importance of the family. One of my students wondered if it could be possible for a Jewish female to lose her identity because, at the very least, "you are always someone's daughter." When I read his comments, I got the sense that he really understood the significance of the Jewish family.

CYNTHIA KALODNER'S REACTION AS A LEADER OF THIS COUNSELING/THERAPY GROUP

If this type of incident would not occur in your group, explain why it would not.

This type of incident could occur if I were a leader in a group like this. It seems to be a very normal discussion among members about how to deal with facing family disapproval when coming out.

Identify the multicultural issues that need to be taken into consideration for you as a leader.

As the leader of this group, the issues that stand out for me are very similar to those that I identified as a member. The primary concern expressed in this group is the conflict between being true to yourself and following parental rules (which may be extensions of cultural demands). It seems unlikely that there is a way to compromise, which might be possible in other circumstances. Rosalie cannot tell her parents and be happy, nor can she not tell her parents and be happy. Therefore, as presently posed, she is in a "no-win" situation. It seems that other group members can relate to this feeling, especially Ashara and Tikki.

Explain how your ethnic and cultural background affected the way you would respond as a leader.

My role as a group leader would be to allow these women to discuss their similar feelings about their situations, while drawing in the other members by asking them to respond to the dilemma presented by Rosalie, Ashara, and Tikki. It would be a wonderful intervention to ask the women to describe how their cultural worldviews might be influencing their feelings, and even more interesting to ask them to wonder aloud about the role of different cultures in terms of the importance of family and secrets. In some ways, being lesbian seems secondary to the family issues described here, and here I wonder if my experience in having to face the disapproval of my parents might influence my choice of interventions. As a leader, I doubt that I would disclose my personal history to this group, since even though I might see my experience as relevant, they might not, since I am not a lesbian in the same predicament. I would need to use my personal history as a guide for myself to understand the extreme difficulty in disappointing parents, but the need to take care of self first. I would need to be careful not to let my values direct this aspect of the group.

Explain how your ethnic and cultural background may or may not inhibit the way you respond to the situation as a leader.

One multicultural issue that I am aware of is the bias associated with gay or lesbian relationships in some cultural and religious groups. Ashara said, "If my parents find out that I am a lesbian, I might be killed. Or something horrible could happen to someone in my family." Since I am accepting of lesbian relationships, I would need to remember that not everyone is. The cultural view toward lesbian relationships could be raised in this group as a way to talk about how we develop our ideas about what is right and wrong. Some cultural messages may become internalized and result in the psychological unrest described by Indira. So while Rosalie's dilemma about her relationship with her parents is being processed, Indira and other members may be facing an internal dilemma about being lesbians. As a leader, I am aware that doing both of these things in a single session might be overwhelming to the members of the group. However, in order to prevent those who are at a different place in their conflicts associated with sexual identity from feeling neglected or misunderstood, I would bring this issue up for discussion. I might do this in the context of describing a model of sexual identity (though I would not make this a long intervention). I think that it might serve a unifying purpose for the members of this group.

Explain how your ethnic and cultural background may have influenced your choice of the response you made over any other that you may have been considering as a leader.

Kalodner's answer to this question can be found in her other responses. See also the Summary/Analysis section at the end of this chapter.

As a result of the response you chose, identify the consequences you might anticipate as a leader.

I hope that my responses to Rosalie and the members of the group struggling with how to tell others about their partners would open the conversation and enable members to process this in greater depth. However, I do not want to neglect those members who are struggling with sexual identity issues. It occurs to me that my attention to Rosalie's request for help is aligned with my cultural world; in other words, I can understand her situation deeply. However, since I do not have a cultural context in which to place a struggle for sexual identity, it may be that I miss the importance of issues felt by Indira, Carla, and Star. I hope that I would not neglect their internal struggles in favor of those that are more interpersonal in focus. The members that are in the midst of this struggle may begin to disengage from the group if their concerns are not addressed in this session.

From your position as a leader, explain what the most glaring or outstanding aspect was of the situation which impacted you from your ethnic and cultural orientation.

The multicultural issue of relevance seems to be the acknowledgment of the importance of the family. One does not like to say that "in my cultural world, family is more important than in yours," since there is clearly much more variability within groups than between them, but the importance of family approval seems to rise to the surface as the multicultural issue of importance. In the Jewish tradition, the word *naches* refers to the pride that parents have in their children. It comes from the things that children do and say and is probably one of the major forces behind the "my son [or daughter], the doctor" jokes. Jewish children learn that they are supposed to provide *naches* for their parents. They can do this by earning good grades, going to college and graduate schools, marrying (a Jew), and having children (the ultimate in *naches*). Given the importance of *naches* in Jewish families, I think that I can understand, at a deeper level, the situation posed by Rosalie and understood by Ashara and Tikki. I do not think that I would lead Rosalie toward either telling or not telling her parents, but I would let the group provide feedback about the situation. A possible way to facilitate this process would be to ask Rosalie to pick members to act as her mother and father and set up a role-play in which Rosalie tries different ways to deal with her parents. She might avoid telling them in one role-play situation, and then discuss with the group what that was like for her. Then she might talk to her parents in a role-play situation, telling them about her partner and their plans, and then process that experience. I do not expect that she would decide what to do based solely on these role-plays, but she could develop a greater understanding of herself in this process. Additionally, other group members would benefit from seeing these role-plays and might be able to get a better sense of Rosalie's situation as well as of their own personal issues with coming out to loved ones.

Based on the composition of this group, what multicultural issues (etic and emic) need to be taken into consideration as the incident is addressed in group?

The group members have come to this group with a variety of assumptions about the importance of parental and extended family relationships in the lives of individuals. I think that this is the primary issue that requires consideration in this group. Developing an understanding of the differences and similarities across religious and cultural backgrounds may be an important way to contribute to the continued group cohesion in this group that seems to be in a transitional stage.

DAYA SANDHU'S REACTION AS A MEMBER OF THIS COUNSELING/THERAPY GROUP

Identify the multicultural issues that need to be taken into consideration for you as a member.

If I were a member of this group and struggling with issues of gender identity and sexual orientation, several multicultural issues would emerge for me. The first and foremost issue would be my religion. In Sikhism, major emphasis is placed on spirituality and reunion with the Supreme Being. Lust is considered one of the five distractions that lead a person astray from the ultimate spiritual path. Even though there is no direct reference to or condemnation of homosexuality in the Sri Guru Granth Sahib (the holy book of the Sikhs), the overall message is clear that perversion is not accepted.

My age would be another cultural barrier. All these participants are much younger than me. As a matter of fact, all the young ladies in this group would be like my daughter, which would make me feel very uncomfortable and ashamed. In my upbringing, such sexual matters were personal concerns that were not discussed openly in the public, as that would bring shame to the family name for many generations to come.

Due to my personal heterosexual orientation, I would feel out of place in this group. As a parent, it would definitely make me concerned about the sexual orientation of my own children. Transference and countertransference would loom large. Dating back several generations and including extended family, my family members have been heterosexual. As a matter of fact, homosexuality in general, and lesbianism in particular, were never discussed. If there were such incidents in my family of origin, I have no knowledge of them. I would also feel very awkward and uncomfortable to participate in this lesbian group as the only heterosexual male participant among all young lesbian women.

Explain how your ethnic and cultural background affected the way you would respond as a member.

As stated earlier, I would feel embarrassed in this group. As homosexuality is a taboo in my culture, I would respond very reluctantly. Even though I have been in the United States for more than 30 years and am clearly a multicultural person (Ponterotto, Jackson, & Nutini, 2001), there are several things in American culture that I have stubbornly rejected, and homosexuality is one of them. With such a negative attitude toward homosexuality and lesbianism, I would definitely terminate my participation in this group.

Explain how your ethnic and cultural background may or may not inhibit the way you respond to the situation as a member.

My ethnic and cultural background as an Asian Indian would definitely inhibit the way I would respond to the situation as a member in this group. In my culture, same-sex attractions may be acknowledged but are not accepted. Family disapproval and traditional religious beliefs strongly condemn homoerotic relationships. Knowledge about a family member's homosexual tendencies generally precipitates a family crisis in Asian cultures. There are so many familial and societal pressures that a homosexual person does not dare to face expulsion from the family and rejection from the parents. The humiliation and shame from the society and religious institutions are so strong, a person will not express homosexual behaviors. Homoerotic feelings are almost always kept strictly discreet.

Explain how your ethnic and cultural background may have influenced your choice of the response you made over any other that you may have been considering as a member.

Both my ethnic and cultural background as an Asian Indian and my religion, Sikhism, do not accept homosexuality, which would certainly influence my choice of the response. I clearly share some cultural similarities with Indira, whose parents are from India, and Ashara, who belongs to a Muslim family. The presence of these two members would certainly make me think of the effects of acculturation on these two young ladies. I would also be predisposed to several transference and countertransference issues in this group. If I were not affected by my cultural background, I might not have even thought about such issues.

As a result of the response you chose, identify the consequences you might anticipate as a member.

As a member of this group with my cultural background, heterosexual orientation, and age difference, I would most likely receive condemnation from all the other members. I might become an object of hatred, isolation, and rejection. Most likely members of this group would describe me as rigid, ignorant, fanatic, and insensitive. These members would have transference issues and consider me as their father figure. They would displace their anger, frustrations, and hatred on me.

From your position as a member, explain what the most glaring or outstanding aspect was of the situation which impacted you from your ethnic and cultural orientation.

As a person from an Asian culture, I was shocked to learn about the lesbian interests of Ashara, a Muslim girl, and Indira, an Asian-Indian girl. During the 26 years of my life in India (including my entire childhood, adolescence, and early adulthood), I never heard of lesbian relationships. Ladies must have kept them discreet. There was a practice of early arranged marriages in my culture. Maybe these early marriages served as a mechanism to curb sexual appetites before youths became too sexually active. (Gandhi, for example, was married at age 13.)

So, the glaring or outstanding aspect of this scenario for me is seeing two young ladies whose parents hail from a culture similar to mine, discuss their lesbian relationships in a group therapy session. It is truly a barometer to assess the level of acculturation of children born in Asian-American families in a free American culture, where everything goes and there are hardly any cultural taboos. That is why America is called a free country. On the contrary, Asian cultures place major emphasis on self-control and restrict self-expressions. Spiritual bliss is stressed as being more important than physical pleasures.

DAYA SANDHU'S REACTION AS A LEADER OF THIS COUNSELING/THERAPY GROUP

If this type of incident would not occur in your group, explain why it would not.

This type of discussion might not happen in my group because of my cultural background and personal discomfort with this subject. I would have referred these young ladies to another counselor or therapist. I am cognizant of my personal biases, negative attitudes, and lack of knowledge about bisexual, gay, and lesbian issues. In my case, it is indicated that I must refer these clients to other counselors who could be more effective.

Identify the multicultural issues that need to be taken into consideration for you as a leader.

I strongly believe that all my cultural variables would play a significant but negative role in this session with lesbian clients. My religion, Sikhism, does not condone homosexuality and considers lust (obsession with sexual matters) a deterrent to spiritual development. Because of my age difference with these clients, I would be a father figure for these young ladies; in that role, I would feel very uncomfortable engaging in discussion about their sexual orientation. My own gender patterns, beliefs, and family values would also be limitations in forming positive therapeutic relationships with these clients. With a strong personal conviction in a heterosexual lifestyle, I would not be honest with myself and my clients if I were to treat these women rather than referring them elsewhere.

Explain how your ethnic and cultural background affected the way you would respond as a leader.

Incompatibility between my traditional values and homosexuality would be a major roadblock to therapeutic efforts. Because of my personal biases, I might end up imposing my personal values on these students. There is a real danger that I might engage in convincing these participants that in the long run, it is not in their best interest to adopt a lesbian lifestyle. Short-term pleasure or sexual gratification may cause them long-term incurable pain. Since imposing therapeutic values is unethical conduct for a therapist, I most probably would refer these clients to other counselors who could help them more effectively than I could.

Explain how your ethnic and cultural background may or may not inhibit the way you respond to the situation as a leader.

I am afraid that my ethnic and cultural background variables would inhibit my efforts to help these clients effectively. My religion, culture, family, social experiences, and avowed traditional beliefs all disapprove of a homosexual lifestyle. Helping these lesbian clients would seem like promoting this alternative lifestyle. As such, it would create internal conflicts in myself. It would also generate guilt in my mind that I would be an accessory to helping these young ladies become estranged from their families of origin.

Explain how your ethnic and cultural background may have influenced your choice of the response you made over any other that you may have been considering as a leader.

As a leader, I should be the facilitator whose heart goes out to these young ladies who are in deep psychological pain due to their struggles with gender identity and sexual orientation. All these young women suffer from internal conflicts about their self-definition. But also, they are tormented due to their conflicts with their parents and feel estranged from their communities and families of origin. The fear of rejection from the loved ones, vulnerability to internalized homophobia, and reprehension about same-sex attractions could become quite traumatic and unbearable.

I would have and should have taken time to actively engage in this group therapy session. However, my ethnic and cultural background would make me apathetic and compel me to refer these clients to some other mental health professional.

As a result of the response you chose, identify the consequences you might anticipate as a leader.

In declining to provide group counseling/therapy to these lesbians, I would anticipate several negative consequences from these young ladies and from myself. These ladies would consider me homophobic, arrogant, apathetic, and an uncaring person. As a professional, I would be looked down upon as someone who is unprofessional, undertrained, ineffective, and an insensitive therapist.

I would feel quite guilty for not being helpful. I would also feel some inadequacy in my training as a therapist. On the positive side, I would feel good about myself for being honest, direct, and open with these clients. I would also feel good about myself for being able to examine my own attitudes and knowledge about gay, lesbian, and bisexual issues objectively. I feel that is incumbent upon me as an ethical professional to make appropriate referrals to provide better help for my clients.

From your position as a leader, explain what the most glaring or outstanding aspect was of the situation which impacted you from your ethnic and cultural orientation.

My ethnic and cultural background in this case became a handicapping condition, a glaring aspect indeed. Due to my religion and cultural background, I have honestly a very limited knowledge about and preference not to work with gay, lesbian, and bisexual clients. My traditional values from my family of origin, avowed religious and cultural proscriptions, and silence around sexuality during my upbringing would discourage me from working with this group. Discussion about sex in my family is shunned as it is considered shameful and demeaning.

I also strongly believe that in the long run, these lesbian clients will have long-term difficulties from many perspectives. Personally, I believe that this choice is for short-term pleasure and is not a wise one in the light of long-term detrimental consequences.

In Asian cultures, adolescents may engage in exploratory homosexual behaviors, but they do not necessarily develop a gay or lesbian identity. These adolescents are still expected to get married to a person of the opposite sex and carry on the name and the lineage of the family. Disclosure of one's gay identity becomes very threatening for Asians, as it rejects continuation of the family and one's culturally proscribed appropriate gender roles (Chan, 1992). Homosexuality in Asian cultures is considered the ultimate expression of individualism, which totally rejects the normative cultural behaviors (Pope & Chung, 1999).

From the professional point of view, this vignette has an outstanding aspect for me to confront my own prejudice and stereotypes against gay men and lesbians. I need to become capable of affirming my clients' gay identity while working with them. I should be able to provide the much-needed caring and safe environment for these lesbians and enable them to explore their painful experiences.

Based on the composition of this group, what multicultural issues (etic and emic) need to be taken into consideration as the incident is addressed in group?

Draguns (1976) distinguished between emic and etic as follows: "Emic refers to the viewing of data in terms of indigenous or unique to the culture in question and etic, to viewing them in light of categories and concepts external to the culture but universal in their applicability" (p. 2). In this group, there are several cultural variations and cultural distinctions that might be considered under emic issues. Even though these ladies have a common sexual orientation, same-sex attractions (lesbianism), they have been raised in very culturally different homes. For instance, here are some culturally distinct backgrounds of these group participants:

- *Religious background.* Clearly, these participants are born and raised in different religious and spiritual traditions. Christianity, Judaism, Islam, Hinduism, and Roman Catholicism are some of the religions that are easily recognized in the backgrounds of the clients in this vignette.
- *Ethnic differences.* These participants belong to various ethnic groups that have unique cultural heritages and traditions. Actually, these participants represent all major ethnic groups, such as European Americans, African Americans, Latin Americans, Asian Americans, and Native Americans.

  There is not enough information available to be sure, but these young ladies seem to belong to different socioeconomic classes. In general, differences in socioeconomic backgrounds lead to differences in attitudes, worldviews, values, beliefs, and behaviors.
- *Language differences.* Language differences in these participants' families of origin are quite explicit. Some of these languages would include English, Spanish, Hindi, some Middle Eastern language (Arabic, Urdu, etc.), and some Native-American tribal language.

In terms of etic issues: Despite numerous cultural differences, the members of this counseling/therapy group share several etic issues. Briefly stated, these issues include:

- *Identity issues.* All these participants are struggling with their lesbian identities. They are in psychological pain from difficulties with acknowledging and accepting their lesbian identities. Most of the pain comes from the difficulty of disclosing their lesbian identities to their significant others.
- *Tri-identity.* Most of these participants are suffering from a tri-identity dilemma. They are all women, a gender minority; they are lesbian, a sexual minority; and many of them are women of color.
- *Family.* Because of the disapproval of their sexual orientation, many of these participants are polarized, alienated, and estranged psychologically from their parents and other family members.
- *Mental.* It is quite obvious that the members of this group are experiencing many psychological problems such as perceptions of rejection, lack of support resources, and internalized homophobia. In addition, these group members suffer from a lack of emotional closeness to their significant others, intense inner conflicts, parental hostility, and social isolation. These participants seem to be undergoing an abundance of confusing and painful experiences that warrant immediate psychological support.

ZIPORA SHECHTMAN'S REACTION AS A MEMBER OF THIS COUNSELING/THERAPY GROUP

I feel quite comfortable in this group. Group members are friendly, intimate, self-revealing, and very interesting. I like it when people feel close to each other and trust each other. I enjoy the postconflict stage, as I do not like conflict, anger, and negative interactions. I am here with another person of Jewish origin, but this does not mean I feel particularly close to her; neither of us practices the Jewish tradition. She seems very confused and unhappy, and does not show much interest in the other group members. Her withdrawal makes me feel uncomfortable, as we are beyond the stage of suspicion.

Several of the group members come from traditional families in which being lesbian is seen as bringing great shame to their families. Ashara, Clara, Rosalie, and Indira have to put up with more cultural restrictions than the others. Although I myself do not have a very traditional family background, I can understand their difficulties, as even confronting parents who conform only to mainstream values can be quite difficult.

I think that my parents would have a hard time accepting me if they discovered who I really am. I would no longer be considered the "good girl" for sure. My father would not confront me openly, but he might decide to just ignore me, which is even worse. It is not that I am afraid I would not be loved anymore; rather, my main concern would be not to put another burden my parents. I feel pity for them, sorry for the unfulfilled lives they have been living, and I am not prepared to make it harder on them. I might choose not to disclose my secret and pay the price of getting emotionally disconnected from my family, rather than revealing my secret. If I were to tell my parents, my sense is that they would not have the strength to cope with the "catastrophe," and I am not willing to pay the price of guilt. In this way, although I do not originate from a very restrictive culture, I can identify with the fears expressed by Ashara and Rosalie.

I feel closer to Ashara, Rosalie, and Tikki, who seem to have made up their minds and now struggle with concrete and practical issues, rather than to the others who are still struggling with questions of sexual identity. I have learned to be efficient and practical, taking little time for self-exploration. Spending time thinking about one's self would be viewed as a luxury in my hard-working family. Hence, I would like to proceed with the sense of helplessness that came up and perhaps help the three girls clarify some possible ways to resolve their problems of acceptance by their meaningful others. The sense of helplessness troubles me: In my family culture, people (and particularly women) have to be decisive and efficacious. I would therefore join their discussion, first trying to learn more about their fears, and then look at what would be some of the consequences if they revealed their secret. Although I would like to share my fears with them, I would be hesitant about revealing my way of thinking, because it may impede their progress. I would probably join them later in the discussion, and meanwhile learn more about how they see the situation. Perhaps they can then help me see things in a less definite way.

On the other hand, I realize that the rest of the group members are quite frightened. They are at a different stage, still trying to clarify for themselves where they are. I do not feel quite comfortable discussing us while they are still so confused. They may not be interested in our problems or may even become judgmental, which would destroy the sense of intimacy in the group. Personally, I do not see a problem with me holding back, for awhile, but holding the other three girls back would be a problem. Ashara is very anxious to find a solution, and letting her down today would be extremely disappointing. My personal preference would be to proceed with the three girls, trying to assist them with the prospective confrontations with their meaningful others. This response suits my own needs and my cultural codes of efficiency. But I would like the other group members to join us in our efforts to help Ashara and the two others.

As I already mentioned, I like the sense of intimacy that has been achieved in the group and would hate to go back to the conflict stage, which I remember as extremely unpleasant. I would therefore state my opinion openly, suggesting that we all try to concentrate on Ashara and her immediate difficulty, prepared to bear the consequences of an angry reaction. I feel quite comfortable in dealing with such confrontation. But to minimize the unfavorable reaction, I guess I would share with the group members my realization of how difficult it is for me to be in a vague and indecisive situation, as well as my need to be efficient. At the same time, I would also share with them my sense of surprise at being able to take a stand in the group, which is not typical of my behavior in group.

I realize that my family culture of immigrants and my social culture as Israeli are influencing my response in a conflicting way: The first inhibits my spontaneity, congruency, and courage; the other enhances all these traits. The culture of my childhood influenced my choice to be practical, to go ahead and solve problems, to be efficient. Dealing with confusion and ambiguity would be considered a waste of time and energy. Moreover, confronting parents with such catastrophic news is an impossible mission for me. I never discussed with them any sexual issue, let alone issues of deviate behavior. In the parent-role, which I took on early in my life, I cannot afford to be that irresponsible. This sense of responsibility is also manifested in my need to help the three girls who are struggling with issues of confrontation. Perhaps I am also curious to see how the others can deal with such difficulty; they may be able to act out my fantasies of communicating openly with my parents. However, joining one subgroup means taking the risk of an angry or disappointed reaction from the other group members. Although I might risk destroying the "good girl" self-image of my early childhood, I would not hesitate to take a stand or confront some group members, or to express my feelings. Here, the influence of Israeli culture is present, suggesting an open and congruent response, though with reservation—honest, clear, but at the same time conveyed with respect and empathy toward group members.

The glaring aspect of the situation is the realization that the different patterns of behavior are restricted to specific situations or people. This is a very optimistic realization, suggesting that people can grow out of impeding cultural codes of behavior.

ZIPORA SHECHTMAN'S REACTION AS A LEADER OF THIS COUNSELING/THERAPY GROUP

This group is dealing with one of the most difficult subjects to discuss in a group. Human sexuality, particularly when it deviates from the mainstream, is a taboo topic in many societies. Traditional and religious cultures or collectivist societies impose more restrictions on their members in terms of values and behavior than do secular or intellectually more open cultures or individualist societies. This particular group is comprised of a majority of members who represent restrictive cultures and families. Within these families, revealing such secrets could have a detrimental effect on everyone. Therefore, the fears, concerns, and confusion of the three engaged persons must be carefully explored. Following this line of thought, I would let them discuss their concerns in more depth. Realizing how difficult the confrontation with the family may be, based on my own experience, I would proceed with great caution, so as to avoid consequences that could be harmful. But I would definitely go ahead and explore how such self-revelation might become possible, despite my own personal concerns not to harm my parents.

Two conflicting cultures have influenced my decision. The culture of my family of origin—that of a hard-working, immigrating family—suggests caution, as strong confrontation may be too much for some of my family members to take. In my family, sexuality was not discussed at all; it was a taboo associated with shame and guilt. "Good girls" were expected to concentrate on their schoolwork and household tasks, and spend most of their time indoors. Dating with boys (only!) would be accepted at a later stage, after high school graduation. Moreover, confronting parents would be irresponsible, and extremely frightening for a child who early on in her life took the role of a parent. However, the culture of Israeli society encourages freedom and openness. Thus, as soon as I joined the army, I opened up to a different world. Here, one was expected to be self-confident and self-sufficient, assertive and direct, and efficient in solving problems. I guess it is this second influence that bears a stronger impact on me at present.

However, as a professional, I realize my responsibility to the rest of the group members and to the group process. Responsibility has always been a typical characteristic of mine, influenced by both cultures but, in this case, also by professional knowledge. Most group members are at a different stage of their sexual identity. They may be frightened, confused, or even feeling left out if the group proceeds with the three engaged girls. Focusing on the advanced stage of sexual identity may steer the group members into the direction of making premature decisions regarding their sexuality, which may bear high risks for people such as Indira, Carla, and others. The fear that someone may be pushed ahead comes from my own fears, I guess, but my decision to act would be professional. I would decide not to risk the significant moments in the group, and to proceed with the three girls.

In addition, I would like to minimize the sense of being left out for the rest, and try to engage all group members in the decision to go ahead and deal with the issue of coming out with their secret and confronting meaningful family members. I would also monitor their feelings during the group process. Such group focus seems to me to be professional, but it may also reflect the double messages that I myself have received from my two conflicting cultures. I think that professionally it is right to engage the whole group, but that entails the risk that the rest of the group will impede the progress of the advanced subgroup, and the whole process may be less efficient. This realization that two different conflicting cultures play a role in my professional decisions is very interesting to me. Yet, I believe I can remain professional and deal with the difficulties of all group members in confronting their families with their sexual identity, whether they are real or only hypothetical.

SUMMARY/ANALYSIS OF RESPONSES

As Members of This Counseling/Therapy Group

Identify the multicultural issues that need to be taken into consideration for you as a member.

As we consider the responses our experts gave to this first question, we are at first struck by the influence that family and culture had on all three of them, even though there is considerable diversity in their answers. Kalodner informs us that being Jewish has taught her to place value on her family; therefore, she must consider how the choices she makes will affect other family members. She identifies with Rosalie. It is not easy to go against family. Thus, to not inform parents is tantamount to engaging in "Jewish denial." That is to say, one ignores undesirable news until it is impossible to do so any longer. Sandhu's response demonstrates that strong family and cultural influences would affect him as a member of the group. He informs us that not only are sexual matters private and their public expression perceived as shameful, but Sikhism views lust as one of five distractions from spiritual growth. In addition, lesbianism is considered a perversion and is not accepted.

Shechtman, like Kalodner, conveys that because she is Jewish, she would also feel guilty about placing an additional burden on her family, especially her parents. For her, being a lesbian would mean bringing shame upon a traditional family. Kalodner and Shechtman have identified additional multicultural issues. Kalodner, for instance, identifies these areas: the need to do what is right for herself and to achieve self-acceptance, the need to reconcile internalized and externalized oppression, the desire to live an honest life, and the need for parental support.

Shechtman's focus falls on other group members. Ashara, Clara, and Rosalie, she claims, have greater cultural restrictions than the other members. She also sees these three members as dealing with concrete issues. She informs us that even though she does not come from a restrictive culture, she can identify with Ashara and Rosalie. Sexual identity is viewed by her to be a transcultural issue in the group.

Explain how your ethnic and cultural background affected the way you would respond as a member.

This question raises for us a process observation regarding how our experts opted to respond. There is evidence that Kalodner and Sandhu were not at ease with what the question asked of them. Kalodner sidestepped the matter of sexual orientation and said that, as a Jew, there would be distance in the relationship with her parents. In other words, they would struggle to overcome their shame and accept her announcement about her sexual orientation, should she make it. Sandhu tells us he would be feeling shame, embarrassment, and the weight of the taboo against discussing the subject matter.

Shechtman seems less inhibited by this group. She states emphatically that being an Israeli woman, she has learned to be decisive and efficacious. Therefore, she would join in the group discussion. Her Israeli experiences would make her efficient and practical as a member. She sees herself eventually reaching out to Ashara, Tikki, and Rosalie. However, her Jewish side would not allow her to pay the price of guilt by disclosing her sexual orientation to her parents. She claims she would rather risk the emotional disconnection that could occur because of her secret.

Explain how your ethnic and cultural background may or may not inhibit the way you respond to the situation as a member.

Here Kalodner is not at all tentative. She conveys that being Jewish would not inhibit her. According to her view, there is no universal Jewish response to gay or lesbian relationships. She adds that she was not raised to believe that such relationships are wrong; however, she is sensitive to how her Jewish background would affect others from less liberal backgrounds.

We infer from Sandhu's response that his background would inhibit him. He restates that same-sex relationships are unacceptable and that family and religious beliefs strongly condemn such relationships. He explains that a strong fear of being expelled from his community would inhibit any public disclosure related to one's sexual orientation.

In her response, Shechtman reveals a unique intrapersonal conflict. Her early childhood Jewish culture directs her to be practical, to solve problems, and to be efficient—but, it also inhibits her spontaneity, congruence, and courage. Consequently, this side of her would not support telling her parents of her sexual orientation. However, her Israeli culture challenges this position: It has her take a stand and confront the other women, and it encourages her to be open, clear, respectful, and empathic. Perhaps we can infer that, from this latter position, she might even risk informing her parents that she is a lesbian.

Explain how your ethnic and cultural background may have influenced your choice of the response you made over any other that you may have been considering as a member.

For Kalodner, the choice between revealing or not revealing her secret to her parents is culturally based. She opts not to reveal her secret to her parents due to having to be responsible for the guilt it may create. As a result, she has an understanding for Rosalie's position.

Again, we experience Sandhu's struggle and his consistency. He presents us with an unequivocal response that is strongly guided by his ethnic, cultural, and religious background. Clearly, for him there is no other choice. He informs us that ethnically and culturally, as an Asian Indian and a Sikh, he would not be able to accept homosexuality.

Once again, we are introduced to Shechtman's intrapersonal bicultural conflict. Her childhood Jewish culture clashes with her Israeli culture. The former tells her to be practical—to solve problems, and to be efficient in helping the other women. Yet the latter presses her to take a stand, confront some members, and express her feelings.

As a result of the response you chose, identify the consequences you might anticipate as a member.

The responses anticipate three very different consequences. Kalodner's response refers to her intermarriage and her effort to relate that to Rosalie's life. She anticipates that the other members would not see from her example that the group's issues are more about gaining parental acceptance and personal life choices, and not as much about the lesbian lifestyle.

Sandhu anticipates strong and harsh consequences. He uses terms such as *condemnation, hatred,* and *rejection* to describe responses from the members. He foresees members describing him as rigid, ignorant, fanatic, and insensitive. Given his age and gender, he also expects members' transference issues, including seeing him as a father figure, along with displaced feelings of anger, frustration, and hatred being projected upon him.

If she risks her "good girl" image of her early childhood for the more assertive Israeli woman, Shechtman anticipates that she would be on the receiving end of anger from the members. She also sees herself as striking a conflictual position between herself and the other members of the group, which could lead to loss of intimacy should she reach out to help Ashara, Rosalie, and Tikki.

From your position as a member, explain what the most glaring or outstanding aspect was of the situation which impacted you from your ethnic and cultural orientation.

The diversity of our respondents is reflected in the diversity of their responses. Of particular interest is that two respondents are women and Jewish, and yet each saw different aspects as outstanding in this situation. Kalodner observed that for her, the centrality and importance of family stands out. She adds the realization that, regardless of circumstances, she will always be someone's daughter. In comparison, Shechtman informs us that she thinks the different patterns of behavior are restricted to specific situations or people. On a more personal note, she states that this awareness is an optimistic observation, suggesting that people can grow out of impeding codes of behavior.

Cultural and ethnic background is particularly evident as an influence in Sandhu's response to this question. He states that he was struck by the fact that two women whose parents' culture is similar to his would discuss their lesbian relationships in a group.

As Leaders of This Counseling/Therapy Group

If this type of incident would not occur in your group, explain why it would not.

Two of the three respondents claimed that this incident could occur in their group if they were the leaders. Kalodner and Shechtman see the issues of sexual orientation and coming out (announcing it to family) as being toxic topics that need to be dealt with. Kalodner is aware members will have to address family disapproval. Shechtman raises our awareness that the majority of the members are from restrictive cultures, and therefore, they need to discuss the subject in depth, but do so carefully to avoid harming themselves.

Sandhu is very candid. He lets us know that due to his cultural background and personal discomfort with the subject, this incident would not occur. He would probably refer these clients to a different counselor.

Identify the multicultural issues that need to be taken into consideration for you as a leader.

Kalodner's response is succinct and brief. She identifies being true to oneself versus following family rules as the multicultural issue being faced by the members. Sandhu and Shechtman elaborate more on this question. Sandhu reiterates that Sikhism does not condone homosexuality, and it is considered to be lust (i.e., an obsession with sexual matters that is a deterrent to spiritual development). His own gender patterns, beliefs, and family values are very present, and he is the only respondent who refers to his age as an issue that needs to be considered.

As a leader, Shechtman sees a number of multicultural issues in this group. There is the clash between traditional and religious cultures, or between collectivistic societies that impose more restrictions and secular or intellectually more open cultures and individualistic societies. She considers that the members are primarily from restrictive cultures and families. Therefore, revealing such secrets could have detrimental consequences on all.

Explain how your ethnic and cultural background affected the way you would respond as a leader.

Kalodner does not refer to her ethnic and cultural background specifically, but she does relate that her personal history would guide her. She has a conscious awareness of the extreme difficulty that exists in disappointing parents.

Sandhu's response is honest and candid. He realizes that his traditional values are in conflict with homosexuality and that they would present a road-block to his therapeutic efforts. His inclination is to advise members to not adopt a lesbian lifestyle, but being aware that to do so would be unethical, he instead would refer the members to another therapist.

Shechtman reintroduces us to the personal conflict she is confronted with because the diversity of her two cultures. Both backgrounds influence her choice of a response in this group. Her family of origin, which is a hard-working immigrant Jewish family, suggests that she should be cautious and that strong confrontation may be too much. In her family, sexuality was not discussed. The subject was taboo and shameful, and would lead to feelings of guilt. Dating with boys (only) came after high school. Consequently, given this background, confronting her parents would be irresponsible.

On the other hand, Schechtman has also been influenced by the culture of Israeli society. It encourages freedom, openness, self-confidence, self-sufficiency, assertiveness, and being direct and efficient in solving problems. Shechtman informs us that this Israeli society is her dominant culture.

Explain how your ethnic and cultural background may or may not inhibit the way you respond to the situation as a leader.

Kalodner's responses to previous questions imply that she would not be inhibited by her background. She informed us earlier that this incident could occur in one of her groups and that she would encourage dialogue among the group members. She views the members as being from more restrictive cultures than hers. Her earlier discussion of the conflict between self and family also implies that she is consciously aware of the struggle for herself, but would opt for being true to oneself while still being respectful of family values. In her response to this question, she states that she is accepting of lesbian relation-ships, implying that her ethnic and cultural background would not inhibit her.

Sandhu does not equivocate. He tells us that his ethnic and cultural back-ground would inhibit him, since all aspects of his culture and ethnic origins disapprove of the homosexual lifestyle. Therefore, if he had led such a group, he would feel like he was condoning a homosexual lifestyle, which would be in direct contradiction to his background.

Shechtman, though faced with potential conflict between her two cultures, states that her Israeli culture would overrule her more conservative family of origin culture. She adds that even though taking responsibility is characteris-tic of both cultures, they still clash with one another.

Explain how your ethnic and cultural background may have influenced your choice of the response you made over any other that you may have been con-sidering as a leader.

Kalodner sees the concerns of Ashara, Rosalie, and Tikki as being aligned with her cultural world; however, she does not have a cultural context for the sexual orientation struggles of Indira, Carla, and Star. Nevertheless, she demonstrates concern that her response would not leave them out. Her response to question four allows us to assume, on the other hand, that she would not be inhibited. Therefore, her ethnic and cultural background would not deter her from encouraging member-to-member dialogue. In all likelihood, she would opt for this more liberal response over a more conservative one that would not encourage dialogue and open exploration of the subject.

Sandhu conveys that if it were for his ethnic and cultural background (which makes him apathetic toward the members' circumstances), he would take time to actively engage the group members.

Shechtman allows that her Israeli culture influenced her choice over that which her family of origin's culture (immigrant Jews to Israel) would have had her make. Her decision to work with the three women first was drawn from her Israeli culture. Her alternative response would have her not push the other group members but still with them. Additionally, she would address the group as a whole. Both interventions would be conservative in nature, and she notes that focusing on the three members (Ashara, Rosalie, and Tikki) as a subgroup could impede the progress of the other members.

As a result of the response you chose, identify the consequences you might anticipate as a leader.

We are given a variety of responses to this question. Kalodner believes that if she were to address Rosalie and the others who are struggling to come out, it would open conversation and lead others to address the problem in greater depth. In addition, she would be mindful of the internal struggles of Indira, Carla, and Star.

Similar to what he expected in his position as a member, Sandhu foresees the members viewing him as homophobic, arrogant, apathetic, and uncaring. As a leader, he also expects that other professionals would see him as being unprofessional, undertrained, ineffective, and insensitive. He discloses the intrapersonal effect his response would have upon him; it would leave him feeling guilty and with some feelings of inadequacy. Yet, even in the face of anticipated criticism, he finds redeeming consequences is his response. He believes he would be left feeling at peace with himself for having remained congruent, honest, direct, and open regarding his position on the issue of sexual orientation.

Shechtman considers how the members are at different stages of sexual identity. Most of the members, she believes, would feel frightened if she were to work only with Ashara, Rosalie, and Tikki. Furthermore, she anticipates that the other members might be led to making premature decisions regarding their sexuality, which could bear high risk for Indira and Carla. Nevertheless, her Israeli culture would dominate her decision; she would focus on the three girls, but try to engage the whole group in the effort to help them.

From your position as a leader, explain what the most glaring or outstanding aspect was of the situation, which impacted you from your ethnic and cultural orientation.

All the respondents approached this question from a personal point of view and were introspective in their responses. The most outstanding aspect of the situation for Kalodner is the fact that family approval emerges as an issue of multicultural importance. From a personal ethnic and cultural view, she discusses how the pride Jewish parents take in their children (referred to as *naches*) can be universalized.

Sandhu's ethnic and cultural background is evident in his response. The Asian perspective regards coming out as threatening, since it rejects continuation of the family and one's culturally prescribed role. He reveals that from a professional point of view, this vignette asks him to confront his own prejudices against and stereotypes of gays and lesbians.

Shechtman is equally insightful in answering this question, stating that the realization of how two different, conflicting cultures (i.e., her immigrant family and Israeli society) play a role in her professional decisions is very interesting to her."

Based on the composition of this group, what multicultural issues (etic and emic) need to be taken into consideration as the incident is addressed in group?

Kalodner identifies the etic issue of the importance of parental and extended family relationships in the lives of individuals. Sandhu identifies the etic issues as: personal identity, tri-identity (female, lesbian, and woman of color), family of origin, and mental health. For Shechtman, the etic issues relate to those things that are similar in most restrictive cultures and families (i.e., revealing sexual secrets can be detrimental to everyone).

In regard to emic issues, Kalodner identifies the need to develop an understanding of the differences and similarities across religious and cultural backgrounds. Sandhu's answer is similar; he feels the emic issues are religious, spiritual, ethnic (European, African, Latin, Asian, and Native American), and language. Though Shechtman does not address this question directly, we can infer that she would see the emic issues as being related to human sexuality, since she notes that sexual topics, those deviating from the mainstream, are taboo in many societies but nonetheless need to be addressed.

Counseling/
Therapy Group
Vignette #4

CHAPTER 11

A Women's Eating Disorders Group—
To Blame or Not to Blame?

You are a counselor in a counseling center at a small southern college. Several of your individual clients have presented with symptoms of eating disorders ranging from subclinical symptoms to bulimia and anorexia. You have decided that a counseling group for these women would be helpful and have invited four of your clients and two other clients at the counseling center to join a counseling group for women with eating disorders and issues. Your group totals six members, with you as a leader making seven.

- Meghan is an 18-year-old Caucasian female of Irish-Catholic descent. Both sets of grandparents immigrated from Ireland soon after their marriages. Her presenting issues are difficulty with academics and depression. Meghan is pursuing a joint degree in psychology and dance, and thus often exercises three to four hours a day. In addition, she only eats a limited amount of food each day, and her range of foods is restricted to about ten items (e.g., rice, milk, fish, chicken).

- Kumi is a 23-year-old graduate student in economics who was born and raised in Japan. She came to the United States as an exchange student in college for a year, returned to Japan for a year, and then decided to pursue a graduate degree in the United States. Her presenting issue is low self-esteem, often expressed as a willingness to defer to others in relationships. Upon exploration, Kumi often refuses to eat for days after a fight with her boyfriend, roommate, or anyone else who matters in her life.

- Cynthia is a 22-year-old African-American female raised as a Baptist in a missionary family. She is about 30 pounds overweight and often engages in severe dieting for a week or two at a time followed by weeks of binge-ing. Her presenting problem is her inability to control her bingeing, which is followed by feelings of inadequacy and being out of control.
- Nyria is a 19-year-old student originally from Puerto Rico. Her family moved to the New York City when she was 10. Her presenting problem is bulimia. She alternates days of restricting her food intake with days of bingeing.
- Phyllis is a 20-year-old student of Orthodox Jewish descent who has drifted away from some of her religious traditions since beginning college. She has been overweight since an adolescent, but has lost a significant amount of weight since beginning college by basically eating one meal a day and exercising every day. Her friends have recently complained that all she talks about is food and exercising; they recommended that she talk to a counselor. Phyllis agreed, but halfheartedly. Her presenting concern is that she is worried about her relationships with friends.
- Shannon is a 22-year-old senior whose mother is of German and Italian descent and whose father is originally from India. She controls her weight by rigidly adhering to a vegan diet and using laxatives daily. Her present-ing concern is her relationship with her boyfriend; he is extremely jealous and wants to know where she is all the time.

This group has been meeting since October. It is now January and the fourteenth session of the group. Group members have recently returned from spending semester break with their families. In this session, they have started to discuss how their families influence their eating behaviors and perceptions of how supportive their families are in general. Several members say that this break was better than Thanksgiving with their families. When asked why, members for the most part indicate that they talked directly with at least one family member or friend about their eating disorder. In addition, each member also spoke to that person about how a person could support the member in trying to overcome this problem. The members congratulate each other for having disclosed to their family and friends. It was something they had dis-cussed before break. Even though they knew it would be hard to do they acknowledged that it was a necessary step toward achieving their wellness.

Kumi has remained silent during this interaction. Nyria turns to her and asks her to comment. Kumi states that she would rather not at this time. Nyria asks her if she thinks her family is helping her to get better. Kumi responds rather defensively, "They don't know about it, so how can I expect them to help me?" Cynthia confronts Kumi about this and asks why Kumi does not directly tell her family about her eating disorder. Kumi continues by saying that it is her duty to take care of her parents and not to embarrass them. She should be able to take care of herself and not have to ask them to help her. She adds that by not eating, she is communicating to her parents that she is upset. Others in the group grumble at this response and respond by making several different kinds of comments such as, "You need to communicate directly with your parents about your feelings," "Your parents should help you if you need help," "Families take care of individuals when they need it," and "It is not healthy not to eat for a couple of days." Kumi responds by saying that these kinds of things do not work in her family or in her culture in general.

Cynthia begins to talk about how food is so important in her family and social network, how it is the basis for most socialization, and that we take care of each other with food. You suggest that it might be helpful for each group member to take some time right now in group and discuss how their families take care of them and help them feel good or bad about themselves. You continue by saying that since all of you recently have spent time with your families, it might be helpful to focus on the members' interactions with their families over the break around food. Kumi, at this point, pulls her chair out of the circle about a foot and looks down at the floor. When asked about her recent experiences, she says she does not want to talk about it. When Shannon asks why, she responds that it is not helpful to talk about her family here, especially since everyone thinks that her family has caused her eating disorder and their families are all helping them to get better. There is a two-minute silence after Kumi says this.

RITA CHI-YING CHUNG'S REACTION AS A MEMBER OF THIS COUNSELING/THERAPY GROUP

Identify the multicultural issues that need to be taken into consideration for you as a member.

The multicultural considerations that need to be taken into account for me as a member of the group are as follows: This group is comprised of six women from various ethnic/cultural backgrounds. Only one of the group members is from an Asian background. Therefore, it is critical that differences in ethnic and cultural backgrounds, including values and communication styles, be addressed.

Furthermore, the focus of the group is eating disorders, which is not a common disorder found among Asians/Asian Americans, or a disorder that is commonly disclosed. It is important to note that the symbolism of food in Asian cultures is a critical multicultural issue. For example, in the Chinese culture, similar to other Asian cultures, food has great importance. During social events, food acts as a vehicle for social interaction, and different types of food are symbolic. In Chinese culture, specific foods are used for particular situations, such as noodles that represent long life, making noodles a part of birthday celebration meals. Food is also used as a medium to "take care" of someone who is emotionally distraught or ill; the food is a means of expressing one's feelings of affection and concern toward others. Food symbolizes affection in terms of how the food is prepared, the ingredients, the type and shape of food, the taste and texture, and the name of the food. For example, *dim sum* translated in English is "little heart," so that to give dim sum is to give some heart, which for Chinese is the soul of the emotions. Specific types of foods in the Asian culture are used for "healing" to restore the balance, or *yin-yang*, and well-being. Therefore, the symbolism surrounding food is of utmost importance for Asian culture and has meaning for the entire family system rather than just the individual. The group leader must understand and be aware of the essence and meaning of food within Asian cultures rather than make presuppositions about causes of eating disorders that are based on traditional Western thought.

Another multicultural issue that needs to be taken into consideration for me as a member of the group is the importance of family, and the interrelationship between individuals and their parents and family. The group members have been discussing how their families influence their eating behaviors and their perceptions of how supportive their families are in general. Topics regarding family are extremely sensitive, especially if there are problems within the family that in Asian cultures are generally not shared with strangers. A group leader must be aware and highly sensitive to this issue, since in Asian cultures it may lead to shame and loss of face. Since a basic premise of Asian culture is the family, an individual's problem with the family causes major shame and loss of face not only for the individual, but also for the family and the community. The individual's problem is seen as a sign of weakness of the entire family, especially the parents. In fact, weakness in the family may be viewed by community members as genetic and therefore stigmatize the entire family, causing problems about suitability for marriage. Community members may go as far as shunning and alienating the entire family. For individuals to bring this problem to their family causes not only loss of face but also extreme feelings of guilt and shame. Disclosing information regarding family dynamics is also considered to be a display of lack of family loyalty, which is a core cultural value.

The group leader also must understand and be aware of the Asian cultural value of filial piety. This concept involves the expectation that children will honor and respect their parents and ancestors, and the obligation to take care of their parents. Kumi's comment that "it is her duty to take care of her parents and not to embarrass them" illustrates filial obligations and expectations.

Explain how your ethnic and cultural background affected the way you would respond as a member.

Although my cultural values enable me to identify and empathize with Kumi, depending on how comfortable I am with the group, I may not speak up or speak in support of Kumi. My culture does not allow me to see my role as a group member to educate other members. I may look to the group leader, as an authority figure, to do this. Since the Chinese culture focuses on harmony and balance, I will definitely feel uncomfortable with the confrontation of Kumi by other group members and may be concerned that they might also confront me. Due to this discomfort, I may approach the group leader privately to discuss my concerns and let the group leader know of the cultural implications. Being in a group with predominantly non-Asians may make it difficult for me to discuss personal and/or family issues, especially due to their lack of knowledge and respect regarding my cultural values.

Explain how your ethnic and cultural background may or may not inhibit the way you respond to the situation as a member.

The cultural concept of loss of face would inhibit the swiftness of my general participation in the group. More specifically, it would also inhibit me in speaking out to support Kumi and to educate group members about the Asian culture. I would be hesitant about disclosing too much information in a group that may not be sensitive and understand my culture to avoid shame and loss of face.

Explain how your ethnic and cultural background may have influenced your choice of the response you made over any other that you may have been considering as a member.

See the responses above.

As a result of the response you chose, identify the consequences you might anticipate as a member.

The consequences for my behavior as a group member are threefold. First, by not supporting Kumi, she may be upset with me and confront me outside the group regarding my lack of support. I may feel guilt for not supporting another Asian person. Second, other group members may confront me as well for not speaking out in general. In addition, they may ask for my reaction or opinion to Kumi's comments, since I am also Asian, to gain a better understanding of Kumi's resistance. Again, I would not like to be placed in the role of educating group members. Also, through speaking out there is the fear that the group may confront me and disapprove of my actions or behaviors, which reflect on my family. Three, if I approach the group leader in private regarding cultural issues related to the situation, the group leader may find this unacceptable and bring the issue to the group, which would cause me embarrassment and loss of face.

From your position as a member, explain what the most glaring or outstanding aspect was of the situation which impacted you from your ethnic and cultural orientation.

Two issues in the situation stand out as the most glaring aspects. First is the direct linkage of family and the problem, as well as the suggestion that the family is not giving support. The second aspect is the supposed lack of understanding and openness to cultural differences displayed by the other group members, as demonstrated by the members' confrontation of Kumi and the critical and disapproving response of the others regarding Kumi's family. It is difficult to witness Kumi being attacked by the other group members, since their comments suggest a lack of support for Kumi and a lack of respect for her culture.

RITA CHI-YING CHUNG'S REACTIONS AS A LEADER OF THIS COUNSELING/THERAPY GROUP

If this type of incident would not occur in your group, explain why it would not.

This situation might not occur because, as a group leader, given the diversity of these group members, I would begin the group by having the members talk about their cultural backgrounds. This would provide a framework from which to talk about cultural differences, and thus establish understanding, sensitivity, appreciation, and respect for cultural issues around the problem of eating disorders. This theme would be revisited throughout the group. An exercise that can be utilized in this situation is for each group member to describe the significance of food in the member's culture.

Identify the multicultural issues that need to be taken into consideration for you as a leader.

The major multicultural issue that needs to be taken into consideration is the development of an awareness, understanding, and appreciation of different cultural perspectives related to eating disorders. This is particularly important with regard to how it relates to families and family dynamics. It is also essential to acknowledge and be aware of the differences in cultural communication styles of each group member and the ensuing problems that may occur as a result of these differences. For example, Kumi is from a culture that tends to be more passive and reflect on issues before talking. In comparison, Cynthia's cultural background may be more direct and outspoken; hence, there may be misunderstanding due to the different cultural styles of communication.

Explain how your ethnic and cultural background affected the way you would respond as a leader.

My cultural background would heighten awareness of cultural influences and dynamics in the group. Coming from a collectivistic culture and from an international background, I would be more in tune to group members' unique cultural backgrounds and the influence of culture on group dynamics. This would lead me to educate myself to understand the social, community, and family context of the origin of eating disorders for each cultural group represented by the group members, and hence not categorize and generalize the problem in the same way for everyone in the group. Thus, I would understand and interpret the meaning of the disorder within a contextual cultural framework that would affect etiology, manifestation, and treatment.

Explain how your ethnic and cultural background may or may not inhibit the way you respond to the situation as a leader.

Due to my cultural background, I may not allow the group members to aggressively confront each other. This would relate to the confrontation of Kumi about her family and the lack of support from her family. Given my understanding of Kumi's worldview and the knowledge about the potential shame and loss of face with her family, I may be protective of Kumi, which could interfere with group dynamics.

Explain how your ethnic and cultural background may have influenced your choice of the response you made over any other that you may have been considering as a leader.
    See the responses above.

As a result of the response you chose, identify the consequences you might anticipate as a leader.
    Group members may perceive me as protective or aligning with Kumi, since we are both Asians, and may perceive this as unfair treatment. Group members may also stereotype me, since my technique is nonconfrontative, stigmatizing me as being a passive Asian woman.

From your position as a leader, explain what the most glaring or outstanding aspect was of the situation which impacted you from your ethnic and cultural orientation.
    The most outstanding aspect of the situation is the lack of sensitivity displayed by the other group members toward Kumi's situation. This is generalized into the group's lack of willingness to explore, understand, and appreciate cultural differences, with an underlying assumption in the group that everyone is the same and should approach the problem of eating disorders in a similar manner.

Based on the composition of this group, what multicultural issues (etic and emic) need to be taken into consideration as the incident is addressed in group?
    See the responses above.

BETH FIRESTEIN'S REACTION AS A MEMBER OF THIS COUNSELING/THERAPY GROUP

Identify the multicultural issues that need to be taken into consideration for you as a member.
    As a Jewish, bisexual, feminist-identified, college-age woman, I would have a number of needs as a member of this therapy group. I feel certain that I would identify with various members of the group around particular individual, familial, and cultural dimensions of their experiences. For example, I would relate to Cynthia regarding the importance of food in her family and the way in which food serves as the fulcrum for most of the socialization in her family. I would probably also identify with Phyllis, her Judaism, and her movement away from the orthodoxy of her beliefs. At the same time, I might actually maintain more distance with Phyllis than I would with other group members because the Orthodox Judaism of her upbringing tends to be very patriarchal and restrictive in its views about women. I could imagine myself

feeling threatened and judged by someone whose upbringing was too much like my father's religious background, a faith tradition that is not at all supportive of lesbian and bisexual women.

A significant issue for me in this group would be the fact that I would be the only openly bisexual member of the group. I would feel unsafe talking about the fact that I was falling in love with my college roommate and that she and I were both coming to identify ourselves as bisexual women. It would be really important to me to feel accepted by the members of this group, and it would be difficult to risk putting forward an aspect of my identity that I seem to share with no other member. As one of two Jewish women in the group, I would feel less isolated than I have felt in many peer groups where I was usually the only person, male or female, of Jewish descent. The sense of being a "double minority" in terms of sexual orientation and religious background would be offset somewhat by the fact that Kumi and Nyria are both foreign-born. My sense is that they would probably feel even more on the outside than I do in this American culture. I could understand that feeling. After all, my father's parents were immigrants, and his mother never spoke English for the entire duration of her life here in the United States.

Explain how your ethnic and cultural background affected the way you would respond as a member.

Please refer to question two for Firestein's response to this question. See also the Summary/Analysis section at the end of this chapter.

Explain how your ethnic and cultural background may or may not inhibit the way you respond to the situation as a member.

As a member of this women's therapy group, I have found a balance between sharing and remaining private. It is my tendency to like to share personal things about myself as a way of getting to know people and becoming close to them emotionally. Everyone in this group has shared a great deal, and I feel I know them pretty well at this point, but I feel really concerned about the way our most recent therapy session has developed. At first, it seemed fine. Almost everyone took the risk of talking to their family members about their eating problems over the holiday break, and I thought that was great. My culture and family really taught me that honesty and openness are important values—even if it often seemed that my parents could not handle the honesty that they invited. In my family, intentional or unintentional "punishing" responses often followed disclosures that parents did not like. I noticed that with other group members, too.

I could see Kumi, our Japanese member, becoming more and more uncomfortable, and that definitely makes me feel uneasy. I remember times when I have been on the "hot spot" myself, and I did not like it one bit. It seems like the group members and leader are behaving in a pushy way toward Kumi. After all, she said right from the start of this topic that she really did not want to comment about the issue of sharing her eating disorder problem with her family when she went home for the holidays. Then it seemed like momentum built, and everyone started grumbling and giving her advice. It did not seem like the members of the group respected her discomfort or her desire to keep her thoughts about this private. In a way, I agree that it would be best if Kumi did open up to her family and friends, but she often opens up to us, and that seems like enough for now. If she is not ready to do more, she should not have to feel bad about that.

Explain how your ethnic and cultural background may have influenced your choice of the response you made over any other that you may have been considering as a member.

I could see what was happening, and it made me feel really tense. Confrontation was common in my family life and seemed to be pretty common in the Jewish family culture more generally, but that does not mean it is fun or comfortable. So I did what I think a lot of people do who have a personal and cultural history of being a scapegoat—I mostly just watched and listened with a growing knot in my stomach. I felt that it was insensitive of the leader to keep directing members back to the issue of how their families take care of them and help them feel good or bad about themselves when it seemed so obvious to me that Kumi was hurting and feeling left out. I have a special sensitivity to people who are being left out of groups. I do not like cliques— "in-groups" and "out-groups"—maybe because I always seem to end up being part of the out-group.

I noticed that when Kumi pulled her chair back from the rest of the group, the other members still did not seem to notice her pain. Both the leader and group members pushed her to respond to the questions that she did not want to answer in the first place. I felt really bad for her. Finally, when Shannon asked Kumi why she did not want to talk about it, Kumi said just about what I thought she would say. It was obvious that she was feeling misunderstood, blamed, and maybe even victimized. I could understand why she might be struggling with feelings of difference and inferiority—she felt different for not wanting to disclose about her eating problem to her parents, different for not wanting to talk about it in group, and bad about herself because she was being pressured by the other members and the group leader. Finally, when Kumi spoke, there was a silence for a long couple of minutes. I debated what to do.

My initial impulse was to remain silent and just continue observing. After all, as a Jew whose family members had fresh memories of WWII and the Holocaust, being invisible is almost assuredly the route to safety. My parents always kept a low profile and tried not to attract attention to our family's differences. I think that is what Kumi was doing too—trying not to attract attention to the way in which she felt culturally different from most of the rest of the group. No one seemed to understand. I really wanted to express anger at the other members of the group and at the leader for being so insensitive and pushy toward Kumi, but that certainly did not seem safe. Finally, I decided that I could only live with my conscience if I at least tried to stand up for Kumi.

I spoke up and said in a clear, quiet voice that I did not think it was fair for the rest of the group to keep pushing their own ideas on Kumi about how she should be with her family. Fairness and standing up for the underdog are two of the paramount values I seem to have gained from my family and my cultural background. I know what it is like to feel like the underdog in a situation, and many times I have wished that someone would recognize my discomfort and my need for support and come to my aid. I wanted to do that for Kumi. It is something I always try to do for people who I think are being discriminated against for being different. I made a plea to the other members to respect Kumi's point of view and her own sense of right action and right timing.

As a result of the response you chose, identify the consequences you might anticipate as a member.

Kumi looked relieved, and frankly, so did a lot of the other members of the group, though a couple of the women looked a little angry about being challenged on the "rightness" of their point of view. I worry that at the next group session, some of the more confident members might retaliate against me by putting me on the spot. I am worried about whether the leader will join with them or respond to protect me. I am afraid that Kumi's cultural differences are not going to be respected, then mine may not be respected either. I really do not know how other members feel about what I did, but they probably know by now that I am always likely to stand up for the underdog in most situations and that fairness is really important to me. It is not that I disagree with the basic points the others were trying to make; it is just that I did not feel good about the way they were going about it. It was more the process than the subject that bothered me in this situation.

From your position as a member, explain what the most glaring or outstanding aspect was of the situation which impacted you from your ethnic and cultural orientation.

I guess the most glaring thing about the whole situation to me was the multiple ways in which Kumi was being excluded from the group in the session. Her difference was being treated as a liability to her healing, as something that made her "wrong" in the eyes of the other members of the group. I did not sense that her cultural differences were being respected. I think there are better ways of helping Kumi want to open up to the group about such an obviously sensitive topic. I really felt sorry for her. I think it is important that we all feel included in the group, not excluded. I think it is important for our differences to be respected, even if they must, at some point, be challenged as well. I do not think scapegoating someone or ganging up on her because her opinion is in the minority is ever really an effective way to help someone heal or grow. People share when they feel ready. They share when they feel safe.

BETH FIRESTEIN'S REACTIONS AS A LEADER OF THIS COUNSELING/THERAPY GROUP

If this type of incident would not occur in your group, explain why it would not.

What Kumi needs in order to feel supported in her individuality is an ally in the group who will affirm her right to set a boundary, whether that boundary is about discussing her eating disorder directly with her family or whether that boundary is about what she is presently willing to disclose to the group. At the same time, Kumi needs to be encouraged to examine her behavior and her motives. Given my perspective and approach to this critical event, it is possible that this incident in group would not have escalated to the point that it did in this vignette. While it seemed appropriate that the leader and members encouraged Kumi to speak about her holidays and her communications with her family, I think that once Kumi physically pulled her chair out of the circle and looked down, a different intervention would have been appropriate. Perhaps at that point, I might have encouraged group members to look at their own need to force this issue with Kumi and what it meant to them that they had taken the actions they had taken while Kumi had made a different choice. We could have explored how each woman's decision served her or failed to serve her in her goals of healing, authenticity, and honoring family relationships.

Identify the multicultural issues that need to be taken into consideration for you as a leader.

In a mature therapy group, members will inevitably progress in an uneven fashion. Some members will be ready to take the "next step" of disclosing their eating disorder to family members and friends, buoyed by the encouragement and progress of other members of the group and the support of the group leader. Others may not progress at the same rate or in the same fashion. In actuality, those members who appear *not* to be "progressing" may, in fact, *be* progressing from within their particular cultural framework, but not when viewed through the lens of the definitional framework for "mental health" normatively applied in Western culture.

In this particular vignette, we have a reasonably mature therapy group. These women have been together and have attended the group regularly for about three and one half months now. The majority of the women attending the group have chosen to take the step of opening up discussion about how their families influence their eating behavior and how their eating behavior influences family members' attitudes toward them and toward one another. In fact, this has been a group topic for some time. Inevitably, these issues surface even more strongly when women return home for holiday breaks. Eating is a significant element in family visits across a variety of cultures, and this tends to be even more the case when holidays are involved. The cultures represented by most of the women attending this therapy group have celebrations, religious rituals, and secular events of one type or another during this time of year that involve food, family, and celebration.

It certainly fit with the group's level of trust, development, and progress that Cynthia, Shannon, Nyria, and others might choose this opportunity to take some new risks in disclosing their difficulties to their families. We talked some about the risks of such disclosures and the potential rewards of taking those risks. We discussed ways to go about sharing information and how to gauge various family members' readiness to hear such disclosures. I tried to help the women prepare for probing questions that might be asked by these women's parents and sisters and brothers. We explored how members of their families might perceive the women who are members of this group. So, from my perspective as a leader, it came as no surprise that many of the members of this group took it upon themselves to take this kind of risk over the holiday break.

Kumi was clearly the least comfortable with this topic and acknowledged that she had not taken any action to disclose her condition to her parents. Several multicultural issues immediately arose for consideration as the situation discussed in this vignette unfolded. First, it is clear that while this is an ethnically diverse group of women, including Nyria, whose family moved here from Puerto Rico when she was 10 years old, Kumi is the only member of the group whose entire upbringing took place in another country—Japan. Despite the racial, ethnic, and cultural diversity of the other women in the group, Kumi clearly has had the least opportunity to achieve any degree of assimilation to American cultural values, and, I would guess, the least motivation for doing so. She only spent one year in the United States as an exchange student before returning to Japan for a year. Now she has returned to the United States to pursue her graduate education in economics, but it is unclear whether she will be remaining in this country once her graduate education is complete.

It is interesting that the reasons Kumi presents for therapy appear to be the product of a clash between our cultural expectations of women and those expectations of women inherent to her own culture. Of course, this is made more complex by the fact that women's roles in Japan are also changing, though not as rapidly as they have changed in the United States. For example, the issue of "low self-esteem" so readily identified as a problem for women in the U.S. university culture is viewed as a problem that manifests as a willingness to defer to others in relationships. Yet, this may be considered extremely appropriate and nonproblematic behavior—even expected and desirable behavior—in Kumi's home community and within her family culture. Her refusal to eat after a conflict with her boyfriend, roommate, or others may well be one of very few acceptable control responses available to her in that culture. Kumi also indicates that it is her way of communicating to her family that she is upset.

In the United States, we problematize her behavior and ask her to exercise control and self-care in ways that are probably exceedingly foreign to Kumi. Her restriction of food intake carries both similar and differing cultural meanings from the restrictive eating behavior of the other group members. For example, Meghan's restricting behavior seems to be more connected to academic performance pressures and her depression, while Cynthia's severe dieting behavior appears to be motivated by the desire to control and decrease her weight. Kumi's restriction appears to serve primarily as a unique form of self-control and indirect social communication with her family. Issues of honor and respect for parents and other family members play a specific role in Kumi's eating disorder that sets her apart from the other women in the group in particular ways.

Explain how your ethnic and cultural background affected the way you would respond as a leader. Based on the composition of this group, what multicultural issues (etic and emic) need to be taken into consideration as the incident is addressed in group?

In the context of this group vignette, and as the leader of this group, I would be concerned that the group had moved into a type of interpersonal confrontation with Kumi that is exactly the type of trigger that resulted in her decision to withdraw interpersonally and refuse to eat. The challenge facing me as a leader of this group in this situation is threefold: First, I need to take a leadership approach that allows me to affirm and support the risks taken by other members of the group without invalidating Kumi's decision not to disclose her eating disorder to her family. Second, I need to attend carefully to both emic and etic perspectives on Kumi's behavior, with the intention of distinguishing to what extent her choices over the holidays, and subsequently in this fourteenth group session, were motivated primarily by her sense of culturally appropriate behavior and to what extent her choices were actually motivated by the same dynamics of disordered eating so clearly and frequently observed across numerous American women who suffer from eating disorders. Third, it is important to highlight the therapeutic significance of Kumi's failure to "defer to the wishes of the other group members." For Kumi, the willingness to voice a dissenting opinion and remain with that opinion in the face of group pressure marks a significant point of progress in defining a "self." Ironically, her failure to follow the group's normative behavior in disclosing to family could actually constitute an act of individuation for Kumi. If she can manage the stress of this encounter without deferring or resorting to refusal to eat, she will have actually accomplished a significant step in her own personal growth and development, at least from the prevailing Western (etic) perspective on mental health.

Explain how your ethnic and cultural background affected the way you would respond as a leader.

For Firestein's answer to this question, see her responses to the other question in this section. See also the Summary/Analysis section at the end of this chapter.

Explain how your ethnic and cultural background may or may not inhibit the way you respond to the situation as a leader. Explain how your ethnic and cultural background may have influenced your choice of the response you made over any other that you may have been considering as a leader.

As a bisexual, Jewish psychologist with a personal and professional history that has sensitized me to issues of inclusion and exclusion, blame and scapegoating, I would probably not have chosen to continue pursuing a group discussion topic that was so clearly alienating one member of the group. I would have been particularly concerned about alienating a member who might already be feeling significantly like an outsider due to her status as a woman from a foreign culture and her obvious sense of alienation during the group's earlier discussion of family interactions over the holiday.

When Kumi pulled her chair out of the circle and physically withdrew from interaction, I would have chosen to shift the focus of the group to the here-and-now of Kumi's experience, with the hope of circling around at another point in time to the group members' experiences with their families of origin. I would have tried to process Kumi's experience of the group members' comments and her emotional reactions to the pressure she might have been feeling from the group. I would have worked to decrease the pressure group members were putting on Kumi while encouraging Kumi to name and describe her own values and experiences with respect to family and how she sees her family members supporting her or presenting her with conflict as she tries to overcome her eating disorder. In this way, I would hope to lessen the intensity of Kumi's experience of feeling blamed or misunderstood by the other members of the group for her cultural differences, while still encouraging her to explore the relevant issues.

As the leader of a therapy group, I always have several choices about how I might intervene in a difficult situation that arises in a group. I think my own "double minority" status as a Jew and a bisexual woman tends to bias me in the direction of actively intervening to attend to the emotional safety needs of a group member whose minority cultural status appears to render her vulnerable to finding herself in such an isolated position vis-à-vis the other members of the group. An alternate response I considered would be to allow the confrontation to fully run its course and then assist Kumi and the group to process the experience, but my fear in doing that would be that the damage potentially done in the process would not be worth the potential therapeutic gains.

As a result of the response you chose, identify the consequences you might anticipate as a leader.

I am not certain how the members of the group would respond to my intervention, but my hope is that in providing for Kumi's immediate needs for validation and emotional safety, I would be modeling a way to balance supportive and challenging behavior to the members of the group. I would hope that they could then use these skills with Kumi and one another in future interactions. I might also anticipate that to the extent group members have bought into normative Western definitions of "mental health" and the treatment of eating disorders, they would remain convinced that Kumi's only route to recovery would lie in the direction of open, honest disclosure and sharing with her family. And perhaps it does. But at this juncture, the risk of alienating a core member of the group clearly seems to outweigh the value of such a confrontation, especially given its potential for harm.

From your position as a leader, explain what the most glaring or outstanding aspect was of the situation which impacted you from your ethnic and cultural orientation.

The most significant aspect of this critical incident from my cultural and ethnic perspective is the recognition that white, Eurocentric, very American notions of mental health pervade our group therapy work and interventions and how little awareness many of us have of our own cultural biases. Group leaders are just as vulnerable as group members to the effects of such cultural biases. At the same time, I do not know whether it is possible to do effective multicultural group therapy from a purely emic perspective. It is not necessary to villianize etic perspectives; we simply need to acknowledge that they exist and be willing to recognize the limitations inherent in operating from a purely etic perspective. If we can thoughtfully blend and balance emic and etic perspectives in our multicultural group psychotherapy work, I believe we shall be successful in attaining our goal of assisting women to higher levels of personal wholeness, self-acceptance, and authentic self-expression that also honor their cultural values and allegiances. This process will be as much art as science, but I have no doubt that it is possible.

MICHAEL HUTCHINS'S REACTION AS A MEMBER OF THIS COUNSELING/THERAPY GROUP

Identify the multicultural issues that need to be taken into consideration for you as a member.

As a group member, I need to know that, even though these other members look different, we have something in common. Just having problems with food is not enough. We must have something more in common.

Also, I need to know that what I say here stops here. In my family, we would not talk about relationship problems or depression, or what is happening for us. The rule is that you do not take family problems outside the family. I need to know what the rules are in the families of the other group members.

I need to know that if I do share what is happening for me, I will not be attacked. That means I need to know what the rules are in this group for giving feedback. In my family, we are not very direct about that. I need to know if I can count on the folks in this group to be direct and caring.

In addition, I need to know what food means for the other group members. In my family, food means many different things. What does it mean for the other group members? Will they understand all the craziness I feel about food because of what it means in my family? Wait, not just in my immediate family, but also in the whole clan. We cannot have a family gathering without people sharing recipes, making sure everyone is "loved" by "eating too much," taking things home from gatherings, and calling to tell stories about how much gets eaten.

Then, when I go home, somebody always makes a comment about how I look. Sometimes, it is a critical one about how much weight I have gained. Sometimes it is about looking like I need to eat more. The messages get very confusing. Do other people in the group get the same messages? How do they deal with the mixed messages?

I need to know what role this counselor is going to play. Is the counselor going to be judgmental or directive? I have been in groups where the counselor just says, "Ummm, hmm." I do not like that. I think a counselor should be more directive. What do the other group members think?

Explain how your ethnic and cultural background affected the way you would respond as a member.

My family is a family that does not share information about ourselves and what is happening in the family. There is little discussion about personal concerns. When such discussion does occur, it is intellectual in nature. We do not discuss feelings. Most of the focus is on behavior when we do discuss anything. We sometimes talk about what people think. Listening is not highly valued in the family, though people will tell you that listening is important.

Historically, there is a strong practice of Roman Catholicism in my family. It is not merely Catholicism, but Irish Catholicism. What comes with that is faith in the local parish priest and the counsel he gives. As a result, I could not tell my parents that I had a problem or they would send me to the priest to talk with him. If I worked hard, I could probably convince my mother that counseling was a good idea. My father would be harder to convince.

That gets to a spirit of independence and "solidarity." In my family, the belief is that we should be strong enough to do things on our own. Not being able to do so is some kind of moral flaw. If my parents knew that I was having a problem, they would probably believe that sin was involved somehow. That would lead to Catholic guilt.

Explain how your ethnic and cultural background may or may not inhibit the way you respond to the situation as a member.

As a result of growing up in a family with parents who lived through the Great Depression, I learned that food is a measure of security and success. Family members were expected to see food as a means of expressing support and affection. Additionally, family members were not expected to discuss emotional concerns with others. My parents were hardworking, blue-collar, lower-middle-class factory workers. They lacked psychological sophistication and were suspicious of mental health professionals. If family members were experiencing psychological stress, the appropriate resource for addressing such issues was the parish priest.

If I were to remain faithful to my family rules and cultural norms, I would not discuss such problems as eating disorders in a group setting. I would not share information about family dynamics and the way the family resolved problems within its structure.

Additionally, I would not seek information or feedback from others about things that occurred within their families. I would need to feel safe enough to speak of guilt and work with the counselor and the others to be clear about the norms and rules. Creating safety would clearly be a concern. I would also assume that such difficulty would be a part of what other group members experienced as well.

I believe that the homogeneity of early life experiences for people of my generation growing up in a small, blue-collar, factory town could make participation in the group more difficult. There was little or no acknowledgment of diversity, and the assumption was that the world experienced life pretty much the same way that folks growing up in this small town in Massachusetts experienced the world. When folks thought about diversity, there was an assumption that other ways of being-in-the-world were, somehow, "less than." In order to fully participate in the group, I would have to transcend these early life worldviews.

What may work to transcend these experiences was the commitment my parents had to making certain that their children had an education. They may not have understood what the implication for education meant. Since I have pursued an advanced degree, my parents have acknowledged that I have lost interest in their world and they do not understand mine. Such acknowledgments may be common for people of my generation in that small town.

Explain how your ethnic and cultural background may have influenced your choice of the response you made over any other that you may have been considering as a member.

As a member, I would be hesitant to provide critical feedback to another group member. As a result of early life experiences, avoiding conflict would be of primary concern. Additionally, sharing information about family holidays on more than a superficial level would be very difficult. While I might want to provide feedback, I might be concerned about hurting another person's feelings.

I might have the intellectual information that sharing feedback is helpful. However, on an affective level, I would be more hesitant. This speaks to rules for safety and confidentiality. It also speaks to accepting norms that are very different from those with which I was raised. In order for me to feel safe in the group, the leader would need to help me explore this dissonance in early group sessions.

If I did provide feedback, I would attempt to share the feedback in the most nonjudgmental fashion possible. This may be awkward, since such sharing is not part of what is expected in my family.

As a result of the response you choose, identify the consequences you might anticipate as a member.

I would hope that my response would invite others to include me in the group. Being an active participant would be important. However, I would want to participate in a way that would not have others in the group "attack" me. As I observe others, I hear them giving advice and telling Kumi what she should do and how her family should behave. I do not like that. In my family, such action would be seen as a betrayal of family norms. I can understand that Kumi does not want to tell her family. Additionally, I can understand that she would not want to talk about what is happening. I would like to be able to tell her that I understand. Furthermore, I would like to tell her in a way that she would hear. I am afraid that I would not be able to do so. I also fear that others in the group would not understand and would "come after" me.

From your position as a group member, explain what the most glaring or out-standing aspect was of the situation which impacted you from your ethnic and cultural orientation.

What stands out is that some group members believe they have the answers to the problems that Kumi is experiencing. It seems that they are telling her what to do with her family. It appears that some of the group members do not understand what it is like to live in Kumi's family and culture. It is not like living in a white, middle-class family. Some of the group members do not seem to understand that.

It could be that in Kumi's family, people do not speak directly to their parents and that, in fact, it is disrespectful. We have not talked a lot about respect in the group. I think that we should. Kumi has said that she does not want to embarrass her family. I do not really understand that; however, I would like to understand that better, because I believe that I think the same thing. I know that my family would be embarrassed if they thought that I had an eating disorder. Furthermore, I believe that my mother would probably think she was, somehow, responsible. There is that Catholic guilt again.

Also, it would be helpful to find out from Kumi if there is another way to address what is going on for her besides sitting around in the group and talking about the holidays and the family. I am not certain, but there might be a more effective way to address the issues. It sounds like the holiday break was pretty traumatic for her. I wonder if there is a way to discuss that in the group without embarrassing the family.

MICHAEL HUTCHINS'S REACTIONS AS A LEADER OF THIS COUNSELING/THERAPY GROUP

If this type of incident would not occur in your group, explain why it would not.

I would like to believe that this incident would not occur in a group that I was leading. I would have attempted to change the group norms by discussing cultural differences early in the group session. I would have had the group participants discuss rules and norms they learned about appropriate ways to behave from early in life. Additionally, I would have had group members do individual time lines that explored messages they learned about thinking, feeling, and doing as they grew up. In doing this, I would hope that we would create a safe environment for the nonjudgmental sharing of feelings, thoughts, and behaviors.

In addition, I would want to help members reach a place in their own development where they can participate without judging themselves or others. I would have tried to find out relatively early in the group if there are ways to share what is occurring that are alternatives to verbal insight-oriented psychotherapy and culturally appropriate for all members of the group. If so, I would have tried to legitimize sharing in these ways, as well as through traditional insight-oriented methods.

Identify the multicultural issues that need to be taken into consideration for you as a leader.

Some of the cultural issues that need to be addressed include the cultural role of sharing feelings in families and in the group. An understanding of different family structures in the different cultures in which the young women were raised is critical to understanding how the group participants think, feel, and behave. What is the appropriate way to express feelings, particularly anger, in different families of origin and cultures? What is the role of food in different families and cultures? Additionally, how do people in different cultures express themselves and give feedback? Is it polite and appropriate to speak directly to someone, or are there other ways to provide feedback? Finally, the age of the participants in the group can be a factor. What are the cultural expectations for young women in the cultures in which these young women were raised?

Explain how your ethnic and cultural background affected the way you would respond as a leader.

I was raised in a family that values privacy, education, and the development of the intellect. Additionally, the family norms include being very vigilant about sharing feelings. As a result, I know the difficulties that many group members experience in sharing feelings and family stories in a "public" setting. Therefore, I work with group members in the early sessions to create safety by having group members share low-risk information about their families of origin. As part of this sharing of stories, I work with group members to reinforce responsibility for one's responses to the environment and the need for moving beyond blame. We also focus on *Gestalt* norms of personal responsibility and distinguishing clearly between thoughts, feelings, and behaviors. We explore how these norms can be applied to people growing up in different cultures and make appropriate adjustments and adaptations.

I have learned that for many young people growing up in diverse cultures, there are options to verbal insight-oriented group therapy. As part of creating safety, I invite group members to participate in experiential collaborative activities that lead to more nonjudgmental processing and that change the focus, allowing the group to create a group culture that is an integration of the norms from the various cultures of group members.

When working with young women with eating disorders, I draw upon the many rules and regulations that were a part of my family as I grew up. There were many rules about food and its role in creating a family. Initially, I invite group members to share food stores, in a nonjudgmental fashion, and relate those stories to family dynamics. Again, it is critical to integrate safety with family histories and the dynamics of different cultural groups.

Explain how your ethnic and cultural background may or may not inhibit the way you respond to the situation as a leader.

Some of the same dynamics that lead to my being able to respond to the issues of privacy, not sharing feelings, and remaining separate are also the dynamics that can inhibit my responses as a leader. In my family of origin and the community in which I was raised, people were supposed to refrain from sharing feedback directly. As a result, I have become accustomed to a less direct way of addressing issues. When this occurs in the group, I may not recognize the need to redirect the group to clarity. As a result, the sense of safety in the group can be jeopardized. Group members may not experience the growth they expect.

In the situation with Kumi, I may not have recognized the need to work with group members earlier in the session to create the safety needed for this group member. It is easy for me, at times, to not attend to quiet members. Additionally, I need to constantly work to be sure that group members are making the interpersonal connections, as well as the intrapsychic learnings, that promote changes of feelings, thoughts and behaviors. I may not always be adept at reading the nonverbal cues that are culturally related. Having grown up in a culture that is relatively "nonaffective," it is particularly important to constantly review the nonverbal and affective dynamics.

Explain how your ethnic and cultural background may have influenced your choice of the response you made over any other that you may have been considering as a leader.

In my family of origin, and in the larger community in which I was raised, the norm was to not discuss family concerns "publicly." To speak up in a group setting may be seen as violating the family's integrity. As a result, I would work to create a safe environment for self-disclosure. As a group, we would spend time sharing less "intimate" stories about families of origin and cultural norms for self-disclosure. My responses would focus on nonjudgmental feedback and teaching/modeling such feedback to/for group members.

Additionally, I have learned from my family that each of us is responsible for our own destiny. I would be tempted to enforce *Gestalt* norms, recognizing that these norms may be culturally inappropriate for some group members. In my family of origin, while we did not discuss affective responses, we did encourage individuation and self-reliance. These values may be culturally inappropriate for some group members. It would be helpful to explore this possibility.

As a result of my upbringing, I am able to examine the possibility that norms for expressing affect may vary from culture to culture. Although my family members may not understand cultural differences, they have begun to learn that "different" does not necessarily mean "less than."

As a result of the response you chose, identify the consequences you might anticipate as a leader.

Hutchins's answer to this question can be found in his other responses in this section. See also the Summary/Analysis section at the end of this chapter.

From your position as a leader, explain what the most glaring or outstanding aspect was of the situation which impacted you from your ethic and cultural orientation.

The most glaring aspect of the situation is that the counselor and the group members do not appear to have a significant understanding of the ways that culture can affect group members. Additionally, it appears clear that at least some of the group members do not understand nonjudgmental feedback and the appropriate expression of feedback, particularly feedback that may have affective attachments. The lack of understanding of diverse worldviews stands out and makes the situation significantly more difficult.

Based on the composition of this group, which multicultural issues (etic and emic) need to be taken into consideration as the incident is addressed in group?

The most significant issues include the structure of families and family rules for behavior. It is important for the leader and the group members to know that the group is a safe place to share information about family dynamics that may be different from the rules group members learned in their families of origin. Additionally, it is important to understand the role of food in different cultures and to understand whether some behaviors that the majority culture identifies as pathological are considered healthy in other cultural groups. If there were a dissonance, it would be important for group members to explore the differences in culturally appropriate ways. I would also want to understand how the young women in the group perceive of themselves as women and to know what they believe the role of women is in families and in this group. In addition, I would want to know the norms for expressing anger and other affective responses, and would want to know where and how the young women learned to express (or not express) such responses. It may also be important to know what the consequences are for speaking about such issues, and what the perceptions are for what happens if one self-discloses on such an intimate level.

It seems most appropriate for the group leader to understand the dynamics of families and young women in different cultural groups. If cultural dynamics are not understood, the group will, most likely, not survive. The leader's role is to help the young women understand cultural dynamics in the group setting and to teach all members to use the group in a culturally appropriate manner to learn new lessons.

SUMMARY/ANALYSIS OF RESPONSES

As Members of This Counseling/Therapy Group

Identify the multicultural issues that need to be taken into consideration for you as a member.

Our respondents cite the central role food plays in their respective cultures and/or families. This is the one issue on which their responses are similar. Firestein sees food as a fulcrum for family socialization. Hutchins feels food has symbolic meaning for other cultures and that it important to understand. In his Irish-Catholic family, food means being loved. Although she does not elaborate, Chung informs us that food holds a variety of symbolic meanings for Asian cultures, especially for the Chinese culture. At this juncture, our respondents separate and give us divergent views of the multicultural issues that are present in this situation.

Firestein underscores how her bisexuality and orthodoxy of Jewish beliefs conflict due to the patriarchal organization of the family. She sees the fact that she is the only open bisexual person as being another issue. She introduces the concept of being a "double minority" as yet another issue. Hutchins believes there are cultural issues related to body size and weight; including weight loss and gain.

Chung elaborates more fully and identifies a multitude of additional issues. She begins with the fact the group consists of six women from various ethnic and cultural backgrounds (included here, then, are gender issues within these cultures). With the diversity of cultures represented, values and communication styles are going to be different. She also raises a number of Asian issues, beginning with the fact that there is only one Asian in the group. We are told that eating disorders are common among Asians and Asian Americans. The fact that there is an Asian in the group means that the importance of family and the interrelationship between individuals and their parents need to be considered. Public disclosure for Asians brings shame to the family as well as the person. Such disclosure also conveys weakness as genetic, which casts parents in a negative light. In addition, disclosure of family matters conveys disloyalty and is a violation of a core cultural value. Consequently, Asian members' silence or reluctance to discuss family matters with strangers presents another issue. A final issue is filial piety. Children in Asian families are required to honor and respect their parents and ancestors, and they are expected to take care of their parents.

Explain how your ethnic and cultural background affected the way you would respond as a member.

The variety of responses to this question reflects the diversity of our experts. Chung allows that Chinese culture prohibits her from educating other members; therefore we assume she means her interactions would be limited. Chinese culture expects women to focus on maintaining harmony and balance. Therefore, the confrontation of Kumi has left her feeling uncomfortable. Firestein offers us a limited ethnic and cultural context in her response when she states simply that her culture and family taught her that honesty and openness are important issues.

Hutchins informs us that his family of origin was closed to discussing matters of gender and feelings. Intimate matters were not shared. In his Irish-Catholic family, people were expected to take such problems to a priest for counsel. A family value required that there be solidarity and independence. Thus, solving problems was done on one's own, and failure to solve one's own problems was considered a moral flaw. Should his parents learn that he has problems, they would view them as being a result of sin, which would lead to Catholic guilt.

Explain how your ethnic and cultural background may or may not inhibit the way you respond to the situation as a member.

The influence of Asian/Chinese culture on Chung is apparent in her response to this question. She discusses the concept of losing face and how it would limit her participation and inhibit her from speaking out in support of Kumi or educating the other group members about Asian culture. Furthermore, the concept of loss of face would make her hesitate to disclose too much in a group that may not be sensitive to or understand her culture.

Firestein states that in her family, intentional or unintentional "punishing responses" often followed disclosures that parents did not like. Perhaps this means she would be hesitant or tentative about sharing her self even though she would be naturally inclined to do so.

Hutchins's Irish-Catholic family consists predominantly of blue-collar, lower-middle-class factory workers who would not support discussing problems in a group. The context he presents allows us to get a deeper appreciation of his ethnic and cultural background. He informs us that in a small, blue-collar factory town, there is little or no acknowledgment of diversity issues. It is assumed that all people experience the world as citizens of the town do and that other ways of being in the world are "less than." Against this background, Hutchins has to transcend these early life worldviews in order to participate fully in the group.

Explain how your ethnic and cultural background may have influenced your choice of the response you made over any other that you may have been considering as a member.

Chung and Hutchins are similar in their responses to this question even though their cultural backgrounds are different. Chung reiterates that the concept of loss of face would inhibit any disclosure or vocal support of Kumi. Therefore, any form of disclosure on her part would be minimal. Hutchins reminds us that his family norms preclude his offering any open, in-depth sharing of information related to his family. So, he might also avoid offering feedback, or he would offer it only in the most nonjudgmental way. To do otherwise, such as to give advice, would be a betrayal of family norms.

Although the are veiled parallels to Chung's and Hutchins's responses in Firestein's answer, the context is different. In Firestein's family and Jewish culture, confrontation is common. She, however, is not comfortable with confrontation, which helps us understand her discomfort with the encounter in the group. Being a Jew, she is aware of family memories of WWII and the Holocaust, and has from those experiences learned that invisibility is a sure route to safety. Her first impulse is to remain silent and just keep observing, as her parents encouraged her to keep a low profile and not draw attention to the family's differences. But even though she chooses not to express anger toward the members and the leader because it would not be safe, she does choose to speak up for Kumi, since she believes in fairness and standing up for the underdog, which are values gained from her family of origin.

As a result of the response you chose, identify the consequences you might anticipate as a member.

Chung anticipates that Kumi might be upset with her and confront her for not being supportive. She admits she might feel guilty for not supporting another Asian person. She expects that the other group members might confront her for not speaking out in general and that they might ask her for her reaction to Kumi's comments, since she is also Asian. Chung considers approaching the group leader in private to address cultural issues, but she thinks the leader could disapprove of that and thus might bring up the issues in the next session. If that were to happen, it would cause embarrassment and loss of face for Chung.

Firestein expects that a couple of the members might be angry for being challenged, but she thinks Kumi and many other members would appear relieved. She sees a possibility that in the next session, some of the more confident members might retaliate against her, in which case the leader would either join them or attempt to protect her.

Hutchins tells us that he would like to express his support of Kumi and that he understands her. He expects that such a response would draw an attack upon him from the other group members.

From your position as a member, explain what the most glaring or outstanding aspect was of the situation which impacted you from your ethnic and cultural orientation.

There is some unanimity in the responses to this question. In addition to noting the existence of a direct link between the family and the problem, as well as the lack of family support, Chung highlights the group's lack of understanding of and openness to cultural differences. She sees the group's nonsupport of Kumi and their lack of respect for her culture as glaring aspects of the situation. Likewise, Firestein considers both the multiple ways in which Kumi has been excluded from the group and the group's disrespect for her cultural differences as outstanding aspects of this incident. Hutchins also points to the fact that the other members do not understand what it is like to live in Kumi's family or culture. This is further emphasized by the fact that some of the members believe they have solutions to Kumi's problems. This is, as Hutchins notes, a reflection of how some members are trying to impose their white, middle-class values on her.

As Leaders of This Counseling/Therapy Group

If this type of incident would not occur in your group, explain why it would not.

All three experts do not think this incident would occur in their groups. Chung and Hutchins would have discussed cultural backgrounds early in the life of the group, and we might infer from Firestein's response that she would have done the same. She tells us that Kumi needs to feel supported in her individuality. One way to achieve this objective for Kumi would be to discuss cultural differences.

Establishing a safe environment is something else the experts would have done to avoid this kind of situation. Hutchins would begin the group by having members discuss rules and norms they learned about appropriate ways to behave in life. He would see that the members would be nonjudgmental of one another so they could feel safe to share feelings, thoughts, and behaviors. Chung would establish early on an understanding, sensitivity, appreciation, and respect for cultural issues related to eating disorders. Firestein conveys that Kumi needs to feel safe to discuss whether it is her eating problem or her family that needs to be addressed, and this can be achieved by gaining allies who will affirm and help her set a boundary for such exploration.

Hutchins also notes a possible limitation with the way this group is designed to function. He proposes finding alternative approaches to insight-oriented psychotherapy that would be culturally appropriate for all members. Doing so could help avoid the occurrence of a situation like this in group.

Identify the multicultural issues that need to be taken into consideration for you as a leader.

Although each respondent identifies different focus issues, they argee on one common issue: the different cultural meanings attendant with eating disorders. Chung notes that the group members need to develop an awareness, understanding, and appreciation of different cultural perspectives related to eating disorders. Firestein also says the members need to understand the different cultural meanings of restrictive eating behavior. She gives examples by stating that Meghan's eating disorder seems to be connected to academic performance, Cynthia's seems to be an issue of control and decreased weight, and Kumi's is a form of self-control and indirect communication with her family. Hutchins joins Chung and Firestein by observing that the group needs to understand the role food plays in each culture. Along the same lines, Chung identifies another issue: the need to acknowledge and be aware of the differences in cultural communication styles in order to avoid misunderstandings.

Feelings are a focus area for Hutchins. He suggests there is a need to understand the cultural role of sharing feelings in families and in the group, as well as the different ways each culture considers appropriate for expressing feelings, particularly anger. He also identifies age and gender as issues, suggesting there are different cultural expectations for young women about which members need to be made aware.

For Firestein, Kumi is a member of a culture that needs explanation. Firestein identifies Kumi as being the member who, above all, has had the least opportunity to achieve any degree of assimilation to American cultural values. Furthermore, she believes Kumi's reasons for being in the group appear to be the product of a clash between Western cultural expectations of women and those of women in the Asian cultures. Finally, she adds that consideration needs to be given to the roles that honor and respect for parents and other family members play in Kumi's eating disorder and how the roles set her apart from the other members.

Explain how your ethnic and cultural background affected the way you would respond as a leader.

In the responses to this question, we can see how the cultures of the leaders truly affected their choice of interventions. Chung's Asian background heightens her awareness of the cultural influences and dynamics in the group. She discusses how she is from a collectivist culture and an international background that makes her more sensitive to the unique cultural backgrounds of the group members. Consequently, her understanding and interpretation of the meaning of an eating disorder comes from a contextual cultural framework from which her intervention would evolve.

Firestein is very candid and forthright in stating that her double minority status as a Jew and a bisexual woman would bias her. She sees herself actively intervening to attend to the emotional needs of Kumi whose minority cultural status appears to render her vulnerable to finding herself in an isolated position. Referring to herself as a bisexual Jewish psychologist, Firestein relates that such a background has given her a personal and professional history that has sensitized her to issues of inclusion and exclusion, blame and scapegoating.

Hutchins's Irish-Catholic family (lower-middle-class, socioeconomically) valued privacy, education, and intellectual development. Family norms discouraged the sharing of feelings, and there were also many rules about food and its role in creating a family. This background has given him the context from which the interventions he would use with these young women with eating disorders would evolve.

Explain how your ethnic and cultural background may or may not inhibit the way you respond to the situation as a leader.

Chung's ethnic and cultural background apparently would not inhibit her. As a fellow Asian, she states that she would not allow Kumi to lose face or feel shame. She would intervene in a protective way, even though it might interfere with the group dynamics.

Firestein does not address this question directly, but we can infer from her other responses that, as a bisexual Jewish psychologist, her professional and personal history would preclude any hesitation. She would follow the influences of her life experiences and intervene immediately; she would not allow the group members to continue dealing with Kumi as they have been.

Hutchins states that in his family of origin and the community in which he was raised, people refrained from sharing feedback directly. Therefore, he developed an indirect way of addressing issues. He adds that growing up in a culture that is relatively "nonaffective" required him to double his efforts to be aware of nonverbal and affective communication. He concludes that some of the dynamics learned from his background regarding the issues of privacy, not sharing feelings, and remaining separate could inhibit him as a leader. He might hesitate to redirect this group to clarity, since doing so might jeopardize members' feelings of safety and member growth.

Explain how your ethnic and cultural background may have influenced your choice of the response you made over any other that you may have been considering as a leader.

Chung explains that saving face and avoiding shame are among the paramount issues for an Asian to regard and respect. Consequently, as a leader, she sees herself intervening to help Kumi save face and not feel ashamed.

Firestein reiterates that her double minority status as a Jew and bisexual woman tends to bias her toward actively intervening in order to attend to the emotional safety needs of Kumi, whose minority cultural status renders her vulnerable. She considers but rejects an alternative response of allowing the confrontation to run its course and then assisting Kumi and the group in processing the experience.

Hutchins reminds us that his family of origin did not reinforce or encourage discussing family concerns in public, as to do so would be to violate family integrity. His family of origin also encouraged self-reliance and responsibility. So, he considers two interventions. The family rule regarding maintenance of privacy would influence him to first establish a safe environment in the group for making self-disclosures. He would also propose the family norm regarding self-reliance and responsibility to the group for exploration, though these values might not be culturally appropriate for all the members.

As a result of the response you chose, identify the consequences you might anticipate as a leader.

Chung foresees her intervention to help Kumi as drawing nonsupportive consequences from the other group members. She believes they may perceive her as being protective of or aligning herself with Kumi because they both are Asians; they may view that as being unfair treatment. In addition, she expects that the members will stereotype her as a passive Asian woman, since her technique is nonconfrontative.

Firestein is less certain about how the other members would respond. She would hope, however, that three consequences would occur as a result of her intervention: (1) that Kumi's immediate needs for validation and emotional safety would be met; (2) that she would have provided a model for the other members of how to balance supportive and challenging behaviors; and (3) that the other members would learn to use these skills in future interactions.

Hutchins anticipates there would be nonjudgmental processing that would change the group's focus, thereby allowing the group to create a group culture that would be an integration of the norms from the various cultures of the members.

From your position as a leader, explain what the most glaring or outstanding aspect was of the situation which impacted you from your ethnic and cultural orientation.

Once again, the leaders, despite their diverse backgrounds, identified similar outstanding aspects in this situation. Firestein notes that a white, Eurocentric, very American notions of mental health pervade group therapy work and interventions and that many group leaders have cultural biases of their own. Similarly, Hutchins believes that neither the group counselor nor the members have a significant understanding of the ways that culture can affect group members. He also identifies a lack of understanding of diverse worldviews. One other concern he raises is that at least some of the group members do not understand nonjudgmental feedback and the appropriate expression of feedback.

Like the other two leaders, Chung sees evidence that the group members lack a willingness to explore, understand, and appreciate cultural differences. Also, there appears to be an underlying assumption that everyone is the same and should approach the problem of eating disorders in a similar fashion. As with Firestein, Chung had strong feelings for Kumi and though the group members demonstrated little sensitivity toward her.

Based on the composition of this group, what multicultural issues (etic and emic) need to be taken into consideration as the incident is addressed in group?

For Chung, the etic issue is the need for group members to be more sensitive to all cultures and the diversity that exists within their own group. Hutchins believes the etic issues regard how young women in the group perceive themselves as women and what the role of women is in their families and in the group.

Hutchins's emic position holds that it is necessary to understand the role food plays in each culture. He also believes it is important to understand that some behaviors identified as pathological by the majority culture are considered healthy in other cultures. Another issue he cites relates to how families are organized (culturally specific) and what their rules of conduct are. A final emic issue for Hutchins regards the need for the leader to understand the dynamics of families and the role of young women in different cultures.

Two emic issues stand out for Chung. The first is specific to Asian women and the need to save face and not be ashamed. The second is understanding the role and meaning of food in Asian culture.

Firestein discusses the emic and etic perspectives together and identifies three challenges facing her as a leader: (1) to affirm and support the other group members without invalidating Kumi's decision not to disclose her eating disorder to her family, (2) to distinguish to what extent Kumi's choices are motivated by her culture and to what extent they are motivated by the dynamics of disordered eating, and (3) to highlight the fact that Kumi's "failure" to go along with the other members could actually constitute a significant point of progress in Kumi's definition of self.

Conclusions

The following chapters are intended to identify the most salient messages that can be drawn from the previous chapters. The objective is to convey how common group factors and processes that have their origins in a Eurocentric view of group work can be applied to multicultural group work. In addition, we offer suggested guidelines for the practice of multicultural group work based on what we have learned.

12 CHAPTER | **What Have We Learned?**

From the outset we stated that interactions between race, culture, community, family, and individual values are incredibly complex and need to be taken into account when conceptualizing multicultural group work. We also said that group stages and group processes are constants that are present regardless of the complexity of group members' experiences and the worldviews of group leaders. In addition, we observed that cultural diversity increases the complexity and diversity of the interactions of members, leaders, and the group as a whole. Therefore, such interactions need to be considered within the context of members' and leaders' personal worldviews. All eleven of our experts confirmed our observations. Each brought his or her personal worldview to the situation both as member and leader. From this we learned that each of our experts did not necessarily represent the whole population, culture, and ethnic group of which he or she is a part.

We feel it is essential to emphasize the complexity of the interactions between personal values, beliefs about effective group work, and cultural and ethnic worldviews. We learned that the same can be said of group members. For instance, in the first counseling/therapy vignette, Molina speaks strongly from her Polish-American background for the need to address the oppression of women (gender) both as a member and as a leader. Shakoor, on the other hand, not only enlightened us about the strong influence women had in his early development, but he also conveyed the need to consider male vulnerability as an issue. It has been made clear that as leaders we need to listen carefully to members' stories, not only when they face a critical moment in the group, but also in terms of how their stories affect the way they interpret events in their lives and subsequently respond to them. In addition, we need to help members explore and understand the influence their culture has had upon their personality and development. For instance, recall Sandhu explaining how India's history with China affected how he might relate to Chinese members. Similarly, Shechtman's early history as an immigrant and her later experiences as an Israeli affected how she might relate to nonassertive group members.

The evidence is clear that leaders need to be aware of their own stories of acculturation and migration, and how these stories may affect the way they experience and perceive the stories presented by group members. Without exception, our experts related how their own personal stories were present as they experienced their group members in each situation. Recall how both Garrett and Chung emphasized the cultural concept of loss of face and respect in their responses to the counseling/therapy vignettes and then again in their responses to the task and psychoeducational vignettes. This conscious awareness of their own stories allowed the leaders to be less inhibited and enabled them to keep their stories from interfering with working effectively in the group.

From this, the age-old adage "Counselor, know thyself" receives reinforcement. Our respondents revealed that by exploring and emphasizing the influences of their personal values, family of origin experiences, and ethnic/cultural backgrounds upon them, they were helped to be more sensitive to the needs and stories of their group members; and accordingly, they were able to implement interventions that reflected cultural sensitivity. Such sensitivity means that our respondents might not always comply with what is custom within their own culture if it means doing so might inhibit their working effectively. For example, in Counseling/Therapy Group Vignette #1, Molina felt she might have to abandon her cultural norm that would encourage her to connect with others lest some of the members did not want to connect at the moment. Remember also how Sandhu opted to withdraw as a leader due to the personal conflict he experienced between the group's purpose and his ethnic and religious background. Even in this case, being self-aware led to the appropriate response.

Also in evidence is the fact that all of our experts have struggled with their dominant culture. As an immigrant to Israel, Shechtman heard the voices from her earlier culture competing with those of her Israeli culture. Shakoor, in a similar vein, heard the voices from his tenement neighborhood in Cleveland conflicting with those of the dominant culture, especially after he left the neighborhood. Hernández also heard the intercultural voices within his family of origin competing with each other, as well as with those of the dominant culture outside of his family. We learned that he thinks of himself as a Latino despite the fact that his mother is of Czechoslovakian decent. Molina's Polish background has her hearing her grandmother's voice telling her to treat clients as though God were a guest in her house, while her dominant American culture, unlike that of her mountain region of Poland, urges her, as a woman, to be assertive. Likewise, Brown heard an early generational voice that told her to not be assertive because she was a girl and to avoid conflict, yet her current personal voice encourages her to counter those early directives.

Further evidence of our experts' struggles with their dominant culture can be seen in Sandhu's acknowledgment of how his Asian-Indian culture and Sikh background often conflicted with that of his dominant American culture, which placed him in the position at times of facing uneasy choices that could cause him to lose face with his professional colleagues. We observed Garrett hearing his Native-American culture directing him to challenge the norms of the dominant culture, and Hutchins's early life experiences in a conservative lower-middle-class, blue-collar, Irish-Catholic family continually challenged his listening to the voice that would have him follow a more liberal and open approach to interpersonal relationships as a member and a group leader. Chung conveyed how she was always aware of her Asian-Chinese background and the voice of her family as she attempted to accommodate her dominant culture's norms. Firestein introduced us to the concept of "double minority." She felt that the voices of her orthodox Jewish family and those of her bisexuality made her continually aware of matters related to exclusion and inclusion, blame and scapegoating. Kalodner hears her Jewish background helping her to give voice in opposition to those voices within the dominant culture that are intolerant of diversity.

We also learned that psychological and emotional intimacy in multicultural groups is determined by what group members can tolerate. Leaders need to be attentive to the acculturation experiences of each member in order to weigh the degree of intimacy that is tolerable for the members and the group as a whole. Also, many individuals appear to have lost their acculturation experiences. In other words, their intergenerational cultural and ethnic stories are not known to them for any number of reasons. Leaders need to realize that such persons can be, at times, considered a cultural minority themselves among those group members who have a grasp of their multigenerational history and that those without such history may feel at a loss if asked to draw upon their own acculturation experiences.

GROUP FACTORS

We learned that regardless of the ethnic and cultural backgrounds of members, what might be considered to be Eurocentric explanations for group phenomena in many cases do apply to multicultural groups. Earlier we mentioned two of these: group stages and group processes. In addition to writing about group stages and group processes, Donigian and Malnati (1997) identified factors that influence leader, member, and group behavior. Those that we will consider here include: systems of communication, history, themes, norms and standards, stages, cohesion, and power and influence.

In all groups, a number of *systems of communication* affect group process and impinge upon leader, member, and group behaviors (Donigian & Malnati,

1997). There are several nonverbal communication systems in which members, leaders, and even the group as a whole engage. All of these communication systems can be identified by actions rather than words.

Proxemics is the emotional and physical distance that exists between and among members. Such distance often can be determined by noting where members and leaders sit in relation to one another over time. Keeping track of which members come late or early to sessions can also reveal how important or how attractive the group is to certain members. When considering proxemics in multicultural groups, leaders need to be cautious and be sensitive to the cultural and ethnic composition of the group's membership. Recall how each of our experts regarded proxemics in their responses to the vignettes. There is clear evidence that they addressed it in different ways according to each expert's own background.

Unconscious behavior, which is behavior that is not made known to the leader, the members, or the group, can be viewed as another form of communication. A possible example of unconscious behavior occurred in the vignette where there were group members who arrived late and others who left early. Recall that the leader did not address these behaviors early on. By delaying the examination of and talking about these events, the leader contributed to the continuation of unconscious behavior, which in itself can be viewed as unconscious behavior that took the form of denial. Thus, not only was an opportunity missed to openly address the behaviors, but also a norm was established that conveyed to the group members that the group was not a safe place to talk about such matters. As a result, unconscious behavior became a system of communication that was reflected throughout the group. Clearly, nipping such behavior early in the life of the group is necessary for the group to function effectively.

The *tense* of communication needs to be in the present. As the members feel safer in the group, communication usually increasingly moves to the present tense. Communication in a there-and-then tense usually means that members may be confronting issues that are not easy to face. However, leaders need to respect that some cultures use metaphor, story, or parable to reflect truth and provide directives; therefore, leaders need to pay attention to there-and-then stories and their underlying messages.

Emotional intensity as a system of communication in multicultural groups can be a barometer of the degree of comfort members feel toward being in the group and with one another. Again, leaders need to use caution when attempting to understand this form of communication, for it is one that varies with and within cultures. For example, we learned from our experts that it is the norm for Asian women to be the peacemakers; therefore, it would not be customary to observe them engaging in verbal or nonverbal communication that is confrontational or openly argumentative.

Silence as a form of communication can convey any number of messages when experienced in a multicultural group. Our Native-American expert used it as a means of conveying his disapproval of the late arriving and early leaving of group members. He informed us that he felt disrespected. It becomes the task of leaders to understand and interpret what group members are trying to communicate through silence. Group silence or member silence may exist for a number of reasons. Donigian and Malnati (1997) offer the following as possibilities:

> Is the silence occurring in the first session? Or in the 12th? Have norms been established to build a group culture that allows members to feel safe about self-disclosure? How is the group composed? Have you as a leader been authoritarian in your interactions? What in the history of the group could be contributing to the group silence? For instance, did a member leave the group prematurely? Was the previous week's session intensely emotional? Does the group as a whole have a common pre-group history that is contributing to the silence? How clear are group goals? Has a member just made a deep emotional disclosure? Have you, as a leader, offered process illumination of the group as a whole? How much extra-group socializing—that is subgrouping—has been going on? Has the group just finished some work and is it in transition? Is the group facing its final session—that is, termination? (pp. 28–29)

Heider (1985) offers another way to view silence. He encourages leaders to "allow regular time for silent reflection. Turn inward and digest what has happened. . . . When group members have time to reflect, they can see more clearly the essential in themselves and others" (p. 23). Asking members about how they view silence and their level of comfort with silence may be useful as well.

When we consider *history* as a factor that influences group process, we are referring to all of the member, leader, and group behaviors that have occurred since the group began. "Pregroup history" refers to the personal histories of the leader and members in other group situations (such as family, work, and social groups) prior to the beginning of the current group. Member and leader pregroup histories do influence the behavior of members and leaders within groups. An essential assumption held by Donigian and Malnati (1997) is that over time a member's behaviors in a group will frequently be a reflection of his behavior in the world outside of the group. Recall the question that asked our experts to address how their background may have influenced their response to the situation first as a member, and then as a leader. In virtually every case, pregroup history influenced how each responded to the situation.

Themes are factors that link one group session to the next and are potential unifiers of the group. When leaders attend to identifying and interpreting themes, they assist the group in its development and progress toward achieving its goals by helping it to break away from narrowly focused issues. In the first counseling/therapy vignette, Molina identified a central issue (i.e., theme) to be trust. She based it on the fact that she considered each member had experienced varying degrees of isolation, oppression, and rejection. Then in Task Group Vignette #2, she reframed issues (i.e., themes) as being related to power and competition. In the same vignette, Brown sought to lessen the differences among members by finding universal themes through which they could find their similarities. In both cases, the leaders' efforts would lead to unifying the members.

Themes also can be observed through behaviors of members and the group as a whole that convey attraction, hostility, intimacy, or flight from conflict. Instead of stating that the group is behaving in a hostile manner, a leader might reframe the behavior as a safe theme. By stating that the group appears to be frustrated and feeling powerless and to be truly at its wits' end, and then asking that the members take some time to share other moments when they felt impotent either in the group or elsewhere, the leader not only diffuses a potentially counterproductive situation but also unifies the members by helping them see that they share a common theme. In the vignette where members were arriving late and leaving early, the opportunity was present to create any number of themes based on interventions related to the struggle for time management, the desire to please and not being able to say "no," trying to meet the needs of others, respecting self and others, and so forth. Identifying themes that were present in the group could lead to group members addressing how they might be resolved, which in turn could lead to finding solutions for the group's current concern regarding everyone being present on time and remaining for the entire session. The effect such an approach would have on the conflictual situation would be to unify the members because, through the discussion of themes, they would identify their commonality by universalizing their shared concerns.

According to Donigian and Malnati (1997), "*Norms* refer to the rules that govern behavior in groups, while *standards* refer to the system of punishment and rewards for violating or cooperating with established or evolving rules of behavior" (p. 37). Norms and standards take the form of explicit rules that the leader determines prior to the group's first meeting. Normally these are viewed as the basic ground rules that the leader expects members and the group as a whole to follow. Norms and standards can also be implicit. That is to say, they can evolve consciously or unconsciously during the group's development as a reflection of individual member's or the leaders' personal set of norms and standards or the group's collective sense of what the norms and standards should be" (Donigian & Malnati, 1997, p. 37). No two groups are alike; therefore, it can be expected that norms and standards will vary from group to group in order to meet each group's particular needs. Similarly, it can be expected that individual member norms and standards will vary from group to group. How often we hear that a person exhibits behaviors in one group, but then we find the same individual exhibiting entirely different behaviors in another.

Norms and standards also provide safety boundaries for members. In all groups, there are existing and developing norms and standards. Existing norms help members realize what codes of acceptable conduct are. If such codes are too rigid, members will not feel safe to risk voicing their points of view, and thus will be inclined to conform. Chapter 3 emphasizes the variability in norms towards disclosure, spontaneous interaction, and respect for elders that may appear as a result of cultural differences; thus, while Eurocentric assumptions about group work are a starting point, they are simply that—a place to begin the discussion about how to make a group safe for all members to achieve their goals.

Another aspect of developing norms and standards is the ever-evolving group culture. Group culture is based on what (content) can be talked about and how (process) it can be talked about in the course of group development. Culture, therefore, is comprised of what is viewed as the behaviors that are deemed acceptable in the group. Healthy, productive groups are those that have an ever-developing and widening culture of tolerable behaviors that test the boundaries of conformity. What can be talked about and how it will be talked about increases, and members also feel a greater sense of safety to participate openly. It is the task of leaders to avoid rewarding conformity. Hulse-Killacky et al. (2001) conveyed that, "Groups work best when time is taken for culture building and learning about differences" (p. 12). The authors relate that in addition to considering race, culture, ethnicity, religion, gender, age, sexual orientation, and disability, leaders need to be sensitive to differences in work styles. For them, "Culture building . . . means developing guidelines for tolerating such differences within the group" (p. 11).

Hulse-Killacky et al. (2001) also stated that leaders who are more concerned about getting their groups started without attending to the members in the group are likely to find that their groups will struggle and not become cohesive. The authors suggest that at the inception of the group, time be given to build the group's culture. Meeting members' needs for safety and building community is imperative. All of this needs to occur early in the history of the group. Recall how Garrett stated that he would begin the group entirely differently by employing the Native-American technique of the talking circle. The intentions of this exercise would be to build safety, coalitions, and a sense of community. Chung, on the other hand, felt that, for Asians, the talking circle did not reflect Asian culture; therefore, she would have opted to begin the group very differently. Notice that both leaders had at least one area of agreement; they both wanted to consider the members' needs and to build a culture that would lead to establishing coalitions and community.

In a number of vignettes, our experts were very cognizant of the value of establishing group norms. For example, in Counseling/Therapy Vignette #2, Garrett and Hutchins both stated that the incident would not be likely to occur in their groups due to their attending to building group norms. Shechtman, in Psychoeducational Group Vignette #2, would strive to first establish group cohesiveness and feelings of safety. Brown also informs us in Task Group Vignette #1 that she would have attended to building group culture and norms, which would have kept the situation from occurring.

Donigian and Malnati (1997) stated, "The knowledge that groups go through identifiable stages of development will help leaders develop a sense of order and expectation (predictability) about group process" (p. 40). The authors added, "An understanding of the stages of group development allows co-leaders to demystify the confusing and highly complex interactive dynamics of a group of diverse individuals" (p. 41).

It is generally accepted that groups go through a series of *stages* (Kottler, 1994). Groups are viewed as developing either along a linear path or through a cyclical process. The former view suggests that the process is fluid and that the group may revert back to an earlier stage at any time. The latter view holds that the group will from time to time repeat certain segments or issues from an earlier stage (Donigian & Malnati, 1997). Hulse-Killacky et al. (2001) presented a model of group development that emphasizes balancing process and content. The model provides leaders with a visual framework from which group development can be understood. Their three-stage model consists of warm-up, action, and closure. At each stage, leaders can assess the effective functioning of their group by ascertaining that there is the expected balance between process and content. According to this model, leaders can readily assess whether there is an imbalance in either content or process focus, and can adjust accordingly. The authors hold that "warm-up, action and closure represent the ebb and flow of group work" (p. 27).

In Counseling/Therapy Group Vignette #1 for instance, Molina believes that the incident could occur in any group because of the group's stage of development, and then again in Task Group Vignette #2 she attributes the incident to natural group processes. In Counseling/Therapy Group Vignette #4, all of our experts made reference to group processes that are related to group stages. Clearly their references to establishing safety refer to the earliest stage of group development.

Group *cohesiveness* relates to the sense of belonging or attraction to the group that is held by each member. Time and again we heard from various experts about the importance of building group cohesiveness, Garrett would do so through the use of the talking circle. Similarly, Hernández attempted to deemphasize his position of authority, and Shakoor tried to help members feel safe to vocally participate and not be penalized if they chose not to.

We have spoken to the need for leaders to learn how to release and manage the *power* of the group. We addressed the fact that the greater the diversity of members, the more effective the group can be. So as leaders come to learn and understand how to use process, they will harness the power of the group in a way that will lead to successful outcomes. It is necessary, therefore, for leaders to realize that theirs is a position of authority, not power, in the group. They can *influence* the groups' direction. A good example of how one of our experts relies on her position of authority to influence the group is found in Chung's intention to disclose first as means for influencing the Asian members to feel safe and not feel they were betraying the Asian custom of saving face. Garrett sought out the *power* of the group as he used his *influence* in forming the talking circle, where norms and standards would be established through the processes of using that technique.

GROUP PROCESSES

Effective group leaders understand the nature of *group process*. Content and process are linked from one session to the next, as is member affect. Therefore, leaders need to view each session as being part of a "continuum rather than a discrete occurrence" (Donigian & Malnati, 1997, pp. 32–33). For example, in Task Group Vignette #2, the incident that occurred in the fourth session was a result of a sequence of issues related to member attendance that began with the first session. Each of our leaders addressed the event in the fourth session from a process perspective. For instance, Garrett viewed the comings and goings of different members during the first few sessions as being disrespectful from a Native American's position. He informs us that not only would he have addressed the incidents sooner, but he also would have dealt with the issue differently, thereby implying that he viewed the moment as being a product of other related occurrences.

Often group events can be viewed as an accumulation of issues that have not been addressed over time. Hulse-Killacky et al. (2001) speaks about leaders needing to balance process and content in order for their groups to function effectively. According to the authors, in order to release the power of the group, knowledge of group processes is paramount. Such knowledge "taps into the power of the collective" (p. 116). Molina's response to the incident in Counseling/Therapy Group Vignette #1 conveys an understanding of group process and taps into the power of the collective. She states that as a group leader, she feels very comfortable as long as leadership is shared. Kline (2003) impressed upon leaders that it is through the interaction of group members that change can take place; therefore, knowledge of group development theory, interactive group theory, general systems theory, and focal conflict theory contributes to group leaders' grasp of group processes.

Agazarian and Peters (1989) also offered words on the significance for leaders to have knowledge of group processes and group development. Although they were speaking about group therapy, consider how their words apply to other forms of group work as well:

> This is why there is a significant difference between the therapy group whose therapist does individual therapy within a group setting of a "group" of people, without the understanding of group development theory, and the therapy group whose therapist understands group process and employs group development theory. The group process therapist is able to influence deliberately the process of group development therapeutically at the same time that he deliberately chooses to influence individual development therapeutically; thus contributing both to the interdependence between the individual therapeutic potential and the potential for the group environment. The individually oriented therapist is not able to influence group development deliberately and will not have that choice until he has become familiar with group process as distinct from individual interests. (p. 128)

According to Donigian and Malnati (1997), *group processes* fall into seven types: emotional contagion, conflict, anxiety, consensual validation, universality, family reenactment, and the instillation of hope. In examining each of these more closely, we find that all of them exist in multicultural groups. Their presence in a group is dependent upon the interaction that occurs between the members, leader(s), and the group as a whole. Consequently, leaders should encourage member-to-member interaction.

Emotional contagion is released when one member's behaviors act as an emotional stimulant to the entire group. For instance, in Counseling/Therapy Group Vignette #1, the effect of Chloe's disclosure/outburst upon the group leads to the members being stunned. In other words, the intensity had the effect of emotionally stimulating each of the group members to act, albeit in a manner that took the form of being immobilized.

"Becoming experientially involved in a group leads inevitably to conflict" (Donigian & Malnati, 1997, p. 6). Generally *conflict* in any group can be found to relate to issues such as one's significance, authority, autonomy, attraction, intimacy, dependence, growth, change, power, control, and loss. The authors claim that the group as a whole, the members, and the leader(s) all are vulnerable to experiencing any of these issues. A good example of conflict is reflected in Task Group Vignette #2 where any number of conflictual issues were present. The early leaving and late arrivals might possibly be related to matters of significance, authority, power, control, and so forth. Note how the members and the leader struggled with these concerns.

Where there is the potential for conflict, there is also the potential for anxiety. *Anxiety* is that continuous state of emotional tension that is the product of unsuccessful attempts at managing internal conflicts that have been stimulated by the interactive experience with one or more members, the leader(s), or the group as a whole. Note that in Counseling/Therapy Group Vignette #1, Chloe's anxiety was really fueled by the emotional tension that had accumulated over the previous two sessions.

Consensual validation is one of the processes that is unique to group work. It allows members to check out and/or validate ideas, behaviors, thoughts, and observations with other members. Validation is better achieved when one receives feedback from the group versus self-assessment. A form of consensual validation occurred in Counseling/Therapy Group Vignette #3. Rosalie's disclosure of her anxious feelings and the reasons for having them was validated as Ashara and Tikki disclosed like concerns and feelings. The effect of the latter two members' disclosures upon Rosalie could be viewed as validating. Likewise, even though it was *ex post facto* (i.e., after the fact), Rosalie's disclosure, when joined with either one of the other two, had a similar effect.

Universality regards the notion that all human beings are fundamentally similar. Finding common ground among members is necessary in order for the group to work effectively. Therefore, it is important for leaders to encourage member-to-member interaction early on. The more they create opportunities for members to realize the universality of their experiences, the more likely they are to succeed in building group unity. We see the concept of universality addressed when Hernández, in Psychoeducational Group Vignette #1, would encourage students to share in order that they would find their commonalities and feel connected.

Donigian and Malnati (1997) related that it is quite common for members to replay their roles from old family scripts. Sometimes the group can represent a family structure that is quite familiar to a member. When viewed in this way, one can easily be seen to *reenact* the role one played in the *family* while in the group. Counseling/Therapy Group Vignette #4 is an example of how members replay their roles from family scripts in the group. Kumi's response to the urgings of the other members appears to reflect how she views herself and her role within her family of origin. That is, she is communicating indirectly that she expects to take care of herself and, therefore, is not receptive to receiving help from group members.

Regardless of the type or purpose of the group, the members need to feel hopeful that the reason for being in the group will be achieved. Thus, it is incumbent upon the leader(s) to be ever mindful of the value of the group's work and of the power of the group. *Instilling hope* and maintaining hope in the members remains a primary function of the leader.

Finally, we once again draw upon Hulse-Killacky et al. (2001, p. 9) to illuminate for us how leaders can maintain a balance between process and content in their groups. The authors offer two sets of questions. The first set regards attending to process:

- Who am I?
- Who am I with you?
- Who are we together?

The second set regards attending to content:

- What do we have to do?
- What do we need to accomplish our goals?

Although these questions are primarily formulated for task groups, leaders can readily adopt them to fit counseling, therapy, and psychoeducational groups.

SUMMARY

In summation, we have learned that multicultural group leaders can benefit from studying their own families of origin and stories of migration and acculturation. For the most part, such knowledge can contribute to developing empathy for diverse individuals. We also found that there is no set definition of multiculturalism, nor is there one set of descriptions for race and culture. *Multicultural* is a most-inclusive term. Therefore, it is important for those who plan to lead multicultural groups to have as many experiential/affective experiences with as many cultures as possible, including their own. In addition, intracultural diversity strongly affirms the need to be sensitive to regional differences and their effects on interpersonal relationships (e.g., mountain versus urban persons of Poland; Asian/Chinese Americans, Asian Indians, and Chinese; etc.). We also learned how the purposes of task groups, psychoeducational groups, and counseling and therapy groups interact with different cultural values and expectations (e.g., face-saving cultures, cultures that value community building versus being strictly goal focused, etc.).

We have been introduced to the power that rests within multicultural groups and how leaders can access that dimension in their groups. This includes understanding the factors and processes that are common to all groups. There is strong support for believing that intercultural connections in multicultural groups are better achieved by giving equal weight to process and content. Finally, after all that has been said, we once again recall the recommendation made by Dyche and Zayas (1995) that multicultural group counselors need to approach each of their groups with a "cultural naiveté."

Suggestions for Best Practices in Multicultural Group Work

We would like to leave you with some suggestions for best practices related to multicultural group work. We all make mistakes, and we all make assumptions about other people. People are different, some of these differences are the results of individual uniqueness, while others result from cultural backgrounds or worldviews. Regardless of their origins, differences need to be acknowledged and respected. When differences in interpersonal style or preference manifest themselves, group members need to discuss the differences and still find a way to be respectful. Safety, cohesion, and universality are essential to group members utilizing the power of groups effectively.

As a framework for the following guidelines, we refer back to Arredondo (1999) and her emphasis on multicultural competence skill development consisting of three domains: (1) the counselor's awareness of personal beliefs and attitudes, knowledge and skills for effective practice; (2) the counselor's understanding and knowledge of the beliefs and attitudes she holds about the worldviews of her clients; and (3) the counselor's ability to provide ethical and culturally relevant counseling to appropriate interventions and techniques. Most, if not all, of what has been written about multicultural counseling competencies has been related to individual counseling. Preliminary research suggests that there is a correlation between clients' ratings of their counselors' multicultural competence and satisfaction with counseling (Constantine, 2002; Pope-Davis, et al., 2002). Even more specifically, Toporek, Davis, Ahluwalia, and Artwohl (2002) reported a significant positive relationship between client perceptions of counselor cultural understanding and client satisfaction with counseling. McCubbin and Coleman (2002) suggested that multicultural counseling competency be defined as the following three specific skills: context empathy, exploring cultural factors, and recovery from insensitive comments. Such skills suggest how important it is for group leaders to acknowledge group members' thoughts and feelings, to explore cultural values and worldviews in defining the problem and making suggestions for change, and to model humanness and understanding of the fact that people make mistakes.

These findings have important indications for multicultural group work. Effective group counseling skills and group work interventions to this point have been largely ignored. So, in this chapter, we attempt to integrate what is known about multicultural counseling competencies from the individual counseling perspective with what we know about effective group work.

AWARENESS OF DIFFERENT WORLDVIEWS AND THEIR IMPACT ON GROUP WORK INTERVENTIONS

Group leaders must have a good understanding of the diversity of cultural worldviews, and of their potential impact on relationships, behaviors, and willingness to participate in therapeutic group work. The message clearly is that it is not essential to research every potential worldview and its implications for behavior, but more important to understand, as a group leader, that each person approaches participation in a group from his own unique perspective.

Dyche and Zayas (1995) emphasized very eloquently the importance of cultural knowledge intertwined with understanding each group member as a unique individual:

> A case might be made that the major benefit to therapists from the study of other cultures is less to understand their clients than to understand themselves. A thoughtful reading of cross-cultural literature can open therapists to the diversity of answers to life's universal questions, and arouse a curiosity that competes with their native ethnocentrism. In the end, the most important application of cultural theory to practice is self-discipline: never assume with a client; always inquire. (p. 391)

Thus, we are not underestimating the importance of learning about and experiencing other cultures. In our chapter on training, we emphasized the importance of reading about and experiencing other cultural traditions. We suggested beginning the process by figuring out who you are as a cultural person, what your cultural traditions are, and how they influence who you are as person. Part of the reason we suggested this examination process is that most of us have been influenced by a variety of cultures, and it is important to analyze how we have integrated these different experiences. A great deal of literature is available, both fiction and nonfiction, that illustrates the themes and worldviews of other cultures. Moreover, the arts often provide insight into other cultures as well. The chapter on training provides many suggestions for books and movies to help leaders learn about other cultures. As the quotation by Dyche and Zayas (1995) emphasizes, part of the value of learning about others is that such knowkedge aids in our own self-understanding.

AWARENESS OF PERSONAL BELIEFS AND ATTITUDES, KNOWLEDGE, AND SKILLS FOR EFFECTIVE GROUP WORK PRACTICE

In earlier chapters, specifically those on training and cultural values, we emphasized how our current use of group work is based on Eurocentric models of counseling. In order to avoid imposing Eurocentric beliefs about counseling and your own cultural values onto group members, we suggest that you consider the following questions: What are your cultural beliefs related to relationships, healing, and mental health? What are your beliefs, as mental health practitioners and group leaders, related to relationships, healing, and mental health? And how many of those beliefs are influenced by and based on the Eurocentric perspective?

The next step is to examine the similarities and differences between your own cultural and therapeutic beliefs, and potentially those of group members from other cultures. Again, it is not essential to identify and explain every potentially different worldview, but more important to be open to different worldviews and realities. The chapter on cultural values suggests potential differences in worldviews and provides questions to guide you in your own self-examination process.

PROVISION OF CULTURALLY RELEVANT GROUP WORK INTERVENTIONS

The third area of emphasis is on group leaders' ability to provide ethical and culturally relevant group leadership. Several steps are suggested within this process.

First, the type of group and the goals of the group must be established, followed by a consensus on the population for which the group is intended. What is the focus of the group? Will it be psychoeducational, task, counseling, or therapeutic in nature? What are the goals of the group? Are the goals consistent with the purpose of the group? Are they culturally consonant with the cultural values of potential group members?

The next decisions focus on the composition of the group. Are similarities desirable among group members in terms of cultural background, problem, and experiences desired? Such homogeneity often promotes the early cohesion needed in psychoeducational and short-term groups. On the other hand, heterogeneity with regard to problems, experiences, and cultural backgrounds may result in different perspectives regarding a problem and a wider variety of alternatives to problematic behaviors. Are there advantages to the group being homogeneous in terms of race or culture? If so, should levels of acculturation be attended to? Resources related to racial identity development models and the impact of acculturation on willingness to seek and participate in counseling and psychoeducational groups should be examined. The possible impact of different levels of racial identity development on willingness to participate in group and attainment of group goals must also be examined. The content of the screening interviews needs to then be tailored to assess factors that may affect group member success and goals in a specific group.

A preparation session and/or written materials may be useful to provide potential members with information and education about process, goals, and interventions. Bowman and DeLucia (1993) suggested a multidimensional framework for preparation sessions that included cognitive, vicarious, and experiential components designed to inform potential group participants about group stages and dynamics, and group member behaviors. Cummins (1996) provided an example of a multidimensional preparation session specifically for eating disorders groups with suggestions about how to adapt the framework to other psychoeducational and counseling groups.

Along with the provision of information about what to expect in group as part of a preparation session for potential group members, it is essential to begin a discussion with group members when you first meet with them about what they expect will happen in group, how they will participate, how other group members may potentially help them, what interactions in group may be like, and how they will deal with disagreements if they occur. Such discussions are good practice in group work in general; however, when working with multicultural groups, it is very important to acknowledge that differences between people based on gender, race, cultural background, and experience will affect how they participate in a group.

Homogeneous Groups

If the decision is made to conduct a psychoeducational or counseling group consisting of a relatively homogeneous group of individuals based on cultural background or lifestyle, there are many resources that address specific types of groups for specific populations. It makes sense to read the literature and utilize the existing knowledge before starting a group. For example, Peeks (1999) provided guidelines for conducting a social skills group of Latina adolescents, while Torres Rivera, Wilbur, Roberts-Wilbur, and Phan (1999) provided specific guidelines for psychoeducational group work with Latino clients. Gloria (1999) based her conceptualization of support groups for Chicana college students on group therapeutic factors. Capello (1994) suggested guidelines for an eight-week group for Latino students focused on stressful educational issues, cultural dynamics, quasi-parenting obligations, and environmental survival strategies. Baca and Koss-Chioino (1997) described a group counseling model specifically targeted for Mexican-American adolescents with behavior problems, including substance abuse, based on the Hispanic Family Project that originated in Phoenix, Arizona. Guanipa, Talley, and Rapagna (1997) described and evaluated the effectiveness of a psychoeducational group for Latin-American women focused on self-concept.

Kim, Omizo, and D'Andrea (1998) described and reported the efficacy of a group for Native-Hawaiian adolescents based on culturally consonant group interventions. In addition, Appleton and Dykeman (1996) described the use of art in group counseling with Native-American youth. Colmant and Merta (1999) described the sweat lodge ceremony, a traditional Native-American healing ritual, as part of group counseling for Navajo youth.

Williams, Frame, and Green (1999) described cultural and spiritual traditions utilizing African-American women's experience as a foundation for group counseling strategies. Brown, Lipford-Sanders, and Shaw (1995) provided guidelines for homogeneous groups for African-American women on predominantly white college campuses. Franklin and Pack-Brown (2001) described a multicultural prevention group approach using the seven principles of Kwanzaa with African-American boys. Brinson (1995) addressed critical issues and provided recommendations for group counseling with black adolescent substance abusers.

With regard to Asian clients and group members, Conyne et al. (2000) discussed their experiences with studying, planning, delivering, and researching group work in China, highlighting the uniqueness of cultural communication styles and attitudes toward leadership. Pan (2000) described and assessed the efficacy of two group approaches for Taiwanese college students using Satir family-oriented groups. Queener and Kenyon (2001) presented an intervention for Southeast-Asian adolescent girls using a primary prevention paradigm within a culturally relevant framework designed to increase self-esteem, increase educational strategies, and teach learning strategies to cope with issues related to cultural identity. Chen (1995) provided general suggestions for working with Chinese clients in group counseling. Bentelspacher, DeSilva, Goh, and LaRowe (1996), based on the process evaluation of five treatment groups, suggested specific interventions for group work with Asian clients.

Very little has been written about counseling, and even less about group work, with some marginalized groups within the United States. However, an article by McCarthy and Mejia (2001) focused on group work with college students from families of migrant farm workers. The authors suggested a prevention approach focused on how to cope with stress within a new environment in this case, college.

Although several examples of psychoeducational and counseling groups designed for persons of specific racial or cultural backgrounds have been highlighted, far less literature has been written about other issues related to diversity. However, a few such resources have been identified. For example, Corrigan, Jones, and McWhirter (2001) suggested guidelines for a group for college students with disabilities that addressed the unique career and employment concerns that confront these students. Firestein (1999) described possible interventions and guidelines for both support and therapy groups for women with diverse sexual identities. She provided guidelines that focus on both homogeneous groups and heterogeneous groups of women of different sexual orientations.

Use of Indigenous Models of Healing

The incorporation of traditional methods of healing and wellness into current group work practices is another way to utilize effective practices and integrate culture. Indigenous, culturally specific healing methods and rituals have been used successfully for centuries. One bias group leaders may often overlook in themselves is the promotion of Western models of counseling over more indigenous healing methods. Caldwell (2002) emphasized that "traditional/majority models of counseling service delivery are based on the social political reality of middle-class Euro-American cultural values (Katz, 1985) and that these models are alternatives to more indigenous forms of helping" (p. 6). In addition, he noted that "counseling and therapy are not culturally universal concepts; therefore it is necessary to identify and learn from culturally indigenous practices of health and healing" (Caldwell, 2002, p. 7).

Some authors have provided specific suggestions about how to incorporate indigenous methods of healing within group work with clients from a particular culture. Several have been mentioned in the previous section. Other authors have suggested the use of cultural rituals, not only with persons of the same culture, but also with diverse groups. For example, Garrett and Crutchfield (1997) provided guidelines for a seven-session group format based on Native-American principles for use with children and adolescents in a preventative way to develop the dimensions of self-esteem, self-determination, body awareness, and self-concept. Roberts-Wilbur, Wilbur, Garrett, and Yuhas (2001) described the use of the Native-American talking circle as an intervention for a peer education program with college students, while Lawrey (2002) described the use of the Native-American talking stick as an icebreaker in college classrooms. Pack-Brown (2002) suggested adaptations of the Afrocentric group work intervention, drumming, with different goals in different groups' stages. Additionally, Brinson and Fisher (1999) suggested the application of a conflict resolution technique known as *Ho'oponopono* and developed by Native Americans to group work in the schools. Garrett et al. (2001) described the use of the inner circle/outer circle, a Native-American technique, with implications for group practice by both Native-American and non–Native American group practitioners.

Heterogeneous Groups Utilizing a Multicultural Theory

Several authors have suggested specific cultural theories and interventions related to group work. Haley-Banez and Walden (1999) suggested the use of optimal theory to understand group process and dynamics and increase diversity in group work based on the group members' racial identity and stage of group development. Related to group work for Asian group members within the United States, Chen and Han (2001) described a model that suggests culturally responsive interventions for Asian members in ethnically mixed groups led by Caucasian leaders based on the racial identity development of both group members and leaders. Merchant and Butler (2003) addressed an area of critical need with a description of a psychoeducational group for ethnic minority adolescents within a predominately white treatment setting. Cheng, Chae, and Gunn (1998) took a slightly different approach to multicultural group counseling theory and focused their discussion of multicultural group work interventions on two specific group phenomena, splitting and projective identification, which the authors suggest are

> two major defenses used in groups to protect significantly against feelings of inadequacy and vulnerability, which underlie racial and cultural prejudice. Filled with feelings of inadequacy and vulnerability, the person or group is unable to assimilate differences and is compelled to simplify the world by splitting it into that which is for one and that which is against one. . . . Projective identification is used . . . to fix all the badness and threat outside oneself by projecting it out onto an identified other (whether an individual or group) (p. 373)

In the area of prevention, Portman and Portman (2002) presented a structured psychoeducational group prevention approach for increasing social justice awareness, knowledge, and advocacy skills for children and adolescents focused on the themes of oppression, prejudice, and racism. Smith, Boulton, and Cowie (1993) suggested a curriculum for classrooms based on an evaluation of a program for white and Asian students that is designed to increase cohesiveness within the classroom and decrease negative stereotypes of other ethnic groups.

Specific Topics and Issues to Be Identified and Addressed in Multicultural Groups

In this section, we suggest general interventions and topics for discussion that promote the open and honest communication between group members with the goal of utilizing diversity within groups to promote more effective problem solving.

Acknowledgment of Group Members' Thoughts and Feelings Each person's uniqueness within the group must be acknowledged. Some general suggestions to group leaders include:

- Treat each group member as an individual.
- Be aware of within-group differences.
- Consider the group members' levels of acculturation.
- Make no assumptions.
- Learn about group members' cultures from multiple sources.
- Acknowledge that you and your members come to group with different perspectives and that all perspectives are valued.
- Admit that sometimes you are ignorant and that you will ask questions to gain knowledge.

- Be aware of multiple sources of oppression such as race, class, nation of origin, and gender.
- Be aware of the differences in attitudes, beliefs, and behaviors related to the concepts of respect and equality in different cultures.

Exploration of Cultural Values and Worldviews on Definition of the Problem and Suggestions for Change Regardless of the specific type of group, population, or setting, all multicultural groups have three goals in common. The first goal is to help the members conceptualize their problems within a personal and conceptual context so that a plan of action can be formulated consistent with individuals' belief systems. Leaders should consider these questions for each member: What is the presenting problem? What are possible interventions? What does this person's culture(s) say about this problem, the cause, and the cure? Each member, with the help of the group, must also examine his own behaviors and belief systems in terms of the influence of culture. Where did he learn this behavior (or belief)? What is its value or relevance to his cultural perspective? Each member must make sense of the behavior for himself, and think about how change might occur.

The second goal is to approach all events and behaviors in the group from a functional perspective. Do they work for that individual? Specifically, individuals must examine their behavior in terms of how it helps them function in relationships. Are they happy with their relationships? If not, how would they like their relationships to be different? What would make their relationships better? Individuals must conceptualize their relationships from this unique perspective. If they are not happy and/or would like to change, then suggestions and interventions can be offered for multicultural perspectives. However, the group must begin by exploring cultural differences without assuming that one way of behaving is necessarily better than others. Each member's perspective must be valued or the group may function as a way to assimilate minority clients (Leong, 1992). With the perspective of the group as a microcosm for the group members' "real life," discussions can begin in group about what group members need, what might be helpful for them, and how they can be helpful to other group members. Recognizing that directly communicating wants, needs, strengths, and weaknesses is a Eurocentric value means that group leaders need to be creative in helping their group members communicate in a way in which they feel comfortable. Metaphors, narratives, and storytelling may all be useful techniques.

The last goal for multicultural group counseling is to help members make sense of new behaviors, beliefs, and skills within a cultural context. As members change and grow, some aspects of cultural, familial, and peer group heritage are assimilated into their identity. As members change and/or learn a new behavior, it must be examined within the cultural framework. What are the cultural implications for this changed and/or new behavior? Does it fit with their present life circumstances? If not, what options are available within their current belief structure? In addition, what new skills, behaviors, and strategies can be learned from other members of the group?

Counselors and members need to learn that they have choices. They also need to understand that

> to act inconsistently with their cultural values may not necessarily mean a denial of a unique cultural heritage. Some members may rationally choose to change their patterns of behavior because new behaviors better align with the kind of person they desire to be, and not necessarily because the changes merely conform to the majority culture's codes. (Greeley et al., 1992, p. 207)

Importance of Group Leader Modeling Humanness and Understanding of Fact That People Make Mistakes   Most theories of group work agree that it is important for the group leader to model essential skills, particularly around communication and relationships, during group sessions so that group members will have an opportunity to observe these skills and then, hopefully, begin to try out new behaviors as well. In integrating, the multicultural literature with effective group work practice, what seems to be most important is the theme that each person is an individual and that each person needs to learn for herself what she wants and needs from relationships, and who she is as an individual. The answers to these questions are unique to each individual, and are influenced by cultural background, race, sexual orientation, education, socioeconomic status, and religion, to name a few factors. The interaction between these factors is different for each person. What makes group work (and life in general) even more complicated, is that each relationship and each set of interactions are uniquely influenced by the two or more people involved in them. Group work helps people learn relationship skills so that they can develop new relationships and enhance current relationships in their lives. The group leaders' role in this process is to model mediation, risk taking, and communication skills—and to encourage members as well. Group leaders will make mistakes, and they will make assumptions. They will ask members to do things that they do not want to do. It is up to group leaders to model how to appropriately respond to such challenges, accept feedback, and make changes in their behavior.

Suggestions for Interventions within Stages of Multicultural Group Work   The orientation stage focuses on the development of trust and cohesion within the group and between group members, and the understanding and acceptance of group norms and group goals. Homogeneous groups often have the advantage of group members having clearly recognizable and sometimes visibly observable similarities, and thus these groups focus on similarities to create cohesion. But real cohesion and a sense of universality come from shared experiences both within and outside of group. Oftentimes, it makes sense, then, for early group sessions to ask members to explore and highlight both similarities and differences in their lives, worldviews, experiences, and values. Even for task and psychoeducational groups, it makes sense to spend some time early on discussing group members' styles of interacting, specifically as they relate to problem solving and giving feedback, which are typically tasks of such groups.

Yalom (1995) suggested that the value of heterogeneous groups is in the diversity of experience, which results in having a multitude of resources available within a group. DeLucia-Waack (1996) suggested that the topics of the uniqueness of individuals and the similarities and differences between group members be explored early on, in the first group session if not before. Discussions using Pedersen's (1991) framework of cultural, demographic, and personal constructs emphasize similarities and differences in worldviews across cultures and groups. It is essential to raise the issue of cultural and demographic differences initially in order to assure members that the subject is not taboo. Freud (1905) postulated that if people talk about an issue, they are less likely to act it out. In this case, as members become aware of and discuss differences, conflict based on stereotypes and prejudice is less likely to occur.

Group leaders need not be afraid to raise the issue of racial and cultural differences. These differences are inherent in any group and must be addressed. Conflict and differences between people are key themes in the transition stage of group. Members need to realize the importance of acknowledging their differences and the impact these differences can have on relationships within the group. Finally, group leaders need to model for members how to introduce and address the issue of cultural differences, and how to respond in a sensitive and open way.

A model of assertiveness may be relevant here. Members can be encouraged to specifically state the behaviors that are upsetting to them, explain how such behaviors affect them personally, and state how they would like the situation to change. To help the group to be accepting of differences, this model of assertiveness may be useful. However, the ultimate goal is for the group to decide on norms that are comfortable and safe. This model of assertiveness is based on making "I" statements and verbal expression of thoughts and feelings directly to others. All cultures do not adhere to these norms, and thus, some members may be uncomfortable being assertive in this manner. In counseling and therapy groups, the task for the group then becomes how each member can communicate with other members comfortably in a way that ensures that the others will receive needed feedback, support, and/or information. This is the ultimate goal for counseling groups: to help individual members balance what they want and need from the group with what other members want and need from them. This balance is crucial because it parallels all other important relationships in their lives. In task and psychoeducational groups, the discussion may focus more on how to problem-solve, brainstorm, evaluate ideas, and so on.

SOME FINAL THOUGHTS

Consuelo Arbona recently presented an address as a newly elected fellow to the American Psychological Association. Her statements resonated with our conclusions at the end of this book. She described how, upon first taking a faculty position, she viewed the teaching of a multicultural counseling course as the easiest part of her job, and scholarship as being much more difficult. In retrospect some years later, as she reflected on these thoughts, she commented that she easily figured out how to publish, but is still redesigning her multicultural counseling course syllabus each year (Arbona, 2002).

We view our experience of writing this book in the same light. Our journey while writing this book has certainly made both of us more aware of multicultural issues and the effect of each member's worldview on group process. It has caused both of us to do some soul-searching in terms of who we are as persons and as group leaders, and how that affects how we intervene in groups. From our experts, we also learned much about how they view themselves as cultural beings and how they sort out their cultural beliefs from their beliefs about groups. Our journey is far from over. Self-awareness as a multicultural person and a multiculturally sensitive group leader is the beginning of the journey toward competence as a multicultural group leader. We hope that this book will serve as a guide for fellow group leaders as they explore and appreciate multicultural differences and their impact on group work, and as they struggle with and try to reconcile who they are as persons and as group leaders in a multicultural world.

References

Agar, M. H. (1996). *The professional stranger* (2nd ed.). Toronto: Academic Press.

Agazarian, Y., & Peters, R. (1989). *The visible and invisible group: Two perspectives on group psychotherapy and group process.* New York: Tavistock/Routledge.

Allport, G. W. (1954). *The nature of prejudice.* Cambridge, MA: Addison-Wesley.

Angelou, M. (1970). *I know why the caged bird sings.* New York: Random House.

Appleton, V. E., & Dykeman, C. (1996). Using art in group counseling with Native American youth. *Journal for Specialists in Group Work, 21,* 224–231.

Arbona, C. (2002, August). *In search of the elusive multicultural competencies.* Paper presented at the national conference of the American Psychological Association, Chicago, IL.

Arredondo, P. (1994). Multicultural training: A response. *Counseling Psychologist, 22,* 308–314.

Arredondo, P. (1999). Multicultural counseling competencies as tools to address oppression and racism. *Journal of Counseling and Development, 77,* 102–108.

Asner-Self, K. K. (2002). Country-of-origin fairy tales. In J. L. DeLucia-Waack, K. H. Bridbord, & J. S. Kleiner (Eds.), *Group work experts share their favorite activities: A guide to choosing, planning, conducting, and processing* (pp. 60–62). Alexandria, VA: Association for Specialists in Group Work.

Association for Specialists in Group Work (ASGW). (1998). Association for Specialists in Group Work best practice standards. *Journal for Specialists in Group Work, 23,* 237–244.

Association for Specialists in Group Work (ASGW) (1999). Association for Specialists in Group Work principles for diversity-competent group workers. *Journal for Specialists in Group Work, 24,* 7–14.

Association for Specialists in Group Work (ASGW). (2000). Association for Specialists in Group Work professional standards for the training of group workers. *Journal for Specialists in Group Work, 25,* 327–342.

Atkinson, D. R., Kim, B., & Caldwell, R. (1998, August). *Validation of the three-dimensional model of multicultural counseling.* Poster session presented at the annual meeting of the American Psychological Association, San Francisco, CA.

Axelson, J. A. (1993). *Counseling and development in a multicultural society* (2nd ed.). Pacific Grove, CA: Brooks/Cole.

Baca, L. M., & Koss-Chioino, J. D. (1997). Development of a culturally responsive group counseling model for Mexican American adolescents. *Journal of Multicultural Counseling and Development, 25,* 130–141.

Baldwin, J. (1980). The psychology of oppression. In M. Asante & A. Vandi (Eds.), *Contemporary Black thought: Alternative analyses in social and behavioral science* (pp. 95–110). Beverly Hills, CA: Sage.

Baloglu, M. (2000). *Counseling expectations of international students.* Unpublished manuscript, Texas A&M University—Commerce.

Banawi, R., & Stockton, R. (1993). Islamic values relevant to group work, with practical applications for the group leader. *Journal for Specialists in Group Work, 18,* 151–160.

Barona, A., & Miller, J. A. (1994). Short acculturation scale for Hispanic youth (SASHY). *Hispanic Journal of Behavioral Sciences, 16,* 155–162.

Bateson, M. C. (1994). *Peripheral visions: Learning along the way.* New York: Harper Collins.

Beck, K. (2002). Walk in my shoes. In J. L. DeLucia-Waack, K. H. Bridbord, & J. S. Kleiner (Eds.), *Group work experts share their favorite activities: A guide to choosing, planning, conducting, and processing* (pp. 102–103). Alexandria, VA: Association for Specialists in Group Work.

Benge, G. (2000, December 5). Where is Indian in "Native American"? *Democrat and Chronicle,* p. 6A.

Bentelspacher, C. E., DeSilva, E., Goh, T. L. C., & LaRowe, K. D. (1996). A process evaluation of the cultural compatibility of psychoeducational family group treatment with ethnic Asian clients. *Social Work with Groups, 19,* 41–55.

Berry, J. W. (1995). Psychology of acculturation. In N. R. Goldberger & J. B. Veroff (Eds.), *The culture and psychology reader* (pp. 457–488). New York: New York University Press.

Bianchi, F. T., Zea, M. C., Belgrave, F. Z., & Echeverry, J. J. (2002). Racial identity and self-esteem among black Brazilian men: Race matters in Brazil too. *Cultural Diversity & Ethnic Minority Psychology, 8,* 157–169.

Boehlen, B. (2000). *The words of the lesson.* Unpublished poem.

Bolyard, K. L., & Jensen-Scott, R. L. (1996). Worldview and culturally sensitive crisis intervention. In J. L. DeLucia-Waack (Ed.), *Multicultural counseling competencies: Implications for training and practice* (pp. 217–235). Alexandria, VA: Association for Counselor Education and Supervision.

Bowman, V. E. (1996). Counselor self-awareness and ethnic self-knowledge as a critical component of multicultural training. In J. L. DeLucia-Waack (Ed.), *Multicultural counseling competencies: Implications for training and practice* (pp. 7–30). Alexandria, VA: Association for Counselor Education and Supervision.

Bowman, V., & DeLucia, J. L. (1993). Preparation for group therapy: The effects of preparer and modality on group process and individual functioning. *Journal for Specialists in Group Work, 18,* 67–79.

Brinson, J. (1995). Group work for black adolescents substance abusers: Some issues and recommendations. *Journal of Child and Adolescent Substance Abuse, 4,* 49–59.

Brinson, J., & Fisher, T. A. (1999). The Ho'oponopono group: A conflict resolution model for school counselors. *Journal for Specials in Group Work, 24,* 369–382.

Brown, D. A. (1970). *Bury my heart at wounded knee: An Indian history of the American west.* New York: H. Holt.

Brown, S. P., Lipford-Sanders, J., & Shaw, M. (1995). Kujichagulia: Uncovering the secrets of the heart: Group work with African-American women on predominantly White campuses. *Journal for Specialists in Group Work, 20,* 151–158.

Caldwell, L. D. (2002, August). *Beyond textbook multicultural competence: Addressing multi-cultural skill development in training.* Paper presented at the annual conference of the American Psychological Association, Chicago, IL.

Calloway, N. O., & Harris, O. N. (1977). *Biological and medical aspects of race.* Madison, WI: American Publishing.

Capello, D. C. (1994). Beyond financial aid: Counseling Latina students. *Journal of Multicultural Counseling and Development, 22,* 28–36.

Carroll, M. R., & Wiggins, J. D. (1997). *Elements of group counseling* (2nd ed.). Denver, CO: Love.

Cavazos, P., & DeLucia-Waack, J. L. (2002). *Relationship between self-esteem and ethnic identity in Latino adolescents.* Paper presented at the annual convention of the American Psychological Association, Chicago, IL.

Chan, C. (1992). Cultural considerations in counseling Asian American lesbians and gay men. In S. Dworkin & F. Gutierrez (Eds.), *Counseling gay men and lesbians* (pp. 115–124). Alexandria, VA: American Counseling Association.

Cheatham, H. E. (1994). A response. *The Counseling Psychologist, 22,* 290–295.

Chen, C. P. (1995). Group counseling in a different cultural context: Several primary issues in dealing with Chinese clients. *Group, 19,* 45–55.

Chen, M., & Han, Y. S. (2001). Cross-cultural group counseling with Asians: A stage-specific interactive approach. *Journal for Specialists in Group Work, 26,* 111–128.

Cheng, W. D., Chae, M., & Gunn, R. W. (1998). Splitting and protective identification in multi-cultural group counseling. *Journal for Specialists in Group Work, 23,* 372–387.

Chung, R. Y. (2000, January). *Groups that work: Global perspectives.* Symposium conducted at the national conference for the Association for Specialists in Group Work, Deerfield Beach, FL.

Chung, R. Y. (2003). Group counseling with Asians. In J. L. DeLucia-Waack, D. Gerrity, C. R. Kalodner & M. T. Riva (Eds.), *Handbook of group counseling and psychotherapy* (pp. 200–212). Thousand Oaks, CA: Sage.

Chung, R. Y., & Okazaki, S. (1991). Counseling Asians of Southeast Asian decent: The impact of refugee experiences. In C. C. Lee & B. L. Richardson (Eds.), *Multicultural issues in counseling: New approaches to diversity* (pp. 107–126). Alexandria, VA: American Association for Counseling and Development.

Coleman, H. K., Morris, D., & Norton, R. (2000, August). *Developing multicultural counseling competencies through the use of portfolios.* Paper presented at the annual meeting of the American Psychological Association, Washington, D.C.

Colmant, S. A., & Merta, R. J. (1999). Using a sweat lodge ceremony as group therapy for special Navajo youth. *Journal for Specialists in Group Work, 24,* 55–73.

Constantine, M. (2002). Predictors of satisfaction with counseling: Racial and ethnic minority clients' attitudes towards counseling and ratings of their counselors' general and multicultural counseling competency. *Journal of Counseling Psychology, 49,* 255–263.

Conyne, R. K. (1998). What to look for in groups: Helping trainees become more sensitive to multicultural issues. *Journal for Specialists in Group Work, 23,* 22–32.

Conyne, R. K., Wilson, F. R., & Tang, M. (2000). Evolving lessons from group work involvement in China. *Journal for Specialists in Group Work, 25,* 252–268.

Corey, G. (1996). *Theory and practice of counseling and psychotherapy.* Pacific Grove, CA: Brooks/Cole.

Corrigan, M. J., Jones, C. A., & McWhirter, J. J. (2001). College students with disabilities: An access employment group. *Journal for Specialists in Group Work, 26,* 339–349.

Costner, K. (Director). (1990). *Dances with wolves.* [Motion Picture]. United States: MGM Studios.

Council for Accreditation of Counseling and Counseling Related Educational Programs (CACREP). (2001). The 2001 standards. http://www.counseling.org/cacrep/2001standards700.htm.

Cross, W. E. (1971). The Negro-to-Black conversion experience. *Black World, 20,* 13–27.

Cross, W. E. (1995). The psychology of nigrescence: Revising the Cross model. In J. G. Ponterotto, J. M. Casas, L. A. Suzuki, & C. M. Alexander (Eds.), *Handbook of multicultural counseling* (pp. 93–122). Thousand Oaks, CA: Sage.

Cuellar, I., Arnold, B., & Maldonado, R. (1995). Acculturation Rating Scale for Mexican Americans–II: A revision of the original ARSMA Scale. *Hispanic Journal of Behavioral Sciences, 17,* 275–304.

Cummins, P. N. (1996). Preparing clients with eating disorders for group counseling: A multimedia approach. *Journal for Specialists in Group Work, 21,* 4–10.

D'Andrea, M. (2003). Considerations related to racial identity development for group leaders and members. In J. L. DeLucia-Waack, D. Gerrity, C. R. Kalodner, & M. T. Riva (Eds.), *Handbook of group counseling and psychotherapy* (pp. 265–282). Thousand Oaks, CA: Sage.

D'Andrea, M., & Daniels, J. (in press). *Multi-cultural counseling: Empowering strategies for a diverse society.* Pacific Grove, CA: Brooks/Cole.

DeLucia-Waack, J. L. (1996). Multicultural group counseling: Addressing diversity to facilitate universality and self-understanding. In J. L. DeLucia-Waack (Ed.), *Multicultural counseling competencies: Implications for training and practice* (pp. 157–195). Alexandria, VA: American Counseling Association.

DeLucia-Waack, J. L. (1997). The importance of processing activities, exercises, and events to group work practitioners. *Journal for Specialists in Group Work, 22,* 82–84.

DeLucia-Waack, J. L., Bridbord, K. H., & Kleiner, J. S. (Eds.). (2002). *Group work experts share their favorite activities: A guide to choosing, planning, conducting, and processing.* Alexandria, VA: Association for Specialists in Group Work.

DeLucia-Waack, J. L., DiCarlo, N. J., Parker-Sloat, E. L., & Rice, K. G. (1996). Multiculturalism: Understanding as the beginning of the process, rather than the ending. In J. L. DeLucia-Waack (Ed.), *Multicultural counseling competencies: Implications for training and practice* (pp. 7–30). Alexandria, VA: Association for Counselor Education and Supervision.

Dhruvarajan, V. (1993). Ethnic cultural retention and transmission among first generation Hindu Asian Indians in a Canadian prairie city. *Journal of Comparative Family Studies, 24,* 63–79.

Donigian, J., & Malnati, R. (1997). *Critical incidents in group therapy.* Pacific Grove, CA: Brooks/Cole.

Draguns, J. G. (1976). Counseling across cultures: Common themes and distinct approaches. In P. B. Pederson, W. J. Lonner, & J. G. Draguns (Eds.), *Counseling across cultures* (pp. 3–21). Honolulu: The University Press.

Dyche, L., & Zayas, L. H. (1995). The value of curiosity and naiveté for the cross-cultural psychotherapist. *Family Process, 34,* 389–399.

Espin, O. (1987). Psychological impact of migration on Latinas: Implications for psychotherapeutic practice. *Psychology of Women Quarterly, 11,* 489–503.

Falicov, C. J. (1995). Cross-cultural marriages. In N. S. Jacobson & A. S. Gurman (Eds.), *Clinical handbook of couples therapy* (pp. 241–252). New York: Guilford Press.

Firestein, B. A. (1999). New perspectives on group treatment with women of diverse sexual identities. *Journal for Specialists in Group Work, 24,* 306–315.

Foeman, A. K. (1991). Managing multiracial institutions: Goals and approaches for race-relations training. *Communication Education, 40,* 255–265.

Folwarski, J., & Morganoff, P. (1996). Polish families. In M. McGoldrick, J. Giordano, & J. K. Pearce (Eds.), *Ethnicity and family therapy* (2nd ed., pp. 658–672). New York: Guilford Press.

Franklin, R. E., & Pack-Brown, S. P. (2001). Team brothers: An Africentric approach to group work with African-American male adolescents. *Journal for Specialists in Group Work, 26,* 237–245.

Friere, P. (1983). *Pedagogy of the Oppressed.* New York: The Continuum Publishing Company.

Freud, S. (1905). On psychotherapy. *Standard Edition, 4,* 257–268.

Fukuyama, M. A., & Coleman, N. C. (1992). A model for bicultural assertion training with Asian-Pacific American college students: A pilot study. *Journal for Specialists in Group Work, 17,* 210–217.

Garrett, M. T. (1996). *Medicine of the Cherokee: The way of right relationship.* Santa Fe, NM: Bear and Co.

Garrett, M. T. (1998). *Walking on the wind: Cherokee teachings for healing through harmony and balance.* Sante Fe, NM: Bear and Co.

Garrett, M. T. (2002). The four directions. In J. L. DeLucia-Waack, K. H. Bridbord, & J. S. Kleiner (Eds.), *Group work experts share their favorite activities: A guide to choosing, planning, conducting, and processing* (pp. 119–122). Alexandria, VA: Association for Specialists in Group Work.

Garrett, M. T. (2003). Sound of the drum: Group counseling with Native Americans. In J. L. DeLucia-Waack, D. Gerrity, C. R. Kalodner, & M. T. Riva (Eds.), *Handbook of group counseling and psychotherapy* (pp. 169–182). Thousand Oaks, CA: Sage.

Garrett, M. T., & Brotherton, D. (2000, January). *Inner Circle/Outer Circle; Cherokee Healing.* Presentation at the national conference of the Association for Specialists in Group Work, Deerfield Beach, FL.

Garrett, M. T., & Crutchfield, L. B. (1997). Moving full circle: A unity model of group work with children. *Journal for Specialists in Group Work, 22,* 175–188.

Garrett, J. T., & Garrett, M. T. (1994). The path of good medicine: Understanding and counseling Native Americans. *Journal of Multicultural Counseling and Development, 22,* 134–144.

Garrett, M. T., Garrett, J. T., & Brotherton, D. (2001). Inner Circle/Outer Circle: A group technique based on Native American healing circles. *Journal for Specialists in Group Work, 26,* 17–30.

Garrett, M. T., & Osborne, W. L. (1995). The Native American sweat lodge as a metaphor for group work. *Journal for Specialists in Group Work, 20,* 33–39.

Gladding, S. T. (1991). *Group work: A counseling specialty.* New York: Macmillan.

Gladding, S. T. (1999). *Group work: A counseling specialty* (3rd ed.). Upper Saddle River, NJ: Merrill/Prentice-Hall.

Gloria, A. M. (1999). Apoyando estudiantes Chicanas: Therapeutic factors in Chicana college student support groups. *Journal for Specialists in Group Work, 24,* 246–259.

Greeley, A. T., Garcia, V. L., Kessler, B. L., & Gilchrest, G. (1992). Training effective multicultural group counselors: Issues for a group training course. *Journal for Specialists in Group Work, 17,* 196–209.

Guanipa, C., Talley, W., & Rapagna, S. (1997). Enhancing Latin American women's self-concept: A group intervention. *International Journal of Group Psychotherapy, 47,* 355–372.

Haley-Banez, L., & Walden, S. L. (1999). Diversity in group work: Using optimal theory to understand group process and dynamics. *Journal for Specialists in Group Work, 24,* 404–422.

Hanson, P. (1972). What to look for in groups: An observation guide. In J. Pfeiffer & J. Jones (Eds.), *The 1972 annual handbook for group facilitators* (pp. 21–24). San Diego: Pfeiffer.

Hardy, K. V., & Laszloffy, T. A. (1995). The cultural genogram: Key to training culturally competent family therapists. *Journal of Marital and Family Therapy, 21,* 227–237.

Heider, J. (1985). *The tao of leadership.* New York: Bantam Books.

Helms, J. E. (1984). Toward a theoretical explanation of the effects of race on counseling: A Black and White model. *Counseling Psychologist, 12,* 153–165.

Helms, J. E. (1990). *Black and White identity: Theory, research, and practice.* New York: Greenwood Press.

Helms, J. E. (1995). An update of Helms' White and people of color racial identity models. In J. G. Ponterotto, J. M. Casas, L. A. Suzuki, & C. M. Alexander (Eds.), *Handbook of multicultural counseling* (pp. 181–198). Thousand Oaks, CA: Sage.

Helms, J. E., & Cook, D. A. (1999). *Using race and culture in counseling and psychotherapy: Theory and process.* Needham Heights, MA: Allyn & Bacon.

Hulse-Killacky, D. (2002). The names activity. In J. L. DeLucia-Waack, K. H. Bridbord, & J. S. Kleiner (Eds.), *Group work experts share their favorite activities: A guide to choosing, planning, conducting, and processing* (pp. 52–53). Alexandria, VA: Association for Specialists in Group Work.

Hulse-Killacky, D., Killacky, J., & Donigian, J. (2001). *Making task groups work in your world.* Upper Saddle River, NJ: Prentice-Hall.

Hulse-Killacky, D., Kraus, K. L., & Schumacher, R. A. (1999). Visual conceptualizations of meetings: A group work design. *Journal for Specialists in Group Work, 24,* 113–124.

Imber-Black, E. (1997). Developing cultural competence: Contributions from recent family therapy literature. *American Journal of Psychotherapy, 51,* 607–611.

Johnson, I. H., Santos Torres, J., Coleman, V. D., & Smith, M. C. (1995). Issues and strategies in leading culturally diverse counseling groups. *Journal for Specialists in Group Work, 20,* 143–150.

Kalodner, C. R. (2002, January). Critical incidents in multicultural group work. Paper presented at the annual meeting of the Association for Specialists in Group Work, St. Petersburg Beach, FL.

Katz, J. H. (1978). *White awareness: Anti-racism training.* Norman, OK: University of Oklahoma Press.

Katz, J. H. (1985). The sociopolitical nature of counseling. *Counseling Psychologist, 13,* 615–624.

Kim, B. S. K., & Atkinson, D. R. (2002). Asian American client adherence to Asian cultural values, counselor expression of cultural values, counselor ethnicity and career counseling process. *Journal of Counseling Psychology, 49,* 3–13.

Kim, B. S. K., Atkinson, D. R., & Yang, P. H. (1999). The Asian Values Scale: Development, factor analysis, validation, and reliability. *Journal of Counseling Psychology, 46,* 342–352.

Kim, B. S. K., Omizo, M. M., & D'Andrea, M. J. (1998). The effects of culturally consonant group counseling on the self-esteem and internal locus of control orientation among Native American adolescents. *Journal for Specialists in Group Work, 23,* 145–163.

Kim, J. (1981). *The process of Asian American identity development: A study of Japanese-American women's perspectives of their struggle to achieve personal identities as Americans of Asian ancestry.* Dissertation Abstracts International, 42, 1551A. (University Microfilms No. 81-18080).

Kincade, E. A., & Evans, K. M. (1996). Counseling theories, process, and interventions within a multicultural context. In J. DeLucia-Waack (Ed.), *Multicultural counseling competencies: Implications for training and practice* (pp. 89–112). Alexandria, VA: Association for Counselor Education and Supervision.

Kitano, Harry H.; Yeung, Wai-tsang. (1982, Spring). Chinese interracial marriages. *Marriage and Family Review, 5*(1), 35–48.

Kline, W. B. (2003). *Interactive group counseling and therapy.* Upper Saddle River, NJ: Pearson Education Inc.

Kottler, J. A. (1994). *Advanced group leadership.* Pacific Grove, CA: Brooks/Cole.

Kwan, K. L. K. (2000). The Internal-External Ethnic Identity measure: Factor-analytic structures based on a sample of Chinese-Americans. *Educational and Psychological Measurement, 60,* 142–152.

Kwan, K. L. K., & Sodowsky, G. R. (1997). Internal and external ethnic identity and their correlates: A study of Chinese American immigrants. *Journal of Multicultural Counseling and Development, 25,* 51–67.

LaFramboise, T. D., Coleman, H. L., & Gerton, J. (1995). Psychological impact of biculturalism: Evidence and theory. In N. R. Goldberger & J. B. Veroff (Eds.), *The culture and psychology reader* (pp. 489–535). New York: New York University Press.

LaFromboise, T. D., Coleman, H. L., & Hernandez, A. (1991). Development and factor structure of the Cross-Cultural Counseling Inventory—Revised. *Professional Psychology—Research and Practice, 22,* 380–388.

Latner, J. (1973). *The Gestalt therapy book.* New York: Julian Press.

Lawrey, J. D. (2002). College classroom ice breaker combined with Native American council process. In J. L. DeLucia-Waack, K. H. Bridbord, & J. S. Kleiner (Eds.), *Group work experts share their favorite activities: A guide to choosing, planning, conducting, and processing* (pp. 52–53). Alexandria, VA: Association for Specialists in Group Work.

Lee, C. C. (1997). *Multicultural issues in counseling: New approaches to diversity.* Alexandria, VA: American Counseling Association.

Leong, F. T. (1992). Guidelines for minimizing premature termination among Asian American clients in group counseling. *Journal for Specialists in Group Work, 17,* 218–228.

Leong, F. T., Wagner, N. S., & Kim, H. H. (1995). Group counseling expectations among Asian American students: The role of culture-specific factors. *Journal of Counseling Psychology, 42,* 217–222.

Leung, P. K., & Boehnlein, J. (1996). Vietnamese families. In M. McGoldrick, J. Giordano, & J. K. Pearce (Eds.), *Ethnicity and family therapy* (2nd ed., pp. 295–306). New York: Guilford Press.

Luhtanen, R., & Crocker, J. (1992). A collective self-esteem scale: Self-evaluation of one's social identity. *Personality and Social Psychology Bulletin, 18,* 302–318.

Marin, G., Sabogal, F., VanOss Marin, B., Otero-Sabogal, R., & Perez-Stable, E. J. (1987). Development of a short acculturation scale for Hispanics. *Hispanic Journal of Behavioral Sciences, 9,* 183–205.

McCarthy, C. J., & Mejia, O. L. (2001). Using groups to promote preventive coping: A case example with college students from migrant farm-working families. *Journal for Specialists in Group Work, 26,* 267–275.

McCubbin, L. D., & Coleman, H. L. K. (2002, August). *Empirical challenge to the distinction between multicultural and general counseling competence.* Paper presented at the annual conference of the American Psychological Association, Chicago, IL.

McDavis, R. J., & Parker, M. (1977). A course on counseling ethnic minorities: A model. *Counselor Education and Supervision, 17,* 146–149.

McGoldrick, M., & Gerson, R. (1985). *Genograms in family assessment.* New York: Norton.

McGoldrick, M., Giordano, J., & Pearce, J. K. (Eds.). (1996). *Ethnicity and family therapy* (2nd ed.). New York: Guilford Press.

Merchant, N. M., & Butler, M. K. (2002). A psychoeducational group for ethnic minority adolescents in a predominately white treatment setting. *Journal for Specialists in Group Work, 27,* 314–332.

Merta, R. J. (1995). Group work: Multi-cultural perspectives. In J. G. Ponterotto, J. M. Casas, L. A. Suzuki, & C. M. Alexander (Eds.), *Handbook of multicultural counseling* (pp. 567–585). Thousand Oaks, CA: Sage.

Meyers, L. J. (1988). *Understanding an Afrocentric Worldview: Introduction to an optimal psychology.* Dubuque, IA: Kendall/Hunt.

Moskos, C. C. (1989). *Greek Americans: Struggle and success* (2nd ed.). Englewood Cliffs, NJ: Prentice-Hall.

Nesdale, D., Rooney, R., & Smith, L. (1997). Migrant ethnic identity and psychological distress. *Journal of Cross-Cultural Psychology, 28,* 569–588.

Olmos, E. J. (Director). (1992). *American me.* [Motion Picture]. United States: MGM Studios.

Organista, K. C., Dwyer, E. V., & Azocar, F. (1993). Cognitive behavioral therapy with Latino outpatients. *Behavior Therapist, 16,* 229–233.

Pack-Brown, S. P. (2002). Drumming. In J. L. DeLucia-Waack, K. H. Bridbord, & J. S. Kleiner (Eds.), *Group work experts share their favorite activities: A guide to choosing, planning, conducting, and processing* (pp. 183–186). Alexandria, VA: Association for Specialists in Group Work.

Pack-Brown, S. P., & Fleming, A. (2003). An Afrocentric approach to counseling groups with African-Americans. In J. L. DeLucia-Waack, D. Gerrity, C. R. Kalodner, & M. T. Riva (Eds.), *Handbook of group counseling and psychotherapy* (pp. 183–199). Thousand Oaks, CA: Sage.

Pan, P. J. D. (2000). The effectiveness of structured and semistructured Satir model groups on family relationships with college students in Taiwan. *Journal for Specialists in Group Work, 25,* 305–318.

Paniagua, F. A. (1998). *Assessing and treating culturally diverse clients* (2nd ed.). Thousand Oaks, CA: Sage.

Parker, A. (Director). (1990). *Come see the paradise.* [Motion Picture]. United States: Twentieth Century Fox.

Pedersen, P. B. (1983). Intercultural training of mental health providers. In D. Landis & R. W. Brislin (Eds.), *Handbook of intercultural training.* Vol. 2: Issues in training methodology (pp. 325–352). New York: Pergamon.

Pedersen, P. B. (1988). *A handbook for developing multicultural awareness.* Alexandria, VA: American Association for Counseling and Development.

Pedersen, P. B. (1991). Multiculturalism as a generic approach to counseling. *Journal of Counseling and Development, 70,* 6–12.

Pedersen, P. B. (2002). Nested emotions. In J. L. DeLucia-Waack, K. H. Bridbord, & J. S. Kleiner (Eds.), *Group work experts share their favorite activities: A guide to choosing, planning, conducting, and processing* (pp. 140–142). Alexandria, VA: Association for Specialists in Group Work.

Peeks, A. L. (1999). Conducting the social skills group of Latino adolescents. *Journal of Child and Adolescent Group Therapy, 9,* 139–153.

Phan, L. T., & Torres Rivera, E. (2003). Language as it impacts group dynamics in counseling and psychotherapy groups. In J. DeLucia-Waack, D. Gerrity, C. Kalodner, & M. Riva (Eds.), *Handbook of group counseling and psychotherapy* (pp. 283–294). Thousand Oaks, CA: Sage.

Phinney, J. S. (1992). The multigroup ethnic identity measure: A new scale for use with diverse groups. *Journal of Adolescence Research, 7,* 156–176.

Phinney, J. S. (1995). Ethnic identity and self-esteem: A review and integration. In A. M. Padilla (Ed.), *Hispanic psychology: Critical issues in theory and research* (pp. 57–70). Thousand Oaks, CA: Sage.

Phinney, J. S., Cantu, C. L., & Kurtz, D. A. (1997). Ethnic and American identity as predictors of self-esteem among African American, Latino and White adolescents. *Journal of Youth and Adolescence, 26,* 165–185.

Ponterotto, J. G. (1988). Racial consciousness development among White counselor trainees: A stage model. *Journal of Multicultural Counseling and Development, 16,* 146–156.

Ponterotto, J. G., Jackson, M. A., & Nutini, C. D. (2001). Reflections on the life stories of pioneers in multicultural counseling. In J. G. Ponterotto, J. M. Casas, L. A. Suzuki, & C. M. Alexander (Eds.), *Handbook of multicultural counseling* (pp. 138–161). Thousand Oaks, CA: Sage.

Pope, M., & Chung, B. (1999). From Bakla to Tongzhi: Counseling and psychotherapy with gay and lesbian Asian and Pacific Islander Americans. In D. S. Sandhu (Ed.), *Asian and Pacific Islander Americans: Issues and concerns for counseling and psychotherapy* (pp. 283–300). Commack, NY: Nova Science.

Pope-Davis, D. B.,Toporek, R. L., Ortega-Villashes, L., Ligiero, D. P, Brittan-Powell, C. S., Liu, W. M., Bashshur, M. L., Codrington, J. N., & Liang, C. T. H. (2002). A qualitative study of clients' perspectives of multicultural counseling competency. *Counseling Psychologist, 30,* 355–393.

Portman, T. A. A., & Portman, G. L. (2002). Empowering students for social justice (ES2J): A structured group approach. *Journal for Specialists in Group Work, 27,* 16–31.

Queener, J. E., & Kenyon, C. B. (2001). Providing mental health services to Southeast Asian adolescent girls: Integration of a primary prevention paradigm and group counseling. *Journal for Specialists in Group Work, 26,* 350–367.

Roberts, R. E., Phinney, J. S., Masse, L. C., Chen, R. Y., Roberts, C. R., & Romero, A. (1999). The structure of ethnic identity of young adolescents from diverse ethnocultural groups. *Journal of Early Adolescence, 19,* 301–322.

Roberts-Wilbur, J., Wilbur, M., Garrett, M. T., & Yuhas, M. (2001). Talking circles: Listen, or your tongue will make you deaf. *Journal for Specialists in Group Work, 26,* 368–384.

Rollock, D., & Terrell, M. D. (1996). Multicultural issues in assessment: Toward an inclusive model. In J. L. DeLucia-Waack (Ed.), *Multicultural counseling competencies: Implications for training and practice* (pp. 7–30). Alexandria, VA: Association for Counselor Education and Supervision.

Rose, S. R. (2001). Group work to promote the occupational functioning of Ethiopian minority men with disabilities who have immigrated to Israel. *Journal for Specialists in Group Work, 26,* 144–155.

Ruiz, Aureliano S. (1990). Ethnic identity: Crisis and resolution. *Journal of Multicultural Counseling and Development, 8,* 29–40.

Sabnani, H. B., Ponterotto, J. G., & Borodovsky, L. G. (1991). White racial identity development and cross-cultural counselor training: A stage model. *Counseling Psychologist, 19,* 76–102.

Scheurich, J. J. (1993). Toward a discourse on white racism. *Educational Researcher, 22,* 5–10.

Scheurich, J. J., & Young, M. D. (1997). Coloring epistemologies: Are our research epistemologies racially biased? *Educational Researcher, 26,* 4–16.

Semmler, P. L., & Williams, C.B. (2000). Narrative therapy: A storied context for multicultural counseling. *Journal of Multicultural Counseling and Development, 28,* 51–61.

Shakoor, M., & Rabinowicz, S. (1978). The sought membership model: A model for conceptualizing person-group relationships in groups where membership is sought. *Small Group Behavior, 9,* 325–329.

Sharabi, H. (1988). *Neopatriarchy.* New York: Oxford University Press.

Silverstein, R. (1995). Bending the conventional rules when treating the ultra-orthodox in the group setting. *International Journal of Group Psychotherapy, 45,* 237–250.

Singh, G. (1978). *Sri Guru Granth Sahib.* Chandigarh, India: World Sikh University Press.

Singleton, J. (Director). (1991). *Boyz 'n the hood.* [Motion Picture]. United States: Columbia/Tristar Studios.

Smith, P. K., Boulton, M. J., & Cowie, H. (1993). The impact of cooperative group work on ethnic relations in middle school. *School Psychology International, 14,* 21–42.

Sodowsky, G. R., Taffe, R. C., Gutkin, T. B., & Wise, S. L. (1994). Development of the Multicultural Counseling Inventory: A self-report measure of multicultural competencies. *Journal of Counseling Psychology, 41,* 137–148.

Sue, D. W. (1981). *Counseling the culturally different: Theory and practice.* New York: Wiley.

Sue, D. W., Arredondo, P., & McDavis, R. J. (1992). Multicultural counseling competencies and standards: A call to the profession. *Journal of Counseling and Development, 70,* 477–486.

Sue, D. W., & Sue, D. (1999). *Counseling the culturally different: Theory and practice* (3rd ed.). New York: Wiley.

Sue, S., & Sue, D. W. (1971). Chinese American personality and mental health. *Amerasia Journal, 1,* 36–49.

Suinn, R. M., Rickard-Figueroa, K., Lew, S., & Vigil, P. (1987). The Suinn-Lew Asian Self-Identity Acculturation Scale: An initial report. *Educational and Psychological Measurement, 47,* 401–407.

Szapocznik, J., Santisteban, D., Kurtines, W., Perez-Vidal, A., & Hervis, O. (1984). Bicultural effectiveness training: A treatment intervention for enhancing intercultural adjustment in Cuban American families. *Hispanic Journal of Behavioral Sciences, 6,* 317–344.

Takahashi, T. (1991). A comparative study of Japanese and American group dynamics. *Psychoanalytic Review, 78,* 49–62.

Tan, A. (1989). *The joy luck club.* New York: Putnam.

Terrell, F., & Terrell, S. (1981). An inventory to measure cultural mistrust among Blacks. *Western Journal of Black Studies, 5,* 180–185.

Thompson, C. E., Neville, H., Weathers, P. L., Poston, W. C., & Atkinson, D. R. (1990). Cultural mistrust and racism reaction among African-American students. *Journal of College Student Development, 31,* 62–168.

Toporek, R. L., Davis, C., Ahluwali, M. K., & Artwohl, R. (2002, August). *Effects of perceived counselor cultural understanding on client satisfaction among white clients and clients of color at a university counseling center.* Paper presented at the annual conference of the American Psychological Association, Chicago, IL.

Torres Rivera, E. (2003). Psychoeducational and counseling groups work with Latinos. In J. L. DeLucia-Waack, D. Gerrity, C. R. Kalodner, & M. T. Riva (Eds.), *Handbook of group counseling and psychotherapy* (pp. 213–223). Thousand Oaks, CA: Sage.

Torres Rivera, E., Wilbur, M. P., Roberts-Wilbur, J., & Phan, L. (1999). Group work with Latino clients: A psychoeducational model. *Journal for Specialists in Group Work, 24,* 383–404.

Vandiver, B. J., Cross, W. E., Jr., Worrell, F. C., & Fhagen-Smith, P. E. (2002). Validating the Cross Racial Identity Scale. *Journal of Counseling Psychology, 49,* 71–85.

Walker, A. (1983). *The color purple.* New York: Pocket Books.

Weeks, W. H., Pedersen, P. B., & Brislin, R. W. (Eds.). (1977). *A manual of structured experiences for cross-cultural learning.* Yarmouth, ME: Intercultural Press.

Williams, C. D., Frame, M. W., & Green, E. (1999). Counseling groups for African-American women: A focus on spirituality. *Journal for Specialists in Group Work, 24,* 260–273.

Worthington, R. L., Mobley, M., Franks, R. P., & Tan, J. A. (2000). Multiracial counseling competencies: Verbal content, counselor attributions, and social desirability. *Journal of Counseling Psychology, 47,* 460–468.

Yalom, I. D. (1985). *The theory and practice of group psychotherapy* (3rd ed.). New York: Basic Books.

Yalom, I. D. (1995). *The theory and practice of group psychotherapy* (4th ed.). New York: Basic Books.

Yau, T. Y. (2003). Guidelines for facilitating groups with international college students. In J. L. DeLucia-Waack, D. Gerrity, C. R. Kalodner, & M. T. Riva (Eds.), *Handbook of group counseling and psychotherapy* (pp. 253–264). Thousand Oaks, CA: Sage.

Ying, Y. W., Lee, P. A., Tsai, J. L., Yeh, Y. Y., & Huang, J. S. (2000). The conception of depression in Chinese American college students. *Cultural Diversity and Ethnic Minority Psychology, 6,* 183–195.

Yinger, J. M. (1976). Ethnicity in complex societies. In L. A. Coser & O. N. Larsen (Eds.), *The uses of controversy in sociology* (pp. 197–216). New York: Free Press.

Index